Plague in the Early Modern World

Plague in the Early Modern World presents a broad range of primary source materials from Europe, the Middle East, North Africa, China, India, and North America that explore the nature and impact of plague and disease in the early modern world.

During the early modern period frequent and recurring outbreaks of plague and other epidemics around the world helped to define local identities and they simultaneously forged and subverted social structures, recalibrated demographic patterns, dictated political agendas, and drew upon and tested religious and scientific worldviews. By gathering texts from diverse and often obscure publications and from areas of the globe not commonly studied, *Plague in the Early Modern World* provides new information and a unique platform for exploring early modern world history from local and global perspectives and examining how early modern people understood and responded to plague at times of distress and normalcy.

Including source materials such as memoirs and autobiographies, letters, histories, and literature, as well as demographic statistics, legislation, medical treatises and popular remedies, religious writings, material culture, and the visual arts, the volume will be of great use to students and general readers interested in early modern history and the history of disease.

Dean Phillip Bell is President/CEO and Professor of Jewish History at the Spertus Institute for Jewish Learning and Leadership in Chicago. His publications include *Sacred Communities: Jewish and Christian Identities in Fifteenth-Century Germany*, *Jews in the Early Modern World*, and *Jewish Identity in Early Modern Germany: Memory, Power and Identity*. He is also editor of *The Routledge Companion to Jewish History and Historiography*.

Plague in the Early Modern World

A Documentary History

Edited by Dean Phillip Bell

Routledge
Taylor & Francis Group

LONDON AND NEW YORK

First published 2019
by Routledge
2 Park Square, Milton Park, Abingdon, Oxon OX14 4RN

and by Routledge
52 Vanderbilt Avenue, New York, NY 10017

Routledge is an imprint of the Taylor & Francis Group, an informa business

© 2019 selection and editorial matter, Dean Phillip Bell; individual chapters,
the contributors

The right of Dean Phillip Bell to be identified as the author of the editorial material,
and of the authors for their individual chapters, has been asserted in accordance
with sections 77 and 78 of the Copyright, Designs and Patents Act 1988.

All rights reserved. No part of this book may be reprinted or reproduced or utilised
in any form or by any electronic, mechanical, or other means, now known or
hereafter invented, including photocopying and recording, or in any information
storage or retrieval system, without permission in writing from the publishers.

Trademark notice: Product or corporate names may be trademarks or registered trademarks,
and are used only for identification and explanation without intent to infringe.

British Library Cataloguing-in-Publication Data
A catalogue record for this book is available from the British Library

Library of Congress Cataloging-in-Publication Data
Names: Bell, Dean Phillip, 1967– editor.
Title: Plague in the early modern world : a documentary
history / edited by Dean Phillip Bell.
Description: Abingdon, Oxon ; New York : Routledge, 2019. |
Includes bibliographical references.
Identifiers: LCCN 2018038024 | ISBN 9781138362482 (hardback : alk. paper) |
ISBN 9781138362499 (pbk. : alk. paper) | ISBN 9780429432057 (ebk)
Subjects: LCSH: Plague–History. | Plague–Social aspects.
Classification: LCC RC172 .P55 2019 | DDC 614.5/732–dc23
LC record available at https://lccn.loc.gov/2018038024

ISBN: 978-1-138-36248-2 (hbk)
ISBN: 978-1-138-36249-9 (pbk)
ISBN: 978-0-429-43205-7 (ebk)

Typeset in Galliard
by Newgen Publishing UK

For Juli, with love and gratitude forever

Contents

2   Religious understanding of and response to plague   72

Figures and tables

Figures

Tables

Figures and tables (sources)

Acknowledgments

This book has evolved over many years. As a result of that time lapse and the broad scope that I have attempted to cover, I have quite naturally sought the assistance of many colleagues and I am most pleased to record here my gratitude for all their help and sage advice. Thanks, as always to my colleagues at the Spertus Institute for Jewish Learning and Leadership, who have provided a supportive intellectual environment and access to a diverse range of materials held at Spertus and in far-flung collections across metropolitan Chicago and the globe. I thank Michael Liu for sharing his extensive research on the history of epidemics in China and A. Tunç Sen and Malynne Sternstein, both of the University of Chicago, for their assistance with some challenging translations from Turkish and Czech respectively. Over the years I have received extremely thoughtful and constructive feedback and encouragement from Carina Johnson, Sander Gilman, and Robert Jütte. I am thankful to Keren Fraiman for her friendship, collegiality and support and to Mike Hogue for his friendship and for many coffee-laden and collegial conversations, as well as for introducing me to the concepts of vulnerability and resilience. Finally, it is my family that deserves the greatest part of the credit for the completion of this book. They have tolerated the early morning work, the frequent diversions, and the stressful interludes that go into the construction of all projects like this. Though they are far away geographically, it is always rewarding and a source of great strength to share ideas and philosophize with Malkaya and Chanan. Roni and Yair have had more on the ground experience with this book, more I am certain, than they would have liked at times. But they have born it with great patience and support. My wife Juli, as always, is my inspiration. She makes everything I accomplish possible, with her remarkable caring and nurturing and her constant faith in and support of me and my work. In this case she has also donned the role of thought partner and so I am doubly appreciative for all that she does for me and our family and all that she has contributed to this work.

Introduction

Trapped somewhat unceremoniously between the medieval and modern worlds the early modern period witnessed many significant developments—from technological innovations, increasing globalization, and religious reform to political centralization. Against this backdrop, frequent and recurring outbreaks of plague and other epidemics around the world helped to define local identities and they simultaneously forged and subverted social structures, recalibrated demographic patterns, dictated political agendas, and drew upon and tested religious and scientific worldviews. The examination of how early modern people understood and responded to plague, therefore, offers extraordinary opportunities to consider early modern society from both local and global perspectives and at times of both distress and normalcy.

Many previous studies have focused on plague in Western and Central European historical and literary narratives. However, few books have examined plague in a broader and more comparative way. What is more, although several books have collected and published primary source documents in English translation, most have focused on the early outbreaks of the plague in the mid-fourteenth century (the Black Death) and most have generally centered their attention on Western Europe.

In this book, therefore, I examine plagues around the early modern world, giving particular attention to important outbreaks of, and responses to, plague in Europe and the lands of Islam, as well as for comparative purposes to other (largely non-plague) disease epidemics in the Americas, Asia, Africa, and India during the period of the Second Pandemic of the bubonic plague. Throughout this book I have tried to balance available sources; however, there are some limitations to a completely global presentation. First, the nature and spread of plague varied considerably in the early modern period. We have no evidence for bubonic plague in the Americas, for example, before the modern period—though contemporaries regularly described a range of other epidemics and the term "plague" was used in important literary contexts—in both cases making a comparison with other diseases and perceptions of disease in the Americas useful for this volume. In Japan and large parts of Africa and India we likewise have little written evidence for early modern bubonic plague. In some cases, these lacunae are the result of the state of documentary remains. In other cases, they reflect different epidemiological histories. Recent genetic research does, in fact, present evidence of plague in the early modern period in parts of Africa, which would be otherwise undocumented. Second, theories of disease (like diseases themselves) crossed political, religious, and cultural borders throughout history and often took a variety of shapes and hues as a result. This was increasingly true in the globalizing early modern period. As a result, local traditions and worldviews often incorporated the thinking of external communities, and many different religious and scientific approaches. Ancient Greek learning and monotheistic religious traditions, for example, seeped into Eastern texts and traditions, or at least affected the inflection and trajectory of many Eastern discussions. As will become clear throughout this Introduction, early modern people understood and responded to plague in ways dictated by their different religious and scientific contexts as well as their encounters with other peoples and traditions. Particular discussions of disease in India, to take only one example, combined a range of views derived from Hindu as well as Muslim and Christian texts and worldviews.

This book includes five chapters that provide overviews and English translations of a wide variety of sources related to: the rise and spread of the plague during the period of the Second Pandemic, including foundational religious and scientific-philosophical texts that provided much of the conceptual context and language for writing about plagues in the medieval and early modern worlds; religious responses to plague; medical understanding and treatment of plague; governmental and political reactions to plague; and social and cultural implications of plague.

This sourcebook provides materials culled from diverse geographical areas and cultures. These include memoirs and autobiographies, letters, histories, and literature, as well as demographic statistics, legislation (local, regional, and national or imperial), medical treatises and popular remedies, religious writings (such as prayers, biblical commentaries, and saints' lives), music, and material culture and the visual arts. Each document includes an introduction that helps the reader to situate and analyze the document.

The range of materials included in this volume is limited by several factors, including the availability and accessibility of documentary evidence in some places and, most significantly, my own language limitations. While I have gathered some sources that have been previously translated from languages I do not work in (for example from Arabic), I have also benefitted from assistance with some short excerpts from texts in Turkish and the research conducted by colleagues on Chinese materials. The vast majority of materials I present in this volume, however, I draw from sources in languages in which I have some facility, particularly Hebrew and Western and Central European languages.

Modern medicine and conditions

The bacterium *Yersinia pestis* manifests itself in various forms of bacterial infection, most notably bubonic plague, which is associated with the appearance of buboes, or swollen lymph nodes, especially, but not only, in the armpit or groin.

Bubonic plague or, often more frequently simply "plague," has been the frequent subject of historical accounts of the Middle Ages as well as rich fodder for the imagination of students, children, and Hollywood productions. Provoking deeply visceral responses, the plague has been somewhat iconic, and something of a metonym for the "dark ages" themselves. In part, this image has been related to the devastating effects of various epidemics (not only bubonic plague) throughout history. The sheer volume of material—from history, to medicine, literature, and art—produced in the midst of, and later in response to, outbreaks of plague makes the task of assessing the physical, social, and cultural impact of plague difficult, however. The rampant death and tumultuous social upheavals associated with the outbreak of plague have nurtured curiosity and compassion, but also fear and marginalization. We have calculated mortality rates and read heart-wrenching personal reflections. At the same time, many civic leaders betrayed concerns that the poor and foreigners infected the rich and they sought ardently for more general societal order amidst the chaos of plague and associated disasters.[1] The varied historical conditions and contexts in which the plague has sprung, and in which it has simultaneously participated and shaped, add further to the dramatic, compelling, and complex nature of the topic.

Despite modern medical advances, plague continues to intrigue and haunt people. Though not generally in epidemic proportions, plague is still present. Various strains and biovars (strain of microorganisms) of the bacterium that causes bubonic plague have emerged over the past 5,000 to 20,000 years.[2] It exists today in at least eight countries in Africa, six in Asia, three in South America, and seven states in the United States,[3] and probably as well in Europe.[4] Since the middle of the twentieth century the successful use of antibiotics has largely mitigated the effect of bubonic plague.[5] Still, a vaccine has not been developed, immunity appears to be short-lived,[6] and mortality can vary significantly depending on local conditions. On average, approximately eight people per year contract the plague in the United States, according to the United State Centers for Disease Control. In 2015, 12 cases of the plague were reported in the United States across seven states, with four proving fatal.[7]

The number of people affected by plague can be substantially higher in other areas around the world, however. Madagascar, for example, is one center of plague persistence today, with an average of approximately 1,250 cases per year.[8] Plague has also broken out in relatively large numbers in other locations over the past several decades, and the overall total number of plague cases has risen since the 1980s.[9] Between 1992 and 1994 alone 1,248 cases were recorded in a Peruvian epidemic and in the decade between 1994 and 2004 there were 630 cases in China, with a fatality rate of 6.67%.[10] An epidemic hit India in 1994, with 876 infections.[11] Between 2000 and 2009, according to the World Health Organization (WHO), some 21,725 cases of plague were reported, with a fatality rate of 7.4%.[12] The vast majority (97%) of these cases, which were primarily in the form of bubonic plague, occurred in Africa. One of the most active bubonic plague areas is the Ituri region of the Democratic Republic of Congo, with approximately 1,000 cases reported annually.[13]

While even these numbers do not generally cause great panic (except for those unfortunate to be in the affected regions or grappling with plague), they should, when seen with the development and spread of other diseases, warn us that disease and serious epidemics are not simply things of the past. They continue to affect human lives and shape social, economic, and political structures and cultural worldviews. They impact humans directly and even comparatively small outbreaks can have lasting consequences. Throughout history, plague could be associated with a range of social, political, and economic challenges. Marginalized groups in the medieval and early modern worlds were at times accused of spreading plague. Such accusations have continued even today, with Muslims in Surat accused of poisoning the city's water system during the 1995 plague outbreak, for example.[14]

While we have come primarily to look for the transmission of plague as occurring through the bite of infected fleas living on rats, and then seeking new, often human hosts when the rat host dies, plague can and has been transmitted through a variety of rodents and even other animals. A recent study that may have surprised some people familiar with well-trodden narratives, noted that it was gerbils, not rats, that helped spread the plague in the Middle Ages—gerbils, whose numbers swelled following favorable climatic conditions, but who died *en masse* with a severe drought that hit Europe a decade or so before the outbreak of the Black Death.[15] Indeed, gerbils are one of many different mammals that have served as important vectors in the transmission of plague throughout history. A larger group of mammals and flea species may be involved in the transmission of plague than was once assumed;[16] some recent studies have even suggested that plague, at different times in history, could have spread between humans (see p. 16), perhaps explaining its quick progression at certain times. The persistence of plague historically and today is generally possible because of reservoirs of host animals, typically burrowing animals such as the great gerbil and marmot,[17] which exist in somewhat protected environments that allow for the survival of infected flea populations.[18] Not surprisingly, then, environmental conditions that encourage flea activity can correspond to plague amplification. Mild and wet winters and wet springs, for example, may provide foliage for small rodents and good climate conditions for flea activity.[19] Some geographical regions, such as Europe's alpine uplands, appear to be particularly good reservoirs for these mammal and flea populations.[20] In addition to the natural characteristics of this area, the link to key Mediterranean plague centers provided further opportunities for the spread of plague.[21]

Biological research, especially that involving ancient DNA (aDNA) extracted from dental and skeletal remains deposited in plague-era graves, has offered significant information about the nature and development of plague in history. As a result, it seems prudent to contextualize the outbreaks of plague and to consider the historical conditions in which it operated and spread, as well as the varying ways that humans have understood and responded to it. In this book, accordingly, I explore the multiple dimensions of plague in the context of the later Middle Ages and early modern period (for the purposes of this study, from the middle of the fourteenth century, as the Black Death was running rampant, until the end of the eighteenth century, when the last major outbreaks were striking Europe and other parts of the globe—generally referred to as the Second Pandemic of plague), a period which converges to a large degree with a wide range of other disease epidemics that have often been seen as significant factors in historical development around the world.

Given this diversity of transmission and response, an approach to the history of plague by definition must be multi-disciplinary.[22] The difficulty of identifying plague (which is described in greater detail in Chapter 1), as well as other diseases, in history supports the argument that although we may suspect the presence of plague in certain periods and locations—because of recorded symptoms and narrative descriptions of the disease progression—it is only in the modern period of the lab that we can determine with certainty the actual presence of plague.[23] Indeed, the etiology of plague, as one recent historian notes, "involves a complex system of entanglements in which every organism (as host, vector, or pathogen) constantly interacts with other organisms, as well as the surrounding environment," and therefore requires an interdisciplinary approach.[24] As indicated above, the history of plague is not only about biology; it has also had other dimensions, notably a political dimension, by which, for example, Europeans associated it with the East (the Ottoman Empire as well as Asia) and used it as a colonial oppositional force against which Europe had to protect itself. Simultaneously, such an argument appeared to demonstrate Europe's superiority and the backwardness of the East (and its associated sanitary conditions),[25] with the Ottoman Empire literally being depicted by Westerners as the "sick man of Europe."[26]

Vulnerability and resilience: conceptual categories and interpretive framework

While early modern plague has been studied from different perspectives for specific regions and periods, the recurrence of plague—which affected many places and people throughout the early modern period—has not received a comprehensive overview. Further, the early modern occurrences of plague have often been linked with the great Black Death of the mid-fourteenth century; however, these outbreaks varied in many ways and the early modern manifestations need to be understood on their own terms.

Given the current medical understanding of plague and the wide scope of the impact of plague in the early modern period, are there any ways to understand the various responses to plague in order to present a more holistic interpretation? The concepts of vulnerability and resilience—which have largely been developed and applied in the fields of psychology, organizational development, political science, ethics, and material sciences—may offer such a possibility.

Vulnerability is often placed within the context of the study of law and public policy as well as in conversations about feminism, discrimination, and post-colonialism. Its emphasis has been simultaneously on ontological vulnerabilities shared by all people on the basis of their humanity and particularized vulnerability that certain groups face at specific times, locations, and conditions. Resilience, frequently associated with material sciences as well as behavioral sciences and psychology, has been employed in a range of studies trying to understand how and why humans bounce back from adversity and even thrive and adapt amid challenges. The concept has been linked with neo-liberal governments and has at times been criticized as a governing tool that dictates how people behave and gives too much power to authorities, which use the assumption that people are in a constant state of vulnerability and need to be protected and taught to be resilient. Recently, both subjects have been applied more broadly to questions of religion and religious experience as well.[27] Given the overlap of these concepts with the analysis of natural disasters and disaster management, their interaction with both science and social and cultural issues, and their intersection with politics, policy, and the law, vulnerability and resilience would appear, on first blush, to offer some useful insights as we attempt to provide an overarching context and framework for plague in the early modern world—a disease that could take many different forms and be associated with a variety of other diseases and conditions, in a world that was changing rapidly, but which contained a remarkable diversity of experiences, practices, and localized conditions.

The term vulnerability is derived from the Latin word "vulnus," wound.[28] Vulnerability is defined in various ways, including: the ratio of risk to susceptibility;[29] the inadequacy of means or ability to protect oneself against adverse events and to recover from them;[30] the capacity to be harmed by a stress or perturbation. Vulnerability is often presented as a counterpoint to or inversion of resilience, though many scholars find resilience to be part of the overall continuum of vulnerability. In the area of disaster studies, for example, vulnerability refers to susceptibility, risk, resilience, and resistance.[31] Vulnerability is, therefore, a process that can change over time and space. Vulnerability includes social, economic, environmental, and institutional dimensions. As a result, both resources as well as networks affect how vulnerable an individual, institution, or community may be. Poverty, social isolation, or marginal status are often indicators of high levels of vulnerability.[32] Social and economic capital are, correspondingly, seen as necessary for successful responses to the vulnerabilities associated with disaster. Individuals and communities may face multiple vulnerabilities in a layered fashion.[33]

Some recent discussions of vulnerability have argued that vulnerability is universal and constant among humans. It is not the characteristic of certain groups, but the result of the very embodiment of human beings.[34] According to this line of thought, the result is that, "While we can attempt to lessen risk or act to mitigate possible manifestations of our vulnerability, the possibility of harm cannot be eliminated."[35] But vulnerability is complex and can take many forms, affected by harm that is beyond individual or human control. As a result, other scholarship has noted that vulnerability is particular and can vary a great deal depending upon individual contexts, characteristics, and resources. For our purposes, it is also important to point out that some have argued that vulnerability is not purely negative. It is not only about harm and injurability; it can also be generative: "It forges bonds between human beings and leads us to create institutions."[36]

Early modern people lived with the plague—if not as a constant state, as a condition that recurred regularly in many places and that had an ongoing impact through related social, cultural, economic, political, legal, and religious developments. Early modern society was highly susceptible to infectious diseases and plague wreaked havoc in both major epidemics and smaller scale outbreaks across Europe and the Ottoman Empire, but also in parts of Asia and Africa. Other early modern diseases, especially combined with natural disasters and man-made catastrophes such as warfare, similarly ravaged early modern societies in these and other locations. Early modern people experienced, understood, and then tried to respond to such devastation. Full recovery did not always occur; and if it did, it could take generations, by which time a new wave of epidemic diseases likely struck again. Nonetheless, most early modern communities did respond with measures to protect their populations and with increasingly effective steps to respond to plague (and other disease) outbreaks. While it may be argued that the disease itself became less virulent over time and that those who survived developed higher levels of immunity, recent studies suggest that the virulence of the plague could vary dramatically. Part of what changed was the way that people perceived of and responded to the plague.

Many early moderns maintained religious worldviews and remained anchored in handed-down scientific and medical sensibilities that were informed by ancient and medieval philosophy. Similarly, practical experience—the creation of what we might call a "learning community"—revealed what traditional models and worldviews might not always, namely that particular behaviors and actions could be beneficial in preventing and combatting the outbreak of plague. At the same time, plague, like other catastrophes, was on occasion leveraged for political agendas. The result could be the stripping of land from natives, the marginal-ization of the poor, or the attacks against, expulsion, or even murder of out-sider groups such as Jews and foreigners. That is, regardless of the nature of the plague, its outbreak, or even the mere threat of an outbreak, plague was regularly harvested as a tool to control society and maintain boundaries, or, at the other extreme, to advance radical new social and political structures.

If early modern society was vulnerable, the nature and implications of that vul-nerability played out differently depending on a host of local conditions. Despite our modern tendency to read uniformity and one-dimensionality back in to the past, early modern society was heterogeneous and multi-valent. The plague was deadly to many who had the misfortune to contract it. However, the poor and the residents of certain locations were more likely to find themselves in contact with the plague and less likely to be able to afford some kinds of treatment; marginalized groups, such as Jews, were more likely to be looked at suspiciously when it was raging in or around an area. Vulnerability, therefore, was a general category that captures both general human susceptibility to the disease as well as the particular susceptibility of certain people or groups under specific conditions. As a result, in contextualizing these vulnerabilities we can learn a great deal about the structures, challenges, and change agents within early modern society writ large and in specific early modern communities.

While plagues could be disruptive and both exaggerate and provoke social and religious tensions, we also find evidence of long periods of normalcy and, especially for survivors, some sense of an ability to cope with the challenges brought about by plague. Early modern plague narratives revealed multi-dimensional responses to crisis and allow us insights into how early modern people perceived and interacted with one another at periods of rupture as well as normalcy.

Whether one sees resilience as a part of a broader system of vulnerability or even as the polar opposite of vulnerability, just as with the concept of vulnerability, there have been a wide range of definitions of resilience, drawn from diverse academic disciplines. How one defines the term, of course, dictates how it can be used and what implications it might have in more formal analysis. In its most basic form, resilience is used to describe the ability to withstand external pressure and return to an original shape, form, or position. In more developed discussions, resilience refers to adaptive capacities that allow for a return to some form of normal functioning (or quality of life), despite, or in the face of, external factors, such as trauma, adversity, or stress.

Seen as part of a process, some research has further suggested that resilience in fact allows people to learn from external conditions and develop improved functioning that leads to greater responsiveness to future challenges. In this case, beyond simply returning to a status quo or a base level of functioning, learning from experiences, developing innate frameworks and resources, and refocusing on larger issues, capacities, and contexts are also characteristics of resilience. Resilience is, therefore, frequently seen as a process but one of many possible trajectories that may follow exposure to trauma or severe stress. While resilience can take on different characteristics and vary in different contexts, some forms of resilience are rather common. Resilience can function at both individual and communal levels; it can also respond to larger disturbances and catastrophes, as well as more everyday occurrences. As a result, resilience arises and can be expressed across multiple domains of life. In addressing this range of concerns, resilience involves some sort of social competence and problem-solving skill.

Given the regularity of their appearance, plagues were seen as part of everyday early modern life. In between outbreaks of plague most people experienced significant periods of normalcy and many communities were able to manage plagues. As a result, despite the number and severity of plague outbreaks, scholarly consensus has begun to emerge that even the most dramatic epidemics did not necessarily constitute watersheds in history, certainly not in the majority of places.[37] As one scholar has noted,

> The people who grew up with the plague in no way panicked when the epidemic approached. Rather one followed intently the path of the plague through more distant and closer cities. They did not panic if the plague broke out in the city. They rather first tried to sustain everyday life as long as possible. They had learned to observe and differentiate.[38]

Even when the plague triggered great disruption, the duration and virulence of the outbreak could vary greatly.

While some scholars, especially in the nineteenth century, equated plague with extreme psychological challenges and long-term change, more recent scholars have downplayed the dramatic dimensions of the plague.[39] The plague seems to have impacted fashion and architecture in some places,[40] but novelty was accompanied by conservatism and continuity as well, not the least in concerns with memory and family.[41] To take but one example, in Marseilles after the plague of 1348, local institutions were both flexible and efficient in handling a wide range of business and inheritance cases—"the social and institutional fabric of the town held together and proved 'remarkably adaptive.'"[42] People "domesticated" the plague and came to terms with it, making meaning as best they could.[43]

Religion, community, and memory have all been linked to the fostering of resilient behavior. Religion and spirituality can help to create a sense of coherence and produce meaning from and the ability to manage crises and difficult situations. Research has shown that community plays an important role in building and exercising resilience. Communal networks and relationships can provide resources and access to them, as well as the redundancy necessary for resilient responses to crisis. They can also provide social support structures. Memory similarly mobilizes schemas that allow individuals and communities to interpret new information and it helps to create explanations that connect new and prior experiences and allows for the assimilation of new experiences or the transformation of previous models.

Early modern religious beliefs, practices, and traditions helped in the response to the challenges of an early modern "age of anxiety." Still, religion never existed in a vacuum—it was defined by theological concepts, central texts, local practices, popular interpretations, and the trappings of political and cultural currents in which it flowed. Civic plague ordinances seamlessly crossed the boundaries between policy and religious behavior in the same way that the language and content of sermons, biblical commentaries, and prayers often recognized the complexity of diseases and the import of natural, as well as supernatural, conditions that helped to create and exacerbate them. The sacred was part of the daily life of many early moderns, though increasingly how one interpreted sacrality was being tested in an age of simultaneous reform from within and increased experience with others from without. Regardless of whether one believed that rituals such as processions, fasts, or even prayers would provide protection or relief from the plague, such actions helped to fashion community and identity, and simultaneously draw boundaries and foster exclusion. At the very least, religious response offered the opportunity for self-reflection and moral improvement at the individual, communal, and even national level. If plague was a punishment for sin, it was in the best interest of people to consider their sins and find ways to improve. The result was far-reaching ordinances and laws that comprehensively reflected communal sensibilities and goals.

If resilience is enhanced through community networks, then early modern social structures were valuable assets during plagues. While response to catastrophe could mobilize people, recent research shows that such mobilization is generally of short duration and that systems tend to return to original conditions after the most pressing period of a catastrophe has passed. Early modern communities did at times show themselves capable of farther-reaching changes, however. In part, this was due to the inclination of humans and human community to absorb lessons from experiences. At the same time, the very nature of the early modern experience—with increasing technology and communication, scientific reconceptualization, internal re-structuring in both religious and social systems, and evolving notions of the State and its increased monitoring and control of individual behavior (famously described by scholars such as Norbert Elias and later Michel Foucault)—forced the creation of stronger networks and communal infrastructures. That is not to say that early modern communities were necessarily more closely knit than medieval or modern ones. There remained significant social disparity and tension in large, sprawling urban centers as well as in more compact towns and villages. However, the increasing early modern ability to mobilize and the tendency to take proactive hygienic measures certainly provided a significant amount of protection from greater devastation.

Memory has been discussed as a key to resiliency. Memory can spark learning, as we recall prior experiences and, hopefully, learn from them. But, memory is also about narration. How we tell the stories of past experiences—how we frame and choose details and story lines—can be an effective tool in both how we change behaviors to enhance resilience as well as how we view the larger context in which we live. Plague was a regular occurrence in some places and so part of normal life. In other places, where plague was more infrequent and large gaps of time separated outbreaks, the memory of plague and reports from other places, combined with changes in medical knowledge and civic legislation, could dictate how people responded to plague when it occurred or to threats of outbreaks, spread through news from other areas. Memories of challenges as well as successes in overcoming the plague, tales of survival, and reflections about measures employed (from religious intercession to medical interventions and communal ordinances) could go a long way in transmitting valuable information and connecting people to something far beyond their immediate challenges and concerns.

The nature and scope of early modern experiences with, understanding of, and responses to plague intersect closely with these discussions of vulnerability and resilience—long before these concepts were clearly articulated. Early moderns were able to learn from their experiences of plague, as demonstrated by discussions of medical treatments and evolving legislative measures in many places. They built on these experiences, which could conflict with inherited worldviews, and slowly developed ways to cope with the recurring challenge posed by plague and disease. Discussing epidemics in historical context, Charles Rosenberg argues that, "When threatened with an epidemic, most men and women seek rational understanding of the phenomenon in terms that promise control, often by minimizing their own sense of vulnerability."[44] The second stage of response to an epidemic involves collective agreement on an explanatory framework, which could serve for both social criticism as well as social control.[45] The story of plague in the early modern world was multi-dimensional. Plagues revealed the structural and conceptual weaknesses of society even as they underscored the internal strength and ability to adapt that characterized, and was played out repeatedly during, a dramatic period of change and growth. This book provides some medical details about the plague—produced by early modern physicians and writers as well as contemporary scholars—but what will receive the bulk of our attention will be the social, cultural, and religious implications of and responses to early modern plagues, for what such responses can tell us about early modern society more broadly.

Notes

1 See John Henderson, "The Black Death in Florence: Medical and Communal Responses," in *Death and Towns: Urban Responses to the Dying and the Dead, 100–1600*, ed. Stephen Bassett (Leicester, 1992), 136–47.
2 Scholars have identified at least eight strains of *Yersinia pestis* and four biovars, which emerged over the past 5,000–20,000 years. Ann G. Carmichael, "Universal and Particular: The Language of Plague, 1348–1500," *Medical History Supplement* 27 (2008): 17–52, 1 of the electronic version.
3 A. Lloyd Moote and Dorothy C. Moote, *The Great Plague: The Story of London's Most Deadly Year* (Baltimore, 2004), 278.
4 Monica H. Green, "Taking 'Pandemic' Seriously: Making the Black Death Global," in *The Medieval Globe* 1 (2014), *Pandemic Disease in the Medieval World: Rethinking the Black Death*, ed. ibidem (Kalamazoo, 2014), 27–61, 53; Ann G. Carmichael, "Plague Persistence in Western Europe: A Hypothesis," in *The Medieval Globe* 1 (2014), *Pandemic Disease in the Medieval World: Rethinking the Black Death*, ed. Monica H. Green (Kalamazoo, 2014), 157–91, here at 161.
5 Zlata Blazina Tomic and Vesna Blazina, *Expelling the Plague: The Health Office and the Implementation of Quarantine in Dubrovnik, 1377–1533* (Montreal, 2015), 45.
6 Ibid.
7 www.cnn.com/2015/08/27/health/utah-plague-death/?iid=ob_homepage_deskrecommended_pool&iref=obnetwork [last visited March 28, 2016].
8 Moote and Moote, *The Great Plague*, 278.
9 Michelle Ziegler, "The Black Death and the Future of the Plague," in *The Medieval Globe* 1 (2014), *Pandemic Disease in the Medieval World: Rethinking the Black Death*, ed. Monica H. Green (Kalamazoo, 2014), 259–83, 265.
10 Ibid., 268.
11 Moote and Moote, *The Great Plague*, 278.
12 Ziegler, "The Black Death and the Future of the Plague," 266.
13 Ibid., 267.
14 Ibid., 261.
15 http://abcnews.go.com/Health/gerbils-rats-caused-bubonic-plaque-study-finds/story?id=29192197 [last visited March 28, 2016].
16 Carmichael, "Plague Persistence in Western Europe: A Hypothesis," 159.
17 Ibid., 179–80.
18 Ibid., 157.
19 Ibid., 174, 177, 158.
20 Ibid., 162.

21 Ibid., 177.
22 Monica H. Green, "Editor's Introduction," in *The Medieval Globe* 1 (2014), *Pandemic Disease in the Medieval World: Rethinking the Black Death*, ed. ibidem (Kalamazoo, 2014), 9–26, here at 14.
23 Andrew Cunningham, "Transforming Plague: The Laboratory and the Identity of Infectious Disease," in *The Laboratory Revolution in Medicine*, ed. Andrew Cunningham and Perry Williams (Cambridge, 2002 (orig., 1992)), 209–44, here at 209ff.
24 Nükhet Varlik, "New Science and Old Sources: Why the Ottoman Experience of Plague Matters," in *The Medieval Globe* 1 (2014), 193–227, here at 194–5; see also Katherine Royer, "The Blind Men and the Elephant: Imperial Medicine, Medieval Historians and the Role of Rats in the Historiography of Plague," in *Medicine and Colonialism: Historical Perspectives in India and South Africa*, ed. Poonam Bala (London, 2014), 99–110, here at 101.
25 Royer, "The Blind Men and the Elephant," 103.
26 See Varlik, "New Science and Old Sources," 201, 204.
27 These concepts have also been tied to discussions of risk and applied to medieval and early modern history in several recent articles and books, for example: Daniel R. Curtis, *Coping with Crisis: The Resilience and Vulnerability of Pre-Industrial Settlements* (Aldershot, 2014); C. M. Gerrard and D. Petley, "A Risk Society? Environmental Hazards, Risk and Resilience in the Later Middle Ages in Europe," *Natural Hazards* 69:1 (2013): 1051–79.
28 Catriona Mackenzie, Wendy Rogers, and Susan Dodds, "Introduction: What Is Vulnerability, and Why Does It Matter for Moral Theory?," in *Vulnerability: New Essays in Ethics and Feminist Philosophy*, ed. ibidem (Oxford, 2014), 1–29, here at 4.
29 Michael J. Zakour and David F. Gillespie, *Community Disaster Vulnerability: Theory, Research, and Practice* (New York, 2013), 17.
30 Katharina Marre, "Components of Risk: A Comparative Glossary," in *Measuring Vulnerability to Natural Hazards: Towards Disaster Resilient Societies*, 2nd ed., ed. Jörn Birkmann (Tokyo, 2006), 569–618, especially 596–603.
31 Zakour and Gillespie, *Community Disaster Vulnerability*, 20.
32 Ibid., 148.
33 Wendy Rogers, "Vulnerability and Bioethics," in *Vulnerability*, ed. Mackenzie et al., 60–87, here at 70.
34 Martha Albertson Fineman and Anna Grear, *Vulnerability: Reflections on a New Ethical Foundation for Law and Politics* (Farnham, 2013).
35 Ibid., 21.
36 Ibid.
37 Ibid., 58.
38 Otto Ulbricht, "Angst und Angstbewältigung in den Zeiten der Pest, 1500–1720," in *Gotts verhengnis und seine strafe—Zur Geschichte der Seuchen in der Frühen Neuzeit* (Wiesbaden, 2005), 101–12, here 102.
39 Paul Slack, *Plague: A Very Short Introduction* (Oxford, 2012), 43.
40 Ibid., 44.
41 Ibid., 45–46.
42 Ibid., 50.
43 Ibid., 52.
44 Charles Rosenberg, "What Is an Epidemic? AIDS in Historical Perspective," *Daedalus* 118:2 (Spring 1989): 1–17, 5.
45 Ibid., 6.

1 The bubonic plague
Historical overview and scope

Terminology

The plague—in myriad forms—recurred in vast swaths of the world, especially in Europe and the lands of the Ottoman Empire, from the fourteenth into the nineteenth century, with many virulent outbreaks. The term "plague" could be a generic word that medieval and early modern people cast around with little precision. In Latin the word *plaga* meant a "blow" or "wound." It was not necessarily associated with disease[1] and when it was it could be a general moniker that might refer broadly to a range of disease epidemics,[2] such as bubonic plague, typhus, small pox, and cholera [see 1.7]. Indeed, at times early modern people had difficulty distinguishing between different diseases and especially between plague and the more general "pestilential fevers,"[3] though some recent scholarship has asserted that early modern physicians could often be quite precise in differentiating various symptoms and diseases.[4] Here it is important to note that the term plague was regularly used in literary, historical, and religious texts. In medical texts, where disease was discussed more precisely, other terms were regnant, including *pestis, mors,* and *magna mortalitas*.

The term plague occurs frequently in the Hebrew Scriptures. The biblical passages in which it was detailed served as prooftexts and fodder for much of the early modern discussion about plague in Jewish, Christian, and Islamic societies. The Hebrew Bible addressed plague in a variety of contexts. Like its Latin equivalent, the Hebrew word "maggefah" (as well as other forms, including *negef, nega, makkah*), denoted "striking" or "smiting." It was associated with the plagues that God famously inflicted upon the Egyptians (as described in the book of Exodus), the punishment of the spies who reconnoitered in the Holy Land,[5] as well as a variety of rebellions,[6] idolatrous practices,[7] and various other transgressive behaviors.[8] Plague might also be associated in biblical texts with other diseases, such as leprosy.[9] Biblical plagues, like those of the early modern period, it should also be pointed out, could affect people as well as animals.

In Arabic, writers utilized several different words to connote communicable disease more generally: *ʿadwā* (contagion); *wabā* (plague); *al-mard al-wāfid* (epidemic); and *tāʿūn* (pestilence). As with both Latin and Hebrew words, the range of Arabic terms is related to hitting or striking.[10] A similar phenomenon could be found in German-speaking lands, where early modern writers described plague in many different ways, focused variably on death, contagion, infection, fever, and regional or localized illnesses.[11] Indeed, the term "pest" or "pestilence" could be used in both a specific sense, often in reference to bubonic plague, and in a more general sense, referring to disease broadly. In the general sense, the term typically indicated diseases that were widespread, contagious, and deadly,[12] and it depicted a wide range of diseases, including ones long known to contemporary society and others that were new and unfamiliar, especially as globalization brought far-flung societies into interaction with each other.

The diversity of words available and enlisted in historical accounts belies the complexity of both the concept and reality of plague. As each of these various examples indicate, how early moderns understood and experienced plague and even the very language they used to describe plague could be diverse and ambiguous. In addition to its connection to specific or general diseases, importantly for this book, early modern people also used it frequently and extensively in a metaphorical sense to represent a variety of political, social, and even religious conflicts. In a mid-sixteenth-century Italian treatise, to take only one of many possible examples, it referred to the invasion of the Turks.[13] As we will see, early modern people did not live in a vacuum. They were affected by contemporary concerns and perspectives, as well as the rich well of images, stories, and lessons they inherited and gleaned from religious and literary writings and social and communal traditions and concerns.

Early modern people drew from and wove into their own accounts some classical discussions of epidemic diseases. From Titus Lucretius Carus (c 99–c 55 BCE), whose *On the Nature of Things* (*De Rerum Natura*) was rediscovered in the later Middle Ages, they possessed an explanatory model that emphasized the role of environmental conditions, regional variations, and associated social conditions. According to Lucretius, whose work drew from other thinking of classical Antiquity and would have great appeal into the early modern period:

> there are many seeds of things which support our life, and on the other hand there must be many flying about which make for disease and death. When these by chance or accident have gathered together, and thrown the heavens into turmoil, the air becomes diseased. And all these diseases in their power and pestilence either come from without down through the sky like clouds and mists, or often they gather together and rise from the earth itself, when through damp it has become putrescent, being smitten out of that novelty of climate and water affects any who travel far from home and country, just because there is a great difference in these things ... Hence different places are dangerous to different parts and members; the variety of air brings that about.[14]

Defining early modern plague

There has been a great deal of discussion about how we should define an "epidemic." Epidemics tend to be events, often of an episodic character, that are both broad (or public) experiences and of a dramatic intensity. In part, it is the social response and framing of an epidemic, along with the consequent search for explanations, which define an event as an epidemic.[15] Reflecting specific cultural attitudes, responses to epidemics reveal social and political considerations. At the same time, defining some event as an epidemic encourages a particular response(s) and can serve to mobilize or inform collective action that helps to shape or bound a particular community or subset of a community.[16] While diseases of course have a pathological reality, they also involve a certain degree of social and cultural construction.[17]

But, given such considerations, what exactly was early modern "plague?" From a medical perspective, it is often quite difficult to distinguish various diseases and epidemics in history. During the course of the 1894 outbreak of the Third Pandemic of the bubonic plague in China, the Swiss microbiologist Alexandre Yersin traveled to China and worked to isolate the disease and develop a serum for its treatment.[18] The disease is commonly referred to as *Yersinia pestis*, after Yersin and his accomplishments. There appear to have been three types of plague manifestations of *Yersinia pestis*. The most common was bubonic (accounting for 75% of the cases), which, without modern treatment, was fatal in 60 to 90% of cases within three to six days after the onset of symptoms.[19] Symptoms of bubonic plague include high fevers, convulsions, vomiting, and severe pain in the limbs. A significant distinguishing factor in bubonic plague, which is frequently mentioned in early modern sources, is the bubo—a swollen mass at key lymph nodes, often in the armpits, groin, or neck area. The presence of buboes often indicated healing—the bursting of the buboes and the release of the encased pus might occur spontaneously or be induced by medical interventions, such as special plasters or surgery—but they gave the plague its unique identifying (and terrifying) characteristic.

An early and detailed description of the symptoms of the plague was provided by the Italian notary Gabriele de' Mussis (c 1280–c 1356), who wrote that:

> For the rest, so that the conditions, causes, and symptoms of this pestilential disease should be made plain to all, I have decided to set them out in writing. Those of both sexes who were in health, and in no fear of death, were struck by four savage blows to the flesh. First, out of the blue, a kind of chilly stiffness troubled their bodies. They felt a tingling sensation, as if they were being pricked by the points of arrows. The next stage was a fearsome attack which took the form of an extremely hard, solid boil. ... As it grew more solid, its burning heat caused the patients to fall into an acute and putrid fever, with severe headaches. As it intensified, its extreme bitterness could have various effects. In some cases it gave rise to an intolerable stench. In others it brought spitting of blood, for others, swellings near the place from which the corrupt humors had arisen—on the back, across the chest, near the thigh. Some people lay as if in a drunken stupor and could not be roused. Behold the swellings, the warning signs sent by the Lord. All these people were in danger of dying. Some died on the very day the illness

took possession of them, others on the next day, others—the majority—
between the third and fifth day. There was no remedy for the vomiting of
blood. Those who fell into a coma, or suffered a swelling or the stench of
corruption, very rarely escaped. But from the fever it was sometimes possible
to make a recovery.[20]

Victims who did not succumb to some of the numerous accompanying medical ailments such as heart failure, internal bleeding, or simple exhaustion, might
begin to recover after eight to ten days.[21] As noted in the Introduction, bubonic
plague can be spread to humans by insects, typically fleas that infect certain
animals (often rodents, such as black rats), as well as by other humans.

A second form of plague associated with the bacterium was pneumonic plague,
which passed directly between humans. In this form, fatalities were generally 100%
within two days of the appearance of symptoms. This was the case, for example,
in Milan during the epidemics of the mid-fifteenth through the early sixteenth
centuries.[22] In a third form of associated plague—septicemic, contracted through
infected insect bites and entering the bloodstream—victims would die within 24
hours, before the outbreak of any symptoms.[23] While scholars have traditionally divided plague into these three different types—bubonic, pneumonic, and
septicemic—some historians have more recently introduced a fourth type, gastro-
intestinal.[24] Each of these types varies in how the pathogen enters the body.[25]

The issue of identifying plague in the early modern world can be complicated.
General symptoms and specific skin disorders associated with *Yersinia pestis* have
varied widely.[26] While bubonic plague has often been associated with swellings
in lymphatic glands (especially in the groin, but also armpits and, less frequently,
cervical glands), swellings can on occasion appear outside of the lymph nodes,
in other parts of the body.[27] The transmission of plague might also affect how it
presents; pneumonic plague does not display the traditional buboes, from which
bubonic plague took its name and bubonic plague transmitted through human
fleas as opposed to rat fleas leads to groin swelling much less frequently.[28] Indeed,
new evidence suggests that plague could be transmitted between humans,
through human lice and human fleas, and this might help explain the very rapid
spread of the disease in some cases.[29]

There have been three major and extended pandemics of bubonic plague in
history. The First Pandemic of the plague ravaged the Mediterranean region and
spread as far east as Persia and as far north as the British Isles between the fifth
decade of the sixth century—beginning in Egypt in 541 and appearing in Gaul
by 546—and lingering in parts of Europe until the middle of the eighth century.[30] During this period there was not a decade that did not experience plague
in some part of this region. Where plague did appear it often returned in intervals
of between six and 20 years.[31] In the Byzantine Empire, for example, the plague
broke out 18 times between 541 and 750, an average of every 11.6 years.[32]

Procopius of Caesarea (c 500–c 560 CE), a well-known scholar who lived in
the Byzantine province of Palaestina Prima and who accompanied Roman gen-
erals into battle, provided a good deal of information about this so-called Plague

of Justinian (because it broke out during that emperor's reign) in Book II of his *History of the Wars*.[33] In his description of the events of the year 542, Procopius expressed what he saw as the unprecedented magnitude and global reach of the plague:

> During these times there was a pestilence, by which the whole human race came near to being annihilated. ... But for this calamity it is quite impossible either to express in words or to conceive in thought any explanation, except indeed to refer it to God. For it did not come in a part of the world nor upon certain men, nor did it confine itself to any season of the year, so that from such circumstances it might be possible to find subtle explanations of a cause, but it embraced the entire world, and blighted the lives of all men, though differing from one another in the most marked degree, respecting neither sex nor age. For much as men differ with regard to places in which they live, or in the law of their daily life, or in natural bent, or in active pursuits, or in whatever else man differs from man, in the case of this disease alone the difference availed naught.

Many of what would come to be seen as typical symptoms of bubonic plague were described by Procopius, who noted that physicians were at a loss to understand the causes of the disease:

> Now some of the physicians who were at a loss because the symptoms were not understood, supposing that the disease centered in the bubonic swellings, decided to investigate the bodies of the dead. And upon opening some of the swellings, they found a strange sort of carbuncle that had grown inside them. ... Death came in some cases immediately, in others after many days; and with some the body broke out with black pustules about as large as a lentil and these did not survive even one day, but all succumbed immediately. With many also a vomiting of blood ensued without visible cause and straightway brought death.[34]

Procopius noted that the outbreak of the disease lasted four months in Byzantium, with greatest virulence in the last three, with thousands perishing daily and many laying unburied as a result.

Some scholars have suggested that the period of the First Pandemic intersected with and most likely also impacted a range of major political changes, including: the shaping of the Byzantine Empire, the rise of the Roman papacy, the beginning of Islam, and the rise of the Carolingian Empire.[35] Recent scholarship is convinced that the disease of the First Pandemic (the Justinian Plague) was, in fact, plague—however, the relative importance of bubonic, septicemic, and pneumonic forms of the disease is still open to discussion.[36] A Third Pandemic spanned the late nineteenth and twentieth centuries, especially in Asia.[37] The medical response to this Third Pandemic has helped to shape a good deal of our understanding of plague.

The focus of this book is on the Second Pandemic, which probably began with the outbreak of plague in central Asia in the fourth decade of the fourteenth century and particularly haunted Europe and the Middle East into the eighteenth century and the nineteenth century in some places. One study now asserts that the bacillus associated with the Second Pandemic originated in or near the Qinghai-Tibet Plateau. The author of the study notes that there were, in fact, major epidemics in south China in 1331, 1333, 1344, and 1345.[38] Indeed, Chinese annals mention a major epidemic in the Hopei province in 1331 that killed 90% of the population[39] and in 1345–46 in other regions. Historical sources also mention an epidemic in southern India in 1344.[40] The confluence of other disasters such as famine, floods, droughts, earthquakes, and climate change further intensified the impact of the plague in many of these locations. Some historians have also explored the possible connections between the Black Death and the previous widespread and deadly famine ("The Great Hunger") that swept much of Europe and other parts of the world between 1314 and 1317.[41] Regardless of the actual impact of other disasters, in the minds of early modern people, who were steeped in and borrowed from the scientific texts of Antiquity, the eruption of disease epidemics was often associated with various environmental conditions, from earthquakes and volcanic eruptions, to weather changes, famine, and bad odors.[42]

How early moderns experienced and described plague could vary. Indeed, the terms for specific swellings may themselves have carried different valence in the early modern period than they do today. More than half of the cases of plague in late fifteenth- and early sixteenth-century Milan, for example, revealed no evidence of skin disorders characteristic of descriptions of plague.[43] In Milan, black, purple, and red bumps were normal features of plague and few accounts revealed swelling in traditional locations associated with bubonic plague. In accounts from Milan, spitting or vomiting blood, common in descriptions of the Black Death elsewhere, was not usual; rather vomiting accompanied by nausea, abdominal bleeding, emissions of fluid, and stomach pains were commonly recorded.[44] Although some scholars have raised the question of whether other diseases might have been recorded as plague, some historians have asserted that early modern physicians were in fact capable of distinguishing between various signs and symptoms—including various swellings, spots, and other associated symptoms.[45]

Although we once assumed that given their backgrounds and particular interests, physicians and civic health boards understood and responded to plague differently—with the former more focused on miasma (the spread of disease through bad air) and the latter on contagion—recent evidence suggests that the reality was far more nuanced.[46] This complexity resulted from the range of contemporary usages of terms for plague (as well as other diseases), the engagement of physicians by health boards to diagnose epidemics, as well as a growing emphasis among early modern physicians on observation and experience and on identifying cures and remedies.[47] As a result, governmental actions reflected familiarity with and responsiveness to different understandings (both miasmist and contagionist—see Chapter 3 for a discussion of these concepts) of plague.[48]

There has been a good deal of discussion among contemporary scholars about whether the plague of the Second Pandemic was actually the bacillus *Yersinia pestis*.[49] Recent molecular and genetic evidence, especially through the examination of DNA drawn from dental remains of individuals in mass graves from the middle of the fourteenth century, has confirmed that it was.[50] Additionally, based on analysis of ancient DNA (aDNA) from burial sites in medieval Germany, we now know that there was long-term persistence of plague in some reservoir hosts within Europe, beyond any reintroduction of plague from central Asia, connecting the Black Death and later outbreaks during the Second Pandemic.[51] Such research has also been helpful in identifying variations of the bacillus, geographic points of origin, and the animal reservoirs that maintain and can transmit the disease.[52] Both biologists and historians have noted that a range of environmental and historical conditions (from poverty, weather, nutrition, and the presence of other diseases, and even land settlement and usage)[53] could affect who contracted plague and how the plague displayed.[54] Weather, in particular, might create conditions favorable for the shift of rat fleas from sylvatic to commensal rodents, allowing them to be maintained for long periods of time, even without contact with wild rodents.[55] What is more, certain environmental landscapes and conditions can better support rodent reservoirs and their associated fleas. These areas include higher altitudes and areas with low annual precipitation (including deserts, semi-deserts, and steppes).[56] It appears now that a wide range of rodents as well as other animals (including cats, dogs, rabbits, goats, and camels) can be infected with the disease and transmit it to humans.[57] *Yersinia pestis* could, moreover, survive in soil and plants and could be transmitted through infected foods, skin lesions, or airborne bacteria.[58]

Throughout the later Middle Ages and early modern period plague was associated with other diseases and catastrophes, which might have preceded, coincided with, or followed it. [See 1.11] Such was the case, for example, in the 1430s in parts of Europe, especially south Germany, when a variety of other disasters, including earthquakes, famines, severe weather, and floods hit together along with plague outbreaks.[59] Such challenging situations could have multilayered impact. They revealed communal and societal vulnerabilities, exasperating social tensions and resulting in extensive poverty, leading in part to the increased legislation about and monitoring of the poor and beggars that was so widespread in the later Middle Ages.[60] But early modern governments and rulers learned from experience and often developed policies and protocols to address what they saw as the key factors in the origin and spread of plague. They devised and enforced various ordinances related to the poor, quarantine of people and goods, restrictions on travel, and policies for food production and prices.[61] Natural disasters could weaken communal infrastructures and populations. Shifting demographics, which could result in great population clusters, as well as declining hygiene and nutrition (particularly when famine hit), might have made certain locations and communities more vulnerable to the plague. Political discord and warfare also frequently facilitated the spread and impeded the treatment of plague, as was the case during the civil war in China that led to the overthrow of the Ming dynasty in 1368.[62]

Plague appears to have traveled through the Black Sea region, Constantinople, and the Middle East, before arriving in Western Europe. While some have suggested a role for the Mongol conquests at the end of the thirteenth century in the spread of the disease,[63] the chronology does not appear likely. Plague was recorded starting in 1347 in Constantinople, Alexandria, and Messina (Sicily), followed by various Italian and French ports, including Genoa, Pisa, Venice, Ragusa, Marseille, and the French Riviera. By 1348 the plague had reached into other parts of Italy, France, Spain, Germany, and England. Between then and 1352 it swept through Switzerland, Holland, Norway, Scotland, Sweden, Poland, and Russia.[64]

The start of the Second Pandemic of the bubonic plague came to be called the Black Death first in the sixteenth century by Danish and Swedish chroniclers[65]— black because of the terror as well as the black pustules associated with the disease. In some locations, the Black Death was indeed quite devastating. It claimed more than 60% of the population in places.[66] It killed some 200,000 people in Cairo alone, for example, at least according to one estimate.[67] In parts of Europe it would take between 100 and 133 years (five to six human generations) for populations to absorb the shock of and rebound from the Black Death.[68] This was the case in parts of Europe as well as the Middle East, where productivity dipped and poverty increased for a long period of time.[69] Still other communities and regions would never fully recover. Nevertheless, many communities proved to be resilient in the face of the plague, which washed over them in regular waves over the course of several centuries. In some areas, including in parts of Italy, the local population began to recover or grow already in the late Middle Ages.

Massive population loss naturally transformed economic and social structures in many areas. Ironically, perhaps, some economic historians have asserted that the dramatic demographic shock of the Black Death was in part responsible for the economic upturn of Western European society in the early modern period.[70] In Western Europe more people gained access to farmland and housing.[71] Due to the reduction in labor, wages and standards of living for those who survived rose in many places. In England, there were new employment opportunities and the purchasing power of wages at least doubled during the century after the Black Death.[72] Of course, the conditions prior to the outbreak of the Black Death were crucial determinants of the conditions afterwards.

The situation in Europe could be quite different from that in other parts of the world. According to one interpretation, due to warfare and urbanization mortality rates and per capita income remained high in Europe. Such changes did not affect China, it has been argued, which did not experience higher permanent death rates after the fourteenth century due to generally healthier conditions in its cities and more uniform political organization.[73] Wars, according to this argument, were fewer in China than in Europe and they also led to fewer epidemics.[74] What is more, China's main population centers were geographically more homogeneous, whereas they were more diverse in Europe and therefore more susceptible to the movement of armies.[75] By this logic, the increased trade of late medieval and early modern Europe also served as a highway for the transmission of plague.[76] Such arguments have been used to explain the apparent lack of widespread plague in early modern China, though as we will see, China was not exempt from deadly epidemics. [**For the later eighteenth century, see 1.9**]

The last major epidemics of the Second Pandemic would strike Austria and Bohemia starting in 1712, Constantinople in 1717 (to return again at the start of the nineteenth century) followed by Hungary and parts of Poland in 1719, Marseilles and Syria 1720–22 [**See 1.6 and 4.9**], Messina in 1743 (claiming 40,000–50,000 people), Russia in 1771–72 [**See 1.8**], and North Africa in 1799–1800 (erupting in Fez in the winter, perhaps claiming one-quarter of the population)[77] and then again in the 1830s, and across the Middle East in the 1830s as well—in Egypt in the first half of the nineteenth century, with plague outbreaks in 20 of the 44 years between 1800 and 1844 in Alexandria and a major epidemic in 1835 that claimed an estimated one-third of the 250,000 people of Cairo.[78]

Recurrence of plague

As a zoonotic disease, plague persists in cycles of exchange of the bacterium between rodent hosts, with fleas typically serving as vectors of transmission. As a result, plague reservoirs may continue to exist in sylvatic (wild) rodent populations even when there is no trace of the disease in humans. When plague is transmitted to humans, plague outbreaks can have different manifestations in terms of location, impact, and duration. The dramatic changes ushered in by the start of the Second Pandemic did not end at the middle of the fourteenth century. Second and third outbreaks would devastate large parts of Europe and the Middle East especially in the 1360s and early 1370s. In the Byzantine Empire, for example, outbreaks occurred nine times between 1361 and 1399,[79] with numerous epidemics in Crete in particular.[80] But, outbreaks continued into the fifteenth century and beyond as well, with plague spread at times by armies on the move. Byzantine chroniclers record epidemics in 1403 and 1416–17. The latter was the subject of an intriguing description by the fifteenth-century Byzantine chronicler Doukas, which linked the plague and the conversion of the youngest son, Yusuf, of the Ottoman Sultan Bayezid (1360–1403).[81]

Outbreaks in the Byzantine lands continued frequently in the fifteenth century,[82] and they might have broad regional implications, as recorded by the chronicler Kritovoulos (c 1410–c 1470) for an episode in 1467. The chronicler described specifically the extent of death and devastation in Constantinople, the dire social conditions, and the inability of contemporaries to address the associated challenges of the massive wave of death.[83]

As already noted, plague was often not an isolated event. A quick overview of some plague events reveals that in many areas prone to such outbreaks plague was a regular part of life. A major plague erupted in Istanbul (Constantinople before the Ottoman conquest in 1453) in 1466, a little more than a decade after the city had been conquered by the Ottomans.[84] It was followed by another outbreak just two years later and again in 1471,[85] presaging what would be centuries of recurring infestation in this bustling cosmopolitan area. These plagues significantly depopulated the city and Ottoman authorities responded with forced resettlement, forming part of a larger political plan often mentioned in historical accounts.[86] The plagues that hit Istanbul almost invariably swept into nearby areas, such as Edirne, as well.[87]

Plague next struck Istanbul in the early 1490s, reaching numerous other Ottoman lands, including Syria and Egypt.[88] Epidemics in and around Istanbul were recorded almost constantly between 1497 and 1533 (including 17 years of major outbreaks).[89] The sixteenth-century Italian businessman Marino Sanudo, who kept extensive diaries of his business and travels, observed in September 1513 that, "there is such enormous plague [in the countryside of the territory of Istanbul] that the inns are closed, and it is incredible how great a number are dying."[90] For October 1513 he noted that, "Business is slack in Constantinople, because the city has lost 60,000 people from plague in the course of one year, including a great number of prominent figures."[91] Additional plague outbreaks would haunt the city in the 1520s, between 1533 and 1549, and again between 1552 and 1567 [See 1.1], culminating in a major epidemic in the 1570s, as well as various epidemics into the seventeenth and eighteenth centuries.[92] In the eighteenth century alone, plague occurred in 68 individual years in Istanbul.

Plague recurred throughout the lands of the Ottoman Empire more generally—throughout the Balkans in the early 1580s[93] and across Anatolia and the Arabian Peninsula in the 1590s. [See 1.2][94] In the seventeenth century, we find references to ten plagues in different parts of the Ottoman Empire.[95] Many places within the Empire faced ongoing cycles of plague during the eighteenth century as well: Aegean Anatolia for 57% of the century; Moldavia-Wallachia for 45%, Egypt for 44%, Albania for 44%, Bosnia-Serbia for 41%, and Syria for 33%.[96] The duration of epidemics might vary considerably. In the period between 1700 and 1850, for example, the largest number of plague outbreaks in the Ottoman Empire lasted one year (45%); 26% lasted two years; and around 4.5% seven years or more (the approximately 25% remaining plagues lasted less than one year).[97] Between 1713 and 1792 there were only 20 years entirely plague free in the large city of Smyrna and during the collective period of epidemic, death tolls reached up to 35% of the total population.[98] These plague years were of a very uneven nature, however, as some plague outbreaks were very serious, as in 1709, 1728, 1735, 1741, 1759, 1762, 1771, and 1788. Five years of outbreaks appear to have been particularly devastating—1740, 1758, 1760, 1765, and 1784. As in Europe, these events were compounded by other calamities, such as famine and major conflagrations, which either preceded or came on the heels of the epidemic.[99] In the Syrian region of the Ottoman Empire, plagues were recorded in 47 years of the eighteenth century, with 34 in the first half of the century alone. Mention of plague was made in Aleppo in 15 years in the eighteenth century[100] [See 1.8] and Damascus in 11 separate years.[101] The port city of Acre (Akko) was hit repeatedly by plague, including in at least 22 years during the eighteenth century.[102]

The majority of eighteenth-century plague epidemics in Ottoman lands have been assessed by one recent historian as "weak" in terms of mortality and long-term impact—81.6% in Istanbul, more than 60% in Salonika, Smyrna, and Alexandria. But, there were still plenty of epidemics that proved to be quite debilitating. In Istanbul, the same scholar has assessed 6.5% of the epidemics as "moderate," 5.4% as "grave," and 6.5% as "terrible." Plagues in Aleppo were more frequently "terrible," according to this metric—with 24% of epidemics there falling into that category.[103] The severity of a plague did not end with the death of large numbers of people. While an extremely devastating plague hit Egypt in 1791, claiming thousands of lives daily, the plague also threatened to unleash social unrest and required significant administrative intervention from the ruling authorities.[104] Although a variety of theories were advanced to explain the severity of the outbreak, it was, not surprisingly, the connection to a cycle of other crises and disasters (such as drought and famine) and corresponding inflation that stoked the difficult conditions.[105]

The plague hit various parts of Russia and Lithuania starting in the fourteenth[106] and well into the fifteenth century.[107] Numerous epidemics would strike Russia again throughout the sixteenth century, including one that may have claimed more than 15,000 lives in Novgorod in 1508, during the last year of a three-year infestation.[108] Significant epidemics also returned in the early 1550s and again in the late 1560s and early 1570s, combining with and increasing the effects of warfare and famine.[109] Seventeenth-century epidemics, such as the one in 1602 similarly combined with other disasters and diseases, such as typhus.[110] A major epidemic hit in 1654, with estimates of death reaching 400,000 in Moscow and 800,000 across central Russia.[111] Various outbreaks erupted in specific locations through the end of the seventeenth century.[112] Several plagues swept across Russia in the eighteenth century. At the start of the second decade of the eighteenth century, plague also devastated a good portion of Eastern and Northern Europe, including Ukraine (1703), Poland, Lithuania, Silesia, and Prussia (1704), with some 280,000 deaths in Prussia and Lithuania alone. The outbreak of 1710 led to the death of an estimated 40,000 people in Copenhagen.

One of the greatest calamities occurred with the major Russian epidemic of 1770–72. [See 1.8] In addition to the significant loss of life, many contemporaries cast the event within the context of the military hostilities between Russia and the Ottoman Empire,[113] with some contemporaries alleging that the plague began in and spread from the Ottoman Empire[114] because of contagion as well as drastic weather conditions.[115] Contemporaries estimated the number of people who died at the hands of this particular plague episode to be 100,000.[116] The plague had the most devastating effects in areas in and closest to the capital. In Moscow in 1771 some 37,000 people died from the plague.[117] Other provinces were also hit heavily. The economic village of Pushkino, northeast of Moscow, for example, lost 537 of 629 inhabitants in fall 1771. Two hundred and twenty-one of 277 inhabitants in Tarsovka died as did 338 of 479 inhabitants in Khomutovo, all around the same time.[118] Largely an urban affair, the plague appears to have killed no more than about 6% of the surrounding rural population.[119] Still, the plague had a dramatic impact on Moscow's economy and manufacturing, in part because of the significant decrease in the number of workers.[120] Connected with various other conditions, the outbreak of plague furthered deteriorating economic conditions, and led to rioting by thousands of people, especially those unwilling to be confined by quarantine.[121] Serfs accounted for the largest number of alleged rioters (more than 50%) examined by government officials.[122]

The plague would return to Europe, as well as other parts of the globe, regularly throughout the later Middle Ages, with an average of 11.6 years between outbreaks. In the early modern period, the time between recurrences of plague would rise slightly to 13.4 years (between 1535 and 1683).[123] Plague, nevertheless remained a regular feature of early modern life in many areas of Europe, Asia, parts of Africa, and the Middle East. In Istanbul, for example, during the Second Pandemic, plague recurred on average every 2.2 years; in Salonika, during that same period, there were 142 outbreaks, equivalent to an average of every 3.5 years.[124]

Plague might also be pervasive in particular territories, affected by regional conditions and contributing to the social, economic, and medical characteristics of a given geographic region, for example in southern Italy in the seventeenth century.[125] There were at least 11 epidemics in Persia during the sixteenth through eighteenth centuries.[126] People living in German-speaking lands experienced deadly waves of early modern epidemics. Consider the example of two major cities in Switzerland. Between 1457 and 1535 there were at least 30 years of plague in Geneva (37.5% of the period). If one were to focus in on the latter part of that period, between 1473 and 1535, there were 28 years (or 44.5% of the period) in which the city was riddled by plague.[127]

In the city of Basel contemporary chroniclers recorded four epidemics in the fourteenth century, six in the fifteenth century, nine in the sixteenth century, and another four in the seventeenth century. The total number of deaths from plague ranged from 800 on the low end (1576–78) to an estimated 5,000 on the high end (1439 and 1502—both higher than the estimated 4,000 for the Black Death of 1348–49). Thus, the average number of deaths per epidemic was 2,217. Mortality ranged from 9.1% (1576–78) to 52.6% (1502), with an average mortality rate of 22.3%.[128] The south German city of Ulm was struck repeatedly in the sixteenth and seventeenth centuries, almost every decade at least once.[129] In the early eighteenth century, in 1713–15, a quarter of the city population died from a plague epidemic. As had been true for some fourteenth-century outbreaks, early modern plague epidemics could have significant population impact. Seventeenth-century Frankfurt am Main, for example, experienced 38,678 deaths as opposed to only 20,224 births between 1622 and 1646, a period which included many active plague years.[130] [See 1.4]

Some areas appear to have been less affected by plague during the Second Pandemic. Bohemia, for example, has generally been seen as somewhat immune to significant plague outbreaks, though recent studies have noted that narration of this alleged escape of plague was often a polemical tool that served political purposes—the suggestion that Bohemia was spared and other places, such as Rome, were punished by the plague could have particularly sharp religious or political utility.[131] In contrast, we now have information that confirms that plague did indeed attack parts of Bohemia with varying intensity in the later fourteenth and early fifteenth centuries, with a notable outbreak in 1380, when an estimated 30% of parish clergy and 15% of the total population of Prague died.[132] In the seventeenth century, regular cycles of plague hit the city of Prague and surrounding regions in six separate decades.[133]

It was not only the number of plagues, but the vicious nature of some epidemics that caused deep-reaching transformation of societies. The total death toll brought on by the plague could range broadly depending on many different factors. Some extremely lethal plagues ravaged some cities in the early modern period. Plague in Paris may have killed 40,000 people in 1466.[134] In 1553 mortality in Paris reached 50,000 and 20,000 in Cologne.[135] A plague in Lisbon in 1569 claimed nearly half of the population, some 50,000 people.[136] At around the same time, 200,000 died in Moscow (1570) and 50,000 in Lyons (1572).[137] The deadly outbreaks in northern Spain between 1596 and 1602 may have killed millions of people; the later plagues in 1648–52 and 1677–85 were also quite deadly.[138] Something like half of the population (150,000 deaths) died in an outbreak of plague in Naples in 1656. [See 1.5 for an image from the plague in Rome in that year] In London, 20% of the population (100,000 people) died in the plague of 1665.

A third or more of the 180,000 people in Venice had been wiped out in the plague of 1575–77. That city was wracked by another significant plague in 1630–31 that swept across much of northern Italy and central Europe.[139] That same plague claimed 61% of the population in Verona, 59% in Padua, and 46% in Cremona and Milan, and it carried off a total estimated 280,000 people throughout northern Italy. In the middle of the seventeenth century plague killed more than 60% of the population in Genoa. A devastating epidemic hit parts of the Ottoman Empire between 1572 and 1589; the plague of 1592 may have taken 70,000 people.[140] Of course, mortality rates could vary a great deal by region and outbreak (see Table 1.1).[141]

Or, consider the more focused statistics for the city of London in the sixteenth and seventeenth centuries (see Table 1.2).

In the 219-year period from 1450–1668 the plague was reported somewhere in Holland in 107 of those years and there were five periods of reports of multi-year outbreaks: 1453–57; 1459–66; 1472–79; 1607–15; and 1638–48.[142] In that same period Amsterdam suffered 37 years of plague;[143] Leiden 34 years;[144] and Rotterdam 30 years.[145] A quick overview of significant plague years and associated mortality in Amsterdam is given in Table 1.3.[146]

Tracing weekly deaths in a single city provides some insight into the progression of an epidemic. Consider Leiden from January 6 through November 12, 1655, claiming 11,591 lives, with significant summer-time spikes (see Figure 1.1).[147]

Table 1.1 Mortality rates in the seventeenth and eighteenth centuries in select major Western European cities

City	Year of plague	Total population	Death by plague	Mortality (%)
Lyon	1628	100,000	50,000	50
Milan	1630	130,000	60,000	46
Verona	1630	53,000	30,000	57
Venice	1631	141,000	46,000	33
Barcelona	1651	44,000	20,000	45
Naples	1656	300,000	150,000	50
Genoa	1657	100,000	60,000	60
Marseille	1720	100,000	50,000	50
Messina	1743	40,000	28,000	70

Note: Information for this table was compiled for comparative purposes from various studies and general overviews, including: Joseph P. Byrne, *Daily Life during the Black Death* (Westport, 2006); Paul Slack, *Plague: A Very Short History* (Oxford, 2012); Mary Lindemann, *Medicine and Society in Early Modern Europe*, 2nd ed. (Cambridge, 2010); and including the article on Plague in the *Encyclopedia Britannica*.

Table 1.2 Mortality statistics for London in the plague years of the sixteenth and seventeenth centuries

Date	Total burials	Plague burials	Mortality (as % of population)
1563	20,372	17,404	24.0
1578	7,830	3,568	7.8
1593	17,893	10,675	14.3
1603	31,861	23,045	22.6
1625	41,312	26,350	20.1
1636	23,359	10,400	7.5
1665	80,696	55,797	17.6

Note: Information as presented in A. Lloyd Moote and Dorothy C. Moote, *The Great Plague: The Story of London's Most Deadly Year* (Baltimore, 2004), 10.

Table 1.3 Death rates in Amsterdam during major plague outbreaks in the seventeenth century

Plague year	Total population	Deaths	Deaths per thousand
1602	104,932	10,700	102
1617	100,000	8,449	84
1623	107,000	5,929	55
1663	195,000	9,732	50
1664	201,000	23,475	117

Note: Based on information provided throughout Leo Noordegraaf and Gerrit Valk, *De Gave Gods: De pest in Holland vanaf de late middeleeuwen* (Bergen, 1988).

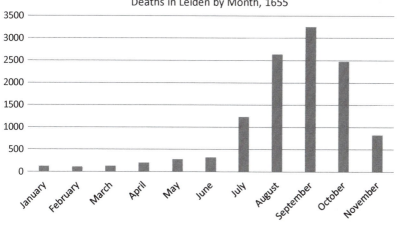

Figure 1.1 Number of deaths in Leiden by month in 1655.

Global dimensions

The Second Pandemic affected broad swaths of the globe. The destructive forces of the plague struck India in the early seventeenth century [**See 1.3**] and again savagely in 1687–90, when one chronicler reported that:

> The plague and pestilence, which for several years had been in the Dakhin as far as the port of Surat and the city of Ahmadabad, now broke out with violence in Bijapar, and in the royal camp. It was so virulent that when an individual was attacked with it, he gave up all hope, and thought only about his nursing and mourning. The black-pated guest-slayer of the sky sought to pick out the seed of the human race from the field of the world, and the cold blast of destruction tried to cut down the tree of life of every being ... The visible marks of the plague were swellings as big as a grape or banana under the arms, behind the ears, and in the groin, and a redness was perceptible round the pupils of the eyes, as in a fever or pestilence. It was the business of heirs to provide for the interment of the dead, but thousands of obscure and friendless persons of no property died in the towns and markets, and very few of them had the means of a burial. It began in the 27th year of the reign, and lasted for seven or eight years.[148]

Based on censuses completed before and after the plague, Bijapur (in south-west India) may have lost more than one-half of its population, or more than one million people, to the epidemic.[149] Plague was devastating in northern India throughout the sixteenth and seventeenth centuries; the south was more prone to the ravages of cholera from the nineteenth century on.

As in other parts of the globe, epidemics involving a variety of diseases occurred in China throughout the later Middle Ages and early modern period. Some historians have maintained that plague did not strike China in earnest again until the nineteenth century, confined until that time in the Yunnan Province in the southwest.[150] While the epidemiological history of early modern China has yet to be written, there are some, limited, contemporary sources that have not received a great deal of scholarly attention to this point, but which reveal episodes of plague in early modern China.[151] In China we have various references to 18 plague outbreaks in the fourteenth century, 19 in the fifteenth, 41 in the sixteenth, 37 in the seventeenth, 38 in the eighteenth, and 40 in the nineteenth centuries.[152]

Although plague appears to have been frequently transmitted along trade routes—across Asia, Europe, and Africa[153]—throughout the seventeenth century it seems to have been less widespread in Asia than was the case in Europe at the same time.[154] However, regardless of the occurrence of plague, it is difficult to write about plague in early modern China—as in other contexts and locations—in part because the terms used to denote plague and epidemic could reflect many different individual or combined diseases. Smallpox, for example, broke out in 1657 (Chaozhou), pox in 1672 (Shauguan), diphtheria in 1736, scarlet fever in 1785 (Qingpu), flu epidemic in 1714, and malaria on numerous occasions, including 1660 (Jiangning), 1766 (Jiukongjiang), and more generally in 1768, to give just a few examples. As in Europe, plague was frequently associated with other calamities, such as famine and drought, as it was in 1691. Major epidemics of one sort or another are recorded in China 20 times between 1644 and 1699. Epidemics with few specific details are noted for 1667 (Shenzhou County) and 1674 (Teng County). Epidemics of plague or pestilence, more generally, were recorded numerous times in the eighteenth century, including: 1738 (Jiangchuan), 1759 (Shicheng), 1760 (Lingao), 1770 (Ning), and 1787. A major plague pandemic appears to have occurred in numerous locations in 1771. Further references to "plague" were made in ten separate years between 1647 and 1771. [See 1.9]

We have generally assumed that the Second Pandemic was not universal (i.e., not truly global), with little evidence of plague in south Asia, southeast Asia, sub-Saharan Africa, Indonesia, or the Americas.[155] Recent research, however, suggests that the Second Pandemic may have reached into sub-Saharan Africa and the Indian Ocean Basin.[156] Speaking to the need for a multi-disciplinary approach, we find that biological evidence may reveal the presence of plague in some areas, particularly in Africa, where documentary evidence is not available. This information suggests, for example, that a strain of *Yersinia pestis* was extant in East and Central Africa (Kenya to Uganda and the Democratic Republic of Congo), with African clades (branches) separating from that of the main Black Death strain between 1377 and 1650, perhaps around the start of the sixteenth century. [See 1.10] The high level of local genetic diversity of the disease in these places also suggests that it had been in the region for a long time.[157] Combined with growth in trade (which may have helped to create a rodent infrastructure important in

the transmission of plague) in the region and some evidence of the sudden aban-
donment of metropolitan centers that had flourished before the middle of the
fourteenth century, we have indicators, even without documentary evidence, of
plague in the region.[158] Similarly, the social upheavals in many areas in Asia in the
fourteenth and fifteenth centuries may point to disruption caused, at least in part,
by plague.[159]

The plague was simultaneously a global phenomenon and a regional affair. The
series of epidemics that raged through Franconia, the Bodensee, and Rhineland
regions of Germany between 1437 and 1439, for example, proved to be devastating in some locations, but less noted in others. Contemporary chroniclers
recorded more than 13,000 deaths in the large city of Nuremberg, resulting in
widespread panic and flight from the city.[160] Chroniclers in Basel reported more
than 4,000 deaths in that city and 1,100 in Bern.[161] The epidemic of the 1530s,
to take another example, struck Western Europe and North Africa, followed
by Venice (1552–53) and Ragusa (1533–34), before circulating more broadly
across the eastern Mediterranean and into Syria. It also hit the western and central parts of the Mediterranean, reaching Istanbul in 1533, and Athens, Anatolia,
and Egypt in 1534.[162] It lingered around the area or re-surfaced throughout the
1530s and into the early 1540s.[163] As recent scholarship has noted, the plague
was a major factor in early modern Ottoman history, and it had significant impact
in many aspects of daily life, as well as long-term religious, social, economic, and
political dimensions.[164]

Plague and other disease epidemics

Bubonic plague did not reach every corner of the early modern world. There is no
evidence of plague in early modern Japan, for example. Indeed, most European
visitors commented on the healthy climate regnant there. Still, there were reports
of other epidemics, particularly smallpox in 1615, which according to one
account claimed more than 2,600 people in Nagasaki.[165] Records of 20 epidemics
in the fifteenth century, 19 in the sixteenth and 16 in the seventeenth century
are frequently of unidentified diseases, but do reveal that medical concerns about
disease epidemics certainly existed in Japan as well.[166]

There were a number of diseases that haunted early modern people, including
smallpox, dysentery, tuberculosis, diphtheria, scarlet fever, whooping cough,
influenza, pneumonia, malaria, typhus, and syphilis, in addition to plague.[167] At
times it was clear to early modern people that these were different diseases. At
other times, the specific dimensions of disease were perceived as less important
than the particular responses and implications. Diseases could, of course, vary a
good deal by location, with some diseases native to certain lands and others transmitted through contact, such as smallpox and measles brought to the Americas
by Europeans or yellow fever which appears to have made its way to America from
Africa and syphilis perhaps transmitted from the Americas back to Europe.[168]

Measles epidemics offer a useful comparison. The outbreak of measles appears
to have occurred regularly in some places during the early modern period. In

eighteenth-century Korea, for example, measles epidemics erupted in ten- to 20-year cycles. The first great outbreak hit in 1668 and the outbreak of 1707 reportedly killed several hundred thousand people. Virulent attacks also occurred in 1730, 1752, and 1775. In one of the last large outbreaks in 1786, the King, Yi San (King Jeongjo, r 1776–1800) instituted both medical and theological responses.[169] He required doctors, especially those with experience with the disease, to hold office hours and to examine the sick. He likewise provided for the distribution of medicines, especially to the poor.[170] Cases of disease were recorded, noting specific symptoms, and medicines were distributed.[171] In addition, the king authored a sacrificial rite to the demons of pestilence. The writing of such works stretched back to the early fifteenth century;[172] in Ming China, it was believed that such sacrificial rites, which were intended for spirits that had not received proper funerary rites, would be effective against plagues.[173]

The situation in the Americas is somewhat more intriguing, particularly since Europeans have typically been seen as introducing devastating new diseases into the "new world." There may, however, have been some epidemic outbreaks of as yet unconfirmed infectious diseases even before the arrival of the Europeans. The term "plague," used below was employed in a broad sense of "disease" and does not in all likelihood refer to bubonic plague. One historian of the time, Guaman Poma, a sixteenth- and early seventeenth-century Quecha nobleman and historian, wrote in his discussion of the military achievements of Pachacuti Inca Yupanqui (1438–71) that:

> The defeat of Chile was made possible by the ravages of plague, which lasted for ten years. Disease and famine, even more than force of arms, brought about the downfall of the Chileans, just as civil war between Huascar and Atahualpa was later to facilitate the Spanish conquest. Peru itself suffered terribly from plague, famine, and drought. For a decade no rain fell and the grass withered and died. People were reduced to devouring their own children and when the stomachs of the poor opened it was sometimes found that they had managed to survive by eating grasses.[174]

The Mexica similarly recounted five periods of epidemic before the conquest, including during the mid-fifteenth century.[175] But Europeans conveyed other deadly diseases with them. A smallpox epidemic (also referred to as "plague," highlighting the multi-valent nature of the term in Europe and across the globe) broke out in 1518. Bartolome de las Casas (1484–1566), the Spanish Dominican historian and social reformer, described it as follows:

> A terrible plague came, and almost everyone died, very few remained alive. This was smallpox, which was given to the miserable Indians by some person from Castile; the feverish Indians, who were accustomed, when they could, to bathing in the rivers, threw themselves in anguish into the water, sealing the illness into their bodies, and so, as it is a destructive disease, they die in a short time: adding to this are the weakness and hunger and the nudity and

sleeping on the floor and overwork and the little health care that those they serve have always taken.[176]

A variety of diseases swept across the New World after the European conquest. In sixteenth-century Mexico, for example, it has been argued that there was a small pox epidemic in 1520–21; a decade later, 1531–32 either a smallpox or measles outbreak; in the mid-1540s typhus; mumps in 1550; influenza or diphtheria in 1559–60; measles in 1563–64; typhus or bubonic plague in 1576–81; Cocoliztli (Aztec) in the late 1580s; and measles again in 1595.[177] The 1576–81 outbreak, which included hemorrhaging and high fevers was associated with particularly high rates of mortality, in some cases half of the native population, according to some reports.[178] In Central America in the sixteenth century, smallpox epidemics appeared in 1520–21, 1527, 1529, and again in 1576–77. Measles erupted in 1532, 1533, 1558–62 with influenza and 1576–77 with smallpox and typhus. Bubonic or pneumonic plague may have hit Honduras and Nicaragua in 1531,[179] though there appears to be no medical evidence that this was in fact plague and not another disease. In response to the latter, the governor of Panama wrote:

> From a ship that has arrived from Nicaragua the *pestilencia* has struck this land, and it has been so great that although it has not yet ended, two parts of all the people that there are in this land have died, native Indians as well as slaves, and among them some Christians. I attest to Your Majesty that it is the most frightening thing that I have ever seen, because even the strongest does not last more than a day and a half, and some two or three hours, and now it reigns as at the beginning, and has become concentrated in Panama. The clerics are organizing processions, and praying, but not even these pleas to Our Lord have lifted his ire, to the point that I don't think there will remain alive a single personal in all the land.[180]

Some historians have speculated that bubonic plague may have similarly hit the Andes in 1531–33 and again in 1546—though again without medical evidence—along with outbreaks of smallpox, influenza, typhus, and measles in 1524–27, 1558–59 and 1585–91.[181]

The sixteenth century witnessed similar disease epidemics in both South and North America. In Brazil, smallpox may have broken out in 1562–63, along with fevers and dysentery in 1552 and 1554 and small pox in 1565, 1575, and 1597.[182] The Jesuit Leonardo do Valle noted in Bahia (Brazil) that:

> When this tribulation was past and they wanted to raise their heads a little, another illness engulfed them, far worse than the other. This was a form of smallpox or pox so loathsome and evil-smelling that none could stand the great stench that emerged from them. For this reason many died untended, consumed by the worms that grew in the wounds of the pox and were engendered in their bodies in such abundance and of such great size that they caused horror and shock to any who saw them.[183]

Smallpox would ravage Florida in the seventeenth century and that and other diseases, including, for example dysentery, typhoid, measles, and perhaps also malaria in the 1530s, typhus from 1576–81, and smallpox and measles in the last decade of the sixteenth century, hit the southwest of North America.[184] Similar diseases would confront the northeastern parts of North America in the seventeenth century.[185] A variety of epidemics broke out in eighteenth-century North America, including smallpox (e.g., South Carolina, 1698–99), scarlet fever (1735), and yellow fever (e.g., Charleston, 1728; New York and Charleston, 1732), described by one contemporary as fatal "Bilious Plague."[186] [See 1.11]

Beyond medical implications, various diseases were regularly leveraged to castigate foreign behavior and people. Responses to the wide range of epidemics could be similar across diseases and cultures. The Dutch minister and writer Philippus Baldeus' (1632–71) description of smallpox in the Malabar region of India in the middle of the eighteenth century provided the author an opportunity to take a jab at the "pagan" culture of the area, even as he began with a familiar discussion of air quality, climate, and symptoms. He wrote that:

> The diseases under which smallpox should be reckoned, were sent by God to punish the sin of the humans, but she has natural causes, she can originate from within and from outside, as air, food, drink, sleep, waking, rest and movement of the body, hunger, forcing and holding excrement, fashions and times of the year ... winds and venomous vapour of the air, as from the scalding fever and pestilence. ... Brahmins also know well, how according to the size of the winds, each period of the year produces various diseases. ... So sees one in spring the Malabaris are attacked by smallpox which without doubt originate from the heat and contaminated blood, and from other vicious humidity and fruits, which the common people mostly partake, who also are attacked by smallpox, for this season is also considered deadly or remediable, after that dampness was found venomous, so that some poxes are cured lightly, while others die in 12 or 18 days. ... The Pagans, thinking that Patragali sends the disease, leave the patient at once. This can be the reason why the image of a woman is [there] among the Pagans, there a child strikes the poor on the neck, as seeking help from this idol, being deserted by men. Because they judge the disease is infectious and sticking: they give the patient over to one of the Comaras, being the devotees of Patragali pagod. Believing that Patragali causes the smallpox they do then many oblations and ceremonies for the sick; to please this idol, cut off the heads of one or two hens, whose blood falling on the earth, was licked up by dogs ... the Malabaris gave this name to the smallpox, which they also hold to be the ulcer and the dagger of Patragali, therefore, when they see a patient with smallpox, they will worship him, because they think that Patragali is in the middle; so they do also to dead-body, calling it Pandara, that is a royal treasure, they know well also that God is good and does harm to none: but that Patragali, because she produces this evil, must be reconciled with offerings.[187]

The great Muslim historian Ibn Khaldun (1332–1406) noted in his universal history regarding the Black Death that:

> Civilization both in the East and the West was visited by a destructive plague which devastated nations and caused populations to vanish. It swallowed up many of the good things of civilization and wiped them out. It overtook the dynasties at the time of their senility, when they had reached the limit of their duration. It lessened their power and curtailed their influence. It weakened their authority. Their situation approached the point of annihilation and dissolution. Civilization decreased with the decrease of mankind. Cities and buildings were laid waste, roads and way signs were obliterated, settlements and mansions became empty, dynasties and tribes grew weak. The entire inhabited world changed. The East, it seems, was similarly visited, though in accordance with and in proportion to [the East's more affluent] civilization. It was as if the voice of existence in the world had called out for oblivion and restriction, and the world responded to its call. God inherits the earth and whomever is upon it.[188]

The bubonic plague was both destructive and long-lasting, in many ways reshaping the way that people understood and interacted with the world and one another. While responses to the plague took many different forms, for convenience, we can divide them into four broad categories of religious, medical/scientific, political, and social/cultural responses. All of these categories of responses could be theoretical and/or practical and they often overlapped across categories. Of course, responses to the plague were also dictated by specific local conditions, social structures, histories, and customs. The texts that follow provide a sample of the narratives and data associated with early modern plague outbreaks, highlighting consistencies and differences as well as the meaning associated with and derived from plague experiences.

Early modern plague could surface regularly in some areas. In many cases it was quite deadly. Many early modern societies proved to be quite vulnerable to the plague and other epidemics, especially in the context of other natural disasters and social and political disruption. At the same time, plague was in many ways a normal occurrence for many early moderns, who found ways to adapt and respond to epidemics. Such responses included legislation and medical treatment, as well as religious practice and polemics against Others, framed variously as contemporary accounts and historical reflections. The documents that follow are intended to provide details about the severity and geographic scope of plague from the sixteenth through the eighteenth century, across Europe and the Ottoman Empire, as well as in India and Africa, and comparatively for other disease epidemics in the Americas.

Sources

1.1 Plague in the Ottoman capital: a diplomatic perspective

Author: Ogier Ghiselin de Busbecq (1522–92)

Title: *The Turkish Letters of Ogier Ghiselin de Busbecq, Imperial Ambassador at Constantinople 1554–1562*[189]

Introduction: Ogier Ghiselin de Busbecq was a Flemish writer, herbalist, and diplomat in the service of the Austrian rulers. He studied at universities in Leuven and in northern Italy. He served as an ambassador to the Ottoman Empire in Istanbul in the 1550s, serving later at the court of Emperor Ferdinand in Vienna as well as subsequent rulers. His letters and accounts were first published in 1581. While a witness to events as they were unfolding and a potentially valuable source for Ottoman and Islamic responses to plague, the author was of course not an objective observer and his preconceptions about other cultures and religions colored his views as much as his political position and work did. As is the case with many early modern narratives, therefore, we must carefully glean bits of information and understand how they are presented and shaped as part of a larger narrative and what broader purposes they might have served. The account contains, for example, a certain sense of Western medical triumphalism, actively contrasting the skill of Western European medicine and doctors and the alleged backwards and unsophisticated practices of the Central and Eastern European population (Christian and Muslim); even the court of the Sultan and regional leaders are presented in somewhat negative light. Despite such cautions, however, we can learn from texts like this a great deal about the outbreak of plague, as well as how people perceived and responded to plague. As we will see, there has been a lot of discussion about whether particular religious responses to plague allowed people to flee from what was seen as God's will (punishment) or whether people were instructed and expected to remain in harm's way, under the assumption that one cannot escape divinely ordained destiny. As biased as the account may be, it reveals a complex and diverse range of responses to and understanding of plague among both early modern Christians and Muslims. The account provides us with some useful observations about how plague spread and displayed—the account of the physician, offering a vivid example of the disease progression. At the same time accounts like this one provide important insights into daily life and broader political, social, and cultural concerns that are at times connected with and times have little to do with plague itself.

Text

If this is not enough to make you think that my path was crossed with evil, I have something more to tell. My colleagues had placed under my care some members of their retinue who were tired of being in Turkey, in order that I might take them back with me. Well, when I had been two days on the road, I saw the head man of his party, whom they called their Voivode, riding in a wagon. He was ill and on his foot was the plague ulcer, which he kept uncovered in order to relieve the pain. This circumstance made us all very uncomfortable, since we were afraid that, this disease being contagious, more of us would be attacked.

On reaching Adrianople, which was not far off, the poor fellow's struggles were terminated by death. Then, as if the peril were not sufficiently great, the rest of the Hungarians seized the dead man's clothes; one took his boots, another his doublet, another, for fear anything should be lost, snatches up his shirt, and another his linen; though the risk was perfectly obvious, we could not stop them from endangering the lives of the whole party. My physician flew from one to another, imploring them for God's sake not to touch articles, contact with which would bring about certain death, but they were deaf to his prophecies.

Well, on the second day after our departure from Adrianople, these same fellows crowded round my physician, asking him for something to cure their sickness, which they described as an attack of headache and general languor, accompanied with a feeling of deep depression; on hearing of these symptoms my physician began to suspect that this was the first stage of the plague. He told them that 'he had not warned them without reason; they had done their best to catch the plague, and they had caught it. In spite of their folly he would do what he could for them; but what means had he of doctoring them in the middle of a journey, where no remedies could be procured.'

On that very day, when, according to my custom on reaching our lodgings for the night, we had set out for a walk in search of interesting objects, I came across a herb in a meadow which I did not recognize. I pulled off some leaves and putting them to my nose perceived a smell like garlic; I then placed them in the hands of my physician to see if he could recognize the plant. After a careful examination he pronounced it to be scordium and raising his hands to heaven offered thanks to God for placing in his path, in the hour of our need, a remedy against the plague. He immediately collected a large supply, and throwing it into a big pot he placed it on the fire to boil; he told the Hungarians to cheer up, and divided the brew amongst them, bidding them take it, when they went to bed, with Lemnian earth and a diascordium electuary; he recommended them also not to go to sleep until they perspired profusely. They obeyed his directions and came to him again on the following day, telling him that they felt better. They asked for another dose of the same kind, and after drinking it they became convalescent. Thus by God's goodness we were delivered from the fear of that dreadful malady. But as if all this were not enough, we were not able to accomplish the rest of our journey without further misfortune.

...

This naval defeat of the Christians, coupled with Bajazet's disaster, caused me great anxiety; I was afraid that I should find the Turks elated by success, and consequently more exacting in my negotiations for peace. Besides the public misfortunes, I also sustained a personal loss; the plague invaded my house, carrying off one of my most faithful servants, and causing a panic among the other members of my household.

...

I now return to the plague, which, as I told you, had attacked our house. When it broke out, I sent to Roostem to ask for permission to remove to some place that was free from infection. I did so with hesitation, as I was acquainted with his character; still I could not incur the imputation of neglecting my own health and that of my servants. Roostem answered, he would lay my request before the Sultan, and the next day sent me back word that his master had made this reply: 'What did I mean, or where did I think of flying? Did I not know that pestilence is God's arrow which never misses its mark? Where in the world could I hide myself, so as to be shielded from the stroke of His weapons? If He ordained that the pestilence should strike me, neither flight nor concealment would be of any avail. To try to escape from the inevitable was a vain attempt. His own palace was not at that very moment free from the plague, but nevertheless he stayed there, and it was likewise my duty to remain where I was.' Thus I was obliged to await my doom in that plague stricken house.

But not long afterwards it came to pass that Roostem was carried off by an attack of dropsy. He was succeeded by Ali, who was then the second of the Vizieral Pashas, the most courteous and sagacious statesman I ever met among the Turks. When I sent him a valuable silken robe with my congratulations on his promotion, I received a gracious rely, for he asked me to treat him as a friend on every occasion, and not to hesitate to apply to him if necessary, and indeed he was as good as his word.

The first occasion on which I experienced his kindness was, when the plague broke out afresh in my house, and, besides attacking other members of my household, carried off the excellent gentlemen, who, under God, had been our chief support in time of sickness. I sent to Ali Pasha to ask the same permission I had formerly asked of Roostem. He replied that he could give me leave to go where I pleased, but it would be more prudent to ask that of the Sultan as well, for fear that if he should happen to fall in with my men going about at large, he should be angry at my being outside my lodgings without his knowledge. Everything, he said, depended on the way in which a matter was brought to the Sultan's notice, and that he would lay the subject before him in such a manner as to leave no doubt of his assent. Soon afterwards he informed me that I had permission to go wherever I thought proper.

The island they call Prinkipo appeared to be the most convenient place for my retirement. It is four hours' sail from the city, and is the most agreeable of the numerous little islands which are in the neighbourhood of Constantinople, for the others have only one village or none at all, but this has two.

As to what I said, that the person on whose skill we had chiefly relied had been taken away from us by death, this was none other than my most excellent and faithful companion during my long sojourn abroad, our doctor, William Quacquelben.

I had ransomed a man, who (though I did not know it at the time), proved to be stricken with the plague. While William was endeavouring to treat him for the disease, being not sufficiently careful of himself, he got infected with the plague poison. On this point he did not agree with the rest of his profession, but declared that, when the plague was rife there was more panic than real danger; his opinion being that, at such times there is about the average amount of different kinds of illness, and that people are then so nervous, that they think most of them are the plague, and that consequently every sort of ulcer or pimple is then regarded as a plague boil, and treated accordingly. And so, although he was already sickening of the plague, he never suspected what was the matter with him, until the sickness, which had been increased by his concealing it, broke out with violent paroxysms. He all but died in the hands of those who ran to support him, and not even then could he be induced to believe it was an attack of the plague. When I sent, the day before he died, to make inquiries, he replied he was better, and asked me to come to him, if I could spare the time. I sat with him a long time, and he told me how very ill he had been. All his senses, he said, and especially his sight, had been so impaired that he could recognize no one. He was now better in this respect and had the command of all of them; the phlegm only continued, which interfered with his breathing, and if this were relieved he would be well at once. As I was leaving him, I said, I heard he had some sort of abscess on his breast. He admitted that such was the case, and throwing back the bed-clothes showed it me, saying, there was nothing bad about it, he had got it from the knots of a new doublet he had put on, which was too tight.

In the evening, according to the rules of my house, two of my servants went to attend him for the night, and were preparing to change his shirt. When he was stripped, he noticed on his body a purple spot which they said was a flea-bite, and then he saw more and bigger ones. 'These are no flea-bites,' said he, 'but messengers to tell me my death is near. Let us therefore profit by this warning.' From that moment he devoted the whole of the night to prayer, pious meditation, and listening to the Scriptures being read, until as morning broke, he departed this life with full assurance of God's mercy.

...

Occasionally friends from Constantinople and Pera and some Germans of Ali's household paid us a visit. When I asked them 'Whether the plague was abating?' one of them replied, 'Yes, in a marked degree.' 'What is the daily death-rate then?' quoth I. 'About five hundred,' said he. 'Good God,' I exclaimed, 'do you call this the plague abating? How many used to die when it was at its height?' 'About a thousand or twelve hundred,' he answered.

The Turks imagine that the time and manner of each man's death is inscribed by God on his forehead, and that therefore they have no power of avoiding the fatal hour, and that till that time there is no need for fear. This belief renders them indifferent to the dangers of the plague, but does not secure them against its attacks. And so they handle the clothes and sheets in which plague-stricken people have expired, while they are still reeking with the death-sweat, and even rub their faces with them. 'If God,' say they, 'has decreed that I shall die thus, it must happen; if not, it cannot injure me.' This of course is just the way to spread contagion, and sometimes whole households perish to a man.

1.2 A visitor's perspective on plague

Author: Baron Wenceslas Wratislaw of Mitrowitz

Title: *Adventures of Baron Wenceslas Wratislaw of Mitrowitz. What he saw in the Turkish Metropolis, Constantinople, experienced in his captivity; and after his happy return to his country, committed to writing in the year of our Lord 1599*[190]

Introduction: Baron Wenceslas served as an ambassador to the Ottoman Empire for the Habsburg Emperor Rudolph II in 1591. Describing his experiences in Vienna in preparation and then in Constantinople (Istanbul) during a period which coincided with plague in the city, the account adds to the extensive travel and diplomatic literature of Europeans traveling to and within the Ottoman capital. This brief excerpt offers a chilling account of the high death rate and the terrifying conditions—the associated stench and fear swirling in the background. The selection highlights the limitations of medicine at the time in combatting the plague and the various medical procedures utilized in attempts to forestall death. It provides some sense of the desperation people—Christians and Muslims alike—felt in the midst of a plague outbreak. As noted in many other sources, it was difficult to find people to bury the dead at times of heavy mortality. While plague outbreaks could vary in terms of total deaths and death rates, the outbreak described here gives us a glimpse into the agonizing reality of a plague event as well as the ongoing threat of plague in many places throughout much of the early modern period.

Text

At that time there was so great a pestilence in Constantinople that, as the Turks told us, 80,000 people died of the plague; and, in fact, as we ourselves saw from our house, people were carried in large numbers, all day long, to the grave, and even in some houses we saw two, three, or four corpses at a time being washed, … and purified with warm water. It is certain that it was very grievous to us when we could see nothing else but a multitude of dead bodies. Out of our own house there died about six persons of the infection of the plague, although we used all kinds of medicines daily. We had the bodies buried in the city of Galata, according to the permission granted us. The corpses were only attended by three or four persons, and the Franciscan monks, who have six convents there, performed the funeral ceremonies. At this time more than half of us fell sick with the stench and with fright. I too, had first an ague, and then a diarrhea, and was so seriously ill for many weeks that the physicians despaired of my recovery, and said that it was impossible for me to get well any more.

…

At that time there was a great plague in Thrace, and in almost all the islands beyond the sea, so that in Constantinople itself, and its suburbs, about 80,000 people died in three months. In the town around our tower, which is called

Genyhyssar, that is, New Castle, many people, and some of our guards, perished. There was great weeping and lamentation. The Turks, learning that there was a surgeon amongst us, sent and requested him to be let out of the tower. He had medicines prepared for them, and let blood by the middle vein of the arm, for he had still kept a lancet or so. Sometimes from twenty to thirty persons of both sexes came to him, and could not sufficiently wonder that our way of blood-letting caused so little pain; for the Turks pierce the vein with an Italian knife, and make a large hole, which cannot be done without considerable pain. And the surgeon began to be the best amongst us, for they gave him plenty to eat, and sometimes sent him money, and, above all, he went into the dear open air and light of day, and refreshed himself—a thing which we poor creatures could not enjoy, but must remain, day and night, in that dark and stinking tower.

1.3 Plague in early modern Hindustan

Author: Jahangir, Emperor of Hindustan (1569–1627)

Title: *The Tuzuk-i-Jahangiri; or, Memoirs of Jahangir*[191]

Introduction: Jahangir, "conqueror of the world" in Persian, was the fourth Mughal Emperor. He ruled for 22 years. He built upon the foundations established by his father Emperor Akbar and advanced political and economic stability along with cultural development. His empire on the Indian Subcontinent was rather open religiously and culturally, though Sunni Islam was the official state religion. Although this account lacks a great deal of demographic detail, it reveals much about the geographic extent and spread of plague in the early modern world and the range of responses to it. Drawing from older histories—and so seeing plague in a long tradition—the author notes the particular intensity of the current outbreak as well as the various explanations for it, including recent drought, as well as "other causes," which only Allah might know. The author describes some of the associated symptoms of plague as well as the spread of plague to animals. At the end of the passage, the chronicler discusses the impact of fire on diminishing the plague; as we know from other contemporary sources, many infected articles and even homes might be burned in efforts to destroy the plague. Even so, the writer finds the appearance of strange circles on houses in the fire to be beyond rational explanation.

Text

OUTBREAK OF PLAGUE

In this year, or rather in the 10th year after my accession [1615], a great pestilence appeared in some places in Hindustan. The commencement of this calamity was in the parganahs [administrative unit] of the Panjab, and by degrees the contagion spread to the city of Lahore. Many of the people, Musulmans [Muslims] and Hindus, died through this. After this it spread to Sirhind and the Du'ab, until it reached Delhi and the surrounding parganahs and villages, and desolated them. At this day it had greatly diminished. It became known from men of great age and from old histories that this disease had never shown itself in this country (before). Physicians and learned men were questioned as to its cause. Some said that it came because there had been drought for two years in succession and little rain fell; others said it was on account of the corruption of the air which occurred through the drought and scarcity. Some attributed it to other causes. Wisdom is of Allah, and we must submit to Allah's decrees!

PLAGUE

On Wednesday, the 17th, I marched 6 kos [each kos between 1–2 miles] and halted at the village of Barasinor (Balasinor). It has already been mentioned that the plague had appeared in Kashmir. On this day a report of the chronicler of events arrived, stating that the plague had taken firm hold of the country and that many had died. The symptoms were that the first day there was headache and fever and much bleeding at the nose. On the second day the patient died. In the house where one person died all the inmates were carried off. Whoever went near the sick person or a dead body was affected in the same way. In one instance the dead body was thrown on the grass, and it chanced that a cow came and ate some of the grass. It died, and some dogs that had eaten its flesh also all died. Things had come to such a pass that from fear of death fathers would not approach their children, and children would not go near their fathers. A strange thing was that in the ward in which the disease began, a fire broke out and nearly 3,000 houses were burnt. During the height of the plague, one morning when the people of the city and environs got up, they saw circles on their doors. There were three large circles, and on the face of these (i.e., inside them) there were two circles of middle size and one small one. There were also other circles which did not contain any whiteness (i.e., there were no inner circles). These figures were found on all the houses and even on the mosques. From the day when the fire took place and these circles appeared, they say there was a diminution of the plague. This has been recorded as it seems a strange affair. It certainly does not agree with the canons of reason, and my intellect cannot accept it. Wisdom is with God! I trust that the Almighty will have mercy on his sinful slaves, and that they will be altogether freed from such calamity.

1.4 Plague statistics in Frankfurt am Main (1622–40)[192]

Introduction: Frankfurt am Main (now Germany) became a central economic hub in the early modern period. Figure 1.4 provides data on the total number of deaths annually, showing the impact of the outbreak of plague in particular years, notably 1627, 1632, and 1634–37. The demographic challenges of this period are also highlighted by the comparison of deaths (38,678) and births (20,224) between 1622 and 1648. The impact of plague could therefore be significant for demographic, economic, and social reasons for shorter as well as longer periods. The recurring cycle of plague in numerous places left social fabrics tattered and economic conditions potentially unstable. With smaller demographic impact in

Data:

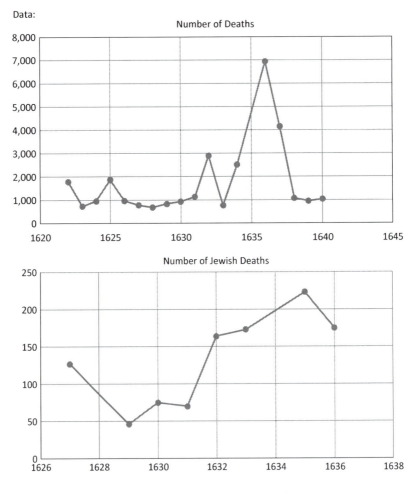

Figure 1.4 Plague statistics in Frankfurt am Main (1622–40).

many plague outbreaks individual communities might bounce back fairly quickly to status quo social conditions or previous production capacities. However, larger demographic shifts or several plague outbreaks combined with other natural disasters and wars could deplete and more permanently damage communities, regions, and entire states.

A separate graph is included in Figure 1.4 that provides information on the demographic impact on the Jewish community in the city. Although at times blamed for the spread of the plague in medieval and early modern Europe, Jews suffered greatly from the plague, as these figures and other documents in this book reveal. In addition, Jews like their non-Jewish neighbors suffered from the outbreak of various other epidemics. Between 1683 and 1697, 1,409 Jews alone fell victim to smallpox and typhus.

1.5 Episodes from the plague in Rome of 1656. Etching[193]

Introduction: The epidemic that lasted from 1656 until 1658 in areas of central and southern Italy may have killed more than 200,000 people in Rome, Naples and even as far north as Genoa, representing more than 40% of those cities' populations combined. In Rome in particular some 23,000 people (19% of the population) perished. The etching (Figure 1.5) shows the funeral procession that was a common sight during the plague, though during periods of high mortality bodies were cast into large pits together, if they were buried at all. With such scenes, the death brought on by the plague was etched into the daily life and consciousness of people in cities where the plague was a regular visitor. Plague was also, thereby, incorporated into the regular structures of religion and society through such rituals and communal responses. In more virulent outbreaks, when such activities could not be conducted—either for lack of personnel or for fear of contagion—writers noted particularly devastating consequences, with corpses rotting in the streets or the use of mass graves, and a tremendous sense of vulnerability as traditional methods of responding to and coping with death were unavailable. Such episodes tested communal systems and cohesiveness; however, through much of the early modern period smaller and more frequent outbreaks were more common and became part and parcel of the early modern experience.

Figure 1.5 Episodes from the plague in Rome of 1656. Etching.
Credit: Wellcome Collection

1.6 Plague death tolls in the early seventeenth century

Author: Richard Bradley, F. R. S. (1688–1732)

Title: *The Plague at Marseilles Considered: With Remarks upon the Plague in General, shewing its Cause and Nature of Infection, with necessary Precautions to prevent the spreading of that Direful Distemper. Publish'd for the Preservation of the People of Great-Britain. Also some Observations taken from an Original Manuscript of a Graduate Physician, who resided in London during the whole Time of the late Plague, Anno 1665* (1721)[194]

Introduction: An English Botanist, Bradley was elected a Fellow of the Royal Society in 1712. In 1724 he became the first Professor of Botany at Cambridge University. He made a number of scientific discoveries and he advanced a biological theory for infectious diseases. The selection below provides his accumulation of death tolls by month during two epidemics in the seventeenth century. The spread of plague to the city of London is noted and the number of deaths recorded by week. Included in this selection are the tables of deaths for the plague outbreaks in 1592 (with more than 44% of the deaths attributed to plague) and 1603 (nearly 82% listed as dead from plague). The author compares the outbreak with other epidemics but also, as with other early modern authors, notes the role of fire in purifying air and killing the "seeds" of plague. He also mentions the steps taken by municipal authorities, such as enlarging streets and improved sanitation, to attempt to avoid or mitigate plague in the future.

Text

The Year 1665 was the last that we can say the plague raged in *London*, which might happen from the Destruction of the City by Fire, the following Year 1666, and besides the destroying the eggs, or seeds, of those poisonous animals, that were then in the stagnating air, might likewise purify that air in such a manner, as to make it unfit for the nourishment of others of the same Kind, which were swimming or driving in the circumambient air: and again, the care that was taken to enlarge the streets at their rebuilding, and the keeping them clean after they were rebuilt, might greatly contribute to preserve the town from pestilence ever since.

But it was not only in the year 1665 that the plague raged in *London*, we have accounts in the Bills of Mortality, of that dreadful distemper in the Years 1592, 1603, 1625, 1630 and 1636, in which years we may observe how many died weekly of the plague, and remark how much more that distemper raged in the hot months, than in the others, and serve at the same time as a memorandum to the curious.

A *TABLE*, Shewing how many Died Weekly, as well of all Diseases, as of the Plague, in the Years 1592, 1603, 1625, 1630, 1636; and the Year 1665.

Buried of all Diseases in the Year 1592		
	Total	*Plague*
March 17	230	3
March 24	351	31
March 31	219	29
April 7	307	27
April 14	203	33
April 21	290	37
April 28	310	41
May 5	350	29
May 12	339	38
May 19	300	42
May 26	450	58
June 2	410	62
June 9	441	81
June 16	399	99
June 23	401	108
June 30	850	118
July 7	1440	927
July 14	1510	893
July 21	1491	258
July 28	1507	852
August 4	1503	983
August 11	1550	797
August 18	1532	651
August 25	1508	449
September 1	1490	507
September 8	1210	563
September 15	621	451
September 22	629	349
September 29	450	330
October 6	408	327
October 13	522	323
October 20	330	308
October 27	320	302
November 3	310	301
November 10	309	209

Buried of all Diseases in the Year 1592		
	Total	*Plague*
November 17	301	107
November 24	321	93
December 1	349	94
December 8	331	86
December 15	329	71
December 22	386	39
		———
	25886	11503

Buried of all Diseases in the Year 1603		*Total*	*Plague*
March	17	108	3
	24	60	2
	31	78	6
April	7	66	4
	14	79	4
	21	98	8
	28	109	10
May	5	90	11
	12	112	18
	19	122	22
	26	122	32
June	2	114	30
	9	131	43
	15	144	59
	23	182	72
	30	267	158
July	7	445	263
	14	612	424
The Out Parishes this Week were joined with the City.			
	21	1186	917
	28	1728	1396
August	4	2256	1922
	11	2077	1745

Buried of all Diseases in the Year 1603		Total	Plague
	18	3054	2713
	25	2853	2539
September	1	3385	3035
	8	3078	2724
	15	3129	2818
	22	2456	2195
	29	1961	1732
October	6	1831	1641
	13	1312	1149
	20	766	642
	27	625	508
November	3	737	594
	10	545	442
	17	384	251
	24	198	105
December	1	223	102
	8	163	55
	15	200	96
	22	168	74
			———
The Total this Year is,			37294
Whereof of the Plague,			30561

1.7 Plague and other diseases in eighteenth-century Aleppo

Author: Alexander Russell (c 1715–68)

Title: *Natural History of Aleppo*[195]

Introduction: Educated in Edinburgh, where he earned a medical degree, Russell lived for a time in London. He went to Aleppo in 1740 and served as the doctor for an English factory, eventually becoming the chief medical figure in Aleppo. He returned to England in 1754, eventually accepting a position at St Thomas' Hospital in London. He published his *Natural History of Aleppo* in 1756. At the start of this selection, Russell describes the appearance of smallpox in Aleppo in 1742—the symptoms of the disease and the treatments. He makes a short notice in passing that Jews were particularly afflicted, but adds no explanation or anti-Jewish comments. He moves on to discuss plague, noting the outbreak of plague in the city every ten years and the general geographical trajectory, seasonal presence, and virulence of the disease. Like many early modern physicians, Russell correlated various environmental conditions with the outbreak and spread of plague. On occasion he remarks about explanations offered by natives or other authors, often to dismiss them, as he does rather polemically at the end of the selection. Russell's careful review of the appearance of buboes and other associated symptoms offers a useful overview of contemporary understandings of plague. His comment that all who contracted the plague had buboes, except for the few who died suddenly without them might point to the presence of other forms of plague besides bubonic.

Text

A.D. MDCCXLII

About the beginning of September, the small-pox made their appearance, especially amongst children; but being of a mild distinct kind, very little assistance was required from medicine. In *October* this disease became more frequent; and much the greater part that were seized, had the confluent sort, attended with hemorrhages, petechiae [small red or purple skin spots], phlyctanae [small pustules], and other the worst of symptoms. Convulsions (always violent) on their first seizure, indicated that the pock would flux, and prove fatal. In this confluent kind the eruptions were often discovered on the extremities as soon as the child was observed to be out of order, and never were later in appearing than the end of the second day. These patients generally died on the beginning of the eleventh, reckoning from the first attack, when the distemper was left to nature, as is commonly the case in this country; or, if they survived, yet many of them were afterwards harassed with corrosive ulcers, carious bones, hard tumors on the glandular parts, difficult either to discuss or bring to suppuration, coughs, and fluxes; which last soon put an end to their miseries. By degrees this great malignancy seemed to wear off; so that by December the disease became mild and favorable, and most of the sick recovered.

The Jews were the most severely afflicted by this sort of small-pox.

Bleeding, bathing the extremities in warm water, with a plentiful use of diluting, antiphlogistic medicines [with the capacity to prevent or relieve inflammation], if used at the beginning, often prevented fatal consequences. Purging in the secondary fever, or after the decline of the disease, is never practiced here by the natives; from the neglect of which, perhaps, the dreadful symptoms above enumerated were more frequent; though they often happened when all possible means had been used to prevent them.

Inoculation is only practiced here among the Christians, and is not yet general even among them. However, it appears to gain ground daily, though their injudicious method of proceeding in it seems to lay this practice under several disadvantages. They do not either prepare the body beforehand, or consider the habit of the child to be inoculated, or the nature of the pock, or other diseases of the party from whom they receive infection, but carry the child to be inoculated into the chamber of the sick; where an old woman opening one of the pustules with a needle, takes a little of the matter upon its point; with this needle she pricks many times the fleshy part of the child's hand, between the first joint of the thumb and the same joint of the fore-finger, taking up a little more matter upon the point of the needle after every two or three punctures; then putting a bit of cotton on the part, it is tied up, and the operation finished.

About the middle of November the plague began to shew itself again in the suburbs called Bankusa(d), and that neighborhood; and before Christmas it was found to be in some parts of the city, though it made little or no progress.

A few pleurises and rheumatisms began to make their appearance in December.

Chapter IV

Of the Plague
Section I
Of the Plague in General

It is common opinion of the inhabitants of Aleppo, that they are visited with the plague about once in ten years, and that it is brought thither from some neighboring city, where it first makes its appearance, as Antab, Ursa, &c. to the northward, or Damascus to the southward; from which last place it is generally alleged that the worst plagues have been brought; though some assert that those which have come from the northward have raged with the greatest violence.

With respect to the intervals between the returns of the plague, though that of 1742 is an exception, yet the common opinion seems in some measure to be founded on experience. And it seems a fact pretty well attested, that it never rages at Aleppo without having first visited some of the above mentioned places; though the first appearance of all is, from what I have been able to learn, always in some town on the coast of Syria. If it first shows itself in Sidon, Byroot, or Tripoly, Damascus is usually the channel through which it comes to Aleppo;

but if in Scanderoon or Byass, then it commonly passes by way of Antab, Killis, Ursa, &c.

During the winter this disease is constantly moderate; as the spring advances it grows more violent, it comes to its height in June, decreases greatly in July, and certainly disappears in August; and this seems to be the constant course of the plague at Aleppo; so that none are ever seized with it in the months of September and October, even in such extraordinary instances as when it has made its appearance for three years successively, as it did in 1742, 1743, and 1744.

A considerable difference is observable, both as to the mortality and number of the infected, in different years; but it does not appear that it has ever raged in this country with the violence that it has often done in Europe.

Extreme heat seems to check the progress of the distemper; for though, during the few first hot days, the mortality, as well as the number of those newly infected, increased, yet a few days longer continuance of that weather greatly diminished the number of the sick. Add to this, that the season wherein it always ceases at Aleppo, is that in which the heats are the most excessive.

Though the natives, as well as several authors, have a notion that the moon has some influence over this distemper, yet experience no ways favored this opinion in the late plague at Aleppo.

Having the distemper once, does not prevent a second seizure, numbers of people being alive when I left Aleppo, who have had it twice or oftener; and I have even seen instances of the same person's having had the disease there several times in the same season.

...

In the years 1742 and 1743, the buboes often appeared as soon as the patients were taken ill, in some not till twelve hours after, and in a few not, till after two or three days; but, in 1744, some perceived the buboes a day or two before they had any other symptom of the disease. And during all the time the plague raged at Aleppo, none of the sick were without them, except such who died suddenly. In general, the sick had but one, and they were more common in the axillary [relating to the armpit] or inguinal [of the groin] glands than in the parotids [salivary gland]. Some few had even two or three, which were not confined to one side of the body. Their first appearance, as hath been mentioned, was like a small indurated gland, deeply seated; in some they were fixed, but more frequently moveable, and most commonly painful to the touch. They would often increase considerably in a few hours with intense pain, and would as suddenly subside; and these changes would frequently succeed each other several-times in twenty-four hours. Sometimes an exacerbation immediately following the decrease of the bubo, would prompt one to imagine this decrease to have been the cause, but this was not so constantly the case as to induce me to think it was so in reality.

The buboes, so far as I could learn, never advanced towards a regular maturation, till a critical sweat had carried off the fever. In ten, twelve, or fifteen days from the first attack, they commonly suppurated with the usual attendants of heat and pain. Sometimes, nay frequently, I have known them to disappear soon after the critical sweat, and disouss without any detriment to the patient. At other times, when grown pretty large, about the height of the disease, they sunk, and mortified without being attended with fatal consequences: for as soon as the crisis was complete, the mortification stopped, and the eschar separated gradually, leaving a large deep ulcer, which healed without difficulty by the usual methods.

The inguinal buboes were seldom single, there being generally two, and the same groin. The superior was the largest, of a long figure, somewhat resembling a cucumber, lying obliquely, but lower than where the venereal buboes appear, and it was this which commonly came to suppuration. Once I met with a case where an axillary bubo divided into two; one part getting under the pectoral muscle, the other sinking deeper into the armpit: both of them grew painful and inflamed; but that in the armpit only suppurated.

I met with no instance of a bubo not followed or preceded by the fever.

...

... As the plague has so often visited that country, one might reasonably have expected among the natives some vestiges of unbiased observation, and attempts at least towards a proper method of cure; but, so far as I have hitherto been able to discover, no traces of anything satisfactory are to be met with among them. The Turks have less faith in medicine for the cure of this disease than of any other, believing it to be a curse inflicted by God Almighty for the sins of the people; and as the chief of those who practice physic are either Christians or Jews, and not so strongly prepossessed with the doctrine of predestination, consequently afraid of catching the distemper, they rather endeavor to confirm the Turks in their false notions. Lest they should be forced to visit the sick. Hence it follows, that the greatest part of those who are seized with the plague, either are left to struggle with the violence of the disorder without any assistance, or must submit to the direction of the meanest and most ignorant of mankind. The practice which seems to prevail most generally amongst them, is to bleed all who apply to them, and in every stage of the disease; after which they endeavor to promote sweat by a few grains of bezoar, in the simple distilled water of scorzonera [a perennial plant]; which is the medicine they chiefly confide in, such is the slender acquaintance they have yet acquired in the *materia medica*.

1.8 Plague in Russia

Author: Charles Mertens (1737–88)

Title: *An Account of the Plague which Raged at Moscow in 1771*[196]

Introduction: Dr Charles de Mertens was a French observer to the great plague epidemic of 1771. Mertens had been a member of the Medical College in Vienna and Strasbourg, an imperial and royal censor, and a corresponding member of the Medical Society at Paris. He had been brought from Vienna to supervise medical services at the Foundling Home in Moscow, already in 1767. The late eighteenth-century plague epidemic in Russia was large and devastating. Set in the context of war between Russia and the Ottoman Empire, Mertens translates a lengthy letter (originally in German) from Baron Asch, who had been a physician in the army and was at the time of the outbreak a physician in Moscow. The letter provides a detailed overview of symptoms experienced by those people contracting plague. The overview also includes a discussion of the activities of a Board of Health, with particular attention to the hospital and Board regulations. These regulations echo many of the measures developed and instituted in other parts of Europe during the later Middle Ages and early modern period, including the separation and disinfection or destruction of clothes and furniture of the dead, quarantine practices, and burial procedures. Importantly, the account details the increased death rate and spread of the plague as well as a major riot that erupted in the fall in response to the curtailment of traditional religious ceremonies (seen by authorities as contributing to the spread of the plague) associated with burial and quarantine (which many people objected to because of separation from their families, loss of work, and fear of contracting plague).

Text

In 1769 war broke out between the Russians and Turks. The year following intelligence was received that the Turks had carried the plague into Wallachia and Moldavia, where it was making great ravages; and that in the town of Jaffy a number of Russians had been carried off by a disorder, which, on its first appearance, was called by some of the faculty, a malignant fever; but which the most eminent physicians in the place declared to be the plague. Baron Asch, first physician to the army, sent an account of this disorder in a letter, written in German, to his brother, a physician at Moscow, who showed it to me. The following is a translation thereof: 'It attacks people in different ways. Some are slightly indisposed, complaining for several days of a headache, sometimes very violent, at other times less so, and now and then ceasing altogether, and then coming on again. The patients are affected with pains in the chest, and particularly the neck; they gradually become languid and dejected, with something like intoxication and drowsiness. They have a particular taste in their mouths, which soon turns to a bitter; at the same time they have an ardor urine. To these success chilly and hot fits, and, lastly, all the symptoms which characterize the plague. The disease sometimes terminates favorably by perspiration, before the appearance of exanthemata, buboes, or carbuncles. The contagion is sometimes more rapid and more violent in action; in that case the infected are suddenly seized after making a hearty meal, after a fit of anger, or too much bodily motion, with head-ach, nausea, and vomiting; the eyes become inflamed and watery (*marmoyans*), and pains are felt in those parts of the body where buboes and carbuncles are about to appear. There is no great degree of heat. The pulse is sometimes full and hard; sometimes small, soft, and scarcely perceptible; it often intermits, and, what should be particularly noticed, it is often feeble. These symptoms are accompanied with lassitude, a white tongue, dry skin, urine of pale yellow color, or turbid, but without sediment; frequently with a diarrhea, which it is difficult to stop; and, lastly, with delirirum, buboes, carbuncles, and petechiae.'

The following summer this disorder spread into Poland, and committed great havoc there; from thence it passed to Kiev, where it destroyed four thousand souls. Immediately on its appearance at the last-mentioned place, all communication between that town and Moscow was cut off; guards were stationed on all the great roads, and all travelers were ordered to perform quarantine for several weeks.

...

On the 22nd of December, we are required to meet at the Board of Health. The first physician to the military-hospital states the circumstances, which I have just related, the truth of which is confirmed by the evidence of three other physicians, who further report, that fifteen among the attendants, including their wives and children, had fallen victims to this disorder since the end of November; that five still continued ill of it; but that it had not yet shown itself in any of the hospital-wards. Eleven physicians were present at this consultation, and we all agreed that the disorder under consideration was the plague, except Dr. Rinder, state-physician, who had visited the sick, several times, in company with Mr. Schafonsky, and who pronounced it to be merely a putrid fever; an opinion which he maintained both in conversation and by writing.

This hospital stands out of the town, near the suburb inhabited by the Germans, from which it is separated by a small stream, called the Yausa. We advised that it should be immediately shut up, and that guards should be placed around it, in order to cut off all communication; that all the attendants upon the hospital-invalids should be removed, together with their wives and children, to a detached situation, care being taken to separate the infected from the healthy and, lastly, that all the clothes and furniture, not only of those who were dead, but likewise of those who still survived, should be burnt.

... Orders were given to the surgeons who had the care of all these people, to transmit daily to the Board of Health a list of the sick and dead. A committee of physicians was appointed to regulate every thing concerning the treatment of the sick, and the keeping of those who were performing quarantine free from infection; and great attention was paid to the interment of the dead. Drs. Erasmus and Yagelsky (now no more!) were entitled to great praise for the manner in which they acquitted themselves in this business. When any one of those who were under quarantine was taken ill, he was put in a separate room, and kept there until the symptoms of the plague showed themselves, when he was conveyed in a carriage, by persons hired for that purpose, to the pesthouse, viz. the convent of St. Nicholas.

The public baths, where the people are accustomed to go, at least once a week, were shut up. The town was divided into seven districts, to each of which one physician and two surgeons were appointed, for the purpose of examining all the sick as well as the dead bodies; in which business police-officers were joined with them. It was forbidden to bury the dead within the city; proper places for burying-grounds were fixed upon at some distance from the town. It was ordered, that whenever any one of the common people should be seized with the plague, he should be sent to the hospital of St. Nicholas, and that, after burning his clothes and furniture, those who had been living in the same apartment should be detained for the space of forty days in some buildings appropriated to that purpose out of the town; that if the like occurrence should happen in the house of a principal inhabitant or person of rank, all the servants who had been in the same room with the patient should perform quarantine, and that the master, together with all his family, should remain shut up in his own house for the space of eleven days. All this was sanctioned and passed into the form of a law by a resolution of the Senate.

We now began to flatter ourselves that the plague had been entirely eradicated by the precautions which had been adopted. Scarcely, however, had we indulged in these fond hopes, when, towards the end of June, some people are taken ill of the same disorder at the hospital of St. Simon, where the quarantine was performed. On the 2nd of July, six people die in one night at a house in the suburb of Preobraginsky; a seventh, who lived with them, absconded.* (*In what manner the contagion got among these people could not be ascertained. Perhaps, through the negligence of the sentinels, they had some communication with the persons under quarantine; or had become infected by burning into used cloths and other effects, which the last-mentioned persons might have concealed under ground before their removal to the quarantine-hospital.) Livid spots, buboes, and carbuncles are found upon the dead bodies. On the following days, many of the common people fall sick in different quarters of the town, and the mortality increases to such pitch, that the number of deaths, which commonly amounted to about ten or fifteen per day, and which, even during the prevalence of putrid fevers (as was the case for the two last years) did not exceed thirty, amounted at the end of July to as many as two hundred in the space of twenty-four hours. The sick, as well as the dead bodies, exhibited large purple spots and ibices; in many there were carbuncles and buboes. Some died suddenly, or in the space of twenty-four hours, before the buboes and carbuncles had time to come out; but the greatest died on the third or fourth day.

In the middle of August, the number of deaths amounted daily to four hundred; and at the end of the same month to as many as six hundred. At this time buboes and carbuncles were more frequent than they had been in July. At the beginning of September there were seven hundred deaths in the space of twenty-four hours; in a few days, there were eight hundred deaths within the same number of hours; and a short time after, the deaths amounted to one thousand in a day!

The havoc was still greater during the time of the riots, which began on the 15th of September, in the evenings; when an outrageous mob broke open the pest-houses and quarantine-hospitals, renewing all the religious ceremonies which it is customary with them to perform at the bed-side of the sick (*Besides praying by them in the ordinary manner, it is customary, in Russia, to carry in great pomp to the sick the images of their saints, which every person present kisses in rotation.), and digging up the dead bodies and burying them afresh in the city. Agreeably to their ancient custom, the people began again to embrace the dead, despising all manner of precaution, which they declared to be of no avail, as the public calamity (I repeat their own words) was sent by God, to punish them for having neglected their ancient forms of worship. They further insisted, that as it was pre-ordained who should and who should not die, they must await their destiny; therefore, that all endeavors to avoid the contagion were only a trouble to themselves, and an insult to the Divinity, whose wrath was only to be appeased by their refusing all human assistance.* (*In their paroxysm of frenzy, the populace attempted to wreak their vengeance upon those who had labored for their preservation. After they had sacrificed one victim to their blind rage, they sought for the physicians and surgeons. Some of the lowest rabble broke into my house, and destroyed every thing they could lay hold of; they also went in search of the other physicians and surgeons, and pursued such as they met with. Providence rescued us all from their hands. Little suspecting what was to happen, I had gone four days before, by order of council, to the Foundling-Hospital, to superintend more closely the health of the children there.) General Yeropkin, with a small party of soldiers drawn together as speedily as possible, dispersed the mob, and restored tranquility in a few days, after which every thing was placed on its former footing. This vast concourse and intermixture of the healthy and infected, caused the contagion to spread to such a degree, that at this time the daily number of deaths amounted to one thousand two hundred and upwards!

For carrying away and burying the dead, criminals capitally convicted or condemned to hard labor, were at first employed; but afterwards, when these were not sufficient for the purpose, the poor were hired to perform this service. Each was provided with a cloak, gloves, and a mask made of oiled cloth; and they were cautioned never to touch a dead body with their bare hands. But they would not attend to these precautions, believing it to be impossible to be hurt by merely touching the bodies or clothes of the dead, and attributing the effects of the contagion to an inevitable destiny. We lost thousands of these people, who seldom remained well beyond a week. I was informed by the Inspectors of Health, that most of them fell ill about the fourth or fifth day.

The plague, as is generally the case, raged chiefly among the common people; the nobles and better sort of inhabitants escaped the contagion, a few only excepted, who fell victims to their rashness and negligence. The contagion was communicated solely by contact of the sick or infected goods; it was not propagated by the atmosphere, which appeared in no respect vitiated during the whole of the time. When we visited any of the sick we* (*I mean those physicians who, with myself, remained in the town; but not such as had the care of the pest-hospitals) went so near them that frequently there was not more than a foot's distance between them and us; and although we used no other precaution but that of not touching their bodies, clothes, or beds, we escaped infection. When I looked at a patient's tongue, I used to hold before my mouth and nose a pocket-handkerchief moistened with vinegar....

1.9 A major plague episode in China in 1770/71[197]

Introduction: China suffered many epidemics in the early modern period, including episodes of the plague. The earliest outbreaks of the Second Pandemic, in fact, are often traced to central Asia and may have impacted parts of China in the fourteenth century. While there are scattered records, the epidemiological history of early modern China is still being researched. More well known are the epidemics of the nineteenth century. However, as the notes below indicate, in the later eighteenth century (and earlier) significant plagues struck large regions of China. These data are presented to suggest the broad range of plague before the nineteenth century. As a review of the list of disease outbreaks makes clear, however, we often have limited sources and it is difficult to distinguish between the appearance of plague and other diseases. The various locations associated with the 1770/71 outbreak are in the north and may be connected with the significant epidemic that hit Russia at the same time, signaling the important regional nature of some epidemics (Table 1.9).

Table 1.9 A major plague episode in China in 1770/71

Year	Location (H)	Geographic region
1770	Lanzhou	Northwest
1770	A County in Gansu	Northwest
1770	Tianshui (Gansu)	Northwest
1770	Ning (Gansu)	Northwest
1770	Ubashi go Gobi	North
1771	Pacific County	Northeast
1771	Jiaxing	North
1771	Qinglong (Jiaxing?)	North
1771	Yongning state area (Gansu)	Northwest
1771	Dingxi Prefecture tongwei (Gansu)	Northwest
1772	Heqing	Northeast?

Note: Based on data assembled and graciously shared with me, by Michael Liu.

1.10 Observing plague in early modern Africa

Author: Johannes Leo Africanus (c 1494–c 1554)

Title: *The History and Description of Africa of Leo Africanus*[198]

Introduction: As noted in the Introduction and in some of the documents above, other diseases appeared at times of plague. In some cases they combined with plague for particularly virulent outbreaks. At other times, we have no evidence of bubonic plague; rather other diseases are described by contemporary writers, or the generic term "plague" is used in reference to other diseases. At times early modern authors and physicians were quite able to differentiate diseases. Yet, many writers, especially those without medical training, with political goals, and simply unconcerned with details, presented "plagues" in certain ways, often for particular purposes. Johannes Leo Africanus was a Berber diplomat from Andalusia who wrote an extensive and popular description of Africa. Born a Muslim, he studied in Fez and served in a number of diplomatic capacities. Captured by Spanish corsairs in 1518, he was eventually baptized in 1520. His scholarship cut across numerous fields, including medicine and grammar. In this account he discusses the spread of syphilis, named the French pox or French disease because its spread was attributed to French armies. While describing some of the characteristics of the disease as well as some of the responses to it in Barbary as well as in Egypt and Syria, Africanus importantly discusses the transfer of the disease, particularly through sexual contact. Sounding what would be a common refrain, Africanus points to the importation of the disease by Europeans into areas where it had not previously been known. He polemically ties it with the expulsion of Spanish Jews at the end of the fifteenth century. Although not plague, the presentation of the disease in this brief case, as well as the narrative use of the description, provides a useful comparison with early modern accounts of bubonic plague.

Text

… If any of the Barbary be infected with the disease commonly called the French pox, they die thereof for the most part, and are seldom cured. This disease begins with a kind of anguish and swelling, and at length breaks out into sores. Over the mountains of Atlas, and throughout all Numidia and Libya they scarcely know this disease. Insomuch that oftentimes the parties infected travel forthwith into Numidia or the land of Negros, in which places the air is so temperate, that only by remaining there they recover their perfect health, and return home sound into their own country: which I saw many do with mine own eyes; who without the help of any physician or medicine, except the aforesaid wholesome air, were restored to their former health. Not so much as the name of this malady was ever known unto the Africans, before Ferdinand the king of Castile expelled all Jews out of Spain; after the return of which Jews into Africa, certain unhappy and lewd people lay with their wives; and so at length the disease spread from one to another; over the whole region: insomuch that scarce any one family was free from the same. Howbeit, this they were most certainly persuaded of, that the same disease came first from Spain; wherefore they (for want of a better name) do call it, The Spanish pox. Notwithstanding at Tunis and over all Italic it is called the French disease. It is so likewise in Egypt and Syria: for there it is used as a common proverb of cursing; the French pox take you. Amongst the Barbarians the disease called in Latin *Hernia* is not so common; but in Egypt the people are much troubled therewith. For some of the Egyptians have their cods often-times so swollen, as it is incredible to report. Which infirmity is thought to be so common among them, because they eat so much gum, and salt cheese. Some of their children are subject unto the falling sickness; but when they grow to any stature, they are free from that disease. This falling sickness likewise possesses the women of Barbary, and of the land of Negros; who, to excuse it, say that they are taken with a spirit. In Barbary the plague is rife every tenth, fifteenth, or twentieth year, whereby great numbers of people are consumed; for they have no cure for the same, but only to rub the plague-sore with certain ointments made of Armenian earth. In Numidia they are infected with the plague scarce once in a hundred years. And in the land of Negros they know not the name of the disease: because they never were subject thereunto.

1.11 Epidemic disease in early modern North America

Author: Noah Webster (1758–1843)

Title: *A Brief History of Epidemic and Pestilential Diseases*[199]

Introduction: The son of a farmer and weaver, Webster was born in Hartford in 1758. He studied at Yale between 1774 and 1778 and worked as a teacher. He wrote a grammar book and after he was married moved to Amherst, MA. A devout Congregationalist, he is perhaps best known for his dictionary, though he was a prolific writer who explored many subjects. Throughout the passage below Webster ties various astronomical (especially the appearance of comets and environmental and geological conditions—including weather conditions, volcanic activity, and earthquake activity) to his discussion of epidemic and pestilential diseases. Here he draws from scientific observations and assumptions inherited from early periods. Webster asserts further that many diseases erupt in different places because of similar atmospheric and geological conditions, but that such eruptions could take diverse forms in various places. The plague in North America in 1763, for example, resulted in typhus and he observes that it only afflicted the native Americans, implying a special predisposition or inability to fight the disease in natives that was not the same for Europeans living in the area.

Text

In 1633 the year of the comet, commenced an eruption of Etna, which continued for four or five years, through this whole pestilential period. London was shaken by an earthquake, and at Halifax in Yorkshire raged a very malignant fever.

In this year also a 'pestilent fever,' invaded the little colony at Plymouth in Massachusetts, and carried off twenty of their number. This was a great mortality for that small settlement. It must have been occasioned by a fever of domestic origin, as the colony had, at that time, no intercourse with foreign countries, except with England. No suspicion has ever been entertained that the disease was of foreign origin.

At the same time, the Indians were invaded by small-pox which swept them away in multitudes. It spread from Narragansett to Piscataqua, and westward to Connecticutt river.

...

We have a remarkable evidence of the extent of a pestilential principle in the elements. The same species appeared, at the same time, in Augsburg, Dresden, London, and in America. Probably the same species prevailed over most of Europe; for we hear of them in every part of Holland the following year. The diseases predominant, previous to the plague, are of eruptive kind: Such was the case in the present instance. In America, the epidemic among the Indians took the form of the small-pox; and also it is the current opinion that the small-pox is communicated only by contagion, yet my investigations have satisfied me that this is a great error. The small-pox is one of the family of eruptive diseases, which belong to almost every pestilential period. Before its origin and progress had been affected by the art of inoculation, it used to be epidemic, in large cities, under the inflammatory condition of the atmosphere, which originated measles, influenza, anginas and plague, and rarely or never at any other time. This disease therefore, though communicable at any time by infection, is generated in particular habits without any infecting cause ab extra; and is the offspring of that state of the atmosphere which generates other eruptive epidemics.

The summer of 1763 was a moist and unkindly season. In August the Indians on Nantucket were attacked by the bilious plague, and between that time and February following, their number was reduced from 358 to 136. Of 258 who were affected, 36 only recovered. The disease began with high fever and ended in typhus, in about five days. It appeared to be infectious among the Indians only; for no whites were attacked, although they associated freely with the diseased. Persons of a mixed blood were attacked, but recovered. Some Indians who lived in the families of the whites, escaped disease; as did a few that lived by themselves on a distant part of the island. I am informed, by respectable authority, that a similar fever attacked Indians on board of ships, at a distance of hundreds of leagues, without any connection to Nantucket.

In December of the same year, the Indians on Martha's Vineyard, distant eight leagues from Nantucket, were invaded by a like fever; not a family escaped, and of 52 patients, 39 died.

In this instance, disease discriminated as nicely between Whites and Indians, as in 1797, it did between men and cats, and as exactly as the plague in Egypt, between the Israelites and Egyptians.

...

In 1764, just after this fatal pestilence among the Indians, a large species of fish, called blue fish, thirty of which would fill a barrel. And which were before caught in great numbers, on every side of Nantucket. Suddenly disappeared, to the great loss of the inhabitants.—Whether they perished or migrated, is not known.

Hist. Col. 3. 158.

In Europe, the year 1763 was remarkable for diseases among various species of animals. In Denmark, an epidemic catarrhal disorder affected horses. In Madrid, a pestilence among dogs swept away multitudes—900 died in one day. In Genoa, the poultry perished in a similar manner. In Italy, horses and swine fell victims to the pestilential principle. In France, horses and mules; in Sweden, sheep, horses and horned cattle perished under the influence of the general cause.

The phenomenon most generally and closely connected with pestilence is an earthquake. From all the facts that I can find in history, I question whether an instance of a considerable plague in any country, can be mentioned, which has not been immediately preceded or accompanied with convulsions of the earth. If any exceptions have occurred, they have escaped my researches. It does not happen that every place where pestilence prevails, is shaken; but during the progress of the disease which I denominate pestilence, and which run, in certain periods, over large portions of the globe, some parts of the earth, and especially those which abound most with subterranean fire, are violently agitated.

By adverting to the foregoing history, the reader will find that those years, in which considerable earthquakes have occurred in America, have been remarkably sickly. These years are 1638, 1647, 1658, 1662 and 3, 1668, 1727, 1755, 1783. See the history and the bills of mortality. Even the slighter shocks, have been attended with considerable sickness, or have introduced a series of epidemics, being contemporary with the measles, influenza or sore throat; as in 1669, 1720, 1737, 1757, 1761, 1769, 1771, 1791, 1797.

To enumerate the instances in Europe and Asia, would be useless repetition of the events related in the preceding history, to which the reader is referred.

Another phenomenon, which, next to earthquakes, appears to be most closely connected with epidemic diseases, is the eruption of fire from volcanic mountains. In this article, history is deficient, or I have not been fortunate enough to find the works necessary to furnish a complete view of these phenomena. There are whole countries in which the books I have consulted, mention no eruption of Etna and Vesuvius. The account of eruptions in Iceland, from the year 1000, taken from Pennant's Arctic Zoology, vol. 1. 331, is probably complete, or nearly so. Of the volcanoes in the Andes, we have very few accounts; as well as of those in the Moluccas. Of those in the Arctic regions of Asia and America, we know very little.

Notwithstanding these diseases, we are able, by the eruptions in Italy, Sicily and Ireland, to arrive at some very important conclusions. The reader must have noticed, in the preceding History, the coincidences in time between volcanic discharges, and winters of unusual severity. These diseases either precede or follow the winter. Thus the eruptions of 1766, 1779 and 1783, were immediately followed by intensely cold winters. The severe winters of 1762–3 and 1779–80, were speedily followed by eruptions. These instances will serve as examples of the ordinary cause of events. Sometimes the eruptions continue or are repeated, for a number of years in succession; but the eruptions when continued are moderate and the seasons variable. When the volcanoes have been, for some years, quiet, and that suspension is followed by a great discharge, it appears to me that severe winters invariably follow or precede the discharge, within a few months. So also when an eruption is continued for a number of years, if at any time the discharge becomes violent, a severe winter attends it; as in 1669. Etna was in a state of eruption from 1664 to 1679; but in 1669, the discharge was immensely augmented, and the winters preceding and following, were very severe.

There are some years in which eruptions are noted, of which I find no account, respecting the seasons. Perhaps some of these will, on further investigation, be found to be exceptions.

It is to be observed that, in some cases, a severe winter extends to both hemispheres, sometimes to one only, and in a few cases, to a part of a hemisphere only. Thus in 1607–08—1683–4—1762–63—1766–67—1779–80—1783–84, the severity extended to both hemispheres. In 1640–41—1739–40, and in other instances, the severe weather in Europe preceded, by one year, a similar winter in America. In a few instances, severe frost takes place in one hemisphere, during a series of mild winters in the other; but this is less common. In general, the severity happens, in both hemispheres at once, or in two winters in immediate succession; and as far as evidence has yet appeared, this severity is closely attendant on volcanic discharges, with very few exceptions.

Another phenomenon which usually coincides in time with severe winters, is the approach of comets. I have been struck with surprise at the coincidences of this kind. There are a few instances on record of mild winters, during the appearance of these bodies; but in these cases, the comets have appeared to be small, or to pass the system at an immense distance from the earth. The large comets and those which approach near to the earth, seem to produce almost uniformly great heat, excessive drought, followed by very cold winters, tremendous storms of wind, rain, snow and hail, unusual tides or swell of the ocean, and usually, volcanic eruptions. How far these are connected, as cause and effect, future observations may determine. Some of them occur so uniformly in the same year, that I cannot resist the evidence of their connection ...

P.S. After this work was prepared for the press, I was favored by Dr. Mitchill, with some extracts from a paper of Mr. Holm, a Swede, on the subject of a volcanic eruption in Iceland, in 1783, by which it appears that the atmosphere is rendered pestilential by discharges of fire and lava from the earth. This effect is supposed to be wrought by a combination of the septous and oxygenous parts, and may confirm and improve Dr. Mitchill's theory of pestilential air.

This eruption I understand to have been bursting of fire from the earth, in a place distant from Heckla. In the neighborhood of the column of flame were generated snow, hail and extreme cold. The water that fell in rain was acid and corrosive; destroying the cattle and men—covering the bodies of cattle with pustules and ulcers, and excoriating the hands and faces of men when it fell on them. It also killed vegetables. The effects were felt not only in Iceland, but in Norway, and other parts of Europe.

Had this treatise fallen into my hands some months ago, I might have been able to illustrate particular parts of my theory by authentic facts, taken from that work. As it is, I must content myself with observing, that Mr. Holm's observations verify my ideas, respecting the agency of electricity in producing pestilence, and extremes in the seasons. On this theory not only pestilence, but severe cold, and extreme heat, hail and snow are all similarly explained, and their connection with volcanic eruptions, and other electrical operations, visible and invisible, demonstrated.

Notes

1 John Aberth, *Plagues in World History* (Lanham, 2011), 1.
2 Ibid., 19.
3 Samuel K. Cohn, Jr and Guido Alfani, "Households and Plague in Early Modern Italy," *Journal of Interdisciplinary History* 38:2 (Autumn 2007): 177–205, here at 182.
4 See Samuel K. Cohn, Jr, "Changing Pathology of Plague," in *Le interazioni fra economia e ambiente biologico nell'Euopa preindustriale, secc. XII–XVIII*, 33–56.
5 Numbers 14:37.
6 Numbers 24, Numbers 14:1–4, 11–12.

7 See Ezekiel 5:8–12; Numbers 25; see also Deuteronomy 28:20–21.

8 David's counting of the people in II Samuel 24.

9 Aberth, *Plagues in World History*, 4.

10 See Michael Dols, *The Black Death in the Middle East* (Princeton, 1977), as well as later, Russell Hopley, "Contagion in Islamic Lands: Responses from Medieval Andalusia and North Africa," *Journal for Early Modern Cultural Studies* 10:2 (Fall/ Winter 2010): 45–64, here at 61, note 23.

11 The various words include: sterbens, Geprästen, pestilenz, pest, Infection, Hauptsucht or Hauptkrankheit, Ungarische Krankheit, hitziges Fieber or hitzige Krankheit, seuch, sucht, Hauptwee, and Contagion. See Annemarie Kinzelbach, *Gesundbleiben, Krankwerden, Armsein in der frühneuzeitlichen Gesellschaft: Gesunde und Kranke in den Reichsstädten Überlingen und Ulm, 1500–1700* (Stuttgart, 1995), 157–8.

12 Lynn A. Martin, *Plague? Jesuit Accounts of Epidemic Disease in the 16th Century* (Kirksville, 1996), 72.

13 Samuel K. Cohn, Jr, *Cultures of Plague: Medical Thought at the End of the Renaissance* (Oxford, 2009), 24.

14 Titus Lucretius Carus, *De Rerum Natura*. Trans. W. H. D. Rouse (Cambridge, MA, 1937), 521ff.

15 Charles Rosenberg, "What Is an Epidemic? AIDS in Historical Perspective," *Daedalus* 118:2 (Spring 1989): 1–17, here 1–6.

16 See Rosenberg, "What Is an Epidemic?," 7–8.

17 See Jo N. Hays, "Historians and Epidemics: Simple Questions, Complex Answers," in *Plague and the End of Antiquity: The Pandemic of 541–750*, ed. Lester K. Little (New York, 2007), 33–56, here at 38, 45.

18 David Herlihy, *The Black Death and the Transformation of the West*, ed. Samuel K. Cohn, Jr (Cambridge, MA, 1997), 20.

19 *The Medieval Globe* 1 (2014), *Pandemic Disease in the Medieval World: Rethinking the Black Death*, ed. Monica H. Green (Kalamazoo, 2014). See also Aberth, *Plagues in World History*, 22.

20 Samuel K. Cohn, Jr, *The Black Death Transformed: Disease and Culture in Early Renaissance Europe* (London and New York, 2002), 83–4, from Rosemary Horrox, trans. and ed., *The Black Death* (Manchester, 1994), 24–5.

21 Herlihy, *The Black Death*, 22.

22 Cohn, Jr and Alfani, "Households and Plague in Early Modern Italy," 180.

23 Aberth, *Plagues in World History*, 22.

24 Monica H. Green, "Taking 'Pandemic' Seriously: Making the Black Death Global," in *The Medieval Globe* 1 (2014), *Pandemic Disease in the Medieval World: Rethinking the Black Death*, ed. ibidem (Kalamazoo, 2014), 27–61, here at 32.

25 Ibid., 32.

26 Cohn, Jr, *Cultures of Plague*, 40.

27 Ibid., 40–1.

28 Ibid., 42.

29 Lilith K. Whittles and Xavier Didelot, "Epidemiological Analysis of the Eyam Plague Outbreak of 1665–1666," *Proceedings of the Royal Society* B 283 (May 2016): electronic download, 2; see also Robert Sallares, "Ecology, Evolution, and Epidemiology of Plague," in *Plague and the End of Antiquity*, 231–89, here at 267.

30 Lester K. Little, ed., *Plague and the End of Antiquity: The Pandemic of 541–750* (New York, 2007), xi.

31 Ibid., 3.

32 Dinonysios Stathakopoulos, "Crime and Punishment: The Plague in the Byzantine Empire, 541–749," in *Plague and the End of Antiquity: The Pandemic of 541–750*, ed. Lester K. Little (New York, 2007), 99–118, here at 105.

33   Procopius, *History of the Wars, Books I and II*. Trans. H. B. Dweing (London, 1971; first printed 1914), XXII–XXIII. www.gutenberg.org/files/16764/16764-h/16764-h.htm#BOOK_II.

34   Ibid., XXII–XXIII. www.gutenberg.org/files/16764/16764-h/16764-h.htm#BOOK_II.

35   Little, ed., *Plague and the End of Antiquity*, xi.

36   Sallares, "Ecology, Evolution, and Epidemiology of Plague," 261, 240.

37   Little, ed., *Plague and the End of Antiquity*; Aberth, *Plagues in World History*, 36–7.

38   Robert Hymes, "Epilogue: A Hypothesis on the East Asian Beginnings of the Yersina Pestis Polytomy," in *Pandemic*, 285–308, here at 285, 299; see also Lester K. Little, "Plague Historians in Lab Coats," *Past and Present* 213 (November 2011): 267–90, here at 271, 282–3.

39   William H. McNeill, *Plagues and Peoples* (New York, 1976), 173.

40   Aberth, *Plagues in World History*, 34.

41   See Bruce M. S. Campbell, *The Great Transition: Climate, Disease and Society in the Late-Medieval World* (Cambridge, 2016); Sharon N. Dewitte, "The Anthropology of Plague: Insights from Bioarcheological Analyses of Epidemic Cemeteries," in *Pandemic Disease*, 97–123; and Herlihy, *The Black Death*, 31–2, 33.

42   See Kristy Wilson Bowers, *Plague and Public Health in Early Modern Seville* (Rochester, 2013), 38–9.

43   Cohn, Jr, "Changing Pathology of Plague," 33–56, here at 43.

44   Ibid., 38–42.

45   Cohn, Jr, *The Black Death Transformed*, 63, 66, 70.

46   John Henderson, "Coping with Epidemics in Renaissance Italy: Plague and the Great Pox," *The Fifteenth Century XII: Society in an Age of Plague*, ed. Linda Clarke and Carole Rawcliffe (Woodbridge, 2013): 175–94, here at 175–7.

47   Ibid., 177; Ann G. Carmichael, "Universal and Particular: The Language of Plague, 1348–1500," *Medical History Supplement* 27 (2008): 17–52, 6–7 of the electronic version.

48   Henderson, "Coping with Epidemics in Renaissance Italy," 178.

49   See A. Lloyd Moote and Dorothy C. Moote, *The Great Plague: The Story of London's Most Deadly Year* (Baltimore, 2004), 279f.

50   Pierre Toubert, "La Peste Noire (1348), entre Histoire et biologie moleculaire," *Journal des Savants* (2016): 17–31, here at 19; Dewitte, "The Anthropology of Plague," 98; Little, "Plague Historians in Lab Coats," 274–6; Monica H. Green, "Editor's Introduction," in *The Medieval Globe* 1 (2014), *Pandemic Disease in the Medieval World: Rethinking the Black Death*, ed. ibidem (Kalamazoo, 2014), 9–11; Maria A. Spyrou et al., "Historical *Y. pestis* Genomes Reveal the European Black Death as the Source of Ancient and Modern Plague Pandemics," *Cell Host & Microbe* 19 (supplemental information): 874–81; Guido Alfani, "Plague in Seventeenth-Century Europe and the Decline of Italy: An Epidemiological Hypothesis," *European Review of Economic History* 17 (2013): 408–30, here at 2 of the online version; Lisa Seifert et al., "Genotyping *Yersinia pestis* in Historical Plague: Evidence for Long-Term Persistence of *Y. pestis* in Europe from the 14th to the 17th Century," *PLOS One* 11:1 (January 13, 2016), online, here at 2; see also Sallares, "Ecology, Evolution, and Epidemiology of Plague," 232, regarding various ways of identifying the pathogen responsible for the Justinian Plague.

51   Seifert et al., "Genotyping *Yersinia pestis* in Historical Plague," 1, 4; Katherine I. Bos et al., "Eighteenth Century *Yersinia pestis* Genomes Reveal the Long-Term Persistence of an Historical Plague Focus," eLife 2016;5:e12994 (online), here at 1, 5, 6.

52   Regarding 1348, see Toubert, "La Peste Noire (1348), entre Histoire et biologie moleculaire," 27–9, for example.

53 See, for example, Green, "Editor's Introduction," 13.
54 Campbell, *The Great Transition*, 209, 329; Zlata Blazina Tomic and Vesna Blazina, *Expelling the Plague: The Health Office and the Implementation of Quarantine in Dubrovnik, 1377–1533* (Montreal, 2015), 6; Pierre Galanaud, Anne Galanaud, and Patrick Giraudoux, "Historical Epidemics Cartography Generated by Spatial Analysis: Mapping the Heterogeneity of Three Medieval 'Plagues' in Dijon," *PLoS ONE* 10:12 (2015): 1–24 (electronic version), here at 1, 3, 12, 20; Alfani, "Plague in Seventeenth-Century Europe and the Decline of Italy: An Epidemiological Hypothesis," here at 19 of the online version; Ann G. Carmichael, "Plague Persistence in Western Europe: A Hypothesis," in *The Medieval Globe* 1 (2014), *Pandemic Disease in the Medieval World: Rethinking the Black Death*, ed. Monica H. Green (Kalamazoo, 2014), 157–91, here at 158, 160; Michelle Ziegler, "The Black Death and the Future of the Plague," in *The Medieval Globe* 1 (2014), *Pandemic Disease in the Medieval World: Rethinking the Black Death*, ed. Monica H. Green (Kalamazoo, 2014), 259–83, here at 271–5; Jo N. Hays, "Historians and Epidemics: Simple Questions, Complex Answers," 33–56, here at 47ff.
55 Campbell, *The Great Transition*, 286; Nükhet Varlik, "New Science and Old Sources: Why the Ottoman Experience of Plague Matters," *Pandemic Disease*, 193–227, here at 207; Alfani, "Plague in Seventeenth-Century Europe and the Decline of Italy: An Epidemiological Hypothesis," here at 6 of the online version.
56 Varlik, "New Science and Old Sources," 209.
57 Ibid., 212–13; Katherine Royer, "The Blind Men and the Elephant: Imperial Medicine, Medieval Historians and the Role of Rats in the Historiography of Plague," in *Medicine and Colonialism: Historical Perspectives in India and South Africa*, ed. Poonam Bala (London, 2014), 99–110, here at 102.
58 Varlik, "New Science and Old Sources," 211; Royer, "The Blind Men and the Elephant," 109.
59 Christian Jörg, *Teure, Hunger, Großes Sterben: Hungersnöte und Versorgungskrisen in den Städten des Reiches während des 15. Jahrhunderts* (Stuttgart, 2008), 9, 56, 58–9, 85.
60 Ibid., 76.
61 Ibid., 168, 209.
62 McNeill, *Plagues and Peoples*, 174.
63 Aberth, *Plagues in World History*, 35; McNeill, *Plagues and Peoples*, 170.
64 See, for example, John T. Alexander, *Bubonic Plague in Early Modern Russia: Public Health and Urban Disaster* (Oxford, 2002), 13.
65 Herlihy, *The Black Death*, 19.
66 Mary Lindemann, *Medicine and Society in Early Modern Europe*, 2nd ed. (Cambridge, 2010), 55–6; Aberth, *Plagues in World History*, 37.
67 Paul Slack, *Plague: A Very Short Introduction* (Oxford, 2012), 62.
68 McNeill, *Plagues and Peoples*, 180–1.
69 Slack, *Plague: A Very Short Introduction*, 39.
70 Nico Voigtländer and Hans-Joachim Voth, "The Three Horsemen of Riches: Plague, War, and Urbanization in Early Modern Europe," unpublished essay; www.anderson.ucla.edu/faculty/nico.v/Research/Horsemen.pdf [last viewed March 29, 2016]. Subsequent publication in the *Review of Economic Studies* 80:2 (2013): 774–811.
71 Herlihy, *The Black Death*, 57.
72 Slack, *Plague: A Very Short Introduction*, 38–9.
73 Voigtländer and Voth, "The Three Horsemen of Riches," 3; Slack, *Plague: A Very Short Introduction*, 41.
74 Voigtländer and Voth, "The Three Horsemen of Riches," 8.

75 Ibid.
76 Ibid., 9.
77 Daniel J. Schroeter, *The Sultan's Jew: Morocco and the Sephardi World* (Stanford, 2002), 36.
78 George Michael La Rue, "Treating Black Deaths in Egypt: Clot-Bey, African Slaves, and the Plague Epidemic of 1834–1835," in *Histories of Medicine and Healing in the Indian Ocean World, The Modern World*, Vol. 2, ed. Anna Winterbottom and Facil Tesfaye (Basingstoke, 2016), 27–59, here at 28–9.
79 In 1361–62, 1363, 1365, 1374, 1376, 1381–82, 1388–89, 1390–91, and 1398–99.
80 Heath W. Lowry, "Pushing the Stone Uphill: The Impact of Bubonic Plague on Ottoman Urban Society in the Fifteenth and Sixteenth Centuries," *Osmanlı Araştırmaları* 23 (2003): 93–132, here at 98.
81 "... Daily he professed to the emperor that he was a Christian and not a believer in Muhammad's doctrines. The emperor did not wish to listen because it might cause scandal. Then when the dreaded disease continued to consume and destroy bodies, neither respecting nor sparing any age, it attacked Bayazid's adolescent son. The stricken youth sent the following message to Emperor John, 'O Emperor of the Romans, you who are both master and father to me, my end is near. Against my wishes I must leave everything behind and depart for the Heavenly Tribunal. I confess that I am a Christian and I accuse you of not granting me the earnest of faith and the seal of the Spirit. Know, therefore, that as I must die unbaptized, I shall bring accusations against you before the Judgment Seat of the impartial God.' Yielding finally to his plea, the emperor sent for him and as his godfather sponsored his baptism. He died the next day. The Emperor buried him with great honor in a marble sarcophagus near the church and within the gate of the Studite Monastery of the Proromos." Cited in Lowry, "Pushing the Stone Uphill," 100–1.
82 In 1420, 1431, 1436, 1440–41, 1455, 1459, 1460, 1467, 1470, 1471, 1472, and 1475. Lowry, "Pushing the Stone Uphill," 105–6, 125.
83 Quoted in ibid., 107–9.
84 Nükhet Varlik, *Disease and Empire: A History of Plague Epidemics in the Early Modern Ottoman Empire (1453–1600)* (Doctoral Dissertation, University of Chicago, 2008), 22.
85 Ibid., 30–1.
86 Ibid., 50. The chronicler Kritovoulos suggested that the famous Ottoman policy of repopulation had not only political dimensions but was related to the very real needs to repopulate the capital city after numerous epidemics claimed the lives of numerous residents (Lowry, "Pushing the Stone Uphill," 111).
87 Varlik, *Disease and Empire*, 47.
88 Ibid., 52–3.
89 In the following seasons/years: winter 1496–97, summer 1497, summer–fall 1500, winter 1500–01, summer 1501, fall 1501, summer 1502, winter 1502–03, summer 1503, winter 1503–04, spring 1510, fall 1512, summer 1513, summer 1514, fall 1514, summer 1516, summer 1518, winter 1518–19, winter–spring 1519–20, summer 1520, summer 1522, summer 1523, winter 1523–24, fall 1525, winter 1525–26, summer 1526, fall 1526, winter 1526–27, spring 1527, summer 1527, summer 1529, summer 1530, spring 1532, summer–fall 1532, winter–spring 1532–33, summer 1533. See Giselle Marien, "The Black Death in Early Ottoman Territories: 1347–1550" (MA thesis, Bikent University, 2009), 37; see also Varlik, *Disease and Empire*, 57.
90 Marien, "The Black Death in Early Ottoman Territories," 143.
91 Ibid.

92 Varlik, *Disease and Empire*, 62, 106ff.
93 Ibid., 137.
94 Ibid., 144.
95 In the years: 1611–13, 1620–24, 1627, 1636–37, 1647–49, 1653–56, 1659–66, 1671–80, 1685–95, and 1697 into the early eighteenth century. See Varlik, *Disease and Empire*, 146.
96 Daniel Panzac, *La peste dans l'empire Ottoman: 1700–1850* (Leuven, 1985), 198.
97 Ibid., 201; see also Alan Mikhail, *Nature and Empire in Ottoman Egypt: An Environmental History* (Cambridge, 2011), 218.
98 McNeill, *Plagues and Peoples*, 171.
99 Panzac, *La peste dans l'empire Ottoman*, 46.
100 1706, 1707, 1712, 1719, 1721, 1729, 1733, 1742, 1743, 1744, 1760, 1761, 1762, 1786, 1787.
101 1710, 1718, 1720, 1721, 1729, 1732, 1743, 1744, 1760, 1785, 1786.
102 1711, 1712, 1713, 1715, 1726, 1730, 1731, 1733, 1735, 1742, 1743, 1744, 1759, 1760, 1762, 1784, 1785, 1786, 1791, 1792, 1798, 1799. See Panzac, *La peste dans l'empire Ottoman*, 30–4.
103 Panzac, *La peste dans l'empire Ottoman*, 216.
104 Mikhail, *Nature and Empire in Ottoman Egypt*, 221ff.
105 Ibid., 229–30.
106 In 1352 and again in 1360, 1363–65, 1369–70, 1374–77, and 1396.
107 In 1401, 1403–04, 1406–07, 1408, and 1417–28. See Alexander, *Bubonic Plague in Early Modern Russia: Public Health and Urban Disaster*, 13–15.
108 Ibid., 16.
109 Ibid.
110 Ibid., 17.
111 Ibid., 17–18.
112 Ibid., 19.
113 Ibid., 24ff.
114 Ibid., 101.
115 Ibid., 102.
116 Ibid., 260.
117 Ibid., 235.
118 Ibid., 236.
119 Ibid., 235.
120 Ibid., 268ff.
121 Ibid., 177ff, 192.
122 Ibid., 198–9.
123 Aberth, *Plagues in World History*, 37.
124 Varlik, "New Science and Old Sources," 206.
125 Alfani, "Plague in Seventeenth-Century Europe and the Decline of Italy: An Epidemiological Hypothesis," here at 9, 22, 33, 35 of the online version.
126 In the following years: 1535, 1571–75, 1595–96, 1611–17, 1666, 1684–86, 1725, 1757, 1760–67, 1773–74, and 1797. McNeill, *Plagues and Peoples*, 334.
127 William G. Naphy, *Plagues, Poisons, and Potions: Plague-Spreading Conspiracies in the Western Alps, c 1530–1640* (Manchester, 2002), chapters 1, 6.
128 Derived from data presented in Frank Hatje, *Leben und Sterben im Zeitalter der Pest: Basel im 15. bis 17. Jahrhundert* (Basel, 1992), 161.
129 1519–20, 1530, 1541–43, 1545–48, 1563–64, 1566–67, 1574, 1576–77, 1583, 1585–87, 1591, 1592–94, 1596–97, 1605–07, 1610–12, 1616–17, 1626, 1630–31, 1634–35, 1639. Kinzelbach, *Gesundbleiben*, 166.

130 Cilli Kasper-Holtkotte, *Die Jüdische Gemeinde von Frankfurt/Main in der Frühen Neuzeit: Familien, Netzwerke und Konflikte eines jüdischen Zentrums* (Berlin, 2010), 266.

131 David C. Mengel, "A Plague in Bohemia? Mapping the Black Death," *Past and Present* 211 (May 2011): 3–34, here at 19.

132 Ibid., 20, 22.

133 1605–13 (with one-tenth of the city population dying in 1613), 1624–26, 1631–35, 1639–40, 1648–49, 1680.

134 *Encyclopedia Britannica.*

135 Martin, *Plague?*, 163.

136 Mark Harrison, *Climates and Constitutions: Health, Race, Environment and British Imperialism in India 1600–1850* (Oxford, 1999), 27.

137 *Encyclopedia Britannica.*

138 McNeill, *Plagues and Peoples*, 181.

139 Ibid., 182.

140 Martin, *Plague?*, 163.

141 Panzac, *La peste dans l'empire Ottoman*, 362.

142 Leo Noordegraaf and Gerrit Valk, *De Gave Gods: De pest in Holland vanaf de late middeleeuwen* (Bergen, 1988), 230–1; 43.

143 1469, 1471, 1483, 1493, 1522, 1534, 1550, 1554, 1557, 1558, 1559, 1573, 1574, 1599, 1601, 1602, 1603, 1616, 1617, 1618, 1623, 1624, 1625, 1626, 1629, 1635, 1636, 1652, 1653, 1654, 1655, 1656, 1657, 1663, 1664, 1665, 1666 (37 years).

144 1483, 1508, 1509, 1515, 1517, 1518, 1519, 1524, 1525, 1526, 1538, 1556, 1557, 1567, 1568, 1572, 1573, 1574, 1599, 1602, 1603, 1604, 1605, 1617, 1624, 1634, 1635, 1636, 1652, 1653, 1654, 1655, 1664, 1666 (34 years).

145 1467, 1468, 1469, 1557, 1573, 1574, 1593, 1594, 1595, 1596, 1598, 1601, 1602, 1603, 1604, 1618, 1624, 1625, 1626, 1634, 1635, 1636, 1637, 1655, 1656, 1657, 1660, 1664, 1665, 1666 (30 years).

146 Noordegraaf, *De Gave Gods*, 233–4.

147 Ibid., 51.

148 Quoted in Cohn, Jr, *The Black Death Transformed*, 18.

149 Cohn, Jr, *The Black Death Transformed*, 19.

150 Michael Shiyung Liu, "Disease, People, and Environment: The Plague in China," unpublished paper, 7.

151 I base the following comments on a massive database compiled by my colleague Michael Shiyung Liu, Associate Research Fellow, Institute of Taiwan History, Academia Sinica, and generously shared with me. Professor Liu has utilized a broad sample of sources exploring epidemics from the middle of the seventeenth century. See also Hymes, "Epilogue: A Hypothesis on the East Asian Beginnings of the Yersina Pestis Polytomy."

152 McNeill, *Plagues and Peoples*, 235–6. More recently, see Hymes, "Epilogue: A Hypothesis on the East Asian Beginnings of the Yersina Pestis Polytomy."

153 Liu, "Disease, People, and Environment," 11.

154 Ibid., 6.

155 Carmichael, "Universal and Particular," 4 of the electronic version.

156 Green, "Taking 'Pandemic' Seriously: Making the Black Death Global," 38.

157 Ibid., 41–2.

158 Ibid., 43–4, 48.

159 Ibid., 50.

160 Jörg, *Teure, Hunger, Großes Sterben*, 147–51.

161 Ibid., 155–6.

162 Varlik, *Disease and Empire*, 102–3.

163 Ibid., 104.

164 See, for example, the valuable works of Ayalon, Bulmuş, Lowry, Mikhail, and Varlik cited in the Bibliography and throughout this volume.

165 Ann Bowman Jannetta, *Epidemics and Mortality in Early Modern Japan* (Princeton, 1987), 31.

166 Ibid., 44.

167 Lawrence I. Conrad, Michael Neve, Vivian Nutton, Roy Porter, and Andrew Wear, *The Western Medical Tradition, 800 BC to AD 1800* (Cambridge, 1995), 217–18.

168 Ibid., 225–6.

169 Shin Dongwon, "Measures against Epidemics during Late 18th Century Korea: Reformation or Restoration?," *Extrême-Orient, Extrême-Occident* 37 (2014): 91–110.

170 Ibid., 94.

171 Ibid., 95.

172 Ibid., 100.

173 Ibid., 101.

174 Suzanne Austin Alchon, *A Pest in the Land: New World Epidemics in a Global Context* (Albuquerque, 2003), 55.

175 Ibid., 56.

176 Ibid., 63.

177 Ibid., 69.

178 Ibid., 70.

179 Ibid., 73.

180 Ibid., 74.

181 Ibid., 76.

182 Ibid., 85.

183 Ibid., 87–8.

184 Ibid., 95.

185 Ibid., 97.

186 John Duffy, *Epidemics in Colonial America* (Baton Rouge, 1953), 148–9.

187 Philippus Baldeus, "Nauwkeurige en Waarachtige," 28–33 in Ishrat Alam, *Smallpox and Its Treatment in Pre-Modern India* (Kumar, 2001), 85–93, here 88–9.

188 Michael Dols, *The Black Death in the Middle East*, 67.

189 *The Life and Letters of Ogier Ghiselin de Busbecq*, 2 vols (London, 1881), vol. 1 163–5, 330–1, 333–6, and 341.

190 *Adventures of Baron Wenceslas Wratislaw of Mitrowitz. What he saw in the Turkish Metropolis, Constantinople, experienced in his captivity; and after his happy return to his country, committed to writing in the year of our Lord 1599* (London, 1862), 107, 162.

191 *The Tuzuk-i-Jahangiri; or, Memoirs of Jahangir*. Trans. Alexander Rogers. Ed. Henry Beveridge (London, 1909), 330, 442–3.

192 Cited in Kaspar-Holtkotte, *Die jüdische Gemeinde Frankfurt/Main*, 266 n. 749.

193 Wellcome Library, London.

194 From the third edition of the work. London, 1721, 10–16.

195 Alexander Russell, *Natural History of Aleppo* (London, 1756), Chapter III (1742), 193–5, 225–8, 237–9, 241–2.

196 1–6, 15–17, 20–3, 33–5.

197 Drawn from data compiled by Professor Michael Liu.

198 *The History and Description of Africa of Leo Africanus*. Vol. 1. London, 1896?, 181–2. The text has been rendered into modern English.

199 Noah Webster, *A Brief History of Epidemic and Pestilential Diseases*, 2 vols (Hartford, 1799), vol. 1, 182–3, 252–3; vol. 2, 11–13, 15–16.

2   Religious understanding of and response to plague

The fear of death brought on by plague was sufficient to launch some religious movements and to deepen religious sensibilities in an age when religion, however broadly defined, was seen to have great power. While plagues were often related to weather conditions and food shortages, and so could be rationalized or approached practically, particularly severe plagues invoked images of the end of days. This was certainly the case with the outbreak of the Black Death in the middle of the fourteenth century, which claimed more than 60% of the population in some places.[1] Such religious intensification could also be associated with more apocalyptic sensibilities or heretical ideologies.

The sixteenth-century Ottoman chronicler Selâniki Mustafa Efendi, who lived during a period of severe and repeated plague outbreaks, frequently referenced the plague as well as other disasters.[2] In most cases he did not employ the standard term *tā'ūn*, with Arabic origins, but rather referred to the plague as "blessed" or "manifest," perhaps euphemistically, though perhaps also suggesting divine origins of plague or simply its appearance, without making a causal connection to the plague as punishment for sin.[3] In his use of particular expressions, one recent scholar suggests that Selâniki emphasized that it was the will of God, not the actual plague, which killed people.[4] [See 2.8]

Textual foundations

Religious worldviews and narratives of plague deeply affected how early moderns understood and responded to plague. Both the Hebrews and the Greeks—to whom early modern Christians, Jews, and Muslims remained indebted—saw plagues, as well as diseases more generally, alternately as either a punishment or a test from God.[5] As a result, the appropriate response to the outbreak of plague could vary, but very frequently involved repentance and prayers to God (or the gods). [See 2.1 and 2.9 for examples]

In the Hebrew Bible plague was associated with divine punishment for human sins and shortcomings—whether the turn to idolatry, neglect of the Law, or poor moral behavior. [See, for example, 2.12 and 2.13] The Hebrew Bible provided a good deal of language and conceptual orientation for understanding and dealing with plague. The plague was of course also famously associated with God's punishment of the Egyptians, whose Pharaoh enslaved and refused to let the Israelites leave Egypt. [See 2.5] Well known was the narrative of the book of Exodus (chapter 9), in which God punished the Egyptian Pharaoh for his intransigence with a multitude of actions, from lice, boils, and burning hail to death of animals (described here) and eventually death of the first born males:

> The Lord said to Moses, 'Go to Pharaoh and say to him: "So says the Lord, the God of the Hebrews: Send my people so they may serve me. For if you refuse to send them and if you continue to hold them, then the hand of the Lord is upon your cattle that are in the field, upon the horses, upon the asses, upon the camels, upon the herds, and upon the flocks, a very heavy pestilence. And the Lord made a division between the cattle of Israel and the cattle of Egypt, and none of all of the cattle of the Children of Israel will die. And the Lord set the time, saying, tomorrow the Lord will do this thing in the land."' And the Lord did this thing on the next day. All the cattle of Egypt died and not one of the cattle of the Children of Israel died. And Pharaoh sent and behold, not one of the cattle of Israel died and the heart of Pharaoh was stubborn and he did not send the people [out].

More generally, however, the "economy of sin," whereby God punished humans for their transgressions against biblical law and directives, would have lasting impact on medieval and early modern sensibilities. As noted in the book of Leviticus (26:14–46):

> And if you remain hostile toward Me and refuse to obey Me, I will smite you sevenfold according to your sins. I will send among you wild beasts, and they will rob you of your children, destroy your cattle, and make you few in number; and your roads will be deserted. And if in spite of these things you do not return to Me but remain hostile to Me, I will also be hostile to you and I will smite you sevenfold for your sins. And I will bring a sword upon you to wreak vengeance for the covenant. And you will be gathered together within your cities, and I will send pestilence among you, and you will be delivered into enemy hands. … Yet in spite of this, when they are in the land of their enemies, I will not reject them or abhor them so as to destroy them completely, breaking My covenant with them. I am the Lord their God. But for their sakes I will remember the covenant with their ancestors whom I brought out of Egypt in the sight of the nations that I might be their God. I am the Lord. These are the statutes, and the laws, and the teachings that the Lord established through Moses at Mount Sinai, between Himself and the Israelite people.

Alternately, God might end a plague because of some virtuous action, as depicted in the book of Numbers (25):

And when Phinehas, son of Eleazar, the son of Aaron the priest, saw this [inappropriate behavior drawing some Israelites to idolatry], he rose up from the midst of the congregation, and took a spear in his hand. And he followed the Israelite into the chamber and stabbed both of them, the man of Israel and the woman through her belly. Then the plague against the Israelites was stopped. Those who died in the plague numbered 24,000.

Similarly, prayer and penitence were presented in the Hebrew Bible as possible ways to end plague and other catastrophes. In an approach that would echo in many early modern narratives, the author of 2 Chronicles 6:28–31 recorded that:

If there is famine in the land, if there is pestilence, blight, mildew, locusts, or caterpillars, or if their enemies oppress them in any of the settlements of their land. In any plague and in any disease, any prayer or supplication offered by any person among all Your people Israel—each of whom knows his affliction and his pain—when he spreads forth his hands toward this House, may You hear in Your heavenly abode, and pardon.

From this perspective, it was trust in God, which, at the end of the day, was most effective in addressing and protecting one from plague. Psalm 91, a frequently quoted text, concluded that,

Whoever sits in the refuge of the most High, he will dwell in the shadow of the Almighty. I will say of the Lord, He is my refuge and my fortress, my God, I will trust in him. For he will deliver you from the ensnaring trap, from the devastating pestilence. With His pinions He will cover you, and beneath His wings you will be protected; shield and armor are His truth. You need not fear the terror of night; nor the arrow that flies by day; nor the pestilence that walks in the dark; nor the destruction that lays waste at noon. **[For Martin Luther's gloss on this Psalm, see 5.4]**

Like the Hebrews, the Greeks (who are discussed in greater detail in Chapter 3) had interpreted plague as punishment for human sins. In the *Iliad*, for example, Apollo sent a plague upon the Greeks as punishment for the insult to his priest Chryses at the hands of Agamemnon,[6] who captured Chryses' daughter and expelled Chryses.[7] Apollo rained down arrows of plague upon the Greeks for nine days—an image that would surface in many European art works on the plague [See 5.3].[8] (Interestingly, Apollo is also known as the mouse god, perhaps making him, even unwittingly, strikingly close to the rats who helped to transmit plague.)

Early Christians and rabbinic authorities discussed plagues in a variety of contexts, revealing the terror associated with, but also the mundane concerns that accompanied, them. In the New Testament plague took on distinctly apocalyptic tones as well, particularly as described in Revelations. Such sensibilities surfaced during particularly disruptive epidemics, when indeed the world seemed to be crumbling and inherited explanations seemed to fall short. According to Revelation 9, to take only one such example, in which plague is taken to refer to a range of punishments (and not disease per se):

> The horses and riders I saw in my vision looked like this: Their breastplates were fiery red, dark blue, and yellow as sulfur. The heads of the horses resembled the heads of lions, and out of their mouths came fire, smoke and sulfur. A third of mankind was killed by the three plagues of fire, smoke and sulfur that came out of their mouths. The power of the horses was in their mouths and in their tails; for their tails were like snakes, having heads with which they inflict injury. ... The rest of mankind who were not killed by these plagues still did not repent of the work of their hands; they did not stop worshiping demons, and idols of gold, silver, bronze, stone and wood—idols that cannot see or hear or walk. Nor did they repent of their murders, their magic arts, their sexual immorality or their thefts.

Plague here had a wide range of associated meaning and imagery, which helps, in part, to explain its multi-valent usage throughout the Middle Ages and into Modernity.

The Rabbis also discussed plague on occasion, defining the scope of an epidemic and suggesting remedies for it. In the Babylonian Talmud, tractate "Taanit" ("Fasting," 18b–19a, 21a–22a Chapter III, in the *Mishnah*), for example, the rabbinic writers explored ways to define a plague:

> What constitutes a plague? If in a city that can supply five hundred foot-soldiers three deaths take place on three consecutive days, this constitutes a plague; less than this is no plague. The alarm is sounded everywhere on account of the following [visitations]: blast, mildew, locust, cricket, wild beasts, and the sword, as they are all plagues likely to spread.

In the gloss on this passage (Gemara), the rabbis took the opportunity to discuss the merits of individuals that could keep the plague (and other disasters) away or cure the victims:

> Once a plague broke out in Sura but it did not affect the locality in which Rab resided. People thought that this was on account of Rab's great merit but in a dream it was made clear to them that this was far too small a matter to need Rab's great merit, but that it was on account of the merit of a certain man who made it a practice to lend shovel and spade for burials.

In this passage, as in others, the practical discussion of how to define and identify a plague merges seamlessly with the connection of or resistance to plague due to human actions.

Late medieval religious orientations

Numerous plague treatises were written in the later Middle Ages and early modern period that explored religious aspects of plague in addition to scientific/medical and policy issues. Consider, by way of example, the plague treatises of Ibn al-Khatīb (d 1374) and Ibn Khatima (the fourteenth-century Granada scholar famous for his historical works as well as his development of the concept of contagion) in 1349. The authors of plague treatises could present a diversity of explanations of plague. One prominent Egyptian scholar asserted that plague had non-natural causes since some people, even in infected houses, did not contract the plague.[9] Indeed, in Islam generally, the role of humans in spreading plague was seen as secondary, since God was believed to have sent the plague.[10] However, the concept of contagion was not dismissed. Ibn al-Khatīb, for example, noted that:

> infection exists, is confirmed by experience, research, insight and observation, and through constantly recurring accounts. These are the elements of proof. For him who has treated or recognized this case, it cannot remain concealed that mostly the man who has had contact with a patient infected with the disease must die, and that, on the other hand, the man who has had no contact remains healthy.[11]

In Islam, the approach to plague was dictated by religious texts and traditions as well as scientific knowledge. In Islam, disease was frequently attributed to the *jinn*, hidden and supernatural creatures.[12] A fourteenth-century Islamic plague treatise, for example, noted that:

> In these days [March–April 1363] the entire story had recurred in dreams of the jinn with lances in their hands with which they pierce mankind. Some people had seen them doing this when they awoke, and more than one had reported this to me.[13]

Various mystical discussions of God's names and meaning were seen as gateways to engagement with God.[14] Other visions and supernatural occurrences were reported, including streams of light said to be emanating from the shrines of various holy figures during the Black Death and the sighting of apparitions during the 1429–30 plague in Egypt.[15] In response, a variety of plague prayers were written that invoked God's divine names in defense against plague.[16] **[On prayer generally is Islam at times of plague, see 2.1 and 2.3]** According to one such prayer,

> Oh God, allay the fearful stroke of the lord of al-Jabarut [absolute Sovereignty] by Thy descending kindness which comes from the abundance of heaven, so that we may cling to the coat-tails of Your Kindness. We seek refuge with You from the events of Your power. You are the omnipotent and universal power. There is no power and strength save in God Almighty.[17]

Some plague responses suggested magical conceptions of disease or revealed apocalyptic sensibilities. Anonymous fifteenth-century Ottoman chronicles, for example, described a magic column constructed in the Hippodrome by the founder of Constantinople (Istanbul) that was of a bronze dragon and a copper statue of himself riding a horse, which was reputed to be effective in warding off the plague.[18] In many cases, the devastation of plague caused radical transformations in worldviews, with many seeing signs of the end of the world. In Islamic traditions, plague and holy war were at times related. According to this line of thought, fleeing from plague was akin to fleeing from battle and martyrdom would be brought about by battle and plague.[19] Regardless of how they were spread, early modern people of all religious backgrounds often saw plagues as portents (along with other signs and wonders, such as comets) of an approaching apocalypse, and they could, as a result be leveraged for a variety of moralistic and polemical ends. [See 2.11] The traditional resort to prayer and repentance, and in many cases religious processions as well, was inflamed by often charismatic preachers who took the opportunity, frequently in an apocalyptic vein to encourage the reform of morals.[20]

In response to the Black Death bands of Christian flagellants inflicted wounds on themselves to redress the moral sins of their day.[21] The Strasbourg chronicler Fritsche (Friedrich) Closener (d 1373), a priest from a noble family, authored a chronicle (1362)—perhaps the oldest chronicle in German focusing on a specific town—in which he described in one passage the movement of the flagellants, which emerged in the fourteenth century as a radical form of penance and took on broader proportions when various groups emerged across Europe. Initially accepted by the Church as practicing a popular expression of piety, flagellants would be later condemned as heretics.

Closener wrote that,

> In 1349, fourteen days after midsummer [July 8], around mass time, about 200 flagellants came to Strasbourg, who carried on in the manner I'm about to describe. First, they had the most precious flags of velvet cloth, rough and smooth, and the finest canopies, of which they had maybe ten or eight, and torches and many candles, which were carried ahead of them when they went into cities or villages. And all bells were rung in alarm then, and they followed their flags two by two in a row, and they were all wearing overcoats and hoods with red crosses. And two or four sang the beginning of a hymn, and the others joined in …
>
> You should know that whenever the flagellants whipped themselves, there were large crowds and the greatest pious weeping that one should ever see. … Thus they make the people believe the flagellants' word more than those of the priests: 'What can you say? These are people who know the truth and tell it.' And wherever they came, many people of the cities became flagellants, both laymen and priests, but no learned priest joined them. Many well-meaning men joined this whipping pilgrimage; in their simple-minded way, they could not see the falsehood which resided therein.[22]

At times, such passionate preaching could lead to scapegoating or the further marginalization of outsider groups, including minorities, such as Jews
and foreigners—even when the plague refused itself to differentiate among its
victims. Under some conditions, the plague could foment anti-Jewish preaching
and lead to anti-Jewish activities, particularly in the form of looting and van-
dalism, as some early modern authors note. Plague narratives—both Jewish and
Christian—provide details about daily life and about the conditions of Jewish life,
including the overcrowding and unsanitary conditions facing some Jews in larger
ghettoized communities. They also reveal multifaceted interactions between and
perceptions of Jews and Christians that make it rather difficult to draw hard and
fast conclusions about Jewish and Christian relations in the early modern world.

Saints, relics, and processions

Proper religious rituals [See 2.2], including communal prayers [See 2.1, 2.3,
2.8, and 2.9], fasts [See 2.3 and 2.14], processions [See 2.10], and pilgrimages
to holy sites [See 2.3] were believed by many early moderns to lead to the end of
the plague and to healing.[23] Early modern people called on saints to intercede on
their behalf with God and to protect them.[24] Some particular saints, such as Saint
Sebastian and Saint Roche [See 2.4] were particularly well known in the early
modern period as powerful intermediaries in the fight against plague, in a certain
way imitating Jesus, who according to Luke 7:21 "cured many who had diseases,
sicknesses, and evil spirits, and gave sight to many who were blind." The Virgin
Mary was also summoned as a protection from or a means to ward off plague.[25]

The Golden Legend, by Jacob de Voragine (c 1230–1298), was translated and
expanded by William Caxton (c 1422–c 1491) in the late fifteenth century.[26]
Throughout the Middle Ages, the text captured the religious belief in the ability
of holy people to serve as intercessionaries with God to protect people and heal
them from the plague. *The Golden Legend* was a collection of hagiographies that
was wildly popular in late medieval Europe, with more than 100 editions, some
with additional tales, published in the last few decades of the fifteenth century.
Saint Roche (Roch, Rocke) was canonized a saint in 1446. [See 2.4] The dates
ascribed for Saint Roche's life have varied from the thirteenth century through
the fourteenth. He appears to have been born in Montpelier. Traditionally he is
said to have died in 1327 and he was reputed to have possessed powers to heal
people from plague. Some scholars question whether he lived and died later than
generally assumed, placing him more squarely with the outbreak of the plague
in 1348 (and dying in the 1370s). In any event, prayers for his intercession were
viewed by many as effective against the plague in the later Middle Ages, for
example, in Italy during the plague outbreak of 1414. The text described the
saint's work at some length:

> ... and Rocke forsook Rome and came to the town of Armine, a noble city
> of Italy, which also he delivered from the said pestilence. And when that
> town was delivered, he went to the city of Manasem in Lombardy, which

was also sore oppressed with sick men of the pestilence, whom with all his heart he served diligently, and by the help of God made that town quit of the pestilence. And from thence went to Piacenza, for he understood that there was great pestilence. Rocke was ever of great study how he might, in the name of Jesus and of his passion, deliver mortal men from the hurt of pestilence. And so a whole year he visited the houses of poor men, and they that had most need, to them he did most help, and was always in the hospital. And when he had been long in the hospital of Piacenza, and had helped almost all the sick men therein, about midnight he heard in his sleep an angel thus saying: O Rocke, most devout to Christ, awake and know that thou art smitten with the pestilence, study now how thou may be cured. And anon he felt him sore taken with the pestilence under his both arms …

Afflicted by plague, he was cast from the city. In the woods, however, Saint Roche suffered patiently, always blessing God—thanking God for the affliction and beseeching God for consolation and comfort. "And his prayer finished," the account continues,

anon there came a cloud from heaven by the lodge that Saint Rocke had made within boughs, whereas sprang a fair and bright well, which is there yet unto this day. Whose water Saint Rocke drank, being sore athirst, and thereof had great refreshing of the great heat that he suffered of the pestilence fever.

In early modern Italy, Saint Sebastian (d 288), as well as Saint Bernadino of Siena (1380–1444) and Saint Charles Borromeo (Cardinal and Archbishop of Milan; 1538–84) [See 2.15], were written about extensively and frequently depicted in art, especially in the context of the plague, starting already in the fifteenth century.[27] The impact of some saints, such as these, could be quite broad geographically. Other saints were more locally known and their impact more locally or regionally focused. Some miraculous cures for the plague were reported in the late fourteenth century, particularly in central Italy. Giovanna of Signa was reputed to have cured several people in the 1360s through the early 1380s.[28] Rosa of Viterbo was said to have performed 82 miracles in the middle of the fifteenth century, primarily in Viterbo (in central Italy) and outlying areas. She allegedly cured victims of leprosy, epilepsy, tuberculosis, sciatica, paralysis, and various snake and insect bites. More than half of her cures, however, involved the plague during the years between 1449 and 1452.[29] Saints could literally be made at times of plague. Descriptions of miraculous healing during the plague associated with Lady Delphine de Puimichel from Provence (1363), were considered as part of her canonization inquest.[30] Or, consider Rosalia of Palermo from the twelfth century. Her relics were found in the seventeenth century and included in a procession that was linked with the cessation of the plague in Palermo in 1624. Jesuit interventions—through hagiographies and sermons— led to the development of her cult.[31] Even in the last major plague outbreaks of the Second Pandemic in eighteenth-century Russia, icons and religious portraits proved to have great appeal and attracted the faithful seeking healing powers.[32]

Processions with saints' relics and other holy objects [See 2.2] were regularly organized against the plague, even in the earliest of plagues. In the epidemic that began in 1348, for example, we find processions with relics of Saint Firenze in Perugia, Saint Waldertrude in Hanover, and Saint Remigius of Rheims.[33] In sixteenth-century Seville (1582), processions with images of the city's patron saints Justa and Rufina and the saints most associated with the plague, Sebastian and Roche, were organized (along with formal health regulations written by the city council scribe) in response to the outbreak of plague.[34]

The inter-relation of religion and politics is clear in a plague ordinance from Innsbruck in 1611, which included a provision that the hospital church must include the reading of a weekly mass on the altar of Saint Sebastian.[35] To take one additional example, the English Plague Orders[36] legislated quarantines and the support of those people quarantined in their houses, as well as for guards, while also including prayers to God.[37]

Other kinds of processions in response to various epidemics and disasters could be found outside the Christian world. During epidemics in the Incan Empire, authorities organized processions of armed men to prevent or drive out diseases. Other ceremonies were also practiced, including a September washing of houses and cleaning of streets, along with fasts, abstinence from sex, and the bathing and rubbing of bodies with bread to absorb and remove illness. Four members of the royal family also ran from the center of the capital city in order to drive away illness. The ceremonials continued into the next day, when torches were carried through the city for the same purpose.[38]

Some Jewish mystics were believed to be able to communicate with God and, with their mystical skills, they at times had the power to intercede in the heavenly court to stop plagues. Israel ben Eliezer, Ba'al Shem Tov (c 1700–60), born in Okp, Ukraine, became a central Hasidic figure, kabbalist, and holy man, who was fashioned as a Bal Shem Tov (Master of the Good Name), the term Bal Shem used throughout medieval and early modern times for various Jewish miracle workers. Medieval and early modern Jewish mystics engaged with God to intercede in different ways. Indeed, much of early modern kabbalah assumed a close relationship between people and God, in which human actions affected the Divinity and some particularly learned and pious men could engage with God and affect conditions on earth and in heaven. In "The Mystical Epistle," his powers related to plague were explicated:

> On the New Year of the year 5510 [=September 1749] I made an ascent to the soul, as you know I do, and I saw a great accusation so that permission was almost given to destroy whole lands and communities. I took my life in my hands and prayed: 'Let us fall into the hands of the Lord but let us not fall into the hands of man.' This they granted to me, that there should be great sickness and an epidemic of unparalleled proportions in all the lands of Poland and in other lands adjacent to ours. And so it came to pass. Sickness

spread over all so that it could not be counted and also epidemics in other lands. I discussed with my company whether to recite the portion regarding the making of the incense in order to nullify the above-mentioned judgments [see Exodus 30:34–38; see also Numbers 17:11–15 and BT Sabbath 89a regarding warding off the plague] but they revealed to me in a vision of the night: 'Behold, you yourself chose the alternative of falling into the hands of the Lord and now you wish to nullify it. An accuser cannot become a defender.' So I then desisted from reciting the incense portion and from praying for this. But on Hoshana Rabba I went to the synagogue together with all the company, uttering the while many conjurations in great dread, and I recited the incense portion just once so that the epidemic should not spread to our districts, and thank God I was successful.[39]

In Muslim lands as well, a variety of religious responses to plague and disease more generally were possible. In Cairo, the response to the plague of 1430—which at its height may have claimed 10,000 people daily—for example, resulted in religious services at mosques, pious activities, and communal processions.[40] [See 2.3] Early modern Muslims could draw from a range of texts and tales in which religious figures encountered and combatted manifestations of plague. The prophet-saint Hizir (a mystical figure described in the Quran), for example, was thought to help those in need and fight against the horseman of pestilence and plague and to heal wounds.[41] The thirteenth-century Anatolian mystic Haci Bektaş utilized apples collected in the dead of winter from a bare tree to treat illness and the fourteenth-century Anatolian mystic Abdal Musa was known to be able to predict and combat plagues.[42] Other mystical or saintly figures with the power to heal were also known in Ottoman society. Such saintly figures could also have the power inflict plagues on others.[43] Murad III (1546–95), to take another example, ordered communal prayers in response to the plague in 1592. Additionally, processions were held, animals sacrificed,[44] and prisoners released all in hopes of God accepting the supplications. An imperial historian noted that the prayers did result in a decrease in the number of plague-related deaths.[45] Similarly, through magical signs, incantations, and talismans individuals pleaded for God's curative interventions, referencing Quranic verses and the knowledge of letters and numerological values of letters.[46] According to Kemaleddin Tasköprüzade (d 1621), for example:

The Name of God is the very kind and very great proof. God is the ruler and does whatever He wants to. There is no power or force but God, the exalted and great. I take refuge in God from Satan the cursed with the name of God the All-Compassionate and All Merciful. O God I take refuge in You from the spear, the plague, calamities, sudden death, from being lost in worldly affairs and from bad actions.[47]

These kinds of spiritual approaches were not without their critics, especially among early modern Protestants, who balked at the ceremonials of the Catholic

Church, as well as what they saw as overly ritualized practices of other religions, such as Judaism. According to Thomas Hastler, in a sermon preached in the Cathedral Church of Saint Paul, London and published in 1615 as *An Antidote Against the Plague*:

> But our Romish doctors, to maintain their invocations of celestial spirits, do cheat [cozen] simple people nowadays (as their predecessors did the Christians in the apostles' time) under the pretense of humility, saying that the God of all things was invisible, inaccessible and incomprehensible: and therefore (as Theodoret testifies) they counselled their followers to procure God's favor by the means of angels: like as the heathen idolaters to cover the shame of their neglecting of God. ... The very same rag our Romanists had borrowed from them to cover their superstition with that wickedness thereof might not appear.[48]

Flight from plague

Adherence to both contagionist and miasmist positions [**See Chapter 3**] often served as the justification for leaving an area of plague in hopes of finding better, healthier air. Given the range of understandings and responses to plague, one of the most frequently debated issues in the early modern world was whether, in fact, one was permitted to flee from one place to another during the outbreak of plague, especially when even movement within a city or town could be highly regulated.[49] In different religious traditions the permissibility of flight in the face of plague was discussed. The Lutheran Nuremberg preacher Andreas Osiander (1498–1552) was fairly representative in identifying "natural" conditions, but ultimately bowing to the power of God. It was God who was the lord of the plague, as well as fever, fire, thirst, and other associated symptoms. According to Osiander, God punishes our disbelief, disobedience, and thanklessness with the plague, as a means both to upbraid and to save us. We must trust in God with a correct and tenacious Christian belief—it is this trust and recognition that saves people—not medication or flight from plague. Similarly, God's word protects us against our chief enemy, the Devil. A true believer in God, therefore, does not fear the plague. The "flight" that Osiander recommended is that which is with seriousness, through penance, and correct belief in the word of God.[50]

Other Christian scholars, under the influence of Greek science, which understood plague as related to air often permitted flight, since fleeing bad air could be a useful strategy in combatting plague.[51] Discussions about flight indeed cut across denominations. As one Jesuit wrote, "On the 16th of October [1571] I wrote to you of my arrival in Vilnius. Now I am forced to write to you of my flight from Vilnius on the 22nd with fourteen brothers," after the plague claimed the life of one Father.[52] Under certain conditions, the Christian reformer Martin Luther also allowed for flight from the plague, though he articulated individual and communal responsibilities, even in times of plague. [**See 2.6; for an example** of the responsibilities and activities of Catholic clergy during plague, see 2.7 and 2.15]

Muslim scholars similarly drew from classical sources, their own traditions, and specific experiences.[53] Early Islamic sources, such as the writings of Khalifa Umar bin al-Khattab (b c 581 in Mecca), the fourth of the "rightly-guided" caliphs who was a companion of Muhammad and was murdered in 644, discussed this issue in his narrative of the expansion of Islam and its military campaigns.[54] He noted that a severe plague broke out in Syria, Egypt, and Iraq in 638–39. The Caliph Umar decided to go to Syria to supervise the measures being taken to suppress the plague, but was advised not to proceed to the infected areas because of the great number of deaths being recorded. After seeking counsel, in which some advisers suggested that he visit the infected areas and others who quoted the Prophet that one should not go to or from infected areas when the plague was raging, Umar opted to remove himself to Medina.

One adviser, Abu Ubaida, "did not feel happy at the decision of Umar. He said: 'O Amir-ul-Mumnin, why are you flying from God's will.' Umar replied that he merely moved from one will of God to another will." The author continues,

> Some Muslims held that the plague was a calamity. Addressing the troops on the occasion of the Friday prayer, Muadh said that the plague was not a calamity; it was a mercy of God. The son of Muadh caught plague. While his son lay on his death bed, Muadh addressing him said, 'My son this is a visitation from God. Let there be no doubt in your heart on this account.' The boy said, 'You will find me resigned to the will of God' and with these words he breathed his last.

Various Islamic Hadith examined the question of flight from plague. According to one, for example, "Narrated Saud, The Prophet said, If you hear of an outbreak of plague in a land, do not enter it; but if the plague breaks out in a place while you are in it, do not leave that place."[55] According to another Hadith,

> Narrated Amir bin Sad bin Abi Waqqas, That he heard Usama bin Zaid speaking to Sa'd, saying, Allah's Apostle mentioned the plague and said, 'It is a means of punishment with which some nations were punished and some of it has remained, and it appears now and then. So whoever hears that there is an outbreak of plague in some land, he should not go to that land, and if the plague breaks out in the land where one is already present, one should not run away from that land, escaping from the plague.'[56]

Islam has generally been presented (in Western scholarship) as being resistant to flight from plague—polemically cast by its opponents as infused with a certain degree of "fatalism" and a more "passive" response to the outbreak of disease.[57] The increasing Islamization of the Ottoman Empire in the sixteenth century, especially with the acquisition of lands in the Islamic heartland, it has been argued, naturally led to a more fatalistic and less pragmatic response to plague, at

least when it came to the decision whether to flee or not.[58] Traditional interpretations have noted that in Islamic thought three basic principles or assumptions
based on teachings of the Prophet shaped response to the plague: plague should
be interpreted as a form of mercy and a means of martyrdom for the faithful,
but a punishment for the infidel; Muslims should not enter into an area with
plague, but also should not flee an area if already there; and the plague was not
transmitted by contagion but rather through God directly.[59] Recent scholarship, however, has complicated these assumptions significantly. Contagion was
not universally rejected by Islamic scholars[60] and the most prominent Ottoman
jurist of the sixteenth century, Ebussuud Efendi (1491–1574), approved flight
as a preventative option against the plague.[61] In support of his position, Efendi
could cite earlier Islamic scholars as well as some sayings of Muhammad and historical examples of Caliph Umar to support his position. Flight from the plague
was certainly practiced at various times. Rulers in Cairo, for example, moved to
avoid the plague in the fourteenth century and emirs in Cairo sent their children
from plague areas to protect them.[62] The Sultan Mehmed II, the Conqueror,
(1432–81) appears to have fled from the plague several times during his reign,
including in 1455, 1467, 1471, 1472, and 1475.[63] Flight was recommended
in some Ottoman medical circles as well. The Jewish physician in the Ottoman
Empire, Ilyas bin Ibrahim al-Yahudi (d after 1512), who had traveled to Istanbul
and converted to Islam at the end of the fifteenth century, wrote a treatise on
"The Refuge from Plague and Pestilence" for sultan Bayezid II. He indicated
flight as the first recommendation against the plague. Absent the opportunity
to flee, however, he identified particular places best suited for refuge—namely,
those in high altitudes and facing north. He also indicated that other related
precautions were beneficial, such as disinfecting the air through the use of vinegar, sandalwood, and rosewater in addition to fumigation.[64] In treating the
plague he also mentioned a variety of remedies that were frequently discussed
in other works.[65]

To take one final example, in his plague treatise the famous Ottoman biog-
rapher Taşköprüzade (1495–1561) discussed the debate between those who
advocated fleeing from plague and those who maintained that one should trust in
God. For Taşköprüzade, the tension between religious incentives not to flee could
be abrogated by the useful measure of the search for pure air. That is, individuals
could leave an infected location not because they were fleeing God's judgment,
but because they were in search of better natural conditions.[66] According to a
recent historian, "His novelty was not only in his bid to wed current medical
knowledge with the principles of Islamic law, but also in formulating an idea that
was practical and applicable."[67] Taşköprüzade concluded that clean air is necessary
for health and corrupt air causes disease. At the same time, he discussed a range
of prayers, talismans, and magical remedies against plague, moving between religious law and medicine. Quoting various Hadith he related plague to sins such
as adultery.[68] Corruption of the air, he maintained, could be caused by celestial as
well as terrestrial factors. Temperature and humidity affected air conditions and
vapors trapped in the earth could cause localized plague. More general plague

conditions of a pandemic, or non-localized plague, occurred, according to this line of thought, when corruption of the air takes place more generally.[69]

Religion played a crucial role in how early modern people understood plague, drawing from a reservoir of texts that addressed the role of disease from the perspective of punishment for sin and the opportunity for repentance and moral regeneration. Human frailty and vulnerability were acknowledged and discussed frequently in this context. But religious traditions were about more than this "economy of sin," and even when early moderns succumbed to plague and other catastrophes, they could prove quite resilient, crafting narratives of strength and salvation. They found comfort in religious values and rituals, which were summoned in caring for and burial of the sick, healing, and community building. From saints to contemporary mystics and holy people, religion provided hope and possible responses to the outbreak of plague, at times even also to the preparation for an epidemic. But religion was never an isolated dimension of life. Social, political, economic, and even environmental conditions worked along with religious principles, texts, and experiences to condition response to plague. The texts below reflect a broad range of religious explanations of and responses to plague, across different faith traditions. There is a good deal that these texts share in common, though there are important differences and nuances as well. Together they provide insights into the complexity of early modern society that transcended plague, but they simultaneously help us to understand that society more generally as well as its interactions with disease.

Sources

2.1 Prayer as a weapon against the plague

Author: Ismail ibn Kathīr (b c 1300–73)

Title: *The Beginning and End: On History* (c 1350–51)[70]

Introduction: Born in Syria in 1300, ibn Kathīr was an accomplished Sunni scholar, known for his Quranic exegesis, jurisprudence, and historical work. He was a teacher of Hadith in one of the religious schools in Damascus on the eve of the 1348 plague. His book *The Beginning and End* is one of the best known books of Islamic historiography, covering world and Islamic history from creation until the end of days. This selection highlights the value early modern Muslims placed on prayer, which was seen as a valuable tool against the plague. The same was true of Christians and Jews, who likewise invoked a range of prayers—some drawn directly from traditional biblical passages and others crafted from an amalgam of biblical texts. Similarly, public fasts were common among early moderns of all religious backgrounds as a means of penance and supplication to God. Combined with a variety of other ceremonials, which might include processions, petitions to saints or holy figures, or even the giving of charity, early modern religious rituals were diverse, but were intended to address the belief that God brought on, or at least allowed, plague, generally as a means to punish people for their sins or to provide them a warning to repent of their poor behavior.

Text

At Damascus, a reading of the *Traditions* of Bukhārī took place on June 5 of this year [1348] after the public prayer—with the great magistrates there assisting, in the presence of a very dense crowd the ceremony continued with a recitation of a section of the Koran, and the people poured out their supplications that the city be spared the plague. Indeed, the population of Damascus had learned that the epidemic extended over the [Syrian] littoral and various points of the province, so that it was predicted and feared that it would become a menace to Damascus, and several inhabitants of the city had already been victims of the disease. On the morning of June 7, the crowd reassembled before the *mihrab* [a niche in the wall of a mosque indicating the direction of Mecca] of the Companions of the Prophet, and it resumed the recitation of the flood of Noah, of which a reading was made 3,363 times, in accordance with the counsel of a man to whom the Prophet had appeared in song and had suggested this prayer. During this month [of June], the mortality increased among the population of Damascus, until it reached a daily average of more than 100 persons. ...

On Monday, July 21, a proclamation made in the city invited the population to fast for three days; they were further asked to go on the fourth day, a Friday, to the Mosque of the Foot in order to humbly beseech God to take away this plague. Most of the Damascenes fasted, several passed the night in the mosque indulging in acts of devotion, conforming to the ritual of the month of Ramadan. On the morning of July 25, the inhabitants threw themselves [into these ceremonies] at every opportunity from 'every precipitous passage:' One saw in this multitude Jews, Christians, Samaritans, old men, old women, young children, poor men, emirs, notables, magistrates, who processed after the morning prayer, not ceasing to chant their prayers until daybreak. That was a memorable ceremony. ...

On Monday, October 5, after the call to afternoon prayer, a violent storm broke over Damascus and its environs, stirring up a very thick cloud of dust. The atmosphere became yellowish, then black and was totally dark. The population was in a state of anguish for about a quarter of an hour, imploring God, asking His pardon and lamenting all the more that it was afflicted by this cruel mortality. Others imagined that this cataclysm marked the end of their misfortunes, but they did not dwell too much on this. Indeed, the number of cadavers brought to the Omayyad Mosque exceeded the figure of 150, without including the dead in the suburbs, and the non-Muslim dead. Now, in the environs of the capital, the dead were innumerable, a thousand in a few days.

2.2 Competition in the religious economy

Author: Michele da Piazza

Title: *Chronicle* (1347–61)[71]

Introduction: Little is known about the fourteenth-century Franciscan Michele da Piazza. The excerpt below provides a fascinating window into community politics and competition for saints' relics, which were thought to have great power to protect people from the plague or to stop the plague after it had broken out. The protective power associated with saints and other holy people was common and highly prized in medieval and early modern societies. Specific saints known for their care for the sick or their ability to cure disease were particularly sought after. In some cases, local patron saints, with a more general set of powers, were called upon at certain times. The Virgin Mary was also viewed by many early modern Christians as a powerful intercessor. Supplications to these protective saints and holy figures might also involve prayers and processions. But the competition over saints' relics could be fierce, as this passage reveals. Such relics were valuable artifacts that had political as well as religious significance. In the competition for them, we see the complex relationships between neighbors and political rivals. In this way, the response to plague could underscore a broad range of conditions and realities that went far beyond plague itself.

Text

Wherefore the Messinese, taking stock of this terrible and monstrous calamity, chose to leave the city rather than stay there to die; and not only did they refuse to enter the city, but even to go near it. They camped out with their families in the open air and in the vineyards outside the city. But some, and they were the majority of the citizens, went to the city of Catania, believing that the Blessed Virgin Agatha of Catania would deliver them from the illness. ... Indeed, very many Messinese were staying in the city of Catania, where with one voice they implored the lord patriarch through the pious petitions submitted to him, that for the sake of devotion he go personally to Messina, bringing with him with all due honor some of the relics of the Virgin Agatha. 'For we believe,' they said, 'that with the arrival of the relics, the city of Messina will be completely delivered from this sickness.' So the patriarch, deeply moved by their prayers, agreed to go personally to Messina with the aforesaid relics. And this was around the end of the month of November in the year of our Lord 1347. The holy Virgin Agatha, seeing through the inward deceit and stratagems of the Messinese—who have always wanted to keep the virgin's relics at Messina and were exploiting the situation for that end—prayed to the Lord to see to it that the whole populace of the city betake themselves to the patriarch, shouting and saying that such a plan in no way pleased them. And wresting the keys away from the churchwarden, they soundly rebuked the patriarch, asserting that he should choose death, before agreeing to transfer the relics to Messina. After this scolding, the patriarch could do nothing else but enter the place where the relics were kept in a spirit of great devotion and honor, accompanied by a monastic choir intoning religious chants and holy prayers, and lave the holy relics with some pure water; it was this holy water which he arranged to be brought to the city of Messina, when he personally crossed over to there by ship. But oh, what a foolish idea you Messinese had, to think you could steal away the relics of the Blessed Virgin Agatha in this secret manner, under cover of a zealous devotion. Have you forgotten that when the body of the virgin was at Constantinople and desired to go back to her own country, to the city of Catania, she appeared in dreams to Gislbert and Goselin and ordered them to bring her body back to the city of Catania? Don't you know that if she had wanted to make her home in Messina, she by all means would have allowed this to happen? What more is there to say? Afterwards, the patriarch came to the city of Messina, bringing with him the aforementioned holy water, and he cured many and various sick people by sprinkling and touching them with the water. ... demons appeared in the city, having changed themselves into the shape of dogs, and they inflicted much harm on the bodies of the Messinese. Struck numb with terror, no one dared leave their homes. Nevertheless, by the general agreement of all and following the wishes of the archbishop of Messina, the citizens resolved to devoutly process around the city while chanting litanies. And as the whole populace of Messina was entering the city, a black dog carrying a drawn sword in its paw appeared among them; growling, it rushed the crowd and broke silver vessels, lamps, and candelabra that were on the altars, and shattered various other kinds of things. At this sight, everyone all at once fell flat on their faces, half-dead with fear. But after a while the men recovered and got up, and they saw the dog leave the church, but no one dared follow it or approach it.

2.3 Islamic religious responses to plague: fasting and sacrifice[72]

Author: Ibn Taghrī Birdī

Title: *History of Egypt 1382–1469 CE*

Introduction: Ibn Taghrī Birdī was a fifteenth-century historian born in Cairo. An aristocrat in Mamluk Egypt and the student of leading scholars, he authored a famous chronicle of Egypt and the Mamluk sultans. In the first selection below, Ibn Taghrī Birdī describes various religious responses to plague, including prayer and other supplications to God and at the tomb of saints, as well as fasting and other pious and humble behavior. As Ibn Taghrī Birdī makes clear, even (and perhaps especially) the sultan engaged in these activities and himself exercised an important leadership role at crucial times, such as during the plague of 1419. The passage details both popular response to the plague and the complex rituals and administration of Islamic religious observance in the early modern period, which had to take into account the outbreak of plague, but which simultaneously shaped the various understandings of and responses to plague.

Text

On Thursday, the 8th of Rabī' II [4 May 1419], it was proclaimed to the people by the market inspector that they were to fast for three days. On the last day, Thursday the 15th, they were to go out with the sultan [al-Mu'ayyad Shaykh] and to beseech God in the desert to lift up the plague … Many of the people fasted on Tuesday, Wednesday, and Thursday, and many of the merchants ceased to sell foods during the fast of the day, as is the custom in the beginning of the month of Ramadān. And on Thursday the 15th it was announced to the people to go out to the desert in the following day. … They spent the night there preparing foods and bread. After the sultan had performed the morning prayer, he rode out to them. He came down from the Citadel dressed in wool, and on his shoulders he wore a woolen shawl hanging down in back as is the custom among the sūfis. On his head was a small turban twisted in the style of the celibate; the end of the turban fell between his beard and his left shoulder. He displayed humility and contrition. His horse was covered in plain fabric—there was no gold or silver. The people drew near to the tomb with him in groups; the Shaykh al-Islām, the chief *qāḍī*, Jalāl ad-Dīn al-Bulqīnī set out from his house walking among a large crowd. The majority of the 'a'yān (notables) set out from their houses either on foot or riding until the sultan came to the desert near the shrine of Bāb an-Nasr. They carried flags and copies of the Qur'ān. And when 'God is Almighty' was proclaimed, there were ringing shouts. The sultan dismounted from his horse and before him and to his right and left were the *qāḍīs*, the men of learning, and the caliph. An innumerable crowd followed him. He spread out his hands and prayed to God, and he cried and lamented. The large crowd saw him and witnessed it for a long time. Then the procession appeared at the courtyard of the tomb of az-Zāhir, and the people surrounded him as he ate what had been prepared. He made a sacrifice there to God of 150 fat rams at the cost of five *dīnārs* apiece. Then the sultan sacrificed ten fat cows, two *jāmūs* and two camels. He wept and his tears were stopped by the fullness of his whiskers. He left the sacrifices, as they were. And he returned to the Citadel. The sultan authorized the wazīr at-Tāj to divide the food properly among the principal mosques, the khawānik, the shrine of as-Sayyidah Nafīsah, and a number of *zāwiyahs*. It was distributed to them equally. He divided it among a number of people in the courtyard, and they portioned the food among the poor. Pure bread was distributed to them which numbered 28,000 *raghīf* [flat loaves of bread] which the poor received from the wazīr. ...

2.4 Seeking saintly intercession: the case of Saint Roche

Introduction: St Roche was believed to have lived in the late thirteenth century. During a plague he went on a pilgrimage, helping to care for those who
had the disease and curing them. He himself was infected. Going in solitude
into the woods so that he would not spread the disease, he was looked after by
a dog, who brought him bread, and therefore, many images of him include a
dog as well. He is generally also pictured pointing to a bubo on his leg (**as in
illustration 2.4B from fifteenth-century Germany**). In addition to figurines,
Saint Roche was a regular in a variety of paintings and stained glass panels (**see
illustration 2.4C**, from the German city of Cologne in the sixteenth century
that includes Saint Roche, the van Merle Family Arms, and a Donor). Tales about
Saint Roche appeared in medieval and early modern collections of saints' lives
and books of miracles, as well as in devotional literature (**Source 2.4A**, which
was a popular late medieval supplication to Saint Roche, included at the end of
the book), which stressed the role of the saint as a protector of man and beast,
with special powers to heal the plague. Such literature drew from a wide range
of religious imagery related to good deeds, divine intercession, and redemption.

2.4A Devotion to Saint Roche

Author: Jehan Phelipot

Title: *The Life, Legend, Miracles of Saint Roch* (1494)[73]

Text

> O protector from the plague,
> Lord Saint Roch, bright light.
> You have cured man and beast.
> Your entire being wants
> to defend us under your banner.
> You are armed for the plague,
> to defend and protect us.
> We appeal to you with crying and tears.
> By your miracle
> the plague has ceased in the country.
> We were rescued joyfully,
> all the inhabitants with faith.
> Guard the kingdom of France
> with the sound of your name and by your good deeds.
> Remember us,
> now and forever.
> [For] the swelling you had in your right thigh—
> The angel from heaven was your doctor.
> Our good will, therefore,
> guards us from the poison of the infection.
> Our burden is the path to paradise.
> Pray for the redemption of the world.
> If we are inclined to sin,
> for the next, as well as for our world.
> Amen

2.4B Saintly intercession

Figure 2.4B Saintly intercession.
Credit: Science Museum, London, Wellcome Images

2.4C Saint Roch in church[74]

Figure 2.4C Stained glass panel with Saint.

Credit: Stained glass panel with Saint Roch, the van Merle family arms and a donor, the Metropolitan Museum of Art

2.5 God punishes Egypt with the Sixth Plague, the plague of boils[75]

Introduction: This image comes from an edition of Luther's German translation of the Old Testament, published in 1523 in Basel, Switzerland. The book of Exodus describes the ten plagues wrought by God (in some cases through the agency of Moses or Aaron) upon the Egyptians. Here we find an illustration of the plague of boils, as described in Exodus 9. As noted in the Introduction to this chapter, for Jews, Christians, and Muslims this influential passage was a proof text for the belief that plague—broadly defined—was a punishment brought by God upon people for their sins. The passage that recounts the plague of boils (Exodus 9:8–12) indicates that:

> Then the Lord said to Moses and Aaron, 'Each of you take handfuls of soot from the kiln, and let Moses throw it toward the sky in the sight of Pharaoh. It shall become a fine dust all over the land of Egypt, and cause an inflammation breaking out in boils on man and beast throughout the land of Egypt.' … The magicians were unable to confront Moses because of the inflammation, for the inflammation afflicted the magicians as well as all other

Figure 2.5 God punishes Egypt with the Sixth Plague, the plague of boils.

Credit: Courtesy of the Richard C. Kessler Reformation Collection, Pitts Theology Library, Candler School of Theology, Emory University

Egyptians. But the Lord stiffened the heart of Pharaoh and he would not heed them, just as the Lord had told Moses.

This well-known passage demonstrated to many early moderns that boils and inflammation were caused by human disobedience (in this case, that of Pharaoh). However, they could be administered through direct or indirect divine agency and the transmission of the ailment through the air could not be overlooked, reinforcing many contemporary notions of the origin and spread of disease. Importantly, this form of divine punishment afflicted even the magicians in Pharaoh's court, despite their own skills. And of course, that the affliction targeted men and beasts and, presumably, like other of the plagues did not impact the Israelites, was further proof of the divinely ordained and inescapable punishments from God. As the biblical story continues, God tells Moses to remind Pharaoh that he has been spared so far, but so that God's power will be manifest and known, neither Pharaoh nor his court will be spared from the next plague, that of heavy hail, if he does not let the Israelites leave. One final observation is in order. The term for plague (magefah) used in the biblical text was multi-dimensional and could refer to a broad range of punishments and afflictions. Not surprisingly, early modern notions of plague and the use of the term to denote a wide range of diseases, as noted above, is not terribly surprising.

2.6 Fleeing from the plague

Author: Martin Luther (1483–1546)

Title: "Whether One May Flee from a Deadly Plague" (1527)[76]

Introduction: Martin Luther rocked the Christian world with a reformation that would impact Europe and the broader world until today. Known for his doctrines of *sola fides* and *sola scriptura*, Luther was a prolific author, whose writings circulated widely and covered a great deal of topics, from biblical interpretation to contemporary issues. In this essay, Luther's approach to the much-discussed question of whether one may flee from the plague reveals both traditional considerations as well as innovative thinking about the various responses of both the individual and the community to the outbreak of plague.

In his 1527 treatise "Whether One May Flee from a Deadly Plague," Luther takes up a common theme, addressed by numerous late medieval and reformation-era writers in Germany and across Europe. The immediate context for the work was a plague epidemic that hit Wittenberg in early August 1527, forcing the relocation of the university faculty and students until April of 1528. Luther had direct and visceral experiences of this tragic event, as several close friends and/or their spouses and children died and Luther's colleague Johannes Bugenhagen and his family even moved into Luther's house for a period of time.[77] The plague also erupted in Breslau in August 1527 and prompted the local clergy there to ask about whether it was acceptable for Christians to flee from the plague. Luther wrote his response after a brief delay as an open letter to Johann Hess, the acknowledged leader of the Reformation in Silesia. His letter was published in 1527 and was widely circulated, printed in 19 editions.

Many medieval and early modern theologians and doctors considered the question of flight from the plague. If plague was caused by God, then what good was flight? If plague was spread by a poor quality of air, then perhaps seeking better conditions would improve one's chance of survival. Throughout such discussions, the practical (often having to do with social class and status, with rich people generally having greater mobility and resources) and experiential (especially the fear associated with a plague outbreak and experiences from previous outbreaks) collided with theological sensibilities. For Luther, flight from the plague revealed weak faith in God, but could be permitted provided that such flight did not leave one's neighbors in peril or did not trump one's civic duties. Here, Luther's notion of the ministry and his concept of public duty took precedence over individual salvation. Luther noted that some people behaved too rashly and took too many risks during times of plague. He was, in fact, not inherently opposed to, nor did he reject, the idea of flight from plague. However, one could contemplate flight only when one was certain that no other person would be harmed nor public functions left unattended to should that person leave. This selection brings together nicely a number of key issues in the discussion about the nature of plague and how people should respond to it, while placing the discussion into the broader context of ministry and communal relations between neighbors.

Text

To begin with, some people are of the firm opinion that one need not and should not run away from a deadly plague. Rather, since death is God's punishment, which he sends upon us for our sins, we must submit to God and with a true and firm faith patiently await our punishment. They look upon running away as an outright wrong and as lack of belief in God. Others take the position that one may properly flee, particularly if one holds no public office.

I cannot censure the former for their excellent decision. They uphold a good cause, namely, a strong faith in God, and deserve commendation because they desire every Christian to hold to a strong, firm faith. It takes more than a milk faith to await a death before which most saints themselves have been and still are in dread. Who would not acclaim these earnest people to who death is a little thing? They willingly accept God's chastisement, doing so without tempting God, as we shall hear later on.

… To put it briefly and concisely, running away from death may happen in one of two ways. First, it may happen in disobedience to God's word and command. For instance, in the case of a man imprisoned for the sake of God's word and who, to escape death, denies and repudiates God's word. In such a situation everyone has Christ's plain mandate and command not to flee but rather to suffer death, as he says, 'Whoever denies me before men, I will also deny before my Father who is in heaven' and 'Do not fear those who kill the body but cannot kill the soul,' Matthew 10 [:28, 33].

Those who are engaged in a spiritual ministry such as preachers and pastors must likewise remain steadfast before the peril of death. We have a plain command from Christ, 'A good shepherd lays down his life for the sheep but the hireling sees the wolf coming and flees' [John 10:11]. For when people are dying, they most need a spiritual ministry which strengthens and comforts their consciences by word and sacrament and in faith overcomes death. However, where enough preachers are available in one locality and they agree to encourage the other clergy to leave in order not to expose themselves needlessly to danger, I do not consider such conduct sinful because spiritual services are provided for and because they would have been ready and willing to stay if it had been necessary. We read that St. Athanasius fled from his church that his life might be spared because many others were there to administer his office. Similarly, the brethren in Damascus lowered Paul in a basket over the wall to make it possible for him to escape, Acts 9 [:25]. And also in Acts 19 [:30] Paul allowed himself to be kept from risking danger in the marketplace because it was not essential for him to do so.

Accordingly, all those in public office such as mayors, judges, and the like are under obligation to remain. This too, is God's word, which institutes secular authority and commands that town and country be ruled, protected, and preserved, as St. Paul teaches in Romans 13 [:4], 'The governing authorities are God's ministers for your own good.' To abandon an entire community which one has been called to govern and to leave it without official or government, exposed to all kinds of danger such as fires, murder, riots, and every imaginable disaster is a great sin. It is the kind of disaster the devil would like to instigate wherever there is no law and order. St. Paul says, 'Anyone who does not provide for his own family denies the faith and is worse than an unbeliever' [I Tim. 5:8]. On the other hand, if in great weakness they flee but provide capable substitutes to make sure that the community is well governed and protected, as we previously indicated, and if they continually and carefully supervise them [i.e., the substitutes], all that would be proper.

What applies to these two offices [church and state] should also apply to persons who stand in a relationship of service or duty toward one another. A servant should not leave his master nor a maid her mistress except with the knowledge and permission of master or mistress. Again, a master should not desert his servant or a lady her maid unless suitable provision for their care has been made somewhere. In all these matters it is a divine command that servants and maids should render obedience and by the same token masters and ladies should take care of their servants. Likewise, fathers and mothers are bound by God's law to serve and help their children, and children their fathers and mothers. Likewise, paid public servants such as city physicians, city clerks and constables, or whatever their titles, should not flee unless they furnish capable substitutes who are acceptable to their employer.

...

Where no such emergency exists and where enough people are available for nursing and taking care of the sick, and where, voluntarily or by orders, those who are weak in faith make provision so that there is no need for additional helpers, or where the sick do not want them and have refused their services, I judge that they have an equal choice either to flee or to remain. If someone is sufficiently bold and strong in his faith, let him stay in God's name; that is certainly no sin. If someone is weak and fearful, let him flee in God's name as long as he does not neglect his duty toward his neighbor but has made adequate provision for others to provide nursing care. To flee from death and to save one's life is a natural tendency, implanted by God and not forbidden unless it is against God and neighbor, as St. Paul says in Ephesians 4 [5:29]. 'No man ever hates his own flesh, but nourishes and cherishes it.' It is even commanded that every man should as much as possible preserve body and life and not neglect them, as St. Paul says in I Corinthians 12 [:21–26] that God has so ordered the members of the body that each one cares and works for the other.

...

Examples in Holy Scripture abundantly prove that to flee from death is not wrong in itself. Abraham was a great saint but he feared death and escaped it by pretending that his wife, Sarah, was his sister. Because he did so without neglecting or adversely affecting his neighbor, it was not counted as a sin against him. His son Isaac, did likewise. Jacob also fled from his brother Esau to avoid death at his hands. Likewise, David fled from Saul, and Absalom. The prophet Uriah escaped from King Jehoiakim and fled into Egypt. The valiant prophet Elijah, I Kings 19

[:3], had destroyed all the prophets of Baal by his great faith, but afterward, when Queen Jezebel threatened him, he became afraid and fled into the desert. Before that, Moses fled into the land of Midian when the king searched for him in Egypt. Many others have done likewise. All of them fled from death when it was possible and saved their lives, yet without depriving their neighbors of anything but first meeting their obligations toward them. ...

...

Others sin on the right hand. They are much too rash and reckless, tempting God and disregarding everything which might counteract death and the plague. They disdain the use of medicines; they do not avoid places and persons infected by the plague, but lightheartedly make sport of it and wish to prove how independent they are. They say that it is God's punishment; if he wants to protect them he can do so without medicines or our carefulness. This is not trusting in God but tempting him. God has created medicines and provided us with intelligence to guard and take care of the body so that we can live in good health.

If one makes no use of intelligence or medicine when he could do so without detriment to his neighbor, such a person injures his body and must beware lest he become a suicide in God's eyes. ...

No, my dear friends, that is no good. Use medicine; take potions which can help you; fumigate house, yard, and street; shun persons and places wherever your neighbor does not need your presence or has recovered, and act like a man who wants to help put out the burning city. ...

...

First, one must admonish the people to attend church and listen to the sermon so that they learn through God's word how to live and how to die. It must be noted that those who are so uncouth and wicked as to despise God's word while they are in good health should be left unattended when they are sick unless they demonstrate their remorse and repentance with great earnestness, tears, and lamentation. A person who wants to live like a heathen or a dog and does not publicly repent should not expect us to administer the sacrament to him or have us count him a Christian. Let him die as he lived because we shall not throw pearls before swine nor give to dogs what is holy [Matt. 7:6]. Sad to say, there are many churlish, hardened ruffians who do not care for their souls when they live or when they die. They simply lie down and die like unthinking hulks.

Second, everyone should prepare in time and get ready for death by going to confession and taking the sacrament once every week or fortnight. He should become reconciled with his neighbor and make his will so that if the Lord knocks and he departs before a pastor or chaplain can arrive, he has provided for his soul, has left nothing undone, and has committed himself to God. When there are many fatalities and only two or three pastors on duty, it is impossible to visit everyone, to give instruction, and to teach each one what a Christian ought to know in the anguish of death. Those who have been careless and negligent in these matters must account for themselves. That is their own fault. After all, we cannot set up a private pulpit and altar daily at their bedside simply because they have despised the public pulpit and altar to which God has summoned and called them. ...

2.7 Clergy and the plague: intercession and activity

Author: Nicolau Gracida

Title: "Letter to Manuel Lopez" (1538)[78]

Introduction: Correspondence was a key mode of communication in the early modern world. Jesuits, who served in a variety of political capacities and as Christian missionaries within and outside Europe, created a formidable international infrastructure that was at times criticized by their enemies, but which also served as a valuable tool for information flow and social services. The work of the Jesuits at the time of plague in Portugal is discussed in this sixteenth-century letter. This letter offers a glimpse into the spread of a "pestilence" with associated fevers in sixteenth-century Spain. The author highlights the contagious nature and quick spread of the disease as well as the social impact of the outbreak. The Jesuit writer notes the physical and spiritual assistance the Jesuits provided to the sick and dying people. Emphasizing the importance of this ministry, the author presents something of a perceived holy protection for the Jesuits involved with helping the infected people, sounding moral and religious tones.

Text

Coimbra, February 14, 1538
Nicolau Gracida to Manuel Lopez
In the parish of São Justa, either because it is too close to the river or because a pond is next to it, Our Lord willed an outbreak of very devastating fevers like *modorra*. The bishop called it a pestilence without a name. It began in São Justa, and it spread to neighboring parishes, but the focus of the disease remained in São Justa, and it spread so much that when it entered a house it struck everyone; quite often a man, his wife, and children were all sick in their house. Seven or eight in bed sick in one small house, and this was not unusual. The colleges that are next to our own had so many sick that they did not have a choir or anyone to say mass. In the college of Saint Augustine the fevers affected everyone from the porter to the rector and from the vice rector to the cook. In the college of the Carmelites brothers had to come from Lisbon to help, because everyone was sick with such fevers that no one gave them many days to live.

Everyone was terrified to see so much death in front of their own eyes, because you did not hear anything all day except the tolling of the bells for the dead, now here, now there. From one side you heard someone mourning, from another the office of the dead. If you walked through the streets you encountered nothing but the dead. Seven deaths in one day were not unusual, and five or six shared the same funeral since there was not enough time for everyone to have their own. While the husband was dying, the wife was receiving extreme unction, and the son was confessing his sins, because there was not enough time for everything. Entire houses became completely empty. If you went through the streets you encountered no one, and if by chance you encountered someone it was not a man but a figure of a man, because everyone was yellow and discolored, incapable of standing, and terrified of death. And the stench was so bad that, according to what was said, they found toads in the houses.

During this time our fathers and brothers coped with much work in assisting the sick and dying. ... Despite the strength of this disease as a result of the mercy of Our Lord only one teacher became sick. Other teachers did become sick due to the extreme cold of winter, but by the goodness of God they never missed a single lesson. As for the others, not nearly as many were sick in comparison to those in other places, but as a result of the closeness of the inferior college to São Justa we could not completely shut the door to illness. As some became sick they began to fill the infirmary. According to the doctors, to a great extent this resulted from the location of the inferior college, so the sick moved to the superior college. So many were consequently there that they filled a very large building. The weather was very cold, and beds so stretched from one side to another that it appeared to be a hospital, but they still did not have room for everyone here. The sick also filled the old infirmary, and even this was not enough until they took large parts of other houses, in such a manner that it was pitiful to see. The number in bed reached more or less thirty, and aside from these another twelve or fourteen and at times twenty were convalescing. Those convalescing seemed to be contesting the beds with the sick, because as one rose another fell in his place ....

2.8 Supplications to God to end the plague

Author: Selanıkî Mustafa Efendi (d 1600)

Title: *Chronicle of Salonika [Tarih-i-Selâniki]*[79]

Introduction: An Ottoman chronicler, Selanıkî was relatively unknown until the eighteenth century. His father died in Salonika, and so his son identified himself with that city. He appears to have had both diplomatic experience and familiarity with religious study. He provides evidence of having been present on military campaigns. His chronicle covered the last four decades of the sixteenth century. The chronicle points to the close relationship between religion and state in the early modern world, with imperial authorities summoning people of all backgrounds to prayer. In large public gatherings, people prayed to God for recovery and delivery from the plague. The positive effects of this mass prayer are recorded by the author, who clearly connected it with decreased rates of death and the recovery of large numbers of people. The mobilization of people points both to the developing and traditional aspects of early modern politics and religion.

Text

People's Supplication addressed to God to repel the bubonic plague

On Thursday, Zilhijja 3 [AH 1000] (September 10, 1592), upon imperial order, all the inhabitants including the pillars of the state [statesmen] and the eminent scholars and Sufis [Muslim ascetics, often with a mystical focus] were present by dawn in the open field of Okmeydanı, located above the Kasımpaşa neighborhood. They asked for God's help by humble entreaty [lit. saying: they smeared the soil of supplication to the dust of poverty and meekness, crying for the abode of oneness and greatness] for deliverance from trouble and obtaining remedy and relief. God, the glorious and the most exalted, with his broad generosity and munificence, accepts the prayers of even his rebellious and sinful servants. Supplications were addressed by saying 'for the sake of, and giving obeisance to, the Prophet Muhammad, His specially selected messenger and beloved one.'

People went up to Alemdağı (a hill in the Anatolian side of the city) to ask for God's help in repelling the trouble and securing the remedy.

By the middle of the month of Zilhijja [late September 1592], the exalted padishah, the refuge of the religion, announced that all the inhabitants of the city, including the scholars, pious people, and dervishes, should go to Alemdağı and address their supplication to the abode of God for recovering of Muslims from the bubonic plague. With the imperial order, the galleys carried the eminent scholars and sheikhs to the district of Anadoluhisarı. Countless people also went there, as none of the stores in the city was open that day. They spent a night there and by dawn's early light started to ask for God's help for deliverance from trouble and obtaining remedy and recovery. In accordance with the Quranic verse, [40:60 "Call upon Me!"], the prayers and requests were addressed to the abode of greatness. With thousands upon thousands humbling themselves and entreating, the chants of 'O God, accept this from us' reached the celestial spirits. Several animals were sacrificed out of the sultan's generosity. The commander of the palace guards [*Bostancıbaşı*] also came and bestowed upon people numerous favors, which were received with blessing and gratitude. [After this] the total amount of deceased people in Istanbul [from the bubonic plague] dropped to 100, while it was [previously] around 350 per day. Those bedridden ones got up and the diseased people found remedy, with the guide and assistance of God, the glorious.

2.9 Prayer to avert the plague

Title: "Prayer for a Time in Which There Is No Plague Arriving"[80]

Introduction: This Hebrew prayer was published in Venice, probably in the seventeenth century. It strings together a variety of biblical passages and follows the form of other supplications in the Jewish liturgy, focusing on protection from the plague. As with the previous document, the author assumes a close connection between religion and healing, praising God and seeking mercy and forgiveness for human sins. The author notes that in the times when the Temple stood, Jews burned incense upon the altar; now, however, after the destruction of the Temple, they rely upon prayers, which are presented to clear away animal pestilence, plague, as well as drought and famine. Such prayers might be recited by individuals or in congregational settings, and the publication and dissemination of such prayers was made possible by the printing revolution of the early modern period, which allowed a range of books and more ephemeral booklets and news items to be published, often in large numbers.

Text

We shall praise You, with goodness and truth we come before You, please do not do evil to us, please do not return us empty-handed from before You. Forgive us and send us mercy from Your [celestial] residence. Today we beseech You, because the source of life is with You, deal with us charitably for the sake of Your name. Please turn away from us pestilence and sword and famine and captives and scorn and the destroyer and the plague and Satan and [the] evil inclination and [the] enemy. We request from You mercy because great mercy is with You. Be charitable to us for the sake of Your name ...

Master of the World, at the time when the Temple stood, the High Priest burned incense before You, an offering of incense spices, and atoned for Your people Israel. And you stopped the plague, as it is written in Your Torah: Then Moses said to Aaron, 'Take the fire-pan, and put upon it fire from the altar. And place incense and go quickly to the congregation and atone for them, for the plague has begun. And Aaron took it as Moses said and ran into the midst of the assembly [kahal] where the plague had begun among the people. And he placed the incense and he atoned for the people. He stood between the dead and the living until the plague stopped [...] And Aaron returned to Moses at the entrance of the Tent of Meeting and the plague stopped.' [Numbers 17:11–13, 15]

And now with our sins, the Temple is destroyed and its service is stopped and we do not have a Priest nor a fire pan nor streaming fire nor altar nor incense of spices. Nothing remains before us, except our lips to talk, as it says: May it be Your will Lord, our God and the God of our fathers, that You remember that You accepted before Your throne of honor, as these our sacrifices before You, incense of spices, and You stopped the plague from upon us and from upon all of Your people Israel, in all the lands and in every place that they dwelled, because it was stopped by the hand of Aaron, the prophet of the holy God, Who turned from the throne of judgment and returned to the throne of mercy. And have compassion upon us and upon our elders and upon our women ... and upon our youth and upon our babies and remove Satan from in front of us and from behind us and do not allow the destroyer to come into our houses to strike (with plague), and crush the animal pestilence [*dever*] and plague and the destruction from upon us and from upon Your people Israel. And so may it be Your will, Lord our God and the God of our fathers, to destroy from upon us and from upon all of Your people Israel, animal pestilence and drought and famine and destruction and plague and all kinds of evil ... and all kinds of punishments that assemble to come to earth, and protect us in our going and coming, now and forever, because You protect Israel ...

2.10 Procession as a response to plague

Artist: Jean Solvain (1600–64)

Title: "The Vow of the Plague, Procession, April 22, 1630"[81]

Introduction: This cathedral painting depicts the inhabitants of the French town of Puy in a procession of thanks to the Black Madonna, an image of the Virgin Mary depicted with dark skin, for having spared them from the plague epidemic in 1630. The Virgin Mary was a popular figure in the early modern period. Many early moderns believed that she had powers to protect people from the plague, similar to the powers thought to be possessed by other, sometimes universal and sometimes local, saints, whose images or relics were prayed to or carried in processions. There were a wide range of religious responses to crises, including the threat or actual outbreak of plague. Processions, which often included locally held relics, provided an opportunity for public supplication and repentance. They also afforded the opportunity for communal cohesion, across social lines—even as they were socially constructed and made visible separations within society. In addition to various civic and medical responses, the religious procession was a traditional form of response, which must have provided some sense of solace

Figure 2.10 Procession as a response to plague. Solvain, Jean (1600–64): Le voeu de la peste, procession le 22 avril 1630 Les habitants de la ville du Puy remercie la Vierge Noire pour les avoir epargnes de l'epidemie de peste. 1630.

Credit: Le Puy, Cathedral. Peinture © 2018. Photo Josse/Scala, Florence. © Photo SCALA, Florence. DIGITAL IMAGE © (2018) The Museum of Modern Art/Scala, Florence

during the particularly brutal epidemic of 1630, which ravaged large portions of northern Italy. Not much is known about the painter, who was born in 1600 in Le Puy in south-central France and died in 1664.

2.11 Religious approaches to illness

Author: Heinrich Grasmüller (b c 1630)

Title: *Sickness-Book, or Prayers and Adages of Consolation for the Sick and Dying* (Hamburg, 1681)[82]

Introduction: Drawing from biblical passages and fiery sermons, throughout the medieval and early modern periods people ascribed plague to punishment for human sins. In the *Sickness-Book* Heinrich Grasmüller, a pastor in Hamburg (in northern Germany), similarly responded to the epidemic of 1680. Grasmüller associated the plague outbreak, as well as other illness, with a range of transgressions—from lack of thankfulness, blasphemy, disobedience, enmity, lack of cleanliness, hatred, lies, etc. The book provided prayers and sermons to counteract all sorts of illness, for every day concerns, and for all members of a household, as well as for magistrates. It provides a valuable example of how early modern Christians thought about and explained plague, weaving it into their broader worldview and engaging with inherited traditions and religious sensibilities. It also offers insights about the prayers that people recited and composed to provide consolation and petitions for healing.

Figure 2.11 Religious approaches to illness.
Credit: Herzog August Bibliothek Wolfenbüttel: M: Th 1054, Kupfertitel

2.12 Monument to the plague

Erasmus Siegmund Alkofer, Regensburg Plague- and Penance-Monument on Account of the Plague and Pestilence Raging Widely in the Year of Christ 1713 (1714)[83]

Introduction: As with other medieval and early modern illustrations, this one associated the plague with biblical passages. In this case, drawing on 2 Chronicles 7:13–14, an angel of God (indicated by the name for God in Hebrew in the upper right corner) threatens the city of Regensburg with a skull, whip, and sword. Penitent people kneel at the bottom. References are made to Psalm 39:11–12, begging God to turn His plague away, and Joshua 24:14–16, in which God demands the people to repent and behave better. The image, a folded leaflet with copperplate engraving was produced in 1714 by Johann Jakob Weisshoff and was shown on the Regensburg plague lazaretto in front of the city gates. The illustration reflects quite clearly the role that religion played in understanding and responding to the plague at the same time that it emphasizes the notion of community represented and the actions taken by civic authorities during plague epidemics.

Figure 2.12 Monument to the plague.
Credit: Herzog August Bibliothek Wolfenbüttel: M: Th 44, Faltblatt mit Kupfertitel

2.13 A memorial of plague in the eighteenth century: religious understandings

Author: Erasmus Siegmund Alkofer (1673–1727)

Title: *Regensburg Plague- and Penance Memorial on the Occasion of the Plague and Pestilence Raging Widely in the Year of Christ 1713*[84]

Introduction: Erasmus Siegmund Alkofer held the degree of Master of Philosophy and was an Evangelical pastor in Regensburg. This brief excerpt exemplifies early modern attempts to balance the power of God and contemporary assumptions about the powers of nature and the stars. On one hand, God is presented as omniscient and a fatherly figure who utilizes the plague as means to upbraid his sinful children. On the other hand, some early modern people associated poor quality of air or other astrological conditions with plague. Regardless, Alkofer stresses that God controls the stars and planets and allows pestilence to occur. Therefore, people must turn their prayers to God in penance.

Text

How and by what means this plague originated in our city, whether through infected goods or through travelers, God knows best. A father, if he wants to upbraid and chastise his child for a transgression can soon find a rod. So also has God, our heavenly Father, because of our sins, sent upon us the pestilential plague. Several people have wanted to attribute the cause of such a poisonous plague to the air; however, all the wisdom and in the natural sciences well-meaning peoples have determined that, thank God, the air was still completely pure and healthy, which I likewise have proven daily with various experiments. And in truth I have found something else known, namely that where the air is infected, the birds fall from the air dead upon the earth; ... Even the well-written ordinance against the plague [from the] Schleswig-Holstein high princely over-guardianship, which appeared in the year of Christ 1711, very appropriately notes that 'if the air is infected, neither people nor cattle remain spared from such infection.' Others have wanted to identify by the calendar makers such poisonous effects of those wondrous light beams and [the] amalgam of the planets, which were observed in this year ...

Such strong light beams create strong movements in the earth, powerful changes in the air, unequal mixing of the humors, or moisture in human bodies. Consequently, all kinds of plagues and virulent illnesses could arise. It is true that the stars do not stand in the heavens in vain (for no reason). They may have meaning, affection, power, and flowing effect.

They may also thereby incline and induce human humors, temperament, and affects. Alone they have no more might and force than God. God created the stars. God has the stars in His Hand. God rules the stars and the stars are obedient to God. The stars' inclination is no compulsion. Just as God has a free hand, so man has free will and can put many things straight through prayers, fear of God, and caution and good ways. Nature can also be master and come further than the stars. At the same time, there is no word in the Scriptures that the planets and their course should govern, cause, compel, or even only proclaim human life and death before and infallibly. God, not Saturn or any other planet, allows a pestilence to come among His people. Indeed, it is, according to Augustine's statement, a superstition and theft from God if one ascribes to creatures what alone is due to God. One who robs God of His honor and gives it to another is a person who has stolen from God....

2.14 Religious responses to other disease epidemics

Author: Jonathan Belcher

Title: "A Proclamation for a Public Fast"[85]

Introduction: Jonathan Belcher, esq., was Captain-General and Governor-in-Chief in and over the English Province of the Massachusetts Bay in New England. Prayers and fasting were typical early modern responses to plague and other disasters, across religions. This proclamation was in response to the Diphtheria Epidemic of 1735. As we have seen in other documents, fasting and prayer to God were considered necessary and at times effective means to combat disease epidemics. The document reveals the extent to which religion and governance overlapped and intersected, as the secular ruler of the province, upon advice from the royal council, selected the day for the fast and exhorted clerics and people alike to fast, confess their sins, and seek God's grace.

Text

Whereas among other tokens of the holy displeasure of Almighty God towards this sinful people, He hath been pleased to visit several of the towns within this province with a very unusual, malignant and mortal distemper, by which great numbers, especially of the younger people, have been removed by death; and there is great danger that the said sickness will become more epidemical so as to spread throughout the land;

I have therefore thought fit, with the advice of Majesty's Council, and at the desire of the representatives, in the present session, to appoint Thursday the eighth day of January next, to be observed as a day of solemn prayer and humiliation with fasting, throughout this province; hereby exhorting both ministers and people devoutly to attend the same, by humble and penitent confession of their sins, and sincere and fervent supplications to the God of all grace, that in his infinite mercy, he would spare this unworthy people, and put a stop to the progress of this mortal distemper, or refrain the malignity thereof, and command the destroying Angel to stay his hand; and above all, that he would sanctify this visitation to the spiritual good and advantage of this people; and that the fruit of all may be to purge away our sin and make us the partakers of his holiness; that he would pour out his Holy Spirit upon all orders of men among us, and especially on the rising generation, that they may see the Lord God of their fathers, and serve Him with a perfect heart and willing wind; and likewise that he would be pleased to give light and direction to the government of this province in all their administrations, and graciously protect all our religious and civil interests: and that he would hasten the coming and kingdom of our Lord and Savior Jesus Christ, and fill the whole earth with his glory.

And all servile labor and recreations are forbidden on the said day.

Given at the Council Chamber in Boston, the Twenty-third Day of December 1735. In the Ninth Year of the Reign of our Sovereign Lord George the Second, by the Grace of God, of Great-Britain, France and Ireland, King, Defender of the Faith, etc.

By His Excellency's Command.

with advice of the Council. J. Belcher

J. Willard, Secr.

God save the King.

2.15 Early modern saints

Artist: Jean-Baptiste Marie Pierre (1714–89)

Title: "St. Charles Borromeo Distributing Communion to the Victims of the Plague in Milan" (c 1760)[86]

Introduction: Jean-Baptiste Marie Pierre was a French painter, who was born and lived in Paris. He was a student of the Rococo painter Charles-Joseph Natoire at the Académie royale de peinture et de sculpture. Charles Borromeo (1538–84) was a Cardinal and Archbishop of Milan. A descendant of a noble family, he was a staunch opponent of the Protestant Reformation and a leader of the Catholic Reformation in the sixteenth century. He was canonized in the early seventeenth century. Like other saints, he was known for particular characteristics and actions, including his ability to heal the sick. Archbishop of Milan (from 1564 to 1584) and also a cardinal, he was noted for his efforts during plague outbreaks in the city and associated with healing and protection from the plague there and in other places as well.

Figure 2.15 Early modern saints. St. Charles Borromeo distributing communion to the victims of the plague in Milan.

Credit: The Metropolitan Museum of Art

Notes

1 Mary Lindemann, *Medicine and Society in Early Modern Europe*, 2nd ed. (Cambridge, 2010), 55–6.
2 Nükhet Varlik, *Disease and Empire: A History of Plague Epidemics in the Early Modern Ottoman Empire (1453–1600)* (Doctoral Dissertation, University of Chicago, 2008), 158.
3 Ibid., 159; see also Daniel Panzac, *La peste dans l'empire Ottoman: 1700–1850* (Leuven, 1985), 47.
4 Varlik, *Disease and Empire*, 159.
5 John Aberth, *Plagues in World History* (Lanham, 2011), 1–2.
6 "And which of the gods was it that set them on to quarrel? It was the son of Jove and Leto; for he was angry with the king and sent a pestilence upon the host to plague the people, because the son of Atreus had dishonoured Chryses his priest. Now Chryses had come to the ships of the Achaeans to free his daughter, and had brought with him a great ransom: moreover he bore in his hand the sceptre of Apollo wreathed with a suppliant's wreath and he besought the Achaeans, but most of all the two sons of Atreus, who were their chiefs" (Homer, *The Iliad*, Book I, Internet Classics Library: http://classics.mit.edu/Homer/iliad.1.i.html).
7 Aberth, *Plagues in World History*, 2.
8 "Thus did he pray, and Apollo heard his prayer. He came down furious from the summits of Olympus, with his bow and his quiver upon his shoulder, and the arrows rattled on his back with the rage that trembled within him. He sat himself down away from the ships with a face as dark as night, and his silver bow rang death as he shot his arrow in the midst of them. First he smote their mules and their hounds, but presently he aimed his shafts at the people themselves, and all day long the pyres of the dead were burning. For nine whole days he shot his arrows among the people, but upon the tenth day Achilles called them in assembly—moved thereto by Juno, who saw the Achaeans in their death-throes and had compassion upon them. Then, when they were got together, he rose and spoke among them" (Homer, *The Iliad*, Book I, Internet Classics Library: http://classics.mit.edu/Homer/iliad.1.i.html).
9 Aberth, *Plagues in World History*, 42.
10 Ibid., 54.
11 Cited in Russell Hopley, "Contagion in Islamic Lands: Responses from Medieval Andalusia and North Africa," *Journal for Early Modern Cultural Studies* 10:2 (Fall/Winter 2010): 45–64, 55.
12 Lawrence I. Conrad and Dominik Wuastyk, *Contagion: Perspectives from Pre-Modern Societies* (Aldershot, 2000), xii–xiii; see Birsen Bulmuş, *Plague, Quarantine and Geopolitics in the Ottoman Empire* (Abingdon, 2012), 70ff; Michael Dols, *The Black Death in the Middle East* (Princeton, 1977), 9–10, 117.
13 Dols, *The Black Death*, 118.
14 Bulmuş, *Plague, Quarantine and Geopolitics in the Ottoman Empire*, 70.
15 Dols, *The Black Death*, 252–3.
16 Ibid., 124.
17 Ibid., 128.
18 Varlik, *Disease and Empire*, 156.
19 Dols, *The Black Death*, 113.
20 Such apocalypticism is generally not considered to have been influential in Islamic circles; ibid., 300–1.
21 See Norman Cohn, *The Pursuit of the Millennium: Revolutionary Millenarians and Mystical Anarchists of the Middle Ages*, revised ed. (New York, 1970), 124–48; see also the work of František Graus.

22 John Aberth, *The Black Death: The Great Mortality of 1348–1350: A Brief History with Documents* (Boston, 2005), 126–31. Trans. from German, *Die Chroniken der Deutschen Städte* 8 (1870): 105–20.

23 Jakob Hornstein, *Sterbens Flucht; Das ist Christlicher vnd Catholischer Bericht/von Sterbenslauff der Pest* (Ingolstadt, 1593), 26, 29; see R. Po-chia Hsia, *A Jesuit in the Forbidden City: Matteo Ricci 1552–1610* (Oxford, 2010), 32 regarding Corpus Christi processions on ships at sea to protect against storms.

24 Samuel K. Cohn, Jr, *The Black Death Transformed: Disease and Culture in Early Renaissance Europe* (London and New York, 2002), 75.

25 Franco Mormando, "Introduction: Response to the Plague in Early Modern Italy: What the Primary Sources, Printed and Painted, Reveal," in *Hope and Healing: Painting in Italy in a Time of Plague 1500–1800*, ed. Gauvin Alexander Bailey, Pamela M. Jones, Franco Mormando, and Thomas W. Worcester (Chicago, 2005), 1–44, here at 28–9; Frank Hatje, *Leben und Sterben im Zeitalter der Pest: Basel im 15. bis 17. Jahrhundert* (Basel, 1992), 59; Joseph P. Byrne, *Daily Life during the Black Death* (Westport, 2006), 108–9.

26 See *The Golden Legend*. The language has been slightly updated. http://catholicsaints. info/golden-legend-life-of-saint-rocke/.

27 Cohn, Jr, *The Black Death Transformed*, 76.

28 Ibid., 75–6.

29 Ibid., 77.

30 Nicole Archambeau, "Healing Options during the Plague: Survivor Stories from a Fourteenth-Century Canonization Inquest," *Bulletin of the History of Medicine* 85 (2011): 531–59, here 532.

31 Mormando, "Introduction," 32–4.

32 John T. Alexander, *Bubonic Plague in Early Modern Russia: Public Health and Urban Disaster* (Oxford, 2002), 186.

33 Cohn, Jr, *The Black Death Transformed*, 75.

34 Kristy Wilson Bowers, *Plague and Public Health in Early Modern Seville* (Rochester, 2013), 48–9; Mormando, "Introduction," 30–1.

35 Bernhard Schretter, *Die Pest in Tirol 1611–1612: Ein Beitrag zur Medizin-, Kultur- und Wirtschaftsgeschichte der Stadt Innsbruck und der übrigen Gerichte Tirols* (Innsbruck, 1982), 234, for the entire ordinance.

36 Lawrence I. Conrad, Michael Neve, Vivian Nutton, Roy Porter, and Andrew Wear, *The Western Medical Tradition, 800 BC to AD 1800* (Cambridge, 1995), 222f.

37 Ibid., 224.

38 Suzanne Austin Alchon, *A Pest in the Land: New World Epidemics in a Global Context* (Albuquerque, 2003), 12–13.

39 Quoted in Louis Jacobs, *Jewish Mystical Testimonies* (New York, 1977), 148–55, here at 149, 152. Original language document printed in M. S. Bauminger, *Sefer Margaliot* (in memory of Reuben Margaliot) (Jerusalem, 1973), 153–74.

40 Dols, *The Black Death*, 215, 206.

41 Nükhet Varlik, "From 'Bete Noire' to 'le Mal de Constantinople:' Plagues, Medicine, and the Early Modern Ottoman State," *Journal of World History* 24:4 (December 2013): 741–70, here at 741–3.

42 Ibid., 748.

43 Ibid., 749.

44 For a reference from Scripture, see 2 Samuel 24:25, when King David atones for a sin that led to the plague: "David built an altar to the Lord there and sacrificed burnt offerings and fellowship offerings. Then the Lord answered his prayer in behalf of the land, and the plague on Israel was stopped."

45 Varlik, "From 'Bete Noire' to 'le Mal de Constantinople,'" 742. Sacrifice is associated with penance at times of plague or punishment; see Leviticus 14:13: "He is to slaughter the lamb in the sanctuary area where the sin offering and the burnt offering are slaughtered. Like the sin offering, the guilt offering belongs to the priest; it is most holy."

46 Bulmuş, *Plague, Quarantine and Geopolitics in the Ottoman Empire*, 70–1; Dols, *The Black Death*, 126–7.

47 Cited in Bulmuş, *Plague, Quarantine and Geopolitics in the Ottoman Empire*, 73.

48 Cited in ibid., 78.

49 Edward Eckert, *The Structures of Plagues and Pestilence in Early Modern Europe: Central Europe, 1560–1640* (Basel, 1996), 26.

50 See also Hatje, *Leben und Sterben im Zeitalter der Pest*, 48ff.

51 Aberth, *Plagues in World History*, 30.

52 Lynn A. Martin, *Plague? Jesuit Accounts of Epidemic Disease in the 16th Century* (Kirksville, 1996), 43.

53 Most recently see John J. Curry, "Scholars, Sufis, and Disease: Can Muslim Religious Works Offer Us Novel Insights on Plagues and Epidemics among the Medieval and Early Modern Ottomans?," in *Plague and Contagion in the Islamic Mediterranean*, ed. Nükhet Varlik (Kalamazoo, 2017), 27–55; and Yaron Ayalon, "Religion and Ottoman Society's Responses to Epidemics in the Seventeenth and Eighteenth Centuries," in ibid., 179–97.

54 Source: *Hadrat Abu Bakr, Umar, Usman, Ali (ra)* 4 Vol. Set www.alim.org/library/biography/khalifa/content/KUM/18/71.

55 *Sahih Al-Bukhari*, Hadith – 7.624.

56 *Sahih Al-Bukhari*, Hadith – 9.104.

57 For a recent reassessment, see Nükhet Varlik, "'Oriental Plague' or Epidemiological Orientalism? Revisiting the Plague Episteme of the Early Modern Mediterranean," in *Plague and Contagion in the Islamic Mediterranean*, ed. ibidem (Kalamazoo, 2017), 57–87.

58 Heath W. Lowry, "Pushing the Stone Uphill: The Impact of Bubonic Plague on Ottoman Urban Society in the Fifteenth and Sixteenth Centuries," *Osmanli Araştirmalari* 23 (2003): 93–132, 129.

59 Dols, *The Black Death*, 23.

60 See Aberth, *Plagues in World History*, 39.

61 Bulmuş, *Plague, Quarantine and Geopolitics in the Ottoman Empire*, 3.

62 Dols, *The Black Death*, 172–3.

63 Lowry, "Pushing the Stone Uphill," 103.

64 Varlik, *Disease and Empire*, 188.

65 Ibid., 189.

66 Ibid., 203.

67 Ibid., 203.

68 Ibid., 200; and Varlik, "From 'Bete Noire' to 'le Mal de Constantinople,'" here 750.

69 Varlik, *Disease and Empire*, 201.

70 'Imād al-Dīn Abū 'l-Fidā' Ismā'il b. 'Umar ibn Kathīr, *The Beginning and End: On History*, c 1350–1351. Quoted in Aberth, *The Black Death: The Great Mortality of 1348–1350*, 110–12. Trans. from the French in Gaston Wiet, "A Grande Peste Noire en Syrie et en Egypt," *Etudes d'Orientalisme dediees a la memoire de Levi-Provencal*, 2 vols (Paris, 1962), 1:381–3.

71 Aberth, *The Black Death: The Great Mortality of 1348–1350*, 100–3. The Italian original is Michele da Piazza, *Cronaca*, ed. Antonio Giuffrida (Palermo, 1980), 82–7.

72 Ibn Taghrī Birdī, "History of Egypt 1382–1469 AD" (an-Nujum az-zahirah fi muluk Misr wal-Qahirah), ed. and trans. William Popper (Berkeley, 1915–63), vols

5–7, 13–14, 17–19, 22–3, 24, here vol. 17, 64–6. Quoted in Dols, *The Black Death*, 248–50.

73 Joël Coste, *Représentations et comportements en temps d'épidémie dans la littérature imprimée de peste (1490–1725)* (Paris, 2007), 375–6, devotion to Saint Roch; from conclusion of J. Phelipot, *La vie, legend, miracles*, fol. 9–10.

74 www.metmuseum.org/collection/the-collection-online/search/463582?rpp=30&pg =1&ft=Plague&pos=17 Met. Medium: Pot metal, white glass, vitreous paint, silver stain.

75 *Das Alte Testament deutsch: Der vrsprunglichen hebreischen Warheit nach, auffs trewlichst verdeütscht. vnd yetzmals in disem Truck, durch den tolmetschen erleüchtet mit vil hübschen der besunder schweren Ortten Außlegungen vnd Erklerung, die keyn ander drück haben.*/M. Luther. http://pitts.emory.edu/dia/detail.cfm?ID=129512.

76 Martin Luther, *Luther's Works*, vol. 43: Devotional Writings II, ed. Gustav K. Wiencke (Philadelphia, 1968), 120–4, 131–2, 134–5; trans. Carl J. Schindler. See *WA* (*D. Martin Luthers Werke: Kritische Gesamtausgabe*. 65 vols. Weimar, 1883–1993) 23(323), 339–79. Reprinted with permission of 1517 Media.

77 115–16.

78 Martin, *Plague?*, 29–31. Original in *Litterae quadrimestres ex universis praeter Indiam et Brasiliam locis in quibus aliqui de Societate Jesu versabantur Romam missae*, 7 vols (Madrid and Rome, 1894–1932), here vol. 5, 949–51.

79 Translated by A. Tunç Sen, 285–7.

80 Venice (1467), 2A, 9A.

81 Location: Cathedral, Le Puy, France; Photo Credit: Scala/White Images/Art Resource, NY.

82 Heinrich Grasmüller (b c 1630): *Krancken-Buch Oder Gebether Und Trost-Sprüche Für Krancken und Sterbenden. Zum andermahl vermehret heraußgegeben* (Hamburg, 1681). Wolfenbuttel: www.hab.de/ausstellungen/seuchen/expo-18.htm. 18 (Kat. Nr. 37).

83 Erasmus Siegmund Alkofer, "Regenspurgisches Pest- und Buß-Denckmahl Wegen Der im Jahr Christi 1713. Allhier grassirten Seuche der Pestilentz/ In sich haltend Einige Pest- und Buß-Predigten" (Regensburg: Seidel, 1714). www.hab.de/ausstellungen/ seuchen/expo-19.htm. 19 (Kat. Nr. 39).

84 Cited in Katharina Kellner, *Pesthauch über Regensburg: Seuchenbekämpfung und Hygiene im 18. Jahrhundert* (Regensburg, 2005), 85–6; Alkofer, "Regenspurgisches Pest- und Buß-Denckmahl Wegen Der im Jahr Christi 1713," 21–2.

85 Boston: Printed by J. Draper, Printer to His Excellency the Governour & Council.

86 www.metmuseum.org/collection/the-collection-online/search/339339?rpp=30&pg =1&ft=Plague&pos=19.

3 Medical understanding of and responses to plague

Early modern conceptions of plague

Early modern people had a number of explanations for the plague. According to one recent study of 250 books held in the Bibliothèque Nationale de France that were exclusively or principally focused on the plague and printed between 1490 and 1725, nearly 70% of the works had content related to causes of disease.[1] A classification of causes was presented in approximately 11% of these works, which distinguished between external and internal causes and between natural and supernatural causes. [See also 3.6] Among the natural external causes, astral conjunctions (42%), comets (16%), and eclipses (12%) were mentioned frequently. Emanations from the earth (27%) and meteorological phenomena (25%) were also regularly discussed. Although temperature was rarely discussed, corruption of the air was a theme in 55% of these works. Other causes of plague were also often cited, including divine wrath (mentioned in 41% of cases). Much less frequent were sorcery (1%) and the role of supernatural beings (5%).

Early moderns clearly understood the significance of contagion (63%)—inter-human contagion (approximately 48%), but also indirect contagion (approximately 26%). Other factors were also connected in the minds of early modern contemporaries. Hunger was linked with plague in 35% of works that discussed the causes of plague. Other factors appeared less frequently, but should be noted. These included: age; gender; heredity; temperament; physical exercise; predisposition to fear; passion; excess sexuality; and poverty (predisposition).[2] [See, for example, 3.7] Many early modern works connected plague and environmental conditions (74%). More than half naturally referenced the buboes (58%) and carbuncles (55%) associated with the disease. Around the same percentage noted fevers (57%), digestive signs (31%), and putrefaction (26%).[3]

The spread of plague: contagion and miasma

Two schools of thought generally predominated in explaining the nature and spread of plague throughout the pre-modern world. Borrowing from Greek medicine as well as biblical writings, many people believed that plague was either transmitted through interaction between people (contagionist) or via the water and air (miasma). The prophylaxis for and treatment of plague could be quite different depending on which of these theories was adopted. According to the former, for example, quarantine and fumigation were preferred methods for redressing plague.[4] This was generally the more common response to plague. Perhaps the first physician to advance a systematic theory of contagion in the early modern period was Girolamo Fracastoro (1483–1533).[5] **[See p. 125 and 3.2]**

From the perspective of the miasma school of understanding, prevention of plague could be associated with regulation of the intake of air, diet, exercise, sleep, repletion and evacuation, accidents of the soul, or mental states.[6] Concern over miasma might also lead to a variety of civic responses, from shooting canons, constructing fires, draining swamps, or applying vinegar and aromatic oils to diseased houses in the hope of purifying the air or water.[7] Various ointments, flowers, and herbs could be prescribed against the plague. **[See 3.3]** An eighteenth-century Egyptian plague treatise continued a long tradition of recommending violets for treatment of the plague.[8]

Plague was often associated with atmospheric conditions.[9] Yet various health regimens published in plague-free years were likewise concerned with air quality, suggesting that it was a general scientific concern and not necessarily associated with or in response to the plague.[10] The interaction between the medical or scientific aspects of miasma and general cultural norms could be closely related. This is perhaps not so surprising, since early moderns crafted a worldview that absorbed plague into their understanding and experiences rather than created new categories for it. Although perfuming of the air had been related to treatment and prevention of plague in the fourteenth and fifteenth centuries, by the sixteenth century, to take one example, it was recommended as a more general means to purify the air and eliminate dangerous vapors.[11] **[See 3.3]** The emphasis on perfuming would decrease by the later sixteenth century, giving way to the use of clothing as a means of protection from the elements and air quality.[12] **[See 3.8]** The emphasis on bad air, which might be attributed to various meteorological or cosmic conditions, was frequently embraced by more learned people—though they also held, sometimes even simultaneously, the contagionist position, which certainly existed across cultures and religions. One interesting example—though directly from a Western source—is the convert to Islam, Ilyas bin Ibrahim, who arrived in the Ottoman Empire at the end of the fifteenth century. He referred in his writings to Hippocrates as well as other classical scientific sources and he noted that disease can be transmitted by direct contact between people through eye contact. True to the somewhat fluid connection between contagion and miasma, he simultaneously asserted that putrefied air can also transmit disease.[13]

While we have generally distinguished between these two approaches to plague (contagion and miasma), they were rarely mutually exclusive concepts and, in some important ways it has been argued, are somewhat anachronistic or over-refined by historians in the study of the early modern period.[14] Contagion, for example, when associated with indirect and direct transmission of harmful material was compatible with the miasmic theory of noxious air.[15] What is more, the precautions taken by physicians when approaching plague victims could address concerns about both contagion and miasma. **[See 3.8]**

The physician Girolamo Fracastoro, in his central works *De contagione* (1546) and the earlier work on *Syphilis* (1530) expressed ideas that were assimilated into the well of medical knowledge of the time and in subsequent generations. For Fracastoro, contagion involved the transmission of a corrupt substance in three ways—direct contact, indirect contact through fomites, and at a distance.[16] [**See 3.2**] Fracastoro did not believe that putrefaction of the humors was enough to cause contagion or disease.[17] He may have been the first to use the term *fomes*, which for him was an infective agent—a seedlet of contagion—that could be deposited on intermediary substances, such as clothes.[18] The type of seed determined the type of disease.[19] The concept served to bridge contagionist and miamist positions, like other concepts such as putrefaction, putrid air, poisonous vapors, and pestiferous odors.[20]

Early modern experiences

How (and how much) early moderns wrote about plague can tell us a great deal about the disease and early modern understanding of it. The great Italian epidemic of 1575–78 led to a significant production of writing about plague—from both literary and medical standpoints.[21] A good deal of this writing was now produced in Italian as opposed to Latin,[22] signaling a shift both of audience and focus. It was also increasingly centered on the duties of princes and magistrates.[23] These writings evinced greater interest in observation and tracing the spread of plague and their authors gave enhanced attention to social causes of plague.[24] While classical texts that dealt with disease, such as those of Galen, were still widely circulated,[25] the new literature had a very practical focus with a concern for recognizing plague signs, such that there was frequently a close correlation between the writings of physicians and various civic health boards.[26] Similarly, while immediate responses to the Black Death in the middle of the fourteenth century included apocalyptic thinking and the examination of celestial forces, by the 1360s in some places, many historians assert, physicians turned from despondency to a new sense of possible human intervention in the treatment and even prevention of plague through surgeries, medicines,[27] and the treatment of patients in hospitals. [**See 3.5, as well as a fuller discussion in Chapter 4**]

Outbreaks of plagues affecting animals, especially cattle, drew from similar treatments to those applied to humans. [**See 3.9**] At the same time, such experiences further enhanced the knowledge of early modern medical professionals. Experiences helped to shape responses and develop familiarity with the disease and other, more natural explanations—such as poverty, warfare, and natural disasters—gained an important role in the discourse about plague.[28]

Scientific traditions and underpinnings

As with religion, medical and scientific understanding of and approaches to the plague drew from a well of classical texts and ideas. Underpinning much of the discussion about plague in the early modern world was the idea that good health was the result of a balancing of "humors;" imbalance of these humors explained disease and a return to health was sought through rebalancing them. Much of the early modern writing on disease was based on key classical sources, most notably the thought and works of the Greek scholars Hippocrates of Cos (460– 377 BCE) and Galen (129–c 200 CE), which associated health and disease with various (im)balances of bodily humors and environmental conditions such as air, water, and climate. According to this system, all things are composed of four elements, each with specific properties: fire (hot and dry); water (cold and wet); air (moist and hot); and earth (dry and cold). Four bodily humors were related to these elements: yellow bile (fire); blood (air); phlegm (water); and black bile (earth).[29] Imbalance caused by excess of any of these elements was a common concern addressed by classical, as well as early modern physicians. Humors might be balanced through changes in climate as well as diet, and medical treatises (scholarly and popular) identified a range of foods to consume and avoid for protection from or in response to the plague.[30] [**See 3.7**] Gentile da Foligno, author of a "Short Casebook" (1348), for example, offered extensive advice about diet and remedies for plague. Foligno was a physician's son from Foligno, near Perugia. He studied medicine at the universities of Bologna and Padua and was later a lecturer in medicine at the University of Perugia between 1325 and 1337. He recommended that people consume food and drink of suitable quality and in moderation. Fish should be avoided, lettuce should not be eaten when cold. "Furthermore," he noted,

> from among various foods, we recommend the eating of good meat, including fowl, chicken, and starlings. But of beef, [we recommend] gelded cows and lactating goats and calves, as well as young pork. Also, we recommend bread carefully prepared and select wines, so that men may live in good cheer as they give vent to their fear.[31]

Beyond food, Foligno also recommended that:

> fires be lit in homes and in places where people are living, and that men rest quietly. Also, fires of any kind of fragrant plant should be set up, and the house and city should be cleansed of foul matter [i.e., excrement], and to counteract the foulness, fruits and spices—which are described below— should be at one's disposal.[32]

Many early modern medical experts similarly viewed the quality of air, often compromised in large urban centers through pollution or lack of sanitation, as a central mechanism in the development and spread of disease.[33] As a result, disease could be associated with particular geographical locations or seasonal conditions. This Greek-based system of thinking dominated European approaches to the plague and through the distillation of major medieval Arabic philosophers and scientists made its way into Islamic culture as well. Commentaries on the work of the famous philosopher Ibn Sina, known as Avicenna (c 980–1037), who had a significant impact on philosophy as well as medicine, advanced the ideas of Galen, which were taken up by later Islamic writers as well. According to the thirteenth-century Egyptian physician Ibn an-Nafis, who likely had no direct experience with plague himself, for example:

> The pestilence resulted from a corruption occurring in the substance of the air due to heavenly and terrestrial causes. In the earth the causes are brackish water and the many cadavers found in places of battle when the dead are not buried and land which is water-logged and stagnant from rottenness, vermin, and frogs. As regards the heavenly air, the causes are many shooting stars and meteorites at the end of the summer and in the autumn, the strong south and east winds in December and January, and when the signs of rain increase in the winter but it does not rain.[34]

Like others of his period, Ibn an-Nafis recognized that at the time of plague rats and other underground animals fled for the surface, though he posited no direct causal link between rats and the plague.[35] Vermin and frogs were not plague carriers—rather this connection, like many others, was transmitted from earlier writers with no direct experience with bubonic plague.

Islamic writers during the Second Pandemic drew from a variety of scientific sources. Abū Ja'afar Ahmad ibn Khātima, a physician from Almeria, on the coast of southern Spain and part of the Muslim kingdom of Granada at the time, wrote his famous plague treatise in February of 1349. He died sometime after 1369. His writing betrays the influence of the classical medical and scientific thought of Hippocrates and Galen, as well as the great Avenzoar (Ibn Zuhr), a highly regarded twelfth-century Muslim physician and surgeon and contemporary of Averroes. His work was also richly influenced by practical experiences during the 1348 plague. Regarding infection, for example, he noted,

> It is clear and obvious that it is the nature of the disease to spread and con-taminate the surroundings. Both experience and observation confirm this. It has not happened yet that a healthy person came into contact with a sick one without contracting the disease. It is a law which God imposed on this matter. God is the first and foremost maker. ... The best thing we learn from extensive experience is that if someone comes into contact with a dis-eased person, he immediately is smitten with the same disease, with identical symptoms. ... Also, the second infected person passes on the disease.[36]

Ibn Khātima offered advice on how to protect oneself from plague. This included making certain to have fresh air—"by living in houses facing north, by filling them with cold fragrances and aroma of flowers, such as myrtle and oriental poplars, by sprinkling the houses with rose water mixed with vinegar, and also use the same on oneself." [See 3.3, for a comparable approach in Christian Europe] In advice that would be followed well into the early modern period, he suggested that people anoint their face and hands with cool fragrances and frequently smell these fragrances as well as sour lemons and limes and cooling flowers, including roses and violets. He recommended food and air that could produce heat. Beyond this, he suggested that one should seek agreeable company; read books on history, humor, and romance; and avoid disparaging others. Bleeding was also of great value. Primarily, however, he exhorted his readers to "Rely on God; He is the best and most compassionate protector."

Outside Christian and Islamic circles, many cultures maintained similar characteristics in their medical systems.[37] As with Islamic approaches to medicine in the medieval and early modern periods, some Hindu texts were influenced by the Greek thought and works of Hippocrates and Galen. Indian Veda texts, for example, associated disease with the imbalance of 3 *dosas*. The Indian school of Ayurveda emphasized humoral balance in a way similar to Buddha's Middle Path. Imbalance could be caused by climate, environment, diet, emotion, as well as sins from previous lives or sins against wisdom.[38] Ayurveda, like other scientific traditions, identified five key elements—earth, water, fire, air, and space.[39] Twenty qualities that formed the elementary composition of a substance were identified and conditions were treated through the use of opposing qualities.[40] Wind (*vata*), bile (*pitta*), and phlegm (*kapha*) were the three *dosas*, whose balancing helped to understand and treat illness.[41] Excessive heat or moisture, for example, prevalent in some places in India, was associated with certain predilections to disease. Of course, diseases could be caused by injury, divinity, providence, as well as natural means.[42] Vedic Indians might, therefore, also see diseases as the cause of human transgressions against other humans or the divine.[43] While contagion was certainly employed as an explanatory factor, disease could also be transmitted through past deeds.[44] The writings of the Caraka (or Charaka, a central compendium of writings dating from before the second century CE, and a key source of Ayurvedic science), note, for example, in ways that resonated with Greek science, that:

> When these four elements [noisome wind, unclean water, insalubrious land, and unwholesome seasons] are abnormal, they are the cause of epidemics; but when they are not, they are wholesome. When properly treated with (prophylactic) medicaments, people do not succumb to disease, even when these four factors are defiled. [45]

Many early modern authors across the globe saw wind, which was considered then as a powerful and elemental force just as it was in Greek science, as playing a pivotal role in the spread of disease. In seventeenth-century Egypt, for example, the warm and southerly winds that blew into that region in late spring and early summer were connected with not only the sweeping dust and sand, but also plague.[46]

The Chinese medical system similarly offered a six-fold classification system that sought a balance between *yin* and *yang* qualities and at times attributed disease to various environmental conditions.[47] Health, like everything else in this system, was dictated by five natural elements—wood, fire, earth, metal, and water (each with specific associations to both seasons and senses).[48] Imbalances in these elements would lead to illness and other problems; reestablishing balance was a key to healing. In classical and early modern Chinese thought, contagion was seen as a real possibility for the spread of disease and epidemics could be triggered by weather and poisonous vapors. Therefore, according to Li Ting, in his *Introduction to Medicine* (1575), when entering a home infected with an epidemic disease, one should first ingest sesame oil or plug the ears and nostrils with paper that has been soaked in sesame oil, orpiment, and cinnabar, in order to protect himself from the polluting poisons.[49] Numerous Chinese treatises examined categories of drugs and herbal and plant remedies more generally—for example, Li Shizhen's *Compendium of Material Medica* (1590) and Wu Qishun's *Investigation on Plants with Illustrations* (1642).[50] During the early modern period, that is, during the Ming and Qing dynasties, Western medicine made inroads into China,[51] and by the seventeenth century some Chinese doctors broke from traditional medical understanding of disease. Wu Youxing (c 1580–1660), for example, offered a new etiological approach in his *Wenyilun* (*Treatise on Warm-Factor Epidemics*, 1642), in response to the major epidemic of 1639–44, which along with famine and other conditions, contributed to a significant population decline in the late sixteenth through the middle of the seventeenth centuries.[52] [See 3.4] Importantly, Wu Youxing included both theoretical as well as clinical descriptions and medical prescriptions.[53] As in other cultures, beyond traditional and innovative scientific explanations, disease could still be seen by many as the result of the work of demons or as punishment for transgressions against heaven or the Emperor.[54]

In some cultures, such as the Aztec in the central Americas, disease was placed within a dualistic system and attributed to higher divine powers; people addressed illness by various prayers, bloodletting, diet, and herbal remedies.[55] [Regarding dressings and cupping, for example, see 3.1] Similarly, in ancient Mesoamerica, illness was associated with punishment by the gods.[56] Medical specialists, such as wise men, utilized a range of physical remedies as well as prayer to divinities in order to seek forgiveness from insults to them during times of pestilence.[57]

The intersection of various systems of thought is perhaps nowhere clearer than in sub-Saharan medicine, which mixed various elements of Greek and Roman scientific models, Islamic beliefs, and the work and thought of Christian faith healers.[58] Disease in this system was caused by changing events in the human or spirit worlds, with natural events caused by God and unnatural events by human or spiritual forces.[59] Plague and other disease could be spread through contagion by animals as well as contaminated substances and the environment.[60] Health was the result of maintaining balance—between individual and larger groups or the community, people, and the natural or spiritual environment.[61]

Plague: between science and religion

When discussing plague many early modern physicians referred back to the authority of Late Antique authors at the same time that they absorbed the scientific, religious, and political characteristics and orientations of their time and location. The German physician Jacob Hornstein (late sixteenth century), for example, referred to the work of Galen,[62] even as his own medical approach was infused with contemporary Christian religious sensibilities. He argued that there are two sources of the pestilential sickness at times of the plague: an inner or natural source and an external source. Within the first he identified "a lazy, poisoned air and the evil humors or damaging humidity of the human body."[63] But it is God who is the *prima causa*, the regent and ruler of all things in heaven and on earth.[64] Plague is a punishment for sin;[65] indeed, as the Bible indicated, God punishes sinners with hunger, war, and pestilence.[66] Hornstein enumerated a full list of sins that warrant punishment, including unbelief, heresy, sectarianism, envy, hatred, anger, enmity, falsehood, lies, usury, blasphemy, and many others.[67] Hornstein also distinguished between spiritual and physical illnesses.[68] True to his Catholic orientations, he viewed sickness of the soul in those who turned from the true Catholic faith and fell from apostolic belief to heresy, in the form of Lutheran, Calvinist, Zwinglian, Protestant, and similarly what he considered other new and false unbeliefs.[69]

A similar blending of religion and medicine, along with policy, could be found in Venice where, for example, the Senate decreed in April of 1464 that:

> Every possible measure must be taken against the plague, and the first of such remedies is to beg for the grace and mercy of our God and savior Jesus Christ. Be it therefore determined that our most reverend Lord Patriarch be requested to have prayers recited unceasingly in all convents and religious houses for the deliverance of this our city from the sudden assaults of such a dangerous disease.[70]

In 1630 the Venetian Senate likewise declared that:

> Be it determined that in honor of Our Lady [who was seen as a protector of the city in previous epidemics], on each of the next fifteen Saturdays, there shall be a devout procession from our church of St. Mark and around the Piazza. The Doge, the magistrates, the Senate and the nobility shall be present, wearing their ordinary robes and carrying, in all humbleness of heart and true contrition, the miraculous image of the Virgin which is preserved in that church, offering up their earnest prayers for the deliverance of this city and of our state from the present sickness, and these prayers shall be accompanied by a universal fast, which shall be an obligation on all these fifteen Saturdays.
>
> On the first Saturday, after the procession, the Doge shall in the name of the commonwealth make a solemn vow to God to build a church in this city and to dedicate it to the most holy Virgin, calling it Santa Maria della Salute; and every year, on the day that this city shall be proclaimed free of the present sickness, the Doge and his successors shall pay a ceremonious visit to that church with the Senate, in perpetual memory of the gratitude of the commonwealth for this great benefit.[71]

The church was a votive church established to end the plague, with annual festivals that have continued until today.

Religious authorities such as John Hooper (c 1495–1555), English religious reformer and an Anglican Bishop of Gloucester and Worcester writing in the middle of the sixteenth century, expressed the common idea that sin was the cause of plague, which would continue to have serious resonance throughout the early modern, and in some cases, well into the modern period. Increasingly since the sixteenth century, however, many early modern writers emphasized other factors related to plague (as well as other disasters), even if God was still seen to be its primary factor. Thomas Sorocold (1591–1617), the Manchester native and author of *Supplications of Saints*, for example, noted that the root cause of disease was divine, but at the same time he argued that we should not rely too heavily on prayer, but rather also trust in other means, such as medicines and geographic location.[72] Like other early moderns, Jews, who participated in a specifically Jewish as well as broader Christian and Islamic cultures, assumed the existence of demons, consulted astrological signs, and relied on amulets at the same time that they engaged with science and medicine.[73]

In late medieval and early modern Islamic plague treatises, a variety of causes of plague were identified, including: natural causes such as the alignment of stars, disasters such as earthquakes, natural conditions related to sanitation of air and water, and human induced causes such as warfare, in addition to divine will.[74] Therefore, beyond religious responses, among some Islamic plague writers, fumigation, diet, folk remedies, and even changes in location were suggested in protecting against or warding off the plague.[75] In the early modern period new emphases on medical over religious or magical approaches to the plague— including the use of quarantine—may be explained by scientific advances, political agendas, as well as greater foreign influences in some places, such as the expanding Ottoman state.[76] Early modern Ottoman authors, in fact, increasingly suggested other means beyond religious practice for combatting the plague, such as medical treatments and fumigation of the air.[77]

Early modern physicians and writers recognized varying symptoms and levels of infection and they recommended many different plague preventions and treatments. [**See 3.10**] They often focused on diet; the control of exercise, sleep, sexuality, and excretions; the avoidance of passions and fear; and the cultivation of general happiness.[78] Preventions related to the air were frequent, as noted above—maintenance of air quality, as well as the use of fires, perfumes, cleaning and washing of houses, preservatives in the mouth, and tobacco.[79] Medical and herbal preventatives and remedies, included various nuts and roots, Armenian bole, and theriac.[80] Medical treatments might be rather general. The widely applied theriac, was an inconsistently prepared remedy that could include a wide range of ingredients depending on time and location and it could be used to treat a plethora of illnesses. Gentile da Foligno in the fourteenth century indicated that the best theriac should be taken when needed at least two or three times per week and that dosages should vary by gender and age. He noted other remedies that he argued were effective against pestilence:

A second question is whether a compound made of Armenian bole, aloe, myrrh, and saffron be effective in this pestilence, which indeed doctors north of the Alps have prescribed. Our response is that this compound, if prudently made up by doctors in accordance with the conditions of each illness, which may be observed in the patient's numbers, and even though true [Armenian] bole may not be seen or found in our country, nonetheless if it were to be found and even if it were not genuine, all the same we could accept its use to counteract a certain blocking of the paths of the spirit [i.e., the arteries], which we have found in those men short of breath in the lungs, and because we have found that a tightness of the chest causes harm throughout the body's trunk. But if it should be discovered that the chest is disposed to be tight at certain times, then there is no cause for concern and its use is not recommended.[81]

The Dutch physician Dr Jacobus Bontius, to take a later example, used human bladder stones and theriac, along with drops of oil of amber or juniper, in place of bezoar stones (expelled concretions of goat stomachs), which were scarce in Leiden during the great plague of 1624–25.[82] Some Ottoman physicians believed in the preventative and curative aspects of a medicinal earth known as *Terra Lemnia* or *Terra Sigillata* (Italian) [Sealed Earth], which could only be found on the Aegean island of Limnos.[83] Certain kinds of clay were prescribed as both a treatment for and prevention of plague when used on the buboes.[84] Medical preventions and treatments of plague built simultaneously on the philosophy of Antiquity, contemporary science, as well as popular culture, practices, and worldviews. Importantly, as we have seen, the separate categories we today ascribe to medicine and religion were highly permeable throughout the early modern world.

Heinrich Steinhöwel (1420–82), the city physician of Ulm in south Germany, to provide but one example, recommended a specific regimen in confronting plague, one should: allow light and air into houses; light bonfires to expel feculence from the atmosphere; scrub rooms with vinegar and water; avoid living near slaughterhouses and cemeteries; shun contact with beggars and vagrants; eat lightly; and exercise moderately.[85]

Still, early modern people—physicians included—continued to resort to prayers, processions, and other religious behaviors (such as those practiced by members of self-flagellation cults) to combat plague. **[See Chapter 2]** Such actions seemed appropriate as most early moderns understood the plague, like other disasters, as God's punishment for human sin.[86] But these simultaneously religious and "civic" rituals could stir the masses and lead to social upheavals (see p. 215ff).[87] Indeed, both supernatural and natural explanations for the plague could be, and frequently were, advanced simultaneously. As one medical historian has argued,

> Even if most people accepted the ultimate divine origin of plague, they also acknowledged the role of other factors, including odd weather patterns (scorching summers or frigid winters), famines, troop movements, wars,

"fetid miasmas," stagnant pools of water, prodigies, monstrous births, and other premonitions.[88]

Or, as another historian of early modern plague has asserted,

> The distinction between natural aspects of epidemics and those related to chastisement by God were not sharply differentiated. Thus, a church service devoted to prayers for forgiveness and assistance might be preceded and followed by smoking-out of the church with juniper or other noxious fumes to prevent natural transmission of the disease. Plague outbreaks were often correlated with unusual events such as deaths among animals, birds falling from the sky, and violent storms and other catastrophes.[89]

Like other natural disasters, plague was seen by early modern people in both scientific and religious contexts. Utilizing a mix of ancient and contemporary medical knowledge, early moderns concocted a range of preventative measures against and treatments for the plague. Sometimes, as in the competing responses of quarantine and flight, some measures advocated appear to have been at cross purposes with other, established, measures.

Medical treatments were discussed in a broad range of treatises and incorporated a diversity of approaches that could vary by the orientation of the author as well as the nature of the intended audience. While there was at times overlap, there could also be significant differences between more popular books of remedies and more professional medical textbooks, designed for physicians and other medical "professionals." This was particularly the case as medicine was increasingly professionalized in the early modern period and into the nineteenth century,[90] when prior systems and methods would be challenged in some parts of the world. New conceptualizations began to affect how people understood and responded to disease. One recent historian writes that:

> Throughout the seventeenth and eighteenth centuries, diseases designated by European as epidemics—that is, sudden and abnormal outbreaks of disease— were generally attributed to some peculiar constitution of the atmosphere. In most cases, it was excessive heat and moisture that were blamed for accelerating the normal process of organic decay and inundating the air with the effluvia of putrefying matter ... During the nineteenth century, these almost exclusively climatic explanations were challenged by a new conception of epidemics that was revolutionary in its implications. European medical men in India began to attribute epidemics increasingly to man-made problems— to the overcrowding and sanitary nuisances produced by urbanization, and to 'ignorance' and uncleanly habits of Indians—rather than simply to 'natural' phenomena.[91]

According to this line of thought, in a certain sense, disease was a social and cultural construct as much as a biological reality.[92] In assessing responses to the plague, therefore, we must also consider political, social, and cultural issues as well. [**See also Chapter 5**]

Early modern medicine involved a diversity of physicians and other healers. It drew from a variety of scientific perspectives, increasingly engaged with observation and experimentation. It also utilized a broad range of preventive treatments and remedies. Although they drew from classical and medieval medical theories and understandings of the body, many early modern people had a good deal of first-hand experience with the plague and other diseases, which recurred regularly in some places. Indeed, observation became a more central practice in the later sixteenth and into the seventeenth centuries in a number of fields, with increasing focus on empiricism and experimentation.[93]

The experiences and responses of early modern people were further conditioned by other environmental conditions and disasters, growing scientific, and more particularly biological, knowledge, as well as broader cultural values and religious worldviews, which each added to and could never really be separated from what we sometimes think of today as medicine. To a very real extent, early modern societies often proved to be quite resilient, learning from experiences and adapting to local and regional conditions. At the same time, they absorbed and applied various medical preventions and treatments, derived from a variety of sources. Though plague—along with other diseases—could be terrifying, early modern people proved quite able to cope with and rebound from even some of the most deadly epidemics.

Indeed, early moderns at times had sophisticated understandings of disease. They were able to distinguish symptoms and intuitively developed responses to plague that could prove to be quite effective. Although we have often divided early moderns into distinct camps, usually around the position of contagion or miasma, it is clear that there could be a good deal of overlap across these categories and across the realms of science, popular culture, and religion. Early moderns, especially across Europe and the Ottoman Empire, engaged a rich lexicon to discuss plague—in classical languages as well as contemporary vernaculars. At the same time, early moderns (like people today) could be less systematic and they frequently lumped diseases together in narrative descriptions. Nor did they always use terms with precision. This was not always due to lack of understanding, but rather because certain terms, like "plague," could be used to express an impressive range of political and social meanings.

Approaches to early modern plague, therefore, are quite helpful in understanding the range of continuity of tradition on one hand and the innovation of an accelerating, globalizing, and increasingly technological world. They also point to different worldviews and experiences as well as shared human concerns and mentalities. Finally, they highlight the significant extent to which medicine and the plague itself could be socially constructed concepts.

Sources

3.1 Applying wound dressings, scarification with cupping glasses

Treatise on the Plague (Tractatabus de Pestilentia) (fifteenth century)[94]

Introduction: Early modern people turned to a variety of healers when confronted with medical problems. Physicians, as well as pharmacists and other more popular healers—whose methods could overlap to some extent—recommended various medical treatments and remedies to protect their patients from or cure the plague. Bleeding was quite common in the medieval and early modern periods, in response to many different ailments and based on medical theories of Antiquity and practices from the Middle Ages. Certain plants and herbs were also considered effective in addressing diseases. In cases of plague, many healers believed that the bursting of the buboes was a condition of healing, and they caused the bursting in different ways, from plasters and hot rocks to incisions.

Figure 3.1 Applying wound dressings, scarification with cupping glasses. Gianni Dagli Orti/The Art Archive at Art Resource, NY, © DeA Picture Library/Art Resource, NY.

Location: University Library Prague

3.2 Tradition and innovation in early modern medicine

Author: Girolamo Fracastoro (c 1478–1553)

Title: *On Contagion and Contagious Diseases and Their Cures* (1546)[95]

Introduction: Born in Padua, Girolamo Fracastoro studied and later taught at the University of Padua. In addition to his work on the "seeds of disease" (see p. 125), which according to some was the predecessor of germ theory, he was also well known for his work on syphilis. In addition to his work in medicine, Fracastoro was also involved with mathematics, geography, astronomy, and poetry. His work, which eventually seems to have been absorbed into medical traditions, reflects a more regular bridging between the miasma and contagion and the efforts of medical professionals and civic administrators. In this important work, which blended different approaches to disease and highlighted some of the key issues being discussed in his day, Fracastoro explores the various means of contagion through direct and indirect contact. Of particular note, he considers the idea of *fomes*, intermediary substances that can preserve and transfer germs (*seminaria*, or "seeds"). While Fracastoro advanced a theory of contagion, it has been argued that this theory was not incompatible with the theory of miasma, or contagion through noxious air. Although there was a range of positive and negative reactions to Fracastoro's argument, his views appear to have been rather easily absorbed into early modern medical writing and models.

Text

Chapter II

There are, it seems, three fundamentally different types of contagion: the first infects by direct contact only; the second does the same, but in addition leaves *fomes*, and this contagion may spread by means of that *fomes*, for instance scabies, phthisis, bald spots, elephantiasis and the like. By *fomes* I mean clothes, wooden objects, and things of that sort, which though not themselves corrupted can, nevertheless, preserve the original germs [*seminaria prima*] of the contagion and infect by means of these; thirdly, there is a kind of contagion which is transmitted not only by direct contact or by the *fomes* as intermediary, but also infects at a distance; for example, pestilent fevers, phthisis, certain kinds of ophthalmia, exanthemata of the kind called variolae, and the like. These different contagions seem to obey a certain law; for those which carry contagion to a distant object infect both by direct contact and by *fomes*; those that are contagious by means of *fomes* are equally so by direct contact; not all of them are contagious at a distance, but all are contagious by direct contact. Hence, the most simple kind of contagion is that by direct contact only, and it is naturally first in order. So I shall treat of this first, and try to discover how and by means of what principle (primary agent) it arises; next I shall treat of the others, in order to see whether there is a certain principle common to them all, or a different principle in each, and what is the peculiar characteristic of each.

Chapter III

CONTAGION THAT INFECTS BY CONTACT ONLY

An especially good instance of the contagion that infects by contact only is that which occurs in fruits, as when grape infects grape, or apple infects apple; so we must try to discover the principle of this infection. It is evident that they are infected because they touch, and that some one fruit decays first, but what is the principle of the infection? Since the first fruit from which all the infection passes to the rest, has putrefied, we must suppose that the second has contracted a precisely similar putrefaction, seeing that we defined contagion as a precisely similar infection of one thing by another. Now putrefaction is a sort of dissolution of a combination due to evaporation of the innate warmth and moisture. The principle of that evaporation is always foreign heat, whether that heat be in the air or in the surrounding moisture; hence, in both fruits the principle of contagion will be the same as the principle of putrefaction, namely extraneous heat; but this heat came to the first fruit either from the air or some other source, and we may not yet speak of contagion; but the heat has passed on to the second fruit by means of those imperceptible particles that evaporate from the first fruit, and now there is contagion, since there is a similar infection in both fruits; the heat that evaporates from the first fruit has power to produce on the second fruit what the air produced in the first, and to make it putrefy in a similar way, all the more because there is analogy ...

Chapter IV

CONTAGION THAT INFECTS BY *FOMES*

Now it is not at once obvious that the germs that transmit contagion by means of *fomes* are produced in the same manner and by the same principle as that above described, for the principle that exists in *fomes* seems to be of a different nature, inasmuch as, when it has retired into *fomes* from the body originally infected, it may last there for a very long time without any alteration. Things that have been touched by persons suffering from phthisis or the plague are really amazing examples of this. I have often observed that in them this virus has been preserved for two or three years; whereas particles that evaporate from putrefying bodies never seem to have the power to last as long as that. Nevertheless no one ought on that account to think that the principle of contagion that is in *fomes* is not the same as the principles that infect by contact only, because the very same particles that evaporate from the body originally infected, after being thus preserved, can produce the same effect as they would have done when they evaporated from the original body. If one desires to be convinced and feel no surprise that they can last and preserve their power so long in *fomes*, he should consider similar cases of this sort. Do we not observe that in wood, clothes, etc., a strange smell may be preserved for a long time, and that not due to some definite quality in them without material basis, but rather to bodies so very small as to be invisible to us? Or take the case of soot and smoke when walls are covered with it; do not these too, by the admixture of very small particles, become a dye that lasts without alteration for a very long time? Surely there are countless examples of this sort, and if one asks what are the conditions on which they all depend, I assert that these are two, namely the fine and volatile nature of the particles, and the strength and resistance of the combination. Because of their fitness and volatility they penetrate and are stored up in the pores of certain objects, so that they are not exposed to the air or to alteration from outside, and, owing to the strength of the combination, they can hold out against many attacks. ...

Now all substances are not suited to become *fomes*, but only those that are somewhat porous, and are warm or tepid. In these, on account of their pores, the germs of contagions can be stored up, and they cannot be altered either by the *fomes* itself or by external factors, unless these are excessively active; for instance they have no defense against fire. It follows that iron, stone and bodies of that sort, which are cold and not porous, are not adapted to become *fomes*, whereas wool, rags, and many kinds of wood are well adapted. From what has been said it is evident that contagions that infect by means of *fomes* and those that infect by direct contact only, have a common principle and a common method of conveying the infection. But they do differ in the kind of combination of the germs, since in the former case the combination is strong and viscous, but in the latter it is weak and not viscous. This is the reason why some germs produce *fomes*, while others do not.

Chapter V

CONTAGION AT A DISTANCE

Even more surprising and hard to explain are those diseases that cause contagion, not by direct contact only, or by *fomes* only, but also at a distance. There is a kind of ophthalmia with which the sufferer infects everyone who looks at him. It is well known that pestiferous fevers, phthisis and many other diseases infect those who live with the sufferer, even though there is no actual contact. It is far from certain what is the nature of these diseases, and how the taint is propagated ...

3.3 Plague precautions

Author: Francois Valleriole (1504–1580)

Title: *Tractate on the Plague* (1566)[96]

Introduction: Francois Valleriole was a physician in sixteenth-century Arles. Assuming the contagious nature of plague, he devoted a chapter of his tractate to presenting the order and regimen that he recommended should be observed by those attending to plague patients. This included prayers, medicines, and precautions to take when visiting the sick, including aeration and perfuming, which appear to have been commonly practiced in the early modern world. The importance of room ventilation and aroma was stressed, in accordance with many discussions (medical as well as in civic legislation) about the danger of putrid smells, which often led to regulations about the disposal of waste and the location of certain businesses.

Text

It is something obvious that those who live constantly with people infected by the plague are in great danger of receiving the infection themselves, by interacting with the sick person night and day, receiving their breath, smelling their stench, and drawing in the infected air of the infected house of the sick person, which is a very dangerous thing, as Galen said [in the] first book of the differences of fevers, second chapter. Therefore, those who deliberately engage with those infected by the plague have to take great care to preserve themselves from the possible evil consequences. And they must first withdraw to God, imploring [Him] to protect the supplicant by the grace of God, so that they may better carry out the act of charity towards the sick person, that he may help and serve with all his power, as is most agreeable and pleasant to God. ...

Preservatives will be prescribed according to the complexion, age, quality, and nature of the humors abounding in him, taking medicine or appropriate pills, powders, opiates, tablets against plague, theriac or metridat, according to the specific conditions and continue this without interruption. When he visits his sick patient, he shall not come too near to him so that he does not receive his breath, to ward off as much as is possible from himself with an empty stomach. Prior to entering the room of the sick, principally in the morning, he ventilates the room, opens the windows some time before he enters, wetting the room with water and vinegar, and making a good fire for a time, taking a mixture of vinegar, rosemary, or juniper. Perfume the room, ahead of the aroma with what is called a regiment of preservative. In entering the room of the sick, he holds in his hand a torch or well lit candles or small fires, full of good and live embers, not placing it before the perfumes written above. He holds in his mouth angelica root or turmeric (zedoaire) or cloves, or the rind of citron, orange, or lemon. Wash the hands, face, and forehead, the temples with good vinegar mixed with rose water or plain water and if he has the means, he should rub the chest and the places of the excretory organs, but this is not too comfortable to do. Change clothes and shirts often, and almost every day, holding in your hands apples, oranges, lemons in order to smell them often. Hold a sponge soaked in liqueur of rose water, red vinegar, white wine mixed together with cloves, turmeric, and angelica root.

… Perfume the whole house and the room of the sick two or three times a day, all day long. When it comes to touching the sick person, make him turn and face backwards, in order that he not face you more. … Be sober in this life, refrain from unnecessary meat and drinking. Be joyous and of good spirit, drive out all kinds of fear, sadness, melancholy.

3.4 Confronting the ancients

Author: Wu Youxing (c 1580–1660)

Title: *Treatise on Acute Epidemic Warmth* [*Wenyilun*] (1642)[97]

Introduction: In Chinese medicine prior to the Ming dynasty most treatises that dealt with disease examined disease induced by coldness. In the Ming and Qing dynasties, a new emphasis on warm disease theory was further developed. Devastating plague struck parts of China in 1641. The physician Wu Youxing published a massive book based on his research of epidemic diseases (*wenbing*) the following year. Diseases, he argued, could be transferred indirectly as well as directly. He described many different symptoms and developed a theory of excessive influences (*liqi*), which caused pestilence by entering the body through the nose and mouth—this was opposed to the traditional assumption that it was exogeneous pathogens, including wind, cold, heat, and moisture. In treating these excessive influences one could use herbs, careful to match remedies with the specific *liqi* of each disease. Throughout the treatise Wu Youxing draws from previous medical research and assumptions, even as he challenges them in his attempts to explain contemporary epidemics.

Text

The diseases that are called epidemics involve warmth and are not due to the wind, nor the cold, nor the heat, nor the humidity; they are contracted by reason of the presence of an extraordinary blowing between heaven and earth. Its transmission occurs according to nine modalities, which have an important connection with the treatment of the epidemic.

How is it that this has never before been put into evidence? Zhang Zhongjing, indeed, wrote his *Shanghanlun* [*Treatise on Cold Damage*]. His reasoning proceeded from *taiyang* [small intestine and bladder meridians]; the transmission occurs either in *yangming* [stomach and large intestine meridians], or in *shaoyang* [heart and kidney meridians], or in [these?] three *yang*, to finally reach the stomach. It thus assumed an outside influence (*waigan*), the wind and cold; this mode of transmission, however, is different from that in epidemics linked to warmth.

Subsequently, the discussions about this subject were numerous, with dozens of schools all thinking in terms of the effect of the cold, and all being very basic regarding signs of epidemics linked to warmth. All of this has been noted and related in many chapters and those who practice medicine have only reported effects of cold. During their clinical observations, however, they are [actually] confronted by epidemics related to tepidity, and only one or two cases out of a hundred are really attained by the cold. ...

As for me, I begin by examining what the medical schools say: the diseases linked to warmth (*wenbing*) occur in spring, summer, or fall, while those attained by the cold must occur in winter. To observe well every year, we note that there are epidemics linked to warmth (*wenyi*) during the four seasons. The examination of those attained by cold show that when a wave of considerable cold arrives [the symptoms are as follows]: headache, pain in the whole body, damage of cold without sweating, bout of fever, all being similar to the signs associated with *taiyang*.

After six or seven days, in the absence of treatment, this is not transmitted to the conduits (*jing* [essence]), and the cure is achieved after sweating, every time that it is used to disperse a medication. Among these conditions, it also necessary that they heal themselves without treatment; moreover, in these cases, if there is no sweat, there is no evidence of worsening with signs such as jaundice, delirium, confusion, or a hot tongue coating. We have, then, [a] matter of illnesses such as common colds (*gammao*) [that] is superficial and not a true cold disease. Common colds and cold diseases are, in an identical manner, related to wind and cold, but there is a difference of severity. Colds are common, cold diseases rare.

There exists in a way a lot more marked distinction—similar to that between the empire and the earth—between contracting an epidemic disease related to warmth (*wenyi*) and contracting a cold disease. Today, if you want quickly to distinguish the deer from the horse, we must see that cold diseases are very rare. Zhang Zhongjing considered cold disease as an acute illness. In haste, inadequate care is given to [the] origin of these disorders. This is the reason for composing this essay, and, in this way, to bring order under Heaven for future generations; this is called virtue of humanity (*ren*). Indeed, cold diseases and epidemic diseases related to warmth are all acute diseases. We meticulously inform future generations about a rare disease, while no discussion is proposed on epidemics related to the warmth, which are a hundred times more frequent than cold diseases: it is difficult to tolerate this. It is said that the origins of the work of Zhang Zhongjing included prescriptions and an essay about the signs of epidemics related to warmth: but the times have passed, and fires and wars have not allowed the fragments of *Shanghanlun* [compiled by Zhang Zhongjing in the third century] to remain. Wang Shuhe [c 180–c 270] gave prescriptions and composed a treatise, but it would be wrong to call this a complete book. It is not impossible that the treatise on the epidemics related to warmth disappeared.

The year *xingsi* of the Chongzhen Era [emperor 1611–44; here 1641], the blowing epidemic (*yiqi*) spread, claiming very many victims in Shandong, Zhejiang, and in the two Zhili, North and South. The worst occurred in the fifth and sixth months, and all the families were affected. At first, the doctors mistook the disease for a cold disease and applied treatment accordingly, without realizing the danger. The sick thought they would recover by themselves within seven days, or, if not, within fourteen days, and they neglected to treat [the disease]; but they died before this period. Drastic medications were also used ... incorrectly, which led to death. One again encountered physicians who understood nothing, full of doubt and indecision, who gave a slow-acting drug for an acute illness; those people did not immediately suffer harm, but ended up dying. If you had been lightly affected, you had a chance to make it through; but if you had been seriously affected, and there were many who were deceived by the treatment, then the unjustified deaths were innumerable.

Alas! To maintain old methods unsuited to the diseases of today, to review the old books about these diseases, you obtain no insight! You then have recourse to ineffective drugs (*bu xiao*), the doctors are hesitant and do not take the correct measures, so that the life of the sick person is in danger. The more acute the disease is the more disordered are the prescriptions; one then dies from the doctors if one does not die from the disease, one dies from the gaps from the classic authors, if one does not die from the physicians. Oh! For a thousand years, how could the people be so miserable?

Although I am a poor ignorant [person], I scrutinized with serenity the reason of things, I thoroughly examined the blowing (*qi*) that is contracted, its ports of entry, the places where it is received, its mode of propagation and transfer. I utilized daily the proven historical methods, I explained in detail all this below, in order to make the best correctives.

It was once thought that the cause of epidemic diseases lay in the accidental character of the climatic conditions. Thus, the spring should be warm and it is on the contrary too cold; the summer was bound to be hot and it is on the contrary too cool; fall ought to be very cool and it is on the contrary too hot; winter ought to be very cold and it is on the contrary too warm. When facing such untimely conditions, the development of the disease resembles the epidemics (*yi*).

My opinion is in disagreement with that. In a general way, the cold, the warmth, the heat, and the cool are the standards of the four seasons, which may slightly decrease or increase due to wind, rain, overcast weather, or sunshine [brightness]. Thus, making autumn hot is a great luminosity; spring is cold because it rains a lot. [These variations] are also normal events of heaven and earth and do not necessarily lead to epidemics. Cold diseases and heat stroke are contracted because of normal blowing of heaven and earth; epidemics are contracted because of pestilential blowing (*liqi* [excessive influences]) of heaven and earth. In the course of a year, there are times of plenty and dearth on earth, there are regional disparities, during the four seasons, there is growth and decline. When pestilential blowing comes, whoever encounters it [becomes] gravely sick, whether they are old or young, strong or weak. The blowing of wind penetrates through the nose and mouth and becomes then [part of] the host body, it is not on the inside in the organs *zang* [yin organs of heart, liver, spleen, lung, kidney] and *fu* [yang organs of Small Intestine, Large Intestine, Gall Bladder, Urinary Bladder, Stomach and *Sānjiaō*] (The Triple-Burner is said to occupy the Thoracic and Abdominal-Pelvic cavities), nor on the outside in the channels [of energy distribution] *jingluo*, [but] it lodges hidden in the spine. ...

3.5 The plague (1649): Hospital del Pozo Santo, Spain[98]

Anonymous, Seville, Spain (seventeenth century)

Introduction: The Hospital del Pozo Santo in Seville was founded in the mid-seventeenth century on a plaza named for the miraculous saving of a boy who fell into a well, after supplications to the Virgin Mary. The hospital was established under the patronage of the Holy Christ of Sorrows by the Beguine Franciscan tertiary. Early modern hospitals were multi-dimensional and they provided a diverse range of treatments for different patients. The conditions in such institutions could vary wildly—some were criticized for their treatment, while others clearly provided valuable resources and care for their patients. The creation of hospitals and the expansion of their services reflected both response to serious epidemics as well as ongoing early modern developments in demography, technology, and government as well as the growth of institutions serving public and civic functions. The scene depicted outside the hospital reveals large-scale death, with some bodies on the ground and others being brought or taken in carriages, and the presence of clergy, merging the sacral and secular needs and functions of the hospital and the broader care for the sick and dying.

Figure 3.5 The plague (1649): Hospital del Pozo Santo, Spain. Photo Credit: Album/Art Resource, NY.

Location: Hospital del Pozo Santo, Spain

3.6 Classifications of plague

Author: M. Chicoyneau, Verney, and Soullier

Title: "A Succinct Account of the Plague at Marseilles: Its Symptoms, and the Methods and Medicines Used for Curing It" (1721)[99]

Introduction: The treatise was written and presented to the governor and magistrates of the French city of Marseilles, where the last plague epidemic hit Western Europe in 1720, claiming the lives of some 100,000 people in and around the city. The treatise was drafted by three physicians—M. Chicoyneau, Verney, and Soullier—who had been sent to Marseilles from Paris by the Duke Regent of France to attend to the sick in that city during the epidemic.

Originally written in French, this account organized plague symptoms and treatments into five categories. These categories coincide both with progression of the plague as well as specific, at times overlapping, symptoms. In each category, the authors identify remedies that are both helpful and harmful in addressing specific issues. In category two, for example, they discuss the appearance of painful buboes in the classically noted locations of the groin area, armpits, and neck. Noting that survival in such cases was rare, they pointed out that survival seemed to be related to the external eruptions of the buboes, with the discharge of blood and "noxious ferment," brought on by nature or remedies. At times, as in the third category there was a mixing of symptoms and display. In the fourth and fifth categories the authors point to cases in which the buboes or carbuncles are of such nature that they can be suppurated to encourage curing. The account is based on many traditional approaches and knowledge as well as the experiences derived from a major late epidemic during the Second Pandemic.

Text

…

All the diseased that we have seen or attended, in this terrible distemper, commonly called the plague, may be reduced to five principal classes; which will take in generally all the cases that we have observed, except a few particular ones, which cannot be brought under any general rule.

First Class

The first class, observed especially in the first period, and in the greatest fury of the Distemper, contains such as were afflicted with the Symptoms that we shall here set down, constantly followed by a speedy death.

These symptoms were for the most part irregular shivering, the pulse low, soft, slow, quick, unequal, concentrated; a heaviness in the head so considerable, that the sick person could scarce support it, appearing to be seized with a stupidity and confusion, like that of a drunken person; the sight fixed, dull, wandering, expressing fearfulness and despair; the voice slow, interrupted, complaining; the tongue almost always white, towards the end dry, reddish, black, rough; the face pale, lead-colored, languishing, cadaverous; a frequent sickness at the stomach; mortal inquietudes; a general sinking and faintness; distraction of the mind; dosing, an inclination to vomit, vomiting, etc.

The persons thus seized, perished commonly in the space of some hours, of a night, of a day, or of two or three at farthest, as by faintness or extinction; sometimes, but more rarely, in convulsive motions, and a sort of trembling; no eruption, tumor or spot appearing without.

It is easy to judge by these accidents, that the sick of this kind were not in a condition to bear bleeding; and even such, on whom it was tried, died a little while after.

Emetics and cathartics were equally here useless, and often hurtful, in exhausting the patient's strength, by their fatal over-working.

The cordials and sudorificks were the only remedies to which we had recourse, which nevertheless could be of no service, or at the most prolong the last moments but for a few hours.

Second Class

The second class of the diseased that we attended during the course of this fatal sickness, contains such as at first had the shivers, as the preceding, and the same sort of stupidity, and heavy pain in the head; but the shivers were followed by a pulse quick, open, and bold, which nevertheless was lost upon pressing the artery ever so little. These sick felt inwardly a burning heat, whilst the heat without was moderate and temperate; the thirst was great and inextinguishable; the tongue white, or of an obscure red; the voice hasty, stammering, impetuous; the eyes reddish, fixed, sparkling; the color of the face was of a red sufficiently fresh, and sometimes inclining to livid; the sickness at the stomach was frequent, though much less than in those of the preceding class; the respiration was frequent, laborious, or great and rare, without coughing or pain; loathings; vomiting, bilious, greenish, blackish, bloody; the courses of the belly of the same sort, but without any tension or pain; ravings, or phrenetick deliria; the urine frequently natural, sometimes troubled, blackish, whitish, or bloody; the sweat, which seldom smelt badly, and which was far from giving ease to the sick, that it always weakened them; in certain cases hemorrhages, which, however moderate, have been always fatal; a great decay in the strength, and above all, an apprehension so strong of dying, that these poor creatures, were incapable of any comfort, and looked on themselves, from the first moment of their being attacked, as destined to certain death. But that which deserves to be well observed, and which has always seemed to characterize and distinguish this disease from all others, is, that almost all had at the beginning, or in the progress of this distemper, very painful buboes, situated commonly below the groin, sometimes in the groin or arm-pits, or in the parotide, maxillar, or jugular glands; as likewise carbuncles, especially on the arms, legs or thighs, small, white, livid, black pustules, dispersed over all the surface of the body.

It was very rare to see any of the diseased of this second class escape, though they supported themselves a little longer than those of the preceding; they perished almost all with the marks of a gangrened inflammation, especially in the brain and thorax; and that which was most singular is, that the stronger, fatter, fuller, and more vigorous they were, the less we had to hope.

As to the remedies, they bore bleeding no better than those of the first class; at least if they were not blooded at the very first Instant of their being taken sick: It was evidently hurtful to them; they grew pale, and fell even in the time of their first bleeding, or a little while after, into such faintings, as could not in most of them be imputed to any fear, repugnance, or distrust, since they demanded with earnestness to have a vein opened.

All emetics, if we except *Ipecacuanha*, were very often more hurtful than useful; causing such fatal irritations and excesses in operating, as we could neither moderate or stop. The cathartics that were a little strong and active, were attended with the same inconveniences.

Such as we prescribed in the form of a laxative Ptisan, as well as plentiful draughts, that were diluting, nitrous, cooling, and gently alexiterial, gave some relief, but did not hinder the return of the symptoms. All cordials and sudorificks, if they were not soft, gentle and benign, did nothing but promote the progress of the inward inflammations.

In short, if any one escaped, which was very rare, he seemed to owe his cure to the external eruptions, when they were very much raised; either solely by the force of nature, or by the assistance of remedies, as well internal as external, that determined the blood to discharge on the surface of the body, the noxious ferment wherewith it was infected.

Third Class

The third class contains the two preceding; seeing we have attended, during the course of this terrible sickness, a great number of persons that have been attacked successively with the different symptoms enumerated in the two former classes, in such a manner, that the most part of the signs described in the second, were commonly the forerunners of those which we have mentioned in the first; and the appearing of these latter symptoms denounced an approaching death.

In these sorts of cases we varied our method according to the diversity of indications, or of the most urgent symptoms; so that without our being obliged to enter into farther particulars, a judgment may be formed of the event of this malady, and of the success of the remedies, from what we before observed on the subject of the diseased of the two preceding classes.

Before we pass on to the fourth class, we believe it will not be improper to observe, that a very great number of different kinds of diseased persons contained in the preceding, had very moderate symptoms, whose force and malignity appeared to be much less, than in those of the same accidents daily observed in inflammatory fevers, or in the most common putrid ones, or in those that are vulgarly called malignant, if we except the signs of fear or despair, which were extreme, or in the highest degree; insomuch, that of the great number of infected persons who have perished, there were very few, who at the very first moment of their being seized, did not imagine themselves lost without relief, whatever pains we took to encourage them: And though many amongst them seemed to us, before the first access of the distemper, to be of a firm and courageous disposition of mind, and resolute under all events, yet as soon as they felt the first strokes, it was easy to know by their looks, and their discourses, that they were convinced that their sickness was incurable and mortal, even at the time when neither the pulse, nor the tongue, nor the disorder in the head, nor the color of the face, nor the disposition of the mind, nor lastly, the lesion of any of the other natural functions mentioned above, gave any fatal Indication, or before there were any grounds to be alarmed.

Fourth Class

The fourth class contains the diseased attacked with the same symptoms with those of the second, but these sorts of accidents lessened or disappeared the second or third day of themselves, or in consequence of the effects of the internal remedies, and at the same time in proportion to the remarkable eruption of the buboes and carbuncles in which the noxious ferment that was dispersed through the whole mass, seemed to be collected together; so that the tumors rising from day to day, at length being open, and coming to a suppuration, the infected escaped the danger that threatened them, provided they had some assistance. These happy events have determined us to redouble our care during the whole course of this sickness, to accelerate, as much as the state of the patient will admit, the eruption, elevation, opening, and suppuration of the buboes and carbuncles, in order to free, as soon as possible, by this way, the mass of blood, from the fatal ferment that corrupts it; aiding nature by a good regimen, and by such cathartic, cordial, and sudorifick medicines, as are proper in the present condition and temperature of the sick.

Fifth and Last Class

This fifth and last class contains all such infected persons, as without perceiving any emotion, or there appearing any trouble or lesion of their natural function, have buboes and carbuncles, which rise by little and little, and easily turn to suppuration, becoming sometimes scirrhous [referring to a hard and slow-growing malignant tumor that contains a good deal of fibrous tissue], or which is more rare, dissipate insensibly, without leaving any bad effect behind them; so that without any loss of strength, and without changing their manner of living, these infected persons went about the streets and public places, only using themselves a simple plaster, or asking of the physicians and surgeons such remedies as are necessary to these sorts of suppurating or scirrhous tumors.

The number of the infected contained in the two last classes, were so considerable, that one may affirm, without any exaggeration, that more than fifteen or twenty thousand persons were found in these sorts of cases; and if the distemper had not often taken this turn, there would not have been left in this city the fourth part of its inhabitants.

We may very well admit a sixth class of such as we have seen perish without any forerunner, or other manifest hurt, than only a decay in strength; and who being asked concerning their condition, answered, that they were not sensible of any disorder, which for the most part denoted a desperate case, and an approaching death; but the number of these were very small in comparison of such as made up the preceding classes.

Besides all these observations, it has happened that amongst so great a number of infected persons, we have seen many particular cases, wherein, contrary to our expectation, and all the appearance of reason, the sick have perished or recovered; but we are of opinion that it would be useless to relate them here, and to give of them a long and tedious account; being moreover persuaded that these sorts of particular events can serve as no sure rule to form a prognostic, or how to proceed in the like distemper. It is therefore more proper to keep to the observations we have made, and that the rather, since they are found conformable to those of our colleagues who have labored in concert with us in this so painful and dangerous work; and who have always professed to relate what they have seen and observed themselves, without suffering themselves to be prejudiced by all the reports that a vain credulity, a popular superstition, the boastings of empericks, and the greediness of making profit by the public calamity, have spread through this city.

To conclude, the medicines we have made use of are such, whose efficacy and manner of operation, are generally acknowledged by a long experience, to be adapted to satisfy all the indications reported above; having moreover not neglected certain pretended specifics, such as the solar powder, the mineral Kernes, elixirs, and other alexiterial preparations, as have been communicated to us by charitable and well-disposed persons; but experience itself has convinced us, that all these particular remedies are at the most useful only to remove some certain accidents, when at the same time they are often noxious in a great many others, and by consequence incapable to cure a disease characterized by a number of different essential symptoms.

3.7 Dietary considerations in preventing plague

Medicina Flagellata (1721)[100]

Introduction: Drawing from classical and medieval scientific knowledge and medical experiences, early modern people understood that a variety of environmental conditions affected the susceptibility to and contraction of disease. They saw diet and hygiene as central to good health, but also to the protection from and treatment of diseases. Specific foods, herbs, and spices were seen as promoting good health or as remedies—other foods were deemed harmful. Cleanliness was also seen as a necessary component of good health. The quality of air was also related to disease, and smell was, therefore, considered an important element in the transmission of disease and, correspondingly, certain aromas were used as preservatives or treatments of disease. This anonymous treatise from the early eighteenth century reviews a number of preventive measures that address these various issues.

Text

And it is here worthy of our first remark, that the last plague, in the Year 1665, as well from the late accounts we have of that at Marseilles, the poorer sort of people were those that mostly suffered, which can only be attributed to their mean and low fare, whereas the most nutritive and generous diet should be promoted, and such as generate a warm and rich blood, plenty of spirits, and what easily perspires, which otherwise would be apt to ferment and generate corruption.

Your greatest care is, to have your meat sweet and good, neither too moist nor flashy, having a certain regard to such as may create an easy digestion, and observing that roasted meats on those occasions should be preferred; as beef, mutton, lamb, venison, turkey, capon, pullet, chicken, pheasant, and partridge: But pigeon, and most sort of wild and sea fowl to be rejected: salted meats to be cautiously used; all hot, dry, and spicy seasonings to be avoided; most pickles and rich sauces to be encouraged, with the often use of garlic, onion, and shallot; the cool, acid, and acrid herbs and roots, as lettuce, spinach, cresses, sorrel, endive, and celery; all windy things, which are subject to putrefaction, to be refrained, as all kind of pulse, cabbage, cauliflower, sprouts, melons, cucumbers, etc., as also most summer fruits, excepting mulberries, quinces, pomegranates, raspberries, cherries, currants, and strawberries, which are of service when moderately eaten of.

Sometimes more fetid substances agree better with some persons than the more grateful scents, of which the most useful compositions may be made of rue, featherfew, *galbanum, assafetida,* and the like, with the oil of wormwood, the spirit or oil drawn and dropped upon cotton, so kept in a close ivory box, though with caution to be used, the often smelling to, dilating the pores of the olfactory organs, which may give greater liberty for the pestilential air to go along with it. A piece of orris root kept in the mouth in passing along the streets, or of garlic, orange or lemon peel, or clove, are of very great service. As also lozenges of the following composition, which are always profitable to be used fasting; of citron peel two drams, zedoary, angelica, of each, prepared in rose vinegar, half a dram, citron seeds, wood of aloes, orris, of each two scruples, saffron, cloves, nutmeg, one scruple, myrrh, ambergrease, of each six grains, sugarcandy one ounce; make into lozenges with gum traganth and rose-water.

I know not indeed a greater neglect than not keeping the body clean, and the keeping at a distance anything superfluous and offensive, to keep the house airy and fresh, and moderately cool, and to strew it with herbs, rushes, and boughs, which yield refreshing scents, and contribute much to the purifying of the air, and resisting the infection; of this kind all sorts of rushes and water flags, mint, balm, chamomile grass, hyssop, thyme, pennyroyal, rue, wormwood, southernwood, tansy, costmary, lime-tree, oak, beech, walnut, poplar, ash, willow, etc. A frequent change of clothes, and a careful drying or airing them abroad, with whisking and cleaning of them from all manner of filth and dust, which may harbor infection, as it is likewise to keep the windows open at sun-rise till the setting, especially to the north and east, for the cold blasts from those quarters temper the malignity of pestilential airs.

Preservative fumigations are largely talked of by all on those occasions, and they with good reason deserve to be practiced. And of the great number of aromatic roots and woods, I should chiefly prefer storax, benjamin, frankinsense, myrrh, and amber, the wood of juniper, cypress and cedar, the leaves of bays and rosemary, and the smell of tar and pitch is no ways inferior to any of the rest, where its scent is not particularly offensive, observing the burning of any or more of those ingredients at such proper distances of time from each other, that the air may always be sensibly impregnated therewith.

Amongst the Simples of the vegetable kind, *virginian* snake-root cannot be too much admired, and is deservedly accounted the most diaphoretic and alexipharmic for expelling the pestilential poison; its dose, finely powdered, is from four or six grains to two scruples, in a proper vehicle; due regard being had to the strength and age of the patient.

The next is generally given to the contrayerva root, (from which also a compound medicine is admirably contrived, and made famous by its success in the last plague;) the dose of this in fine powder is from one scruple to a dram, in angelica or scordium water, or in Wine, etc.

There are other roots likewise of which many valuable compounds are formed in order to effect that with an united force which they could not do singly; in this class are the roots of angelica, scorzonera, butterbur, masterwort, tormentil, zedoary, garlic, elicampane, valerian, birthwort, gentian, bitany, and many others, which may be found in other Writings.

Ginger, whether in the root, powdered, and candied deserve our regard; for it is very powerful both to raise a breathing sweat and defend the spirits against the pestilential impression.

From these roots may be made extracts, either with spirit of wine or vinegar, for it is agreed by all, that the most subtle particles collected together, and divested of their grosser and unprofitable parts, become more efficacious in medicinal cases.

The leaves of vegetables most used in practice are scordiam, rue, sage, veronica, the lesser cataury, scabious, pimpinel, marygolds, and baum, from which, on occasion, several *Formuae* are contrived.

3.8 Protective clothing

Author: Jean-Jacques Manget (1652–1742)

Title: *Treatise on the Plague* (Geneva, 1721)[101]

Introduction: In attending to the plague-stricken sick, people (whether medical practitioners, servants, or family) had to take significant precautions to keep from becoming infected themselves. As the contagions of the plague were thought to enter through the nose and mouth through infected air, a special head covering, mask, and other protective clothing were developed as means of protection. This image comes from the early eighteenth century, from a book compiled by the Genevan doctor Johann Jacob Manget, Dean of the University of Valence medical faculty and personal physician to Frederick III, Elector of Brandenburg. Many early modern discussions of treating the plague addressed the challenges of interacting with patients and the measures that could be taken to avoid the disease. While measures could be taken to limit susceptibility to plague, doctors and others who came into contact with infected people could themselves contract the disease, leading to concerns about caring for the sick and dying as well as tending to the bodies of those who died.

Habit des Medecins, et autres personnes
qui visitent les Pestiferes, Il est de
marroquin de leuant, le masque a les yeux
de cristal, et un long nez rempli de parfums

Figure 3.8 Protective clothing.
Credit: Herzog August Bibliothek Wolfenbüttel: M: Mi 139, Frontispiz

3.9 Cattle plague

Author: Richard Bradley, F. R. S. (1688–1732)

Title: *The Plague at Marseilles Considered* (1721)[102]

Introduction: See 1.6. Plague not only affected people. Animals suffered during various plague and other disease outbreaks and the infection and death of animals, especially cattle, could have dramatic impact on both the animal and surrounding human populations.[103] Early moderns struggled to understand how disease was contracted and progressed in animals and how to treat sick animals. In many respects the medical approach they took mirrored that utilized in the treatment of humans, even as it had some specific aspects that took into account the physical nature of animals. For example, many of the same kinds of environmental conditions were seen as bringing on disease in animals and some of the same herbal treatments were recommended as for people. At the same time, doctors understood that different conditions, from food to insects, had an impact on animals.

Text

The Method of Cure for the Cattle

As soon as ever there was any suspicion of the contagion upon any one of the herd, the tongue of that beast was carefully examined, and in case they found any aptha or blisters whether white, yellow, or black, then they were obliged to rub, and scratch the tongue with a silver instrument (being about the breadth and thickness of a six-pence, but indented on the sides, and having a hole in the middle whereby it is fastened to a stick, or handle,) til it bleed, then they must wipe away the blood with new unwashed linen. This done, a lotion for the tongue is used, made of salt and good vinegar.

The antidote for the diseased cattle is thus described.

Take of soot, gun-powder, brimstone, salt, equal parts, and as much water as is necessary to wash it down, give a large spoonful for a dose.

The following Account we have from Dr. Bernard Ramazzini, concerning the contagion among the black cattle about Padua, translated from *Acta Erudit.*

In the Year 1712 a dreadful and violent contagion seized the black cattle, which, like an increasing fire, could neither be extinguished nor stopped by any human means.

This first was observed in *Agro Vincentino*, and discovered itself more openly in the Country, spreading every way, even to the very suburbs of Padua, with a cruel destruction of the cows and oxen. It was also in Germany, in many places; and is not yet wholly conquered.

Of this distemper, Dr. Ramazzini [referring to the Italian doctor, Bernardino Ramazzini (1633–1714)] made a particular dissertation; in which he inquired into the causes of the distemper, and what remedies might be used, to put a stop to its violent course.

It is evident, that this distemper in cows and oxen was a true fever, from the coldness of the cattle at first, which was soon succeeded by a violent burning, with a quick pulse. That this fever was pestilential, its concomitant symptoms plainly show, as difficulty of breathing, a drossiness at the beginning; a continued flux of a nauseous matter from the nose and mouth, fetid dung, sometimes with blood, pustules breaking out over the whole body on the fifth or sixth day, like the Small-Pox; they generally dyed about the fifth or seventh day.

The author tells us, that out of a great drove, such as the merchants bring yearly into Italy out of Dalmatia and the bordering countries, one beast happened to straggle from the rest, and be left behind; which a cowherd brought to a farm belonging to the Count Borromeo: This beast infected all the cows and oxen of the place where he was taken in, with the same distemper he labored under; the beast itself dying in a few days, as did all the rest, except one only, who had a rowel put into his neck.

'Tis no strange thing therefore, if from the effluvia, proceeding from the sick and dead cattle, and from the cow-houses and pastures where they were fed, and perhaps from the cloth of the cowherds themselves, this infection falling upon a proper subject, should diffuse itself so largely. When therefore this subtle venomous exhalation happens to meet with any of the cow-kind, joining itself with the serous juices and animal spirits, 'tis no wonder it should disorder the natural consistence of the blood, and corrupt the ferments of the viscera; whence it follows, that the natural functions of the viscera are vitiated, and the requisite secretions stopped. For Dr. Ramazzini not only supposes, but asserts, that a poison of this kind, rather fixes and coagulates, than dissolves the blood: For beside the aforementioned symptoms accompanying the disease, the eye itself is a witness; since the dead carcasses being opened while they are yet hot, little or no blood runs out; those animals having naturally a thick blood, especially when the fever has continued so many days. And he adds, that whether this plague came first from the foreign beast, or any other way, it only had its effect upon some animal, in which there was the morbid seminary or ground prepared for it.

In the dead bodies of all the cattle, it was particularly observed, that in the omasus, or paunch, there was found a hard compact body, firmly adhering to the coats of the ventricle, of a large bulk, and an intolerable smell: In other parts, as in the brain, lungs, etc., were several hydatides, and large bladders filled only with wind, which being opened, gave a disagreeable stink: there were also ulcers at the root of the tongue; and bladders filled with a serum on the sides of it. This hard and compact body, like chalk, in the omasus, the author takes to be the full Product of the contagious miasma. He adds a prognostic, believing that from so many attempts and experiments, and the method observed in the cure of this venom, at last a true and specific remedy will be found out to extirpate the poisonous malignity wholly: He also expects some mitigation of it, from the approaching winter and north winds. He does not think this contagion can affect human bodies, since even other species of ruminating animals symbolizing with the Cow-kind, are yet untouched by it; nor was the infection taken by the air, after the dead bodies had been carefully buried.

As for the cure of it: From the Chirurgical part, he commends bleeding burning on both sides the neck with a broad red-hot Iron, making holes in the ears with a round Iron, and putting the root Hellebore in the hole, a rowel or seton under the chin, in the dew-laps; he also orders the tongue and palate to be often washed and rubbed with vinegar and salt.

He recommends the use of *Alexipharmics*, and specific cordials; and three ounces of Jesuits bark, infused in ten or twelve pints of cordial water or small wine, to be given in four or five doses; which is to be done in the beginning of the fever, when the beast begins to be sick. Or else two drams of *sperma-Caeti* dissolved in warm wine. Again he prescribes *Antimonium Diaphoreticum*. Against worms breeding, an infusion of quicksilver, or petroleum and milk is to be given. And lastly, as to the food, he directs drinks made with barley or wheat flower or bread, like a *ptisane*, fresh sweet hay made in May and macerated in fair water. In the meantime the cattle must be kept in a warm place, and clothed, daily shaking fumigations in the cow-houses with juniper berries, galbanum, and the like. As to prevention, he enjoins care in cleaning the stalls, and scraping the crust off from the wall; Care also is to be taken of their food, the hay and straw not spoiled by rain in the making; and he judges their food ought to be but sparing: He likewise recommends currying, with a comb and brush; with setons under their Chin, made with a hot iron run through the part, and kept open with a rope put through it.

After which we have the receipt: Or the ingredients of a medicine for the speedy cure of that mortal distemper amongst cows; sent over from Holland, where a like distemper raged among the black cattle.

...

Bleed the cow, and give her three or 4 mornings successively, an ounce of this powder, with a horn, in warm beer.

If the Cow continues distempered, after the omission 2 or 3 days, repeat the medicine for 3 or 4 days again.

I cannot help taking notice likewise of the raging distemper which was among the cows about London, Anno 1714. It was so violent and infectious, that if *one* had it, all others that came within scent of her, or even eat where she grazed, were surely infected; it seized their heads, and was attended with running at the nose, and a very nauseous breath, which killed them in three or four days. The herdsmen would not allow it to be the *Murrain*, nor could give any account from whence it did proceed, or could find out any remedy against it; they only tell us the unusual dry summer, and the continued *East*-winds, were the occasion of it. This distemper had been for two or three years before it came to us, in Lombardy, Holland, and Hambrough, to the loss almost of all their cattle. The states of Holland caused a medicine to be published for the good of those who had their cattle thus distempered; but having been tried here, 'twould not cure one in seven, but rather increased the Infection by keeping the distempered cattle longer alive (by some days) than they would have been without it. 'Tis remarkable, that no oxen had this distemper, but only milch-cows, which were more tender than the *males*. The herdsmen to keep their cattle from the infection, let them blood in the tail, and rubbed their noses and chaps with *tar*; and when any happened to die of it, they were burnt, and buried deep under ground. It began at Islington, spreading itself over many places in Middlesex and in Essex, but did not reach so far westward from London as twenty miles.

The most general opinion concerning the cause of this distemper, was, that the cattle were first infected by drinking some unwholesome standing water, where 'tis probable some poisonous insects were lodged and bred; the summer having been extremely dry, attended almost constantly with easterly winds, the grass almost burnt up, and the herbs of the gardens destroyed by insects; but such as they were, (unfit for table use) were given to the cattle. There was likewise so great want of water, that many were forced to drive their cows five or six miles to it.

The electuary published upon this occasion by the states of Holland, was composed of most, if not all the drugs used in the most serviceable medicines that were made use of against the plague among men; most of which ingredients we know to be mortal to insects, as strong scented roots and herbs; but above all, aromatic gums and saps of plants; as rhue, garlic, pitch, tar, frankincense and olibanum. These ingredients are much used in France and Italy to prevent or destroy Infection, by burning them and smoking such bodies, letters, or any other things as are brought from infected places, after they have made quarantine, and are not suffered to come on shore 'till they have undergone this operation.

It is not against experience, that insects can live and increase in animal bodies: How often do we find men, women and children troubled with worms? What varieties of those insects are often voided by them? And how should that be, if they were not either sucked into the stomach with the breath, or taken into it with some unwholesome food? For they cannot breed in such bodies from nothing, without either their eggs or themselves are brought thither by some Accident: For if they were the natural Produce of Animal Bodies, they would then be alike common to all, which we know they are not.

I have been informed, that in the Year 1714, when this mortality among the cows was at its height, that towards the end of the summer, some farmers brought in fresh cattle, and turning them into the same fields, where many cows had died before, they took the infection and died likewise; but the following spring those fields were void of infection, and the cows that were put into them did very well, but what were then put into the cow-houses, where the sick cows had been the year before, were seized with the distemper, and died; which seems to inform us, that it was the effect of insects, which thro' the warmth of those stalls were preserved from the severity of the winter's frost; but such as were left in the open fields were destroyed by the cold. I have heard that a woman about Camberwell cured six in seven of her cows, by giving them once a week an Infusion of rhue and ale-wort.

3.10 Comparing diseases and treatment

Author: Richard Mead (1673–1754)

Title: *A Discourse on the Plague* (1744)[104]

Introduction: Richard Mead, who studied at prominent institutions of higher learning in Utrecht, Leiden, and Padua, returned to London and in 1703 was admitted to the Royal Society and was a physician at St Thomas' Hospital. He attended to the royal family and was involved with the creation of the Foundling Hospital, a home for abandoned children. In this passage he compares and contrasts plague and Small Pox, which he asserts are both contagious diseases originating in Africa. He notes the similarities in types and manifestations, as well as treatment and remedies for each. Mead points to the reality that while early modern people had a good deal of experience with certain diseases, and at times showed a remarkable understanding of the symptoms and possible treatments for them, they also often placed different diseases within the same general framework, and regularly approached them in similar ways despite the often real inherent differences between them. This explains, in part, why some early moderns could be quite precise in how they described disease, while others utilized rather general blanket terms and observations in their discussion of disease.

Text

CHAPTER III

OF THE CURE OF THE PLAGUE

It appears, from what has been said in the beginning of this discourse, that the plague and the Small-Pox are diseases, which bear a great similitude to each other: both being contagious fevers from Africa, and both attended with certain eruptions. And as the eruptions or pustules in the Small-Pox are of two kinds, which has caused the distemper to be divided into two species, the distinct and confluent; so we have shewn two sorts of eruptions or tumors likewise to attend the plague. In the first and mildest Kind of the Small-Pox the pustules rise high above the surface of the skin, and contain a digested pus; but in the other, the pustules lie flat, and are filled with an indigested sanies. The two kinds of critical tumors in the plague are yet more different. In the most favorable case the morbific matter is thrown upon some of the softest glands near the surface of the body, as upon the inguinal, axillary, parotid, or maxillary glands: the first appearance of which is a small induration, great heat, redness, and sharp pain near those glands. These tumors, if the patient recover, like the pustules of the distinct Small-Pox, come to a just suppuration, and thereby discharge the disease. In worse cases of the distemper, either instead of these tumors, or together with them, carbuncles are raised. The first appearance of them is a very small indurated tumor, not situate near any of the fore-mentioned glands, with a dusky redness, violent heat, vast pain, and a blackish spot in the middle of the tumor. This spot is the beginning of a gangrene, which spreads itself more and more as the tumor increases.

But, besides the agreement in these critical discharges, the two distempers have yet a more manifest likeness in those livid and black spots, which are frequent in the plague, and the signs of speedy death: for the same are sometimes found to attend the Small-Pox with as fatal a consequence; nay, I have seen cases, when almost every pustule has taken this appearance. Moreover, in both diseases, when eminently malignant, blood is sometimes voided by the mouth, by urine, or the like. And we may farther add, that in both death is usually caused by mortifications in the viscera. This has constantly been found in the plague by the physicians in France: and I am convinced, from accounts I have by me, of the dissection of a great many, who had died of the Small-Pox, that it is the same in that distemper.

This analogy between the two diseases, not only shows us, that we cannot expect to cure the plague any more than the Small-Pox, by antidotes and specific medicines; but will likewise direct us in the cure of the distemper, with which we are less acquainted, by the methods found useful in the other disease, which is more familiar to us.

In short, as in the Small-Pox, the chief part of the management consists in clearing the *primae viae* in the beginning; in regulating the fever; and in promoting the natural discharges: so in the *plague* the same Indications will have place. The great difference lies in this, that in the *plague* the fever is often much more acute than in the other distemper; the stomach and bowels are sometimes inflamed; and the eruptions require external applications, which to the pustules of the Small-Pox are not necessary.

When the fever is very acute, a cool regimen, commonly so beneficial in the Small-Pox, is here still more necessary. But whenever the pulse is languid, and the heat not excessive, moderate cordials must be used.

The disposition of the stomach and bowels to be inflamed, makes vomiting not so generally safe in the plague as in the Small-Pox. The most gentle emetics ought to be used, none better than *Ipecacuanha*; and great caution must be had, that the stomach or bowels are not inflamed, when they are administered: for if they are, nothing but certain death can be expected from them: otherwise at the beginning they will be always useful. Therefore upon the first Illness of the patient it must carefully be considered, whether there appear any symptoms of an inflammation having seized these parts: if there are any marks of this, all vomits must be omitted; if not, the stomach ought to be gently moved.

The eruptions, whether glandular tumors, or carbuncles, must not be left to the course of nature, as is done in the Small-Pox; but all diligence must be used, by external applications, to bring them to suppurate. Both these tumors are to be treated in most respects alike. As soon as either of them appears, fix a cupping-glass to it without scarifying; and when that is removed, apply a suppurative cataplasm, or plaster of warm gums.

If the tumors do not come to suppuration, which the carbuncle seldom or never does; but if a thin ichor or matter exudes through the pores; or if the tumor feel soft to the touch; or lastly, if it has a black crust upon it, then it must be opened by incision, either according to the length of the tumor, or by a crucial section. And if there is any part mortified, as is usually in the carbuncle, it must be scarified. This being done, it will be necessary to stop the bleeding, and dry up the moisture with an actual cautery, dressing the wound afterwards ...

The next day the wound ought to be well bathed with a fomentation made of warm aromatic plants with spirit of wine in it; in order, if possible, to make the wound digest, by which the sloughs will separate. After this the ulcer may be treated as one from an ordinary abscess.

Farther, in the glandular tumors, when they suppurate, we ought not to wait, till the matter has made its way to the outer skin, but to open it as soon as it is risen to any bigness: because these tumors begin deep in the gland, and often mortify, before the suppuration has reached the skin, as the physicians in France have found upon dissecting many dead bodies.

This is the method in which the plague must be treated in following the natural course of the distemper. But the patient in most cases runs so great hazard in this way, notwithstanding the utmost care, that it would be of the greatest service to mankind under this calamity, if some artificial discharge for the corrupted humors could be found out, not liable to so great hazard, as the natural way. To this purpose large bleeding and profuse sweating are recommended to us upon some experience.

Dr. Sydenham tried both these evacuations with good success, and has made two very judicious remarks upon them. The first is, that they ought not to be attempted unless in the beginning of the sickness, before the natural course of the distemper has long taken place: because otherwise we can only expect to put all into confusion without any advantage. His other observation is, that we cannot expect any prosperous event from either of these evacuations, unless they are very copious: there being no prospect of surmounting so violent a malignity without bolder methods than must be taken in ordinary cases.

As for bleeding, by some accounts from France, I have been informed, that some of the physicians there have carried this practice so far, as upon the first day of the distemper to begin with bleeding about twelve ounces, and then to take away four or five ounces every two hours after. They pretend to extraordinary success from this method, with the assistance only of cooling *ptisanes*, and such like drinks, which they give plentifully at the same time. Such profuse bleeding as this may perhaps not suit with our constitutions so well as with theirs; for in common cases they use this practice much more freely than we: Yet we must draw blood with a more liberal hand than in any other case, if we expect success from it. I shall excuse myself from defining exactly how large a quantity of blood is requisite to be drawn, for want of particular experience: but I think fit to give this admonition, that, in so desperate a case as this, it is more prudent to run some hazard of exceeding, than to let the patient perish for want of due evacuation.

As for sweating, which is the other method proposed, it ought, no doubt, to be continued without intermission full twenty-four hours, as Dr. Sydenham advises. He is so particular in his directions about it, that I need say little. I shall only add, that theriaca, and the like solid medicines, being offensive to the stomach, are not the most proper sudorifics. I should rather commend an Infusion in boiling water of Virginia snake-root, or, in want of this, of some other warm aromatic, with the addition of about a fourth part of *aqua theriacalis*, and a proper quantity of syrup of lemons to sweeten it. From which, in illnesses of the same kind with the goal fever, which approaches the nearest to the pestilence, I have seen very good Effects.

Whether either of these methods, of bleeding, or of sweating, will answer the purpose intended by them, must be left to a larger experience to determine; and the trial ought by no means to be neglected, especially in those cases, which promise but little success from the natural course of the disease.

Notes

1 See Joël Coste, *Représentations et comportements en temps d'épidémie dans la littérature imprimée de peste (1490–1725)* (Paris, 2007).
2 Ibid., 81–2.
3 Ibid., Table 5, 83.
4 See also Edward Eckert, *The Structures of Plagues and Pestilence in Early Modern Europe: Central Europe, 1560–1640* (Basel, 1996), 24.
5 David Herlihy, *The Black Death and the Transformation of the West*, ed. Samuel K. Cohn, Jr (Cambridge, MA, 1997), 72. See Vivian Nutton, "The Reception of Fracastoro's Theory of Contagion: The Seed That Fell among Thorns?" *Osiris* 6 (1990), 2nd series: 196–234.
6 John Aberth, *Plagues in World History* (Lanham, 2011), 38.
7 Mary Lindemann, *Medicine and Society in Early Modern Europe*, 2nd ed. (Cambridge, 2010), 51–3.
8 Michael Dols, *The Black Death in the Middle East* (Princeton, 1977), 107.
9 Sandra Cavallo and Tessa Storey, *Healthy Living in Late Renaissance Italy* (Oxford, 2013), 77.
10 Ibid., 77.
11 Ibid., 103.
12 Ibid., 105.
13 Nükhet Varlik, *Disease and Empire: A History of Plague Epidemics in the Early Modern Ottoman Empire (1453–1600)* (Doctoral Dissertation, University of Chicago, 2008).
14 Nutton, "The Reception of Fracastoro's Theory of Contagion," 198.
15 Ibid., 198.
16 Ibid., 200.
17 Ibid., 201.
18 Ibid., 200.
19 Ibid., 201.
20 Ibid., 232.
21 Samuel K. Cohn, Jr, *Cultures of Plague: Medical Thought at the End of the Renaissance* (Oxford, 2009), 4.
22 Ibid., 5.
23 Ibid.
24 Ibid., 6–7.
25 Ibid., 24.
26 Ibid., 6, 15.

27 Samuel K. Cohn, Jr, *The Black Death Transformed: Disease and Culture in Early Renaissance Europe* (London and New York, 2002), 10.

28 Ibid., 10–11; Lester K. Little, "Plague Historians in Lab Coats," *Past and Present* 213 (November 2011): 267–90, here at 287.

29 Guy Attewell, "Islamic Medicines: Perspectives on the Greek Legacy in the History of Islamic Medical Traditions in West Asia," in *Medicine across Cultures: History and Practice of Medicine in Non-Western Cultures,* ed. Helaine Selin (London, 2003), 325–50, here at 326; Dols, *The Black Death,* 85–7.

30 See Dols, *The Black Death,* 99, for ninth-century Islamic suggestions of sucking acrid pomegranates and plums and consuming lentils, Indian peas and pumpkin seeds to guard against plague; later doctors noted the value of certain breads and meats, especially when the latter were cooked with lemon, grape leaves, and served with vinegar. Corn and heavy foods were to be avoided. Ibid., 101.

31 John Aberth, *The Black Death: The Great Mortality of 1348–1350: A Brief History with Documents* (Boston, 2005), 47–50. Trans. from German in Karl Sudhoff, "Pestschriften aus den ersten 150 Jahren nach der Epidemie des 'schwarzen Todes' 1348," *Archiv für Geschichte der Medizin* 5 (1911): 84–6.

32 Ibid.

33 Mark Harrison, *Disease and the Modern World: 1500 to the Present Day* (Cambridge, 2004), 39ff; Herlihy, *The Black Death,* 71.

34 In Dols, *The Black Death,* 88–9.

35 Ibid., 89.

36 Aberth, *The Black Death: The Great Mortality of 1348–1350,* 55–63 (citations here from 55–60). Trans. from German in Tah Dinanah, "Die Schrift von Abi G'far Ahmed ibn 'Ali ibn Mohammed ibn 'Ali ibn Hatimah aus Almeriah über die Pest," *Archiv für Geschichte der Medizin* 19 (1927): 49–87.

37 Mark Harrison, *Climates and Constitutions: Health, Race, Environment and British Imperialism in India 1600–1850* (Oxford, 1999), 35.

38 Deepak Kumar, ed., *Disease and Medicine in India: An Historical Overview* (New Delhi, 2001), xv.

39 Ananda S. Chopra, "Ayurveda," in *Medicine across Cultures,* ed. Selin, 75–83, here at 75; see also Michael Pearson, "Medical Connections and Exchanges in the Early Modern World," *PORTAL Journal of Multidisciplinary International Studies* 8:2 (July 2011): 1–15, here 3–4.

40 Chopra, "Ayurveda," 75.

41 Ibid., 77; Kenneth G. Zysk, *Medicine in the Veda: Religious Healing in the Veda* (Philadelphia, 1996), 85.

42 Zysk, *Medicine in the Veda,* 86.

43 Ibid., 81.

44 Ibid., 87–8; see also, Pearson, "Medical Connections and Exchanges in the Early Modern World," 4, 5.

45 Caraka Vi.3.7–8 (see http://en.wikipedia.org/wiki/Charaka_Samhita; http://www.britannica.com/EBchecked/topic/94520/Charaka-samhita).

46 Alan Mikhail, *Nature and Empire in Ottoman Egypt: An Environmental History* (Cambridge, 2011), 220.

47 Aberth, *Plagues in World History,* 5–6; Cai Jingfeng and Zhen Yan, "Medicine in Ancient China," in *Medicine across Cultures,* ed. Selin, 49–73, here at 56.

48 Jingfend and Yan, "Medicine in Ancient China," 56.

49 Shigehisa Kuriyama, "Epidemics, Weather, and Contagion on Traditional Chinese Medicine," in *Contagion: Perspectives from Pre-Modern Societies,* ed. Lawrence I. Conrad and Dominik Wujastyk (Aldershot, 2000), 1–22, here at 8.

50 Jingfend and Yan, "Medicine in Ancient China."

51 Ibid., 55.

52 Frédéric Obringer, "Wu Youxing and Pestilential Epidemics: A Medical Expert in Late Ming China," *Revue de synthèse/Centre international de synthèse* 131:3 (2010): 343–72, here at 343, 345, 348.

53 Ibid., 351.

54 Kuriyama, "Epidemics, Weather, and Contagion on Traditional Chinese Medicine," 2.

55 Aberth, *Plagues in World History*, 81.

56 Carlos Viesca, "Medicine in Ancient Mesoamerica," in *Medicine across Cultures*, ed. Selin, 259–83, here at 270.

57 Ibid., 273–5.

58 John M. Janzen and Edward C. Green, "Continuity, Change, and Challenge in African Medicine," in *Medicine across Cultures*, ed. Selin, 1–26, here at 1.

59 Ibid., 9, 12.

60 Ibid., 15.

61 Ibid., 14.

62 M. Jacobum Hornstein, *Sterbens Flucht; Das ist Christlicher vnd Catholischer Bericht/ von Sterbenslauff der Pest* (Ingolstadt, 1593), 7.

63 "ein fauler/vergiffter Lufft/und die bose humores oder schadliche Feuchtigkeit dess menschen Leibs," Hornstein, *Sterbens Flucht*, 8.

64 Hornstein, *Sterbens Flucht*, 11.

65 Ibid., 12–13.

66 Ibid., 14.

67 Ibid., 18.

68 Ibid., 21.

69 Ibid., 22.

70 David Chambers and Brian Pullan, eds, *Venice: A Documentary History, 1450–1630* (Toronto, 2001), 114.

71 Ibid., 415.

72 Alec Ryrie, *Being Protestant in Reformation Britain* (Oxford, 2013), 128.

73 Nimrod Zinger, " 'Our Hearts and Spirits Were Broken': The Medical World from the Perspective of German-Jewish Patients in the Seventeenth and Eighteenth Centuries," *Leo Baeck Institute Yearbook* 54:1 (2009): 59–91, here at 62, 69, 90, 66; for a discussion of Jewish uses of Christian saints in the Middle Ages, see Ephraim Shoham-Steiner, "Jews and Healing at Medieval Saints' Shrines: Participation, Polemics, and Shared Cultures," *Harvard Theological Review* 103:1 (2010): 111–29.

74 Varlik, *Disease and Empire*, 179.

75 See Russell Hopley, "Contagion in Islamic Lands: Responses from Medieval Andalusia and North Africa," *Journal for Early Modern Cultural Studies* 10:2 (Fall/Winter 2010): 45–64, at 56–8.

76 Birsen Bulmuş, *Plague, Quarantines, and Geopolitics in the Ottoman Empire* (Abingdon, 2012), 3.

77 Ibid.

78 Coste, *Représentations et comportements*, 84.

79 Ibid.

80 Ibid.

81 Aberth, *The Black Death: The Great Mortality of 1348–1350*, 7–50. Trans. from German in Karl Sudhoff, "Pestschriften aus den ersten 150 Jahren nach der Epidemie des 'schwarzen Todes' 1348," 84–6.

82 Harold J. Cook, *Matters of Exchange: Commerce, Medicine, and Science in the Dutch Golden Age* (New Haven, 2007), 191.

83 Heath W. Lowry, "Pushing the Stone Uphill: The Impact of Bubonic Plague on Ottoman Urban Society in the Fifteenth and Sixteenth Centuries," *Osmanli Araştırmaları* 23 (2003): 93–132, here at 104.

84 Dols, *The Black Death*, 103, 107.

85 Lindemann, *Medicine and Society*, 62.

86 See Eckert, *The Structures of Plagues and Pestilence in Early Modern Europe*, 22.

87 František Graus, *Pest, Geissler, Judenmorde: Das 14. Jahrhundert als Krisenzeit* (Göttingen, 1987); see also Lindemann, *Medicine and Society*, 60.

88 Lindemann, *Medicine and Society*, 60.

89 Eckert, *The Structures of Plagues and Pestilence in Early Modern Europe*, 22–3.

90 See Varlik, *Disease and Empire*, 181.

91 Harrison, *Climates and Constitutions*, 153.

92 Aberth, *Plagues in World History*, 20, citing McNeill.

93 See Gianna Pomata, "Observation Rising: Birth of an Epistemic Genre, 1500–1650," in *Histories of Scientific Observation*, ed. Lorraine Daston and Elizabeth Lunebeck (Chicago, 2011), 45–80.

94 www.artres.com/C.aspx?VP3=ViewBox_VPage&VBID=2UN365CFKDZSU&IT =ZoomImageTemplate01_VForm&IID=2F3C2SDP4IQ&PN=445&CT=Search &SF=0.

95 Hieronymi Fracastorii, *De contagione et contagiosis morbis et eorum curatione, Libri III*. Trans. Wilmer Cave Wright (New York, 1930), 7, 9, 13, 15, 17, 19 in the English. The Latin text is provided on 6, 8, 12, 14, 16, 18.

96 Coste, *Représentations et comportements*, 720–1.

97 From the French translations provided in Obringer, "Wu Youxing et les Épidémies pestilentielles," here 353, 354, 355, 356, 357 (coming from 7–9 of the introduction of *Wenyilun*).

98 www.artres.com/C.aspx?VP3=ViewBox_VPage&VBID=2UN365CFKDZSU&I T=ZoomImageTemplate01_VForm&IID=2UN39YYHAVJ&PN=9&CT=Search &SF=0.

99 *A Succinct Account of the Plague at Marseilles, its Symptoms, and the Methods and Medicines used for Curing it. Drawn up and presented to the Governor and Magistrates of Marseilles, by M. Chicoyneau, Verney and Soullier, the Physicians who were sent thither from Paris by the Duke Regent of France, to prescribe to the Sick in the Hospitals, and other Parts of that Town, during the Progress of that Calamity. Translated from the French by a Physician* (London, 1721), 6–18.

100 The language has been standardized and updated. *Medicina Flagellata*: OR, THE Doctor Scarify'd. Laying open the Vices of the Faculty, the Insignificancy of a great Part of their *Materia Medica*; with certain Rules to discern the true Physician from the Emperick, and the Useful Medicine from the Noxious and Trading Physick. WITH An ESSAY on HEALTH, Or the Power of a Regimen. To which is added, A Discovery of some Remarkable Errors in the late Writings on the PLAGUE, by Dr. *Mead, Quincey, Bradley*, &c. With some useful and necessary Rules to be observed in the Time of that Contagious Distemper (London, 1721), 215–24.

101 www.hab.de/ausstellungen/seuchen/expo-24.htm. 24 (Kat. Nr. 55).

102 THE PLAGUE AT *MARSEILLES* CONSIDER'D: With Remarks upon the Plague in General, shewing its Cause and Nature of Infection, with necessary Precautions to prevent the spreading of that Direful Distemper. Publish'd for the Preservation of the People of Great-Britain. Also some Observations taken from an Original Manuscript of a Graduate Physician, who resided in London during the whole Time of the late Plague, *Anno* 1665. By Richard Bradley, F. R. S. The Third Edition. *LONDON*: Printed for W. Mears at the *Lamb* without *Temple-Bar* (1721), 21–40.

103 For a recent discussion of the plagues affecting cattle in the Ottoman Empire, see Sam White, "A Model Disaster: From the Great Ottoman Panzootic to the Cattle Plagues of Early Modern Europe," in *Plague and Contagion in the Islamic Mediterranean*, ed. Nükhet Varlik (Kalamazoo, 2017), 91–116.

104 *Medicina Flagellata*, 151–64.

4 Political and policy responses to plague

Early modern people were able to distinguish short and long-term effects of the plague.[1] As a result, they differentiated immediate responses and more long-term prophylaxis. Increasingly, some late medieval and early modern governments formed health boards or commissions to respond to plague outbreaks in planned and cohesive ways. In 1486 Venice established a permanent Commission on Public Health [See 4.1], though there were earlier examples of governmental responses to plague already in the fourteenth century, as in the creation of the first recorded Health Office to implement plague controls in Dubrovnik in 1390.[2] Similarly, health boards were established in attempts both to prevent the plague and, when it did erupt, to limit its impact, treat the sick, and bury the dead.[3] Such boards could have rather broad powers, often hiring communal physicians and dictating access to the city and trade. [See 4.6] On June 21, 1630 the Padua Health Board, for example, ordered all Friars to remain in their convents.[4] Under the advice of health boards different policies and practices were established in many early modern cities. By the middle of the sixteenth century, for example, the city of London had standardized the recording of death and burials. [For a later period, see 4.7]

Governmental actions: quarantines, lazarettos, hospitals

Governmental measures included the organizing of processions—dipping into more "religious" responses—, prohibitions on traveling, the creation of quarantine areas, and regulations about the transport of particular goods (such as wool). Many governments also created or expanded the number and scope of hospitals and pharmacies, and often they hired hospital or communal physicians. Naturally, they initiated and implemented legislation related to cleaning of infected homes and the cleaning or burning of infected materials.[5]

Civic authorities took other plague-related measures as well, including the establishment of quarantine houses, or lazarettos, to separate the sick from the healthy population in hopes of stemming the spread of the disease.[6] [See 4.2, 4.3, 4.4, and 4.8] In Europe quarantine houses emerged first in Mediterranean lands in the fifteenth century, for example in Ragusa (today in Croatia) in 1465 and Venice in 1485,[7] and subsequently in many other early modern places, developing into one of the most widespread measures in Europe. In the German city of Bremen, to take only one example, two structures were allocated for a lazaretto in 1582. Lazarettos served many people during the great epidemic of 1630. In Bologna, one lazaretto housed over 500 people and a second some 400; at Florence there were more than 900 people placed in the lazaretto; in Verona over 4,000; and in Padua, by August 1631, some 2,000.[8] Conditions in such facilities could be quite bleak. [See 4.2 and 4.4] One doctor serving in the early modern Roman lazaretto admitted that he was:

> shocked and amazed that people in Rome [outside the lazarettos] could actually be laughing, much less playing music and singing, for if they stayed in [a lazaretto] for just one day, they would come out very different people, and would not feel like laughing any more. … All the babies sent there died; at times they were fed goat's milk with sugar to quiet them at night because they cried continuously, while the wailing of the women, who had lost loved ones, pierced one's heart with compassion.[9]

On the other hand, some contemporaries noted that the survival rates of these inmates might be higher than those who fled the plague and, in some cases, they were afforded larger daily food rations than might be expected by people outside the lazaretto.[10]

Governments, as noted above, at times organized hospitals to treat the sick.[11] [See 4.3] In Venice, a Senate decree of 18 July 1468 authorized the construction of a hospital on the Vigna Murata on the island of Sant' Erasmo as a kind of quarantine holding pen for those cured at an institution on the island of Santa Maria di Nazareth. Those who left Nazareth were to remain at the hospital for 40 days—a common period of time for quarantine (related to the Italian for 40, the number of days that people were often separated), based on the work of Hippocrates, as well as the Bible, and even principles of alchemy.[12] The construction of the hospital was to be funded by rental income from shops and quays owned by the government.[13]

Debates about the contagious nature of plague and the value of quarantine and specialized hospitals would continue into the eighteenth century. Richard Mead (1673–1754), who studied at prominent institutions of higher learning in Utrecht, Leiden, and Padua, returned to London and in 1703 was admitted to the Royal Society and was a physician at St Thomas' Hospital. He attended to the royal family and was involved with the creation of the Foundling Hospital, a home for abandoned children. In his *A Discourse on the Plague* (1744), he rued that,

> All this abundantly shows how inexcusable the foresaid physicians in France are, in their opposing the common opinion that the plague is contagious. … for if this opinion were a mistake, quarantines, and all the like means of defense, ought to be thrown aside as of no use. But as I continue persuaded, that we have the greatest evidence, that the plague is a contagious disease;

so I have left, without any alteration, all my directions in respect to quarantines.[14]

Magistrates and Councils of Health, like other civic officials, he noted, should be accountable to provide responsibly and humanly for the sick as well as those who might be exposed to plague. Criticizing the management of some hospitals, Mead observed that, "in many places the sick have chosen to lay themselves in fields, in the open air, under the slightest coverings, rather than to fall into the barbarous hands of those who have had the management of these hospitals."[15]

Quarantine was not necessarily limited to special facilities or to the segregation of humans. To keep people out of houses confirmed to have housed plague victims, infected houses were locked and bolted from the outside and in some cases guarded and marked with various signs, such as red crosses.[16] On May 18, 1631 alone, the Padua Board ordered 137 houses closed, with 771 people confined (5.6 average per house).[17] This and other works required a good deal of staff and administration. Accordingly, by July 1631, the Padua Health Board employed 110 people to serve the 100,000 inhabitants of the city.[18]

Still, quarantines were not always fully enforced. While the Seville Health Commission initiated travel bans and established quarantines, for example, its members also had to deal with complex realities rather than maintain blanket policies. As a result, as in other cities, they investigated a wide range of individual cases and reviewed numerous petitions for exclusion from quarantine from many different people, particularly those who depended on trade and travel for their livelihoods, or who were simply horrified by the prospects.[19] Forced quarantine was a terror filled proposition for many people, who sensed they were being consigned to death. According to one early modern Egyptian writer,

> Quarantine ... increased the people's anxiety and fear of the plague. Rumors spread that whoever was struck by the disease in a place discovered by the French, would be taken to a French quarantine, his family getting no news from him, unless he recuperates and returns home in good health. Otherwise his family will never see him again nor learn anything about him. For if he dies, the quarantine attendants seize him and bury him in a hole, and the clothes he is wearing.[20]

In this, as in other matters, state response to plague varied depending on context, understanding of the nature of plague, as well as competing social and political powers and interests.[21] As one historian has noted for early modern Seville,

> Officials in Seville, like many others across Europe, responded to epidemics with what seems to us a strange balance of fear and disregard. They imposed regulations, then allowed frequent exceptions; they banned travelers they feared might bring disease with them, then sent their own colleagues traveling to the very areas where disease was reported and allowed them to return

to the city unimpeded. They asked physicians and surgeons for professional advice and then, often as not, chose to act against that advice.[22]

Not just people, but various goods, including food and animals, could also be regulated and quarantined from time to time. The health board in Seville in 1582 established formal regulations that controlled the entry of both people and goods through the city gates, in addition to legislating other plague prevention measures, such as the cleaning of the streets and the purification of the air through the public burning of rosemary and thyme.[23] **[See 4.5 and 4.6 for discussion of these issues, as well as other forms of disinfection]** Upon medical advice, the outbreak of plague prompted the avoidance of textiles, which were seen as potential conveyers of infection.[24] As a result, cargo was often stranded onboard ships that were not permitted to dock in harbors, raising challenges for crews and financial loss for merchants. In Morocco in 1800, for example, British authorities noted that many articles in cargoes were susceptible to infection, pointing especially to goat skins, and would not allow them to be unloaded and stored on land. Crews and passengers from such ships were to be put onboard other ships and placed under quarantine for 14 days. The ships themselves were taken far out in the water and sunk. The British had followed such protocols already since the early eighteenth century.[25] Similarly, French forces ordered a quarantine for all infected individuals during the severe plague of 1791 in Egypt:

> An address to the people of Cairo, Būlāq, Old Cairo and vicinity. You shall obey, uphold and observe, without opposition, the orders. Anybody opposing them will encounter abundant vengeance, painful punishment, and severe retribution. They are precautions against the disease of plague. In the case of anybody whom you know certainly, or believe, imagine, or suspect to be suffering from this illness in any place, house, caravansary or building, it is your duty and obligation to establish a quarantine, and the place must be closed off. The elder of the quarter or street in which this occurs must immediately inform the French officer who is the district supervisor. He, in turn, will report it to the *shaykh al-balad*, the commandant of Cairo and its districts.[26]

Governmental authorities, however, did not always agree about the policy of quarantine—due in part to economic considerations, especially the loss of stock, revenues, and taxes.[27]

Beyond the contentious and challenging issue of quarantine, early modern governments developed a wide range of plague-related policies. Plague ordinances were developed and circulated in many cities and regions in the early modern period. They specified the practical measures taken by governments, such as campaigns to clean city streets, waterways, and even the air. [See 4.5] Often such ordinances provided for the appointment of officials for various work and they frequently included what we might consider more religious elements, such as establishing fast days, processions, and public prayers. The Austrian Plague Ordinance of 1534, for example, began in a rather spiritual vein:

> First, praise God the Almighty and conduct a procession of all burghers, mountain laborers, residents, and those house people, young and old, men and women, with prayers and discipline, as has been done previously when emergencies have occurred. And everyone should go with such procession or cloister, the men and the women separately, and diligently beg God the Almighty, all together with prayerful hearts, to forgive us for our sins and to stop His godly wrath.
>
> Each and every person, young and old, in the middle of the day, should kneel down and beg God the Almighty with prayer for mercy and the cessation of the punishment of this cruel plague; and everyone should say an 'Our Father,' an 'Ave Maria,' and a declaration of faith. Every householder should make certain that his people conduct themselves in this way as well, and neglect nothing; if they do not do it they should be punished by the authorities.[28]

The question of sanitation in civic ordinances

City ordinances treated the provision and price of foodstuffs, often with specific attention to the quality of animals prior to slaughter.[29] This was in many ways a quite logical step, given the concern with sanitation in much of the medical discussion about plague and the number of disease epidemics that struck cattle and other animals throughout the early modern period.[30] We know, by way of example, of cattle plagues in the south German cities of Ulm and Überlingen 11 times between 1583 and 1632.[31] This issue would impact other areas at different times. One local witness noted that the plague in Egypt in 1787 affected people and cattle, leading to a tremendous stench throughout the land due to the decaying cattle carcasses.[32] The plague had other tangible results as well, as food prices rose drastically.[33]

The city of Geneva represents a useful example of how governments responded to the plague. Genevan legislators issued a series of laws in the fifteenth century. Concerned with unsanitary conditions in the city that might lead to epidemics, in August 1409 the city developed controls on animals, markets, and refuse. Later that year, Jews were banned from selling meat, but allowed to trade in "whole animals"—a measure that was perhaps related to growing accusations of Jews spreading the plague.[34] In 1411, specific ordinances were issued regarding the inspections and disposal of meat. In 1428, city legislation revealed increased interest in food sanitation and the butchers' trade and growing concern to control the presence of animals and carcasses. In 1430, pigs were required to be kept in pens and fines were threatened for people who allowed pigs to roam the streets.[35] There were similar regulations for sheep and later attempts to regulate the fish trade. In the 1460s, a civic dumping ground was created close to the slaughterhouse. Responding to miasmic concerns, in 1410 decrees regarding the building and repair of city latrines and the prohibition of construction of "malodorous" edifices were passed.[36] Between the 1440s and the 1460s numerous ordinances were related to fountains and wells and a general concern for safe water sources.[37] Despite these various ordinances, the city's response to sanitation and hygiene remained primarily sporadic and reactive. There were, as of yet, no formal or permanent health boards in Geneva in the first half of the fifteenth century.[38]

The outbreak of a severe plague in Geneva around 1458 further stimulated legislation and the development of civic functions.[39] Preparations apparently were beginning already in 1457 with moral and social reforms, such as transferring prostitutes off the street into a semi-official brothel.[40] Early sixteenth-century ordinances related to cleaning, fumigation, disinfection of infected houses continued the trajectory of the preceding century.[41] But, a review of the legislation suggests that it was not all related to plague and that the Genevan authorities were certainly not in a state of panic. According to one historian:

> In many instances, the city's actions during 1473 are to be expected and explicable as the 'normal' response to plague. However, the detail of information available in the Genevan records forces one to be cautious about associating every state action as a response to plague or about viewing a late medieval, early modern city-state as a place wholly and narrowly consumed with crisis. Although the magistrates were clearly preoccupied with the need to respond to and control these twin crises [plague and grain prices], there is no sense that the city was in a state of panic.[42]

In Germany, connections were clearly perceived between health and cleanliness and between stench and disease and pestilence. The Dominican monk Felix Fabri (c 1441–1502) from Ulm, Germany, wrote that,

> with great enthusiasm the city was maintained in cleanliness, and there was no stench of the sewers and privies as elsewhere, rather everything exited through sealed passageways. ... There was nothing that so dirtied the streets and polluted the air than the crowd of swines, which brought all over their garbage; I believe that if the swines were not there that one would not find so clean and healthy a city.[43]

Such connections between stench and disease were clearly made by civic leaders as well, who passed numerous ordinances in various German towns.

Governments frequently enacted health and plague ordinances to address these and related issues,[44] that called upon physicians and apothecaries to prescribe and administer a variety of remedies,[45] and that often sought to regulate communal gatherings and they hired workers for such tasks as grave-digging as needed. A good example of the scope of plague ordinances is the December 1606 measures enacted in the electorate of Mainz, which included 14 items, such as: beseeching God to turn His anger from the sinful living of people through

His mercy, by means of prayer, fasting, giving of alms, and other godly works; not hosting foreigners, avoiding infected people, and turning beggars away at the city gate; fumigating living quarters and rooms and keeping streets and alleys clean; showing moderation in food and drink; not conducting business in used clothing; digging graves deeper than usual; and the closing of public baths.[46] The ordinance belies traditional medical notions of contagion and diet. At the same time, the marginalization of foreigners and the poor, combined with limitations on public activities had a significant impact on daily life [See Chapter 5].

As in Christian Europe, in Muslim Ottoman lands, state public health interventions continued to increase during the early modern period. Preventive actions such as street cleaning, sanitation (garbage collection and regulations for slaughter houses)—resulting in the appointment of a variety of communal overseers and functionaries to monitor street conditions, etc.[47]—urban planning, regulation of the medical profession, establishment of hospitals and hospices, city-wide inspections, and, during outbreaks of plague, oversight of burial practices (including the use of lime in graves) and monitoring of death tolls, were developed.[48] In the Ottoman Empire, it has been argued, starting in the sixteenth century growing concerns of sovereignty and the State's role in saving people during epidemics combined with increased emphasis on natural explanations of plague (as opposed to more "supernatural" ones),[49] led to the replacement of saints and holy men (as mystical intercessionaries)[50] by civic regulations and ordinances.[51]

Religious dimensions of political responses to plague

Still, throughout much of the early modern world governmental regulations continued to take seriously the religious response to plague as part of a broader civic concern. Not only ecclesiastical, but also secular authorities responded to the outbreak of plague by railing against what they castigated as lapses in morality, such as widespread gambling and overly ostentatious living, and in response they called for communal prayers and issued and re-issued sumptuary laws dictating the social behavior of local residents. Plague, or even the mere threat of plague, could lead to legislation against vagabondage, begging, and prostitution (similar notions that plague was punishment for sins such as fornication and prostitution circulated in Islamic plague treatises in the fifteenth century).[52]

In Europe, like their Christian neighbors, early modern Jews frequently attributed the devastation of the plague to sin. As in the realm of medicine, in the area of policy, political and social responses to plague often overlapped with religious responses and sensibilities. Moses ben Hayim Eisenstadt, in his Yiddish manuscript account of the plague in Prague in the early eighteenth century, pleaded that:

> Almighty God, in the Heavenly realm, You always come to our aid when we are in peril: You brought us out of exile in Egypt and out of exile in Babylon, You have preserved us from all Evils. Merciful God, in the third exile, again

You defend us, and in the fourth exile You will also protect us. Our hopes turn toward You, and we hope in these times that You will not try us so harshly.[53]

Formulaically, he called for prayer and penance:

Holy community of Prague, you must do penance! And remember this punishment for many years to come; and let us pray to God whom we love and in whom we hope, that He may never again send us such punishment.[54]

In Prague, Jewish communal leaders enacted penitential rules, fast days, and special prayer sessions in response to the plague of 1611. They also spoke out against blasphemy and expelled all prostitutes from the Jewish community.[55] Although most Jews perceived the plague as "divine punishment for individual and collective sins," there is evidence that not everyone linked sin and affliction so directly.[56]

The collective actions of early modern governments to establish and enforce various medical policies, especially at times of plague have been connected by some scholars with the broader social disciplining of society that occurred in the wake of the Reformation and that affected society and culture beyond the Christian world. One scholar, for example, asserts that:

The social disciplining stood in close connection with the process of increased concern with hygiene. Both processes were expedited with the help of the multi-faceted conceptions of medical policies in the interest of the authorities. As a consequence, social discipline and hygienic measures often went hand in hand and mutually reinforced each other.[57]

In the eighteenth century, the concept of cleanliness was predominant. Initially, this concept carried a religious orientation, referring to the internal, spiritual condition of a person. By the end of the century the notion of inner purity was increasingly secularized and was transformed to a bourgeois value and more closely linked with moral concepts, eventually serving as social markers.[58]

Early modern governments responded to the outbreak and even the threat of plagues in a variety of ways. At times, they continued policies that had been developed and implemented in the later Middle Ages. At other times, they initiated new, and often extensive, interventions that attempted to limit the spread of plague or to distance it from the city gates and territory. Such measures included quarantining of individuals and goods and the closure of houses with infected residents; the creation of lazarettos and plague hospitals; various cleaning measures—from the fumigation of buildings and public spaces to ordinances about sewage, animals, and butchering; inspection of trade goods; and restrictions on travel. Due to many different factors, including economic considerations and the protests of local populations, early modern authorities were not always consistent in their development or enforcement of these policies. Still, life continued on even amid significant epidemics and, *en masse*, such measures eventually had a positive impact in many locations. The resilience demonstrated in many early modern cities and territories was advanced through both innovations and regulations that helped to limit the extent of the spread of plague, even when it could not be eliminated. Early modern society remained vulnerable to disease epidemics, at times cataclysmic ones made worse on occasion by the confluence of other natural and man-induced disasters and crises. Nevertheless, anticipating more recent discussions of preparedness and disaster management, early modern people identified mechanisms to help them grapple with the recurrence of plague.

In addition to setting policies, early modern authorities frequently hired people to carry out their orders, including staff to run extant and newly created institutions, physicians and other medical personnel, as well as cemetery workers. As part of the larger bureaucratization of early modern society, such measures and oversight are not surprising and they highlight the rapidly changing nature of society and government in the early modern period.

Governments involved themselves in ruling and in daily life in a diversity of ways that extended beyond the formal policies and procedures just noted. On occasion, they extended their powers into more religious realms as well, organizing processions and prayers and casting communal ordinances within a larger framework of early modern religion and society. To that extent, it is somewhat artificial to separate out political from religious responses to plague. Still, increasingly in the early modern world, practical responses to plague, based on scientific advances and especially practical experiences over a long period of time, inflected and even dictated people's understanding of and response to the plague. Even more literary sources noted the practical steps of public policy and religious writers, such as Martin Luther, interwove theological and governmental dimensions in their writings about plague. In this regard, the early modern world was both one of transitions and continuities. There were, indeed, variations, in many locations, but increasingly common approaches to plague—in Europe, the Ottoman Empire, and in relation to other diseases, in other parts of the globe— intersected with broader changes and developments in society and culture.

Sources

4.1 Civic examinations

Title: "The Plague Orders of 1541," Venice[59]

Introduction: Venice was a large and powerful early modern city state. Its bustling trade and cultural efflorescence extended onto the Italian mainland and its policies reached beyond the immediate borders of the city. Venice was at the forefront of communal organization and the creation of health boards, hospitals, and quarantine houses, as well as other preventive and response measures at times of epidemic that would be emulated across the early modern world. This city ordinance describes briefly the system of examinations and notifications related to possible contagion at the time of plague deaths. As such, it reveals the growing work of public health officials and the civic efforts to curb the spread of plague.

Text

Ordinances to be observed when plague is discovered in the city, that steps may be taken to ensure that, by God's grace, it does not spread further.

When the [Health] Office has been notified that a death has occurred in the city within a few days or hours [of the onset of illness], the doctor of the Office must be sent to view the body, and examine it thoroughly to see if there is an abscess, carbuncle or other symptom. If plague is found, the whole house must immediately be placed under a ban, with all its inhabitants and others too who have had contact with it. Then the notary and an attendant at the Office must be sent to examine the inhabitants on oath and under threat of punishment. The master of the house must first be examined, and then the others separately, to establish the likely provenance of this disease. The notary must take special care to ask if the sick or dead person has been in any house where anyone has died; whether foreigners have lodged with him; whether goods have been brought to him from foreign parts; for how many days he has been ill; how many times the doctor has visited him; from which pharmacy he obtained the medicines; whether the patient was bled from a vein or by cupping-glasses; whether the parish priest or [other] priests and friars have been to the house to hear confession and given the rites of the Church; whether any relative or friend has been there to visit and how many times; whether they have been at the bedside or merely in the house; whether any of the neighbors has come in to help around the house, as often happens; whether any goods have been taken out of the house, and where, and to whom. This examination, which must be performed thoroughly and shall exact other information as seems appropriate to those responsible, shall be carried out in the presence of the parish priest or sacristan of the parish church, together with two residents of the parish. The last-named must sign [the record of] the examination, which must then be presented to the Provveditori alla Sanità, who will issue such orders as they see fit.

If the doctor has made only one visit to the sick person, no matter whether he has taken his pulse or merely stayed at the door and examined the urine, he shall be placed under a ban for twenty-two days. ...

4.2 Running a plague house

Author: Paul Hector Mair (1517–79)

Title: *Chronicle from 1547–1565*[60]

Introduction: Paul Hector Mair was a civil servant and chronicler in the key imperial free city of Augsburg—home of the noted banking family of the Fuggers—in Bavarian Swabia. Augsburg was a major center for finance, art, and politics, as well as a flashpoint for both religious conflict and rapprochement during the Reformation. In addition to his historical chronicle, Mair wrote a noted compendium related to martial arts, with a specific emphasis on the art of fencing. Found guilty of embezzlement and misappropriation of city funds during his tenure as city treasurer, he was hung at the age of 62. Here he provides valuable information about the function and scope of an early modern plague house. Mair notes the public nature of plague—in the knowledge of its appearance as well as the increasing efforts to address those infected and precautions to limit the spread of the disease. A system of institutions, complete with associated personnel and administrative tasks, developed or expanded in the early modern world to address these concerns, and Mair provides valuable information about these matters, including job descriptions and salaries. He also points to occasional abuses within the system and the need for a series of rules to govern the function of the plague house and the behavior of the people residing in and working there.

Text

How one should behave in the plague house during the plague.

1563. Always with God.

Since God, the Almighty, afflicted us with the serious sickness of plague in this year, and although much effort and work had [previously been] exerted in [addressing] the matter, one did not have the experience [of the plague to know] about how it was handled previously, therefore I decided to record a few things about how people conducted themselves and proceeded in this year of the plague, so that one would know better what to do should it sooner or later be sent [again], may God mercifully prevent it.—Written by Michael Reischlin, caretaker of the plague house and pox house.

First, it happened that in March, a few people were ... afflicted with plague. One would have liked to keep this quiet, but it could not be hidden, because a maid became sick, so that they did not want to keep [her] in the house. She was placed in the upper part of the building Gotsacker [God's field] by Dr. Schludy, and we, the directors of the pox house, were informed that we should provide [her] with food and other things.

By order of the steadfast lord Burgomaster Haintzle (whom we had informed), the caretakers sent out for the gravedigger and his wife, and gave both 1 gulden and 30 kreuzer per week for overseeing [the sick] and for [providing] food. In no more than a week, five people came; we [provided] food from the pox house—meat, bread, rolls, wine, ... which the gravedigger had to buy and then settle accounts every Saturday. We had to have a surgeon immediately, and we had to pay him 2 Gulden per week. This we reported to the supervisors, Matheus Rechlinger and Bartholomeus Mai; they thought that it was too much, and that a gulden would be enough, but the surgeon would not accept it, therefore we gave him a crown.

Afterward, we had beds made for ten or twelve people. Immediately after the first week, on the 17th of April, four more people arrived, who we received like the first, and there were more people as time went on; there were ten people, so that we caretakers had to appoint attendants.

We reported to the supervisors, and also to the Burgomasters, and since we could no longer house any more [people], asked if we should open the plague house. ...

In the upper level of Gotsacker we housed the sick for seven weeks. Then on the 18th of May we came into the small plague house. As soon as we came there we had to pay two doctors 2 Gulden every week. ... We housed [sick people] in the small plague house for three weeks. Then there were 30 people, and we could no longer provide for them. The caretakers reported this to the Burgomasters, who consented to us opening the large plague house. ...

When we had now housed [sick people] for several weeks in the outer plague house, we, the caretakers, ordered that all of the food, such as meat, bread, lard, flour, and seasonings, bedclothes, sheets, sackcloth, linen for bandaging and plasters, and other things as needed [be brought in], all of which was managed by the pox father. Regarding only the wine, when the one barrel we bought was empty, the Pox Father presented an invoice and another was purchased. We also took on a manager [chaplain?], by the name of Johannes Meer, who comforted the people and instructed them in the Christian faith; the ministers [predicanten] ordered that he be sent for that purpose. We caretakers also had two gilded vessels made for administering the Lord's Supper, which cost 16 Gulden, including the case.

We also had two doctors, named Dr. Schludy and Dr. Trincklin; one went in the plague house in the evening, and the other in the morning, and there was a lot of discord between them; what one wanted, the other didn't want, leading to so much irritation that the plague father complained that he did not know what to do ... This we reported to the Burgomasters and indicated that we wanted to dismiss one doctor. ...

The manager who I mentioned previously, Johannes Meer, did not live long, only into the third week, and then he died. Since his wife was in the plague house at his death, she therefore had to remain in her house for 4 weeks. We paid her 1 Gulden each week, until the month was over. Afterwards, the ministers appointed another [manager], named Balthas Kon, a weaver.

We caretakers also appointed 8 women to care for the people sick with the plague by lifting them, bedding them down, and whatever [else] was needed, and also to sew up the dead [in their shrouds]. They were also needed when the parents of a child died; in that case one of them was concerned with the children or the children [were put] in the women's quarters, such that each one had three children [in their charge]. The Alms Lords distributed the food. We retained the caregivers for four weeks, and afterward the Alms Lords provided for them. When it was possible, however, they had to provide for themselves [or] their friends [had to support them]. And when someone became sick anywhere and needed an attendant, that person should only come to the caretakers, if one was available or where one could find her. Even when there was no service to be had, she reported to the caretakers so that she could be sent to another area. When all of the 8 women were in service, several [more] women were also brought in who were also needed; we eventually need those who were loaned out. There was a great, unceasing unrest. And a midwife was also brought into the plague house. We paid her every week ½ Florin and when she went to a woman in the plague house we paid her [an additional] 15 kreuzer. ...

The Plague Father and Mother were also afflicted with the sickness, so that they lay intensely [ill]. A lot of complaints were registered that things were entirely disorderly. As a result, we went to the plague house and demanded that every servant and maid handle themselves seriously in all matters. It was not long before the Plague Mother was well and could again go about her inspections. She was very quarrelsome with the servants, who complained bitterly. Therefore, we went back and questioned the servants, as well as both parties. The sick people also complained that their food came completely cold, and that usually no order was maintained there. We appointed a man who was always to be present during the preparation [of meals] and [who was] to go around into all of the rooms when the sick people were eating, and see what was wrong; he was then to report to us so that we could take care of it. The same person also had to watch over and do whatever else was needed [for the sick people].

Afterwards, the third manager, by the name of Leonhard Leyer, became sick and it was thought that he would die. Then another, by the name of Hanns Bader, also a weaver, [and] a much younger man, was placed by the minister. He was in the plague house for a long time and he was not clumsy when it came to [religious] instruction. But we had a servant, a married man, and they associated with one another. They went into a wrong room, one as brazenly as the other; for the [servant] laid himself down with a woman on her bed, and the manager lay on the bed of another woman, who was watching [over the sick] that night. After midnight, she came back and also lay down with him on the bed, and they lay together until three or four o'clock. Whether they were both innocent, I will leave to you [the reader to decide].

When we, as caretakers, found out about such a thing, we summoned them along with other keepers and Dr. Schludy, as well as the Plague Father and Mother and several [other] people, to tell us everything they had seen, heard, or experienced regarding the servant and the manager. Although they could not deny it, they made the matter out to be as negligible as they could, [but] we put both of them on leave. This greatly offended the manager, who said he would seek further counsel.

It was also reported to us that two maids were out drinking most impudently in the company of young men at night, and that they saved up their [rations of] wine and drank it with the men and otherwise behaved badly. Therefore, we immediately went out [to the plague house] and placed them both on leave. And there we heard of fornication and lechery among servants and the sick, which caused us to issue an ordinance and construct a plaque, as follows:

> God, the Almighty, strikes us, as before, daily with the heavy sickness of the plague in his great mercy in order that we undergo penance and improvement of our lives; but still few want to better themselves, and because of this God may therefore punish us more severely; and now our Lords, an honorable Council, have at great expense prescribed [that] a house [be designated], in which the poor who are burdened with this sickness can be maintained; however, there are some who do not recognize this good deed, and some among the employees and those sick people in that same house prove themselves to be completely impudent, completely mischievous and quarrelsome, and in another way more disobedient (until good will prevails), and practically no one any longer will be upbraided with words. This has often come to [the attention] of the caretakers, as a result of which they have become very displeased, such that in order to address and stop it, this ordnance has been created:
>
> Ordinance
>
> First, when a sick person is brought into the house, he should be laid upon a clean bed without any delay and be given a sweat inducing drink, and afterward he should be treated according to the doctor's advice. And there should always be available several beds, [with] freshly washed [sheets], for women and men, so that no sick person has to wait. Grace should also be said when one wants to eat, in all of the rooms ... And when someone is in danger of death, the healthy people should recite a faithful common prayer that God will mercifully deliver [the dying person]. But where there is mischievousness or impudence among the employees or the sick people, whether with words or deeds, or through blasphemy, the offender or offenders (employees or sick people) should as a result be punished for the action reported, as follows: First, they will receive no wine on the day of the incident; and if the matter is great, then they should also be given no meat. If the matter is really wicked, they should immediately be put out of the house; if it is a sick person, he should be put out of the house (and the city), and not come in to the city for a month. The doctor, the manager, and the father of the house [Plague Father] should impose such punishment. And if it happens that the Plague Father and Mother also behave improperly, one or more of the employees should report this to the caretakers, who will know how to handle the impropriety. The Father at the Plague House should make known to the Father of the Pox House such matters, and thereupon the Pox Father [should make it known] to the directors, so that it's known how it is being handled and where complaints about the Father or Mother should be made.

House employees or others should make such complaints without any motivations. No one is to abuse another, upon [pain of] the penalties reported above. This ordinance should be read every week in all rooms in the presence of the employees. Such ordinance is passed by an honorable Council, the 14th of August, [15]63.

4.3 The ideal plague hospital

Author: Francois Valleriole (1504–80)

Title: *Trafficking of the Plague* (1566)[61]

Introduction: See 3.3. As in other early modern contexts, Valleriole stresses the need to cordon off those people infected with plague and the role of civic officials and institutions in that work, reflecting the developing notions of public space and the broadening scope of civic authority in early modern society. The author of the treatise displays a wide range of contemporary understandings of the nature of plague and infection, drawn from classical texts (dealing with air quality, for example) as well as practical experiences, which informs the physical layout and structure of the plague hospital. As with a number of documents in this collection, in this one Valleriole demonstrates the balance between theory and practice in addressing plague and the numerous issues that needed to be considered in constructing spaces to care for the sick in early modern society.

Text

The most necessary thing in good cities is to have a definite place delegated for the removal of the plague disease when it pleases God to send His scourge upon us. And it belongs to the public police, before the need arises, to provide a well-built house according to the standard that will be described after, in order to receive those people attacked by the plague disease and who have no other means to help themselves, except to withdraw to the hospital to be cared for in their need. So the house must be situated outside the city, in a place separated from areas frequented by people and along a public road or common way ... to prevent passersby from contracting the infection. The house should be ample and able to accommodate several sick people in times of need. Its position should be between the eastern equinoctial and the northern, so that the midday heat is not too hot, and it is capable of coolness—so it will be built.

Such a house must liberally receive the wind of the north that is popularly called the right weather, the one that is the drier, healthier, and the more purged and flushing of all poor vapors and infections of the air, and is cold and dry and more consuming of the superfluities of the body. As according to Hippocrates and Galen in the third book of the aphorisms, and as the same Hippocrates learnedly testifies ... regarding the manner of living.

That is what Avicenna wrote more fully when he spoke of the nature of this northern wind, to which he attributed this property to correct all corrupted and pestilential air. And by this, it is necessary to mention another aspect. The length [of the building] must be more extended than the width, in order to be able to build 25 or 30 rooms above and as many below, because of the multitude of sick people who might hasten [there] because of need. The rooms should be separated from each other and nevertheless connected, just as the chambers of the religious [orders] are in their dorms.

And each should have its fireplace … and it is necessary that the said chambers open on two sides, having one window toward the rising sun, the other toward the north. And each should have two beds in order to move the patient from one to the other, which is most needed for this disease. The hospital should be in healthy air, windy and not in a place of a lagoon and ponds, but in a place removed from such quality and dry, having, however, water, either from a fountain or from a flowing stream around, if possible, in order to clean their cloths and other soiled things. And if the nature of the region is such that there is not any flowing water, it is necessary to construct a reservoir of good water along a large table, long and big enough to clean as needed.

The rooms of the surgeon and of the priest appointed at the time of the plague should be separated from those of the diseased, in a corner apart, just as also is that of the apothecary, which should have a place apart from his shop, and it should maintain a supply of necessary drugs and ointments in such strength that are generally observed in well-policed cities. It is also necessary that in the square of the rooms there is a long and open path or gallery, where the patient can walk when he begins to recover and which runs up and down until the end of the house. This gallery is not only necessary as said, but also a covered bed, gowns, and other coats that are useful in such cases.

Along the side of the hospital and at a distance of about fifty paces, another lower part of the house should be constructed … to serve as a [place] to disinfect the sick after they are healed. In order that they not remain with the more ill, it is necessary and reasonable to change their location so that they do not interact with the sick and be in separate and healthier air, to be completely protected from the danger, and return, with the help of God, to their original health. It is also necessary to construct a chapel that should be separated from the main part of the house and located in such a place that from a distance the sick people can hear those who offer the word of God. This is the order and construction of the house, which should be furnished with good beds, blankets, mattresses, and other necessary things for the sick with as much liberality of the city in common as is in its power.

4.4 Tales of the lazaretto

Author: Rocco Benedetti (active 1556–82)

Title: "Account of the Plague of 1575–1577" (1630, Bologna; originally published in 1577 in Urbino)[62]

Introduction: Rocco Benedetti was a sixteenth-century Venetian notary and chronicler, who published various civic ordinances and accounts. The quarantine house, or lazaretto, could be a dismal place, where the sick were lumped indiscriminately and sent to live out the last days of their lives. Benedetti offers a colorful picture of a pest house that is replete with smoke, confusion, and indifference. Of course, not all plague houses were as gruesome as depicted here; however, the account provides an important perspective on the challenges and limitations facing even the most highly organized early modern governments as they grappled with the contagious and deadly plague, especially during major epidemics.

Text

... I say truly that on the one hand the Lazzaretto Vecchio seemed like Hell itself. From every side there came foul odors, indeed a stench that none could endure; groans and sighs were heard without ceasing; and at all hours clouds of smoke from the burning of corpses were seen to rise far into the air. Some who miraculously returned from that place alive reported, among other things, that at the height of that great influx of infected people there were three and four of them to a bed. Since a great number of servants had died and there was no one to take care of them, they had to get themselves up to take food and attend to other things. Nobody did anything but lift the dead from the beds and throw them into the pits. It often happened that those who were close to death or senseless, without speech or movement were lifted up by the corpse-bearers as though they had expired, and thrown onto the heap of bodies. Should one of them then be seen to move hand or foot, or signal for help, it was truly good fortune if some corpse-bearer, moved to pity, took the trouble to go and rescue him. And many, driven to frenzy by the disease, especially at night, leapt from their beds and, shouting with the fearful voices of damned souls, went here and there, colliding with one another, and suddenly falling to the ground dead. Some who rushed in frenzy out of the wards threw themselves into the water, or ran madly through the gardens, and were then found dead among the thornbushes, all covered with blood.

On the other hand, the Lazzaretto Nuovo seemed a mere Purgatory, where unfortunate people, in a poor state, suffered and lamented the death of relatives, their own wretched plight and the break-up of their homes. Sometimes at the height of the plague 7000–8000 sick persons languished at the Lazzaretto Vecchio. Pray consider, Your Excellency, how many medicines, syrups, plasters, ointments and cloths were required to treat them, and how much broth and pap and how many distillations and other things were required to restore them. It was truly impossible to provide for so great a need, there being so few to serve so many. We should not be surprised if scarcely one in ten survived …

4.5 A window onto early modern Jewish life

Title: "Prague Plague Ordinance" (1607)[63]

Introduction: Prague is the capital of the modern Czech Republic. Early modern Bohemia was a complex political stage, with rival Catholic and Protestant groups in conflict, and a cultural center that became home to the eclectic Habsburg emperor Rudolph II in the late sixteenth and early seventeenth century. The city was also at the heart of the start of the Thirty Years War, with the famous "defenestration of Prague" in 1618. Devastating plagues struck the city throughout the early modern period. In the seventeenth century alone regular cycles of plague hit the city and surrounding regions in 1605–13 (with one-tenth of the city population dying in 1613), 1624–26, 1631–35, 1639–40, 1648–49, and 1680. In the early eighteenth century, in 1713–15, a quarter of the city population died from a plague epidemic.

Jews had lived in Prague since at least the tenth century. Despite significant setbacks, including a devastating massacre of thousands of Jews in 1389, the Jewish community developed into one of the largest and most sophisticated in early modern Europe. In the midst of recurring anti-Jewish campaigns and attempts to expel Jews from the city and from the region in the sixteenth century, Jews enjoyed a good deal of economic opportunity and intellectual engagement, with an enviable range of scholars in rabbinics, mysticism, and the sciences. With more than 1,100 Jews in 1540 and about ten times that many by the start of the eighteenth century (comprising almost 29% of the total city population), Prague was one of the largest and most important centers of Jewish life in Western or Central Europe. The Jewish residents were not without their challenges, as political and military conflicts merged with occasional anti-Jewish sentiments and pressures. Still, there were real opportunities, especially within the upper strata of Jewish society, for engagement with non-Jewish culture and society. We possess a number of sources written by Prague Jews at times of or in response to plague—various prayers and historical songs in Yiddish, communal ordinances (in Hebrew and Yiddish), memoirs, and other materials, as well as various medical treatises (generally in Latin and German) and governmental decrees (in German and Czech). These sources address theological concerns along with communal, governmental, and scientific issues.

This text provides important insights into the activities, and the regulation of activities and movement, of Jews during the early seventeenth-century plague years. A veneer of anti-Jewish sentiment permeates the text, which nevertheless also reveals that Jews were involved in a broad range of professions and functions in the city and beyond. The economic work of the Jews is particularly stressed, but the daily and apparently at times friendly social interaction of Jews and Christians emerges in the document. The text reveals typical early modern understandings of and responses to the plague—airborne contagion, the value of quarantine and the restriction of foreigners who could carry the plague, and the need for cleanliness and sterilization to slow the spread of the disease.

Text

Statute in the name of His Imperial Majesty concerning the plague scourge.

... In the case of the plague scourge, inasmuch as in many places the divine pestilence has penetrated, His Imperial Majesty deigns to mete out and order sternly that from these places, wherein that plague scourge circulates, no one should be received at another's home nor in any public house. It is heard how even in the homes of Jews the same plague scourge has penetrated, so that no one ventures into the homes of these Jews, nor keeps or suffers them. 22 August 1607.

In strict accord with and on behalf of the recommendations of His Imperial Majesty's governor [hetman] of the Old Town of Prague, made in the course of the previous articles, actual distraints must be attended to and carried out with diligence. In the case of the Jews, it is so commanded that no one may depart from their town [district], go about from home to home, nor on the streets or the tarmarce [area in old Prague], nor sell anything, and may not wander hither and thither, since they are shameless—as credible people say even those who are infected with plague are not ashamed to run hither and thither into homes and about the streets. Last, in the case of white crosses made on homes and seals [indicating presence of the plague], those shall remain according to previous regulations. *Actum in consilio feria 2. post s. Bartholomaei 27 August anno 1607.*

A decree from the office of His Imperial Majesty for a specific statute that Jews are able once again to exit their streets.

For delivery to the Honorable Mayor and Aldermen of Prague's Old Town.

His Majesty the Roman Emperor and Hungarian and Bohemian King, Our Most Gracious, Honorable Mayor and Aldermen of Prague's Old Town, deign to make known that it has come to pass that Jews may once again come out from their streets, by dint of their gracious permission, in the following manner:

In the first place, that no one of them may go onto the bridge nor cross to the Little Quarter (Malá strana) by ferry, even if it is empty.

Second, that neither may anyone roam hither and thither about the market nor about the streets of Old or New Town, especially about homes with carpeting, nor may anyone walk about selling any goods, except those who are given permission to do so by someone of the higher estates.

Third, the garments of pedestrians, particularly old and plumed, be they those of Jews or Christians, should not be sold, especially on the tarmarce.

Fourth, that they may not discharge their goods from Krámský from their cellars outside onto stalls, but must sit and sell in the basement, with doors open.

Fifth, whosoever makes a living from threadwork, lacework, saddle-cloth, and other whites [white textiles], are permitted to do so, so that the time-honored mandate to sell is upheld, indeed under the arches in the tarmarce.

Sixth, Jewish drifters and mercenaries, whom purchasers put up for work, cannot be tolerated and are completely proscribed.

Seventh, where Jewish butchers are concerned, they are authorized to purchase livestock on Friday [on the fifth day] till 5:00pm and not later.

Eighth, no pantries or rooms in Christian homes may be used for transactions or rented, but should be left empty.

Ninth, inasmuch as they are proscribed, they may not frequent the houses of Christian innkeepers for beer.

Tenth, whatsoever Jews have left here must have their names marked and no one will be received further or welcomed here according to this recommendation without the express will of higher authorities.

Eleventh, regarding the cleanliness in the homes of Jews and especially about the streets, from whence most disease arises out of the air. These areas are to be sterilized. All mire, uncleanliness, which is emitted from their homes into the street, onto the banks and then carried further, are to be subjected to immediate punishment. Their elders must be especially attentive and one person should be specifically charged to supervise and foster this behavior.

Twelfth, spas are forbidden for Christians, insofar as they are proscribed, so that they are not drowned.

Thirteenth, in whatsoever home the ill might have died, this [house] must be immediately sealed and instead of a white cross a yellow circlet [should] be placed on the doors.

Fourteenth, the graves for their dead are to be dug to a further depth, a piece of unslaked lime embedded on the corpse, unslaked lime scattered on the grave, and in addition the walls in the homes whitewashed.

If any of the Jews should act against any of these statutes, they should first be taken to prison and then duly penalized and punished accordingly. And accordingly, it is commanded to the pleasure of the offended Mayor and Aldermen, that the above-written statutes be made known in whole to the Jews and over this mandate His Imperial Majesty's indisputable hand of the leaders is sustained, and that in this the certain and gracious will of His Imperial Majesty is fulfilled. *Decretum in consilio bohemico Pragae 14. Septembris anno 1607.*

4.6 Practical policies and approaches to the plague

Author: Abraham Catalano (d 1642)

Title: "A World Turned Upside-Down"[64]

Introduction: Firmly under Venetian rule for most of the period between 1405 and 1797, Padua was acclaimed for its medical college. Many Jews had come to Padua to study at the university, which boasted 80 Jewish students between 1517 and 1619 and 149 between 1619 and 1721. Jews had first settled in remote parts of the town, but eventually made their way to more central locations. The Great Plague epidemic of 1629–31 resulted in the deaths of about 280,000 people throughout northern Italy. The plague had a devastating effect on the Jews of Padua, where two-thirds of them succumbed to the disease.[65] The plague in Padua began in spring of 1630.[66] Initially it did not affect the Jews; but it fell on the inhabitants of the ghetto during the ten days of repentance between Rosh Hashanah and Yom Kippur. By Rosh Hodesh [start of the new month of] Adar 5391 [1631] 170 Jews had died. After that there was a lull in deaths, but in the month of Sivan the plague began anew across the city.[67] In Padua 19,000 out of 32,000 people died (59%).[68] The Padua Jewish population witnessed a proportionally significant decline. In 1585 there had been 280 Jews in Padua and by 1603 439, out of a total population of 35,263.[69] In 1630–31 there were 721, of whom 634 were afflicted by plague and 421 died.[70]

Rabbi Abraham Catalano (d 1642) studied Torah and medicine at Padua (where he earned a medical degree). He was not registered as the rabbi of the community, even though he taught Torah and sat on the *bet din* (rabbinic court). His wife Sarah died during the plague, after 21 years of marriage. Their son Moshe Hayyim authored a liturgical poem (*piyyut*) appended to the account and read on Tisha b'Av (a fast day commemorating the destruction of the Temple). In 1602 a ghetto was established for Jews in Padua, which remained in operation until the French destroyed it in 1797. The text is quite long and covers a great deal of material. The author stressed the notion that God punishes with the plague, but he also discussed at great length the practical means to address the plague and the means by which one can save his family and community. He recorded various rules and regulations from the Jewish community and from the local and territorial authorities. Catalano reviewed the timing of the outbreak and spread of the plague and he described in detail the death of many individuals, including his own family members. The text also points to the complex relationship between Jews and Christians. Although there were some tensions, relations between Jews and Christians in the region were generally good during the crisis. Jews who fled from the city were able to find lodgings among non-Jews outside the city.[71] Jews in Padua also received support from other Jewish communities, especially from communities in Venice and Ferrara.[72]

Text

... I will speak and moan, I will complain from the bitterness of my spirit (I am Abraham Catalano), to inform the generations to come and the children who should be born of things as they happened. And I will faithfully make known to the generations three useful lessons from this story.

The first lesson is to understand that this is God's way. Our God's wrath is kindled and there is no one who can save us from His hand. The living being will take it to heart to end transgression and limit sin lest the evil adheres to him and he dies for his sins.

The second lesson is that the generations to come will know how to behave and properly prepare for a devastating plague in the world in their days as we did at this time. In this report I will describe not only everything that we did, but also all that is appropriate to be done to be saved from the plague in general and after it dissipates.

The third lesson is to save children naturally from pestilence that prowls in the darkness and to make known to them in this report how specifically a family should behave in order to survive.

... And the plague stopped. And the number of dead in the plague was four hundred and twenty-one. Two hundred and thirteen recovered from the plague and seventy five people were not affected by the plague, including me, the young writer, praised be to God. Twelve people ran away from the Ghetto before the plague started, none of whom died. Among them were the young men Reb [Mr.] Moses Jacob and Reb Joseph bar Shalom, who had stayed in the house of one of the townsmen, from the Bigolini family in the village of Bigolina. For a while they were imprisoned in Cittadella and they had to pay a fortune to free themselves. The Jews who resided there treated them well and assisted them. Reb Moses Shalom, the runaway, was saved from a fire in his father's house, as were all the members of the household except an eight-month old baby. At that time, there was a certain Jew who was imprisoned with his sons [in the] jail who was not afflicted, since almost all the prisoners in the jail would not touch him. And among the rest who were not struck who fled from the midst of the plague was, for example, Jacob Lustro—who lost all his family in the plague and ran away with his son. And after the quarantine he was followed by the three sons of Samuel Cohen Tzedek from the Cantarini family, who left after their father died and after their two scholarly brothers died. And all the rest here from their family died. My mouth will speak the praise of God that their brother, the important and leading doctor, our honored master and teacher Rabbi Judah Cohen Tzedek, who married a woman in Venice, came back to help our community. And the people mentioned above, asked one minister from Venice in Montebelluna to transport them there for a fair compensation. And after some time they were expelled from the adjoining property of the minister and thanks to the efforts of the Jews in Casteifranco, the ministers of health were willing to give them permission to stay in a house three quarters of a mile from Casteifranco.

And on the next day, three of them were struck with fever. There was a great panic in Casteifranco because of this and all the people were embittered against them when they found this out; when they learned that it was only a simple case of fever and that it was not a plague people calmed down. And [Isaac ben Simon] Lustro and his sons ran away to Venice because they were afraid of the sick people of the Cantor's family, because they were infected upon their sick bed. In the darkness of the evening burglars came upon them, beat them, and captured all that they had. They threw the sick people down furiously from their beds just to find out whether or not they were hiding money in the beds. And while Lustro was in Venice he also became sick with a high fever; in the end he and the Cantors recovered. After my son Moses, our wise rabbi, returned to the Ghetto he visited the house of an urbanite Leandro Porcellino in the village Corte. He stayed there for a few days and became sick with a fever. When he returned home the city gate keepers did not know that he was sick, and he recovered after many days.

Experience proved that young children are more prepared for this disease and next the young men and women. Such was not the case for the elderly and the pregnant women, almost all of whom died. Many of those who were infected and recovered became sick with tertian and quatran fevers for many days, and there was not a house in the Ghetto without someone sick or dead. There were only two widows in whose households no one became ill. The name of the first was Esther, the widow of Nachman Katz the Sephardi, and two of her sons, and the name of the second was Gioia, the widow of Chaim ben Shushan, and their four sons. This was a miracle since their houses were surrounded by contaminated houses. Among the men, two hundred and fourteen died and among the women two hundred and seven died, including thirty-eight couples. Thirty women and twenty men were left widowed, and in fifteen houses no soul was left and in many houses only one was left. In the house of Rabbi Gabriel di Negri eight died and only a nursing baby survived; and in the house of Asher Kastel Franko ten died and only one survived; and in the house of the sage Moses Grasito eleven died and only one grandson, who had no share or inheritance, survived and he inherited everything, and many were like this. And the estates moved from one to another, this one inheriting the property of the householder, and another one inheriting his wife's dowry; there were also many who lived in other places who were entitled to an inheritance. And I have foreseen a world turned upside-down, as I said.

And when the plague stopped I was called by the commissioner (of health) [provveditore] and the minsters asked me to choose a place to disinfect our belongings and if there was no place, then everything we have would be burnt, and no Gentile would be allowed in our places until we had done so. Then we sought out a place and I rode by horse outside the city, to see a place in the village of Mandriola, on the river bank, which was particularly well-suited because bricks were baked there. I was pleased with the place and I rented it for ninety scudi and a boat for twenty scudi to transport our belongings. Still, we needed the good will of the commissioner, and when the approval of the commissioner and ministers was requested they were not willing to listen because they said that this place was too far from the lazaretto and that we would spread the disease. They told us that we should build a place near our lazaretto or use the place Brentelle that we had rented. And we told them that whenever the plague had occurred in the past sixty years the Jews had disinfected their belongings in the village of Montà, which was far away from the lazaretto, and that the place Brentelle was too small and insufficient (for our needs).

They responded and told us to build wooden houses or pay them the cost for using the wooden houses that they have. The cost was more than five hundred ducats and we grew angry and disputed what had been done to us and complained. [Others?] rented the place Brentelle, and they benefited from us in many new (ways). They imposed heavy expenses upon us and the wooden houses were also far from the place. We pleaded [our case] and he exempted us from the expenses except (those related to) the place. It was for the disinfection that the ministers destroyed the wooden houses and we knew for sure that it was a place where we could not conduct the disinfection and we requested of them that they accept our belongings in their lazaretto that they used for disinfection and we would pay all the expenses that would be incurred. They refused, saying that it was not enough [space] even for them. Then we were forced to use the Brentelle. The commissioner and the ministers forced us to send all the belongings that were found in the Ghetto, except those that had been signed and sealed by the health authorities to the disinfection place.

We demanded to know why such requirements were made for us but not for the rest of the people of the city, who had to send only those items that were in the room of the sick person, or everything from the houses in which nobody resided. Why do they take our beds from underneath us and why can't we hold on to our clothes of white linen, as is customary in the entire world. We demanded that a copy of this decree be sent to Venice and we requested from the ministers there its cancellation. The commissioner heard our voice and said that each person could claim his bed and clothes of white linen, but that the rest should be sent outside the camp for disinfection. All this was achieved only after intervening and negotiating and after I went many times before the advocate and before the commissioner and the ministers, because there could not be found then an advocate for us, as they had all died or run away.

When we saw that the commissioner intended to enforce the decree delaying the entry of the Gentiles into the Ghetto until after all of our belongings were sent for disinfection and the Ghetto cleaned, we proceeded as fast as we could and we started sending all our belongings outside the Ghetto. On Rosh Hodesh Elul we started sending everything that had been sentenced to be burned— [made of] feather [and] hides, and all the moveable goods and the like, which had been handled by the dead or sick or that was in the room of the dead or the sick. We sent the gravediggers to the houses that had no inhabitants because their residents had died or were sent to the lazaretto. Reb Joseph Treves, who was sick but recovered, received wages in the amount of seven liras per day. The moveable goods that needed to be burned were selected on a house by house basis and they were piled up heap by heap, bundle by bundle, and tied together so that nobody would [be tempted to] behave foolishly with the goods. What was suitable for disinfection was placed in the corner and the house was cleaned well. When they were done the possessions that were to be burned were taken to the city walls by wagons and everything was burned there. Those things that needed to be burned from the remaining houses [were collected] and all the preparations were made before the wagons returned to the Ghetto in order not to delay the disinfection of the goods. The goods to be burned were placed in fifty wagons, four each day, two in the morning and two in the evening, because we did not want them to come in the heat of the day. All the items that were designated for burning in each and every house were written down in a book. Reb Isaac Israel Coronel the Sephardi and Reb Abraham Ferrarese, who were sick and [had] recovered, marked all the goods in the first house with the letter 'A' and in the second house the letter 'B' and so on from house to house. The goods were taken on carts to the ship that we rented for twenty scudi. Reb Isaac Da Fano took the goods with him for one ducat per day, and with him went thirty Gentiles and one Jew, for three liras per day for each one of them, and the place was too small and insufficient, as said.

The process lasted for three months and five days and we received back our possessions here, still soaking wet and some became moldy, especially mattress covers. The possessions were placed in the lazaretto here by the authority of the ministers. We paid a Jew in the disinfection place one hundred ducats to dry the wool there in the lazaretto and to repair the mattress covers. The expense was very great and it cost four thousand and five hundred liras. We appointed a committee of three men to assess the goods, appraised at ten liras for each mattress cover, two liras for each linen, two liras for each robe, and three liras for each mattress. All the people started complaining that the value of the goods was not equal to the expense of the disinfection, which was true. Azriel Katz, one member of the court, agreed to burn all the contaminated goods because he was afraid that the expenses would be more than the value of the goods, or to give the goods as a gift to the lazaretto of the Gentiles. However the rest of the members of the community refused to do so, and I did not want to express my opinion on this matter, either in favor or in opposition—because the disinfection of my contaminated goods and those of my in-law's in Academia occurred there by the authority of the ministers and also our contaminated goods in the Ghetto that we sent secretly there by carts and post for burning—nor how I determined which goods would not be burned.

After all the goods were sent for disinfection we cleaned all the contaminated houses of the holy community. I applied tar and sulphur and after plastering each and every room, the windows were left open for several days. We signed a testimonial from our board to the commissioner that all of the contaminated goods had been taken from the Ghetto and been fumigated properly and requested to bring into the Ghetto the people from quarantine; however, they were not to go out from their houses for eight days in order to see whether something would happen or not. And still Christians were forbidden to enter into the Ghetto and the ministers stood firm in their decision because they said that the days of the quarantine for the Ghetto had not passed since the last death. We said to them, 'why do you decide to close the Ghetto based on one case of death? If one person is sick close his house, not the whole Ghetto.' They did not want to listen and they said that ['[']if in a few days nothing happens in your courtyards, we will give you permission to open all the gates and the Christians may come and go.['] We were very afraid to bring the people who were in quarantine into the Ghetto, lest the plague break out again and the ministers close the entire Ghetto again. Despite our fears, all the unfortunates were returned to the Ghetto, despite the fact that some of them were sick with high fevers. They returned to their homes on the fifth of Tishrei 5392 [October 1, 1631].

The next day we received permission from the ministers also to bring [back] the people who resided in the lazaretto once [there was] a doctor's testimony regarding their health. The doctor Francesco Bianchini saw them and testified that they were healthy and that even if they had long-standing fevers there was no fear that they were seriously ill.

The first lazaretto was divided into two; in one section were the sick who had recovered and in the second section were the people who were still sick. In this section of sick people there was only one woman who was too weak to see the doctor. The ministers avoided coming to this part of the Ghetto. After the eight days in which the contaminated people were not allowed to leave their houses, the wife of Shmaria Muggia died and a blister was found under her arms and they sent her husband and his son to the lazaretto again, along with one woman and her son who had visited her.

And after three days the Christians were allowed to come and go in the Ghetto and all the gates were open as before. After three days the rest of the people who stayed at the lazaretto also returned to the Ghetto, except Shmaria Muggia and his friends, who stayed there for a few days. And on the fifteenth of Tishrei 5392 [October 11, 1631] a scribe of the health office came to the Ghetto by order of the commissioner with keys to the sealed rooms, and he commanded us to inspect the seals to make sure they were intact and he gave each person the key to his room telling them to take their goods but not to sell anything until the time when the word of the commissioner arrived. On the 23rd of Tishrei [October 19, 1631] the commissioner permitted the reopening of the stores on the condition that for a period of eight days all vendors report to the scribe of the health office their daily sales and swear that the goods had been in the sealed rooms.

This is the chronicle of the matter and its outcome. If the doctor tells you to take these drugs—Elettuario, Conservi, Preservativi—and you would be protected from the plague, do not believe him, as this is not going to help you and not going to save you. I saw many who followed this course and died bitterly and many others who did not take any of them and were not infected, or were sick and recovered, and the plague did not distinguish between them. Many important doctors contracted plague and many were unaffected. I saw at that time that there were many who always placed a citron under the nose to filter the vapors leaving or temper impurities, which I thought was nonsense. Who knows if the smell from breathing the air resulting from those vapors stimulates good health. Although I was adorned with the crown of medicine and I know what the doctors say about Preservativi I did not look to record anything from the writings in their books. I only wrote what I remembered and thought would be useful for future generations.

When a plague surrounds your house, do not rent your house, just let it stand empty. If there is pestilence inside your house you must leave the house. If you do not own another house, rent a house to ameliorate your condition. And if you are poor and you cannot afford any on these, separate yourself in your house from the sick there or run away.

Prepare enough food that will last for many days—grain, wine, oil, and everything needed for you and your household, and also [from the smallest and most mundane things], from a thread to a shoe lace, so that you will not get close to where the plague is and you will be protected from all that is evil.

If a plague strikes your town, take your precious belongings and seal them in the room with the health stamp; [take] only a change of clothes if you slip.

And if someone gives his friend money or the equivalent of money to guard in his room, he should have written proof lest he dies from the plague and no one can help him. If brothers or a father and his sons dwell together the inhabitants of the house should divide into two houses, for when the plague is found in one house it may be closed up [the inhabitants of the second may go out into public]. Two should not dwell together lest the one become infected and hurt his friend.

If someone in your household is found sick, do not leave him alone with a man or woman from your house or hire a caretaker for a full price, in case he dies with a bitter spirit. The sin will be upon you and you must take yourself to your place of refuge, so that bloodguilt will not come upon your house.

And you, people of my community, remember and do not forget, before a plague reaches you, send a delegate to the holy community of Venice and pay his salary, so that he can help you when you are in trouble and if a matter comes up against you before the ministers, which is not religious [in nature], whether [for example] to hand over the Ghetto or a single person, this one can stand there in the breach.

4.7 London plague ordinances (1665)

Author: Daniel Defoe (1660–1731)

Title: *Journal of the Plague Year* (1722)[73]

Introduction: Daniel Defoe was an English writer, known especially for his novel *Robinson Crusoe*. A colorful personality and a prolific writer, he was often in debt and had several brushes with the authorities that led him to prison. Defoe published *Journal of a Plague Year* in 1722, which was purportedly about the great plague in London in 1665–66. That plague took the lives of an estimated 100,000 people—building upon several significant other outbreaks in the first half of the seventeenth century—and has appropriately been seen as a major force in social and historical change, especially given a number of other major political events and natural disasters in the middle of the seventeenth century. Most scholars would not take Defoe's work as an accurate historical source, reflecting as it does conditions of his own age and particular artistic and literary concerns. Still, Defoe did compile a number of documents and related materials, including the ordinances related below. Despite his extensive journalistic background and production, we must take Defoe's work as a literary construct, but one that can simultaneously tell us about the cultural and social understanding of plague in the early eighteenth century and one that preserves traces of material from an earlier period that can shed light on the understanding of and response to plague. In this passage, Defoe presents ordinances from seventeenth-century London enacted in response to the outbreak of the plague. These ordinances addressed the work of numerous government officials, from examiners to medical staff. They also outlined procedures for dealing with infected individuals, goods, and houses, including the examination, closure, and cleaning of houses and public spaces. Dipping into moral and religious sensibilities, the selection concludes with several decrees related to moral behavior and restrictions on begging and festivities during the period of the devastating disease.

Text

These orders of my Lord mayor's were published, as I have said, the latter end of June, and took place [effect] from the 1st of July, and were as follows, viz.:

ORDERS CONCEIVED AND PUBLISHED BY THE LORD MAYOR AND ALDERMEN OF THE CITY OF LONDON CONCERNING THE INFECTION OF THE PLAGUE; 1665.

WHEREAS in the reign of our late sovereign King James, of happy memory, an act was made for the charitable relief and ordering of persons infected with the plague: whereby authority was given to justices of the peace, mayors, bailiffs, and other head officers to appoint within their several limits examiners, searchers, watchmen, keepers, and buriers, for the persons and places infected, and to minister [administer] unto them oaths for the performance of their offices; and the same statute did also authorise the giving of their directions, as unto them for the present necessity should seem good in their directions. It is now upon special consideration thought very expedient for preventing and avoiding of infection of sickness (if it shall so please Almighty God), that these officers following be appointed, and these orders hereafter duly observed.

Examiners to be appointed in every Parish

First, it is thought requisite, and so ordered, that in every parish there be one, two, or more persons of good sort and credit chosen and appointed by the alderman, his deputy, and common-council of every ward, by the name of examiners, to continue in that office for the space of two months at least: and, if any fit person so appointed shall refuse to undertake the same, the said parties so refusing to be committed to prison until they shall conform themselves accordingly.

The Examiner's Office

That these examiners be sworn by the aldermen to inquire and learn from time to time what houses in every parish be visited, and what persons be sick, and of what diseases, as near as they can inform themselves, and, upon doubt in that case, to command restraint of access until it appear what the disease shall prove; and if they find any person sick of the infection, to give order to the constable that the house be shut up; and if the constable shall be found remiss or negligent, to give notice thereof to the alderman of the ward.

Watchmen

That to every infected house there be appointed two watchmen, one for every day, and the other for the night, and that these watchmen have a special care that no person go in or out of such infected houses whereof they have the charge, upon pain of severe punishment. And the said watchmen to do such farther offices as the sick house shall need and require; and if the watchman be sent upon any business, to lock up the house and take the key with him; and the watchman by day to attend until ten o'clock at night, and the watchman by night until six in the morning.

Searchers

That there be a special care to appoint women-searchers in every parish, such as are of honest reputation, and of the best sort as can be got in this kind; and these to be sworn to make due search and true report to the utmost of their knowledge, whether the persons whose bodies they are appointed to search do die of the infection, or of what other diseases, as near as they can; and that the physicians who shall be appointed for cure and prevention of the infection, do call before them the said searchers, who are, or shall be, appointed for the several parishes under their respective cares, to the end they may consider whether they be fitly qualified for that employment, and charge them from time to time as they shall see cause, if they appear defective in their duties.

That no searcher, during this time of visitation, be permitted to use [hold] any public work or employment, or keep any shop or stall, or be employed as a laundress, or in any other common employment whatsoever.

Surgeons [Chirurgeons]

For better assistance of the searchers, forasmuch as there has been heretofore great abuse in misreporting the disease, to the farther spreading of the infection, it is therefore ordered that there be chosen and appointed able and discreet surgeons besides those that do already belong to the pesthouse; amongst whom the city and liberties to be quartered as they lie most apt and convenient, and every of these to have one quarter for his limit; and the said surgeons in every of their limits to join with the searchers for the view of the body, to the end there may be a true report made of the disease.

And farther, that the said surgeons shall visit and search such like persons as shall either send for them, or be named and directed unto them by the examiners of every parish, and inform themselves of the disease of the said parties.

And, forasmuch as the said surgeons are to be sequestered from all other cures [duties], and kept only to this disease of the infection, it is ordered that every of the said surgeons shall have twelve-pence a body searched by them, to be paid out of the goods of the party searched, if he be able, or otherwise by the parish.

Nurse-keepers

If any nurse-keeper shall remove herself out of any infected house before twenty-eight days after the decease of any person dying of the infection, the house to which the said nurse-keeper doth so remove herself shall be shut up until the said twenty-eight days be expired.

ORDERS CONCERNING INFECTED HOUSES, AND PERSONS SICK OF THE PLAGUE.

Notice to be given of the Sickness

The master of every house, as soon as anyone in his house complaineth, either of blotch, or purple, or swelling in any part of his body, or falleth otherwise dangerously sick without apparent cause of some other disease, shall give notice thereof to the examiner of health, within two hours after the said sign shall appear.

Sequestration of the Sick

As soon as any man shall be found by this examiner, surgeon, or searcher, to be sick of the plague, he shall the same night be sequestered in the same house, and in case he be so sequestered, then, though he die not, the house wherein he sickened should be shut up for a month after the use of the due preservatives taken by the rest.

Airing the Stuff

For sequestration of the goods and stuff of the infection, their bedding, and apparel, and hangings of chambers must be well aired with fire, and such perfumes as are requisite, within the infected house, before they be taken again to use. This to be done by the appointment of an examiner.

Shutting up of the House

If any person shall have visited any man known to be infected of the plague, or entereth willingly into any known infected house, being not allowed, the house wherein he inhabiteth shall be shut up for certain days by the examiner's direction.

None to be removed out of Infected Houses, but, etc.

Item [Likewise], That none be removed out of the house where he falleth sick of the infection, into any other house in the city (except it be to the pesthouse or a tent, or unto some such house, which the owner of the said house holdeth in his own hands, and occupieth by his own servants), and so as [except] security be given to the parish whither such remove is made, that the attendance and charge [responsibility] about the said visited persons shall be observed and charged [looked to] in all the particularities before expressed, without any cost of that parish to which any such remove shall happen to be made, and this remove to be done by night; and it shall be lawful to any person that hath two houses, to remove either his sound or his infected people to his spare house at his choice, so as if he send away first his sound, he do not after send thither the sick; nor again unto the sick the sound; and that the same which he sendeth be for one week, at the least, shut up, and secluded from company, for fear of some infection at the first not appearing.

Burial of the Dead

That the burial of the dead by this visitation be at most convenient hours, always before sun-rising, or after sun-setting, with the privity [consent] of the church-wardens, or constable, and not otherwise; and that no neighbours nor friends be suffered to accompany the corpse to church, or to enter the house visited, upon pain of having his house shut up, or be imprisoned.

And, that no corpse dying of infection shall be buried, or remain in any church in time of common prayer, sermon, or lecture. And that no children be suffered at time of burial of any corpse, in any church, church-yard, or burying-place, to come near the corpse, coffin, or grave; and that all the graves shall be at least six feet deep.

And farther, all public assemblies at other burials are to be forborne during the continuance of this visitation.

No Infected Stuff to be uttered [put into circulation]

That no clothes, stuff, bedding, or garments, be suffered to be carried or conveyed out of any infected houses, and that the criers and carriers abroad of bedding or old apparel to be sold or pawned, be utterly prohibited and restrained, and no brokers of bedding or old apparel be permitted to make any public show, or hang forth on their stalls, shopboards, or windows towards any street, lane, common-way, or passage, any old bedding or apparel to be sold, upon pain of imprisonment. And if any broker or other person shall buy any bedding, apparel, or other stuff out of any infected house within two months after the infection hath been there, his house shall be shut up as infected, and so shall continue shut up twenty days at the least.

No Person to be conveyed out of any Infected House

If any person visited do fortune [chance], by negligent looking unto, or by any other means, to come or be conveyed from a place infected to any other place, the parish from whence such party hath come, or been conveyed, upon notice thereof given, shall at their charge [injunction], cause the said party so visited and escaped to be carried and brought back again by night, and the parties in this case offending to be punished at the direction of the alderman of the ward, and the house of the receiver of such visited person to be shut up for twenty days.

Every visited House to be marked

That every house visited be marked with a red cross of a foot long, in the middle of the door, evident to be seen, and with these usual printed words, that is to say, 'Lord have mercy upon us,' to be set close over the same cross, there to continue until lawful opening of the same house.

Every Visited House to be watched

That the constables see every house shut up, and to be attended with watchmen, which may keep them in, and minister necessaries to them at their own charges [expenses], if they be able, or at the common charge if they be unable. The shutting up to be for the space of four weeks after all be whole.

That precise order to be taken that the searchers, surgeons, keepers, and buriers are not to pass the streets without holding a red rod or wand of three foot in length in their hands, open and evident to be seen, and are not to go into any other house than into their own, or into that whereunto they are directed or sent for, but to forbear and abstain from company, especially when they have been lately used in any such business or attendance.

Inmates

That where several inmates are in one and the same house, and any person in that house happens to be infected, no other person or family of such house shall be suffered to remove him or themselves without a certificate from the examiners of health of that parish, or in default thereof, the house whither she or they remove shall be shut up as in case of visitation.

Hackney-Coaches

That care be taken of hackney-coachmen, that they may not, as some of them have been observed to do after carrying of infected persons to the pesthouse and other places, be admitted to common use till their coaches be well aired, and have stood unemployed by the space of five or six days after such service.

ORDERS FOR CLEANSING AND KEEPING OF THE STREETS SWEPT.

The Streets to be kept Clean

First, it is thought necessary, and so ordered, that every householder do cause the street to be daily prepared before his door, and so to keep it clean swept all the week long.

That Rakers take it from out the Houses

That the sweeping and filth of houses be daily carried away by the rakers, and that the raker shall give notice of his coming by the blowing of a horn, as hitherto hath been done.

Lay-stalls [rubbish heaps] to be made far off from the City

That the lay-stalls be removed as far as may be out of the city and common passages, and that no nightman or other be suffered to empty a vault into any vault or garden near about the city.

Care to be had of unwholesome Fish or Flesh, and of musty Corn

That special care be taken that no stinking fish, or unwholesome flesh, or musty corn, or other corrupt fruits, of what sort soever, be suffered to be sold about the city, or any part of the same.

That the brewers and tippling-houses be looked into for musty and unwholesome casks.

That no hogs, dogs, or cats, or tame pigeons, or conies [rabbits], be suffered to be kept within any part of the city, or any swine to be or stray in the streets or lanes, but that such swine be impounded by the beadle or any other officer, and the owner punished according to act of common-council, and that the dogs be killed by the dog-killers appointed for that purpose.

ORDERS CONCERNING LOOSE PERSONS AND IDLE ASSEMBLIES.

Beggars

Forasmuch as nothing is more complained of than the multitude of rogues and wandering beggars that swarm in every place about the city, being a great cause of the spreading of the infection, and will not be avoided notwithstanding any orders that have been given to the contrary: it is therefore now ordered that such constables, and others whom this matter may any way concern, take special care that no wandering beggars be suffered in the streets of this city, in any fashion or manner whatsoever, upon the penalty provided by the law to be duly and severely executed upon them.

Plays

That all plays, bear-baitings, games, singing of ballads, buckler-play [exhibitions of skill with swords or bucklers], or such-like causes of assemblies of people be utterly prohibited, and the parties offending severely punished, by every alderman in his ward.

Feasting prohibited

That all public feasting, and particularly by the companies [guilds] of this city, and dinners at taverns, ale-houses, and other places of public entertainment, be forborne till farther order and allowance, and that the money thereby spared be preserved, and employed for the benefit and relief of the poor visited with the infection.

Tippling-Houses

That disorderly tippling in taverns, ale-houses, coffee-houses, and cellars, be severely looked unto as the common sin of the time, and greatest occasion of dispersing the plague. And that no company or person be suffered to remain or come into any tavern, ale-house, or coffee-house, to drink, after nine of the clock in the evening, according to the ancient law and custom of this city, upon the penalties ordained by law.

And for the better execution of these orders, and such other rules and directions as, upon farther consideration shall be found needful, it is ordered and enjoined that the aldermen, deputies, and common-council-men shall meet

together weekly, once, twice, thrice, or oftener, as cause shall require, at some one general place accustomed in their respective wards, being clear from infection of the plague, to consult how the said orders may be duly put in execution, not intending that any dwelling in or near places infected shall come to the said meeting while their coming may be doubtful. And the said aldermen, and deputies, and common-council-men, in their several wards, may put in execution any other good orders, that by them at their said meetings, shall be conceived and devised for preservation of his majesty's subjects from the infection.
SIR JOHN LAWRENCE, Lord Mayor.
SIR GEORGE WATERMAN
SIR CHARLES DOE, Sheriffs.

4.8 The lazaretto and medical services to the community

Author: Jacob ben Isaac Zahalon (1630–93)

Title: "The Treasure of Life" (1683)[74]

Introduction: Jacob ben Isaac Zahalon was born in Rome in 1630 and died in Ferrara in 1693. He was both a physician and a Talmudic scholar, called to serve as rabbi in Ferrara. He authored the medical work "The Treasure of Life" (Oẓar ha-Ḥayyim) as well as commentaries on various biblical books. In this selection he discusses the procedure for responding to the outbreak of plague in the Jewish Ghetto in 1656. He notes the various offices and institutions in the Ghetto as well as the role of both Jewish and non-Jewish physicians. Zahalon also points to the impact on the community in things such as closure of the Ghetto and restrictions on synagogue attendance.

Text

5416 (1656) from creation in the month of July [the plague appears to have arrived already in June], prior plague illness called *morbilli* began among the children and most of them died. After the illness broke out the adults became feverish with blotches on the skin, called *petechiae*, and in three days they were dead. The plague began three months earlier among the Gentiles and afterwards appeared among the Jews. It ended among the Gentiles before the Jews. And the plague continued in the Ghetto for nine months and approximately 800 children and adults died. And then the Jews were forbidden to go outside the Ghetto or go around the city, as was their custom. And two cardinals went into the Ghetto to prepare a decent place to construct there a lazaretto, in which to place all the sick people, to separate them from the others in order not to spread the plague among them. And they ordered that the selected place should be the houses along the river next to the Ghetto gate, known as the Gate of the Bridge, and there they [the sick people] should be closed in until they are healed. They appointed one bishop called minister Negroni, who came two times a day to investigate matters of the community and to assure that they do not mix [with healthy people], under [punishment of] a great fine. And they constructed a gallows in the street next to the large gate, to hang on it by rope anyone who transgresses against these orders. They also appointed one Gentile physician, who was closed up in the Ghetto with the Jews to see who was sick with the plague, [and] who should be placed in the above-mentioned lazaretto.

And the physician Samuel Gabai, may God protect and preserve him, was positioned there with the sick people sent there, and with his father, Cirocico, who after several days died and were taken from there in peace to the cemetery. They divided all the houses into three parts, and in each one a Jewish physician was appointed. ... Blessed be the Lord who did kindness to me, showed mercy to me, revived me, and saved me in order to do His will. I raise the cup of salvation and call upon the name of the Lord. Praises to the Lord for He is good, for His mercy endures forever.

At that time it happened to me that one patient, whose name was Sabbatai Cohen, of blessed memory, became ill with fever and he had a swelling in the groin, but I did not think it was a bubo. When he died I said that he did not die of the plague; but the Gentile physician said that he had died of the plague because he saw the swelling in the groin, which I said was a hernia of the intestines. There was therefore a great disagreement regarding whether the house should be closed up, as was customary when one died of the plague. What did they do? They brought the corpse to the Gentile physician, cut it open at that place, and saw that it was as I said, and not a bubo, as according to the Gentile physician, and I was saved. Blessed be He who redeems and saves.

And this was the practice: The Jewish physician visited the sick person, and if he saw signs of the plague, such as a black carbuncle or a bubo in the groin, [along] with fever or other serious symptoms, especially if the tongue was white as snow, he would tell the Gentile physician to come and examine [the patient], and it was an order to take the bed [and patient on it] to the place mentioned above of the lazaretto, to the physician Rabbi Samuel Gabai, of blessed memory. If the patient could not rise from his house, he would be treated there. At the time when the physician visited the sick, he would take in his hand a large candle of tar, burning it night and day to purify the air for his protection, ... and he also had theriac in his mouth. It was also very helpful, with God's help, that I made on my upper left arm a cautery, from which flowed much blood and bad moisture. In the nine months during which the plague occurred, there died, among young and old, about 800; including a young scholar, expert in the science of surgery, Rabbi Isaac Zahalon, son of my father's brother, of blessed memory. At that time all the souls in the holy community, may God protect and preserve it, four thousand and one hundred, all of whom may God protect and preserve. They brought the dead to the river in small boats and carried the bodies to the cemetery outside the city to a place called Pian de Devisori. ...

Because none of the people were able to go to the synagogue, therefore on Sabbath of the Torah portion 'Toledot Isaac' [Generations of Isaac] on the second day of the month of Kislev 5417 from creation [November 18, 1656], I, Jacob Zahalon, preached a sermon in Catalana Street, in the corner of the street in the house of Rabbi David Gategni, may God protect and preserve him, in the window of his house, and the community, may God protect and preserve them, and the people were standing in the street to hear the sermon. ...

No one was permitted to go out all day on the street except for physicians, but at certain appointed times they were able to do so to get food; even at night no one was allowed to leave from his house, and guards circulated around the city and if they found anyone they would put him into a prison set up in the Ghetto.

And after nine months the Holy One blessed be He remembered His people because of the merit of their forefathers and the plague ended and they were well and the gates were opened and Israel returned to the synagogues to pray as in former times. And they gave thanks and praise to God on High, whose kindness never ceases and whose mercy never ends.

4.9 An eighteenth-century epidemic in Western Europe

Artist: Etching by J. Rigaud after M. Serre

Title: "The Port of Marseille during the Plague of 1720" (1720)[75]

Introduction: One of the last major outbreaks of bubonic plague in Western Europe hit Marseilles in 1720, killing some 100,000 people in the city and surrounding area. As in other cities, various health measures were instituted by the city—from increased sanitation to quarantines. The etching provides a vivid illustration of the chaos and confusion caused by the large number of deaths in this port city. The plague in Marseilles spawned a great quantity of writings about the specific details of the plague, general reflections about plagues, and broader cultural and artistic reflections on disease and society.

VUE DE L'HOSTEL DE VILLE DE MARSEILLE ET D'UNE PARTIE DU PORT

Figure 4.9 An eighteenth-century epidemic in Western Europe.
Credit: Wellcome Collection

Notes

1 David Herlihy, *The Black Death and the Transformation of the West*, ed. Samuel K. Cohn, Jr (Cambridge, MA, 1997), 59.
2 Zlata Blazina Tomic and Vesna Blazina, *Expelling the Plague: The Health Office and the Implementation of Quarantine in Dubrovnik, 1377–1533* (Montreal, 2015), 3.
3 Regarding Health Boards, see Jane L. Stevens Crenshaw, *Plague Hospitals: Public Health for the City in Early Modern Venice* (Farnham, 2012).
4 Herlihy, *The Black Death*, 40.
5 See Blazina Tomic and Blazina, *Expelling the Plague*, 52, 68, 69, 85ff, 108, 113, 166, 170, 219.
6 In Korea, apparently during the early centuries of the Joseon dynasty (1392–1910), medical clinics were established outside the capital's gates to lock out infected people.

Don Baker, "Oriental Medicine in Korea," in *Medicine across Cultures: History and Practice of Medicine in Non-Western Cultures*, ed. Helaine Selin (Dordrecht, 2003), 133–53, here at 139.

7 William H. McNeill, *Plagues and Peoples* (New York, 1976), 181.

8 Carlo M. Cippola, *Cristofano and the Plague: A Study in the History of Public Health in the Age of Galileo* (Berkeley, 1973), 80.

9 Quoted in Franco Mormando, "Introduction: Response to the Plague in Early Modern Italy: What the Primary Sources, Printed and Painted, Reveal," in *Hope and Healing: Painting in Italy in a Time of Plague 1500–1800*, ed. Gauvin Alexander Bailey, Pamela M. Jones, Franco Mormando, and Thomas W. Worcester (Chicago, 2005), 1–44, here at 16.

10 See Samuel K. Cohn, Jr, *Cultures of Plague: Medical Thought at the End of the Renaissance* (Oxford, 2009).

11 See Herlihy, *The Black Death*, 62.

12 Joseph P. Byrne, *Daily Life during the Black Death* (Westport, 2006), 133. The idea of separation, of course, also had specific biblical roots. Consider Leviticus 14:1–5: "The Lord said to Moses, These are the regulations for any diseased person at the time of their ceremonial cleansing, when they are brought to the priest: The priest is to go outside the camp and examine them. If they have been healed of their defiling skin disease, the priest shall order that two live clean birds and some cedar wood, scarlet yarn and hyssop be brought for the person to be cleansed. Then the priest shall order that one of the birds be killed over fresh water in a clay pot."

13 David Chambers and Brian Pullan, eds, *Venice: A Documentary History, 1450–1630* (Toronto, 2001), 115.

14 The language has been updated. Richard Mead, *A Discourse on the Plague*, 9th ed. corrected and enlarged (London, 1744), i–iii; xiii–xx, xxii–xxv, 41–2.

15 Ibid.

16 Cippola, *Cristofano and the Plague*, 29–30.

17 Ibid., 158.

18 Ibid., 133.

19 Ibid., 56–7.

20 Alan Mikhail, *Nature and Empire in Ottoman Egypt: An Environmental History* (Cambridge, 2011), 232.

21 Kirsty Wilson Bowers, *Plague and Public Health in Early Modern Seville* (Rochester, 2013), 3.

22 Ibid., 2–3.

23 Ibid., 49.

24 Ibid., 50.

25 Daniel J. Schroeter, *The Sultan's Jew: Morocco and the Sephardi World* (Stanford, 2002), 48–9.

26 Mikhail, *Nature and Empire in Ottoman Egypt*, 230–1, for the full document.

27 Yaron Ayalon, *Natural Disasters in the Ottoman Empire: Plague, Famine, and Other Misfortunes* (Cambridge, 2015), 82–3.

28 Heinz Flamm, *Die ersten Infektions- oder Pest-Ordnungen in den österreichischen Erblanden, im Fürstlichen Erzstift Salzburg und im Innviertel im 16. Jahrhundert* (Vienna, 2008), 26.

29 Annemarie Kinzelbach, *Gesundbleiben, Krankwerden, Armsein in der frühneuzeitlichen Gesellschaft: Gesunde und Kranke in den Reichsstädten Überlingen und Ulm, 1500–1700* (Stuttgart, 1995), 110. See also Annemarie Kinzelbach, "Infection, Contagion, and Public Health in Late Medieval and Early Modern German Imperial Towns," *Journal of the History of Medicine and Allied Science* 61:3 (2006): 369–89; Ernst

L. Sabine, "Butchering in Medieval London," *Speculum* 8:3 (July 1933): 335–53, as well as Philip Slavin, "The Fifth Ride of the Apocalypse: The Great Cattle Plague in England and Wales and Its Economic Consequences, 1319–1350," in *Economic and Biological Interactions in Pre-Industrial Europe from the 13th to the 18th Centuries*, ed. Simonetta Cavaciocchi (Firenze, 2010), 165–79. See also Carole Rawcliffe, *Urban Bodies: Communal Health in Late Medieval English Towns and Cities* (Woodbridge, 2013).

30 Kinzelbach, *Gesundbleiben, Krankwerden, Armsein in der frühneuzeitlichen Gesellschaft*, 147. See also Kinzelbach, "Infection, Contagion, and Public Health in Late Medieval and Early Modern German Imperial Towns."

31 In 1583, 1585, 1586, 1591, 1592, 1596, 1597, 1610, 1611, 1628, 1632. See Kinzelbach, *Gesundbleiben, Krankwerden, Armsein*, 148.

32 See also John Henderson, "Coping with Epidemics in Renaissance Italy: Plague and the Great Pox," in *The Fifteenth Century XII: Society in an Age of Plague*, ed. Linda Clarke and Carole Rawcliffe (Woodbridge, 2013), 175–94.

33 Mikhail, *Nature and Empire in Ottoman Egypt*, 219.

34 William G. Naphy, *Plagues, Poisons, and Potions: Plague-Spreading Conspiracies in the Western Alps, c 1530–1640* (Manchester, 2002), chapter 1, 2.

35 Ibid., chapter 1, 3.

36 Ibid., chapter 1, 3.

37 Ibid., chapter 1, 3–4.

38 Ibid., chapter 1, 4.

39 Ibid., chapter 1, 5; including: the location of bakeries and types of loaves to be produced; the control of food prices; the repair of fountains and procurement of safe water; as well as increased anti-Jewish activity. See also ibid., chapter 1, 7.

40 Ibid., chapter 1, 6. Ironically, the Ottoman traveler, Evliya Celebi noted an episode in which the Pasha banished all prostitutes from Sofia in a reforming move. Celebi noted that rogues and brigands, out of carnal pleasure, associated the banishment of the prostitutes with famine and plague. (Evliya Celebi, *An Ottoman Traveller: Selections from the Book of Travels of Evliya Celebi*, ed. and trans. Robert Dankoff and Sooyong Kim (London, 2010), 10.)

41 Naphy, *Plagues, Poisons, and Potions*, chapter 1, 13.

42 Ibid., chapter 1, 9.

43 Kinzelbach, *Gesundbleiben, Krankwerden, Armsein*, 99.

44 Ibid., 100–3.

45 See Christopher R. Friedrichs, *The Early Modern City 1450–1750* (London, 1995), 281–5.

46 Walter G. Rödel, "Pestepidemien in Mainz im 17. Jahrhundert," *Scripta Mercaturae* 15:1 (1981): 85–103, here at 92–3.

47 Katharina Kellner, *Pesthauch über Regensburg: Seuchenbekämpfung und Hygiene im 18. Jahrhundert* (Regensburg, 2005), 160ff.

48 Nükhet Varlik, *Disease and Empire: A History of Plague Epidemics in the Early Modern Ottoman Empire (1453–1600)* (Doctoral Dissertation, University of Chicago, 2008), 206, 217–18, 221–2; for Europe see Kinzelbach, *Gesundbleiben, Krankwerden, Armsein*, 98ff.

49 Nükhet Varlik, "From 'Bete Noire' to 'le Mal de Constantinople:' Plagues, Medicine, and the Early Modern Ottoman State," *Journal of World History* 24:4 (December 2013), 741–70, here at 751, 756–7.

50 Ibid., 762.

51 Ibid., 763.

52 See Michael Dols, *The Black Death in the Middle East* (Princeton, 1977), 114.

53 Sylvie Anne Goldberg, *Crossing the Jabbok: Illness and Death in Ashkenazi Judaism in Sixteenth- through Nineteenth-Century Prague*, trans. Carol Cosman (Berkeley, 1996), 163.

54 Ibid., 169.

55 Joseph M. Davis, *Yom-Tov Lipmann Heller: Portrait of a Seventeenth-Century Rabbi* (Oxford, 2004), 48.

56 Chava Turniansky, "Yiddish Song as Historical Source Material: Plague in the Judenstadt of Prague in 1713," in *Jewish History; Essays in Honour of Chimen Abramsky*, ed. Ada Rapoport-Albert and Steven J. Zipperstein (London, 1988), 189–98, here at 196–7.

57 Kellner, *Pesthauch über Regensburg*, 218; see also Frank Hatje, *Leben und Sterben im Zeitalter der Pest: Basel im 15. bis 17. Jahrhundert* (Basel, 1992), 63f, 153–4.

58 Kellner, *Pesthauch über Regensburg*, 11–12.

59 Chambers and Pullan, eds, *Venice: A Documentary History, 1450–1630*, 115–16. Record of the Health Office: ASV Provveditori alla Sanità, reg 2, ff 103r–104v.

60 B. Ann Tlusty, *Augsburg during the Reformation Era: An Anthology of Sources* (Indianapolis, 2012), 266–9. Trans. from German, *Paul Hector Mairs 1. Chronik von 1547–1565*, Beilage VIII, 485–94.

61 In Joël Coste, *Représentations et comportements en temps d'épidémie dans la littérature imprimée de peste (1490–1725)* (Paris, 2007), 740–2; "Traicte de la peste," 103–8.

62 Chambers and Pullan, eds, *Venice: A Documentary History, 1450–1630*, 117–19, here 118–19. The Plague of 1575–77 from an account of the epidemic by a Venetian notary, Rocco Benedetti, 1630.

63 Source: G. Bondy, ed., *Zur Geschichte der Juden in Böhmen, Mähren und Schlesien: von 906 bis 1620*, 2 vols (Prague, 1906), here vol. 2, no. 1024, 805–7. Trans. Malynne Sternstein (University of Chicago).

64 Source: Abraham Catalano, "A World Turned Upside-Down," ed. Cecil Roth, *Kobetz al Yad* (1946): 67–101. See the translation by Alan D. Crown, "The World Overturned: The Plague Diary of Abraham Catalano," *Midstream* XIX:2 (February, 1973): 65–76, some of which I have included in this translation.

65 Columbia University exhibition, https://exhibitions.cul.columbia.edu/exhibits/show/hebrew_mss/communities/x893_ab8 [last accessed July 15, 2014].

66 This particular outbreak of plague in 1630–31 claimed 46,000 of 140,000 residents in Venice. Similarly, there was a 61% mortality rate in Verona where 38,000 died.

67 Catalano, "A World Turned Upside Down," 67.

68 Kohn, George C., *Encyclopedia of Plague and Pestilence: From Ancient Times to the Present* (New York, 2001), 201.

69 Catalano, "A World Turned Upside Down," 68.

70 Ibid., 68.

71 Ibid., 69.

72 Ibid., 69.

73 *Daniel Defoe's Journal of the Plague Year*, ed. George Rice Carpenter (New York: Longmans, Green, and Co., 1896), 38–48.

74 Translated from the excerpts in Joshua Leibowitz, "The Plague in the Roman Ghetto (1656) according to Zahalon and Cardinal Gastaldi," *Korot* 4:3–4 (1967): 155–69, here at 156–61. For a slightly different translation, see Jacob Zahalon, "The Treasure of Life," trans. in Harry A. Savitz, "Jacob Zahalon, and His Book 'The Treasure of Life,'" *NEJ of M* (July 25, 1935) 213:4: 167–76, here at 175–6 (Chapter XII; see also Chapter II).

75 Wellcome Library, London; published: chez l'auteurParis (ruë St. Jacques).

5 Social responses to plague
Memory, society, and culture

The impact of plague epidemics could vary a great deal by location and social conditions,[1] and different people might experience plague differently, depending upon their geographic location, social status, and type of exposure to the pathogen. It has been argued that although the Black Death did not discriminate in terms of the social status and gender of its victims, the later medieval and early modern plagues of the Second Pandemic increasingly, especially after 1400, more frequently affected the poor, women, and children.[2] As the historian Samuel K. Cohn, Jr writes,

> Historic plague was not as stable with fixed characteristics over its near-five century history as historians and scientists often assume. Rather, it evolved in its pathology over the late medieval and early modern periods (even if less dramatically than diseases such as syphilis or tuberculosis) but more so in the socio-economic characteristics of its victims and its demographic consequences.[3]

While higher mortality rates appear to have prevailed among the wealthy in some cases, as in early fifteenth-century outbreaks of plague in Dijon (France),[4] for example, during later plagues in the same city lower mortality was associated with wealth. Similarly, in seventeenth-century London there is evidence of lower mortality rates among the wealthy, perhaps related to their residing in stone buildings, which offered greater cleanliness and protection from rats and associated fleas.[5] In 1611 in the south German city of Constance, to take another example, 300 people died from the plague between September 17 and October 12. Of the 700 houses within the city, 355 were quarantined at some time. But the disease had a particularly dire effect on the "have-nots," who had a mortality rate of 39%; the very rich, by contrast, had a mortality rate of only 4%. Not surprisingly, the southern part of the city, with many poor areas, was particularly hard hit. In Milan in 1523, to cite one final example, four out of 60 parishes accounted for 42% of plague-related deaths and the victims of plague came typically from poorer families—none had a noble title and only 15% possessed a family name, indicating a higher social and economic level.[6]

The occurrence of plague does appear at times to have correlated with professional occupations and associated sanitary conditions, with certain groups such as bakers, millers, and butchers suffering higher death rates in certain cases, perhaps related to their work and the possible presence of rats in areas where food processing took place.[7] Throughout the Middle Ages and into the early modern period, stench—especially related to bad meat or the disposal of blood and entrails from butchered animals—was regularly associated by contemporaries with plague outbreaks.[8]

Age might also be a significant factor determining the scope and impact of a plague outbreak. The percentage of victims who were children in the plague of Bremen in 1713 was nearly 47%.[9] The same was true in Basel in the early seventeenth century, where 43% of those who contracted the plague were children, but 51.4% of those who died from the plague were children. What is more, although the mortality of men who contracted the plague was 62.1% and women 49.7%, the mortality of children was highest of all, regardless of gender, at 77.5%.[10]

Impact on daily life

Exposure to plague does not appear to lead to "a long-lasting immunological memory that will protect exposed individuals from future plague infections."[11] Because of the complexity of the immune system, the individual level of immune competence can vary based on biological as well as social and environmental conditions (including famines and associated malnutrition, as well as the presence of other infectious diseases).[12] Even within families, individual family members might have different experiences (and express or display the disease differently), depending on their own health and the particular people and pathogens they encountered.[13]

Many late medieval and early modern writers recounted the ravaging effects of plague, often in gruesome detail. [See, for example, 5.2] Of course, the devastation could depend a great deal on localized conditions—including the concurrence of other disasters (such as food shortages or particularly harsh weather) and the scope and effectiveness of local civic and health policies [See Chapter 4]—as well as the specific virulence of the disease. As we have seen, a good deal of civic and territorial legislation attempted to address epidemics and numerous modern state policies and interventions were born in the context of early modern plagues. In the end, plagues affected daily life for many people and they had an enduring impact on the psyche of early modern people writ large. [See 5.2, 5.3, 5.9, 5.10, and 5.11] The mere fear of plague spreading into an area from another place where it was observed could instill terror,[14] as in southern Italy in 1575 when one contemporary reported that although Syracuse was free of the plague people were greatly concerned by rumors of the plague in other parts of Sicily.[15] Still, vulnerability to and reports of the plague did not impede people's day-to-day existence, even if they engendered genuine concern. In any event, plague rarely caught a population completely by surprise in the early modern world, especially given increasing networks and vehicles of communication.[16] [See 5.9] What is more, in many places we find evidence of long periods of normalcy and freedom from plague and, especially for survivors of the disease, some sense of an ability to cope with the challenges brought by plague.

Plague could infiltrate late medieval and early modern society in a variety of ways. Early modern court records provide valuable evidence about prescriptive legislation as well as actual events. [See 5.9 and 5.11] While they must be read with caution, understanding that they present specific perspectives and identify issues adjudged important by contemporaries, such sources offer insights into communal norms and transgressions and the interaction of individuals. During times of crises, especially plagues, some communal and social bonds could break down or be used to mask nefarious plots or behavior. [See 5.7] The Court of Justice in Florence, for example, tried the siblings Francesco and Tomasia for an alleged plot against Tomasia's wealthy stepdaughter in the early fifteenth century:

> Francesco brought a notary and certain witnesses to Lena's house while she was lying ill [of the plague] in bed. And after being persuaded by Francesco and by Tomasia, Lena was interrogated by the notary and she consented to have Francesco as her husband. [They were quickly married.] Then two days later after the wedding Francesco had a conversation with certain persons from whom he sought counsel about arranging that Lena would not recover from her illness but instead would die. And since the pestilence was then (and still is) raging, he would never be suspected by anyone. Having received advice on this matter, Francesco went personally to the shop of Leonardo di Betto, a druggist in the Mercato Vecchio, and bought from him eight portions of arsenic and took it home. With Tomasia he placed that arsenic in a small loaf of bread and gave it to Lena to eat, for the purpose of poisoning and killing her. Lena ate that mixture and on the second day she died.
>
> The pair confessed to the crime and was sentenced to death. Francesco was executed but pregnant Tomasia's sentence was first postponed and later cancelled.[17]

Plague catastrophes also helped to create and inform communal memory and they often led to civic and religious rituals, including processions and pilgrimages.[18] [See 5.2, as well as Chapters 2 and 4] Various plague monuments were erected across Europe—in Vienna in 1693 and in Budapest in the late seventeenth or early eighteenth century, for example. The "Milan Column of Infamy," to take one prominent example, recounted a story from the plague of 1630 in Milan in which a woman spied a scrivener unwittingly wiping ink on a wall and accused him of spreading poison. Apprehended, he first denied any evil actions but then broke down in torture and confessed his guilt, "revealing" that the inkhorn in his belt was from Guglielmo Piazza and that he had obtained the "ointment" from Giangiacomo Mora. The column of infamy was erected with the following inscription (in Latin):

> Here, where this plot of ground extends, formerly stood the shop of the barber Giangiacomo Mora, who had conspired with Guglielmo Piazza,

Commissary of the Public Health, and with others, while a frightful plague exercised its ravages, by means of deadly ointments spread on all sides, to hurl many citizens to a cruel death. For this, the Senate, having declared them both to be enemies of their country, decreed that, placed on an elevated car, their flesh should be torn with red-hot pincers, their right hands cut off, and their bones be broke; that they should be extended on the wheel, and at the end of six hours be put to death, and burnt. Then, and that there might remain no trace of these guilty men, their possessions should be sold at public sale, their ashes thrown into the river, and to perpetuate the memory of their deed the Senate wills that the house in which the crime was projected shall be razed to the ground, shall never be rebuilt, and that in its place a column shall be erected which shall be called Infamous. Keep afar off, then, afar off, good citizens, lest this accursed ground should pollute you with its infamy. August, 1630.[19]

Other structures, such as churches, might be constructed as thanksgiving for the end of the plague, as was the case in Venice in 1576 and again in 1630.[20] Memorials could serve other purposes as well. In sixteenth-century Florence, a column and gallows were set up in the middle of the city as a means to deter robbers or others who mixed with healthy people to infect them.[21] [See also 5.7] Various communal rituals carried out in public spaces also evolved in the early modern period. The "Black Wedding" emerged in some Jewish communities in Eastern Europe, notably Berdichev, by the 1770s and is attested to by ethnographic accounts from the twentieth century. In this uncommon ceremony, a wedding was held in the cemetery, to curry the favor of the dead, who could act as intercessionaries with God to halt raging epidemics.[22]

Marginalization: plague as polemical tool and boundary marker

Plagues could be localized, but they might also extend beyond individual communities and regions, with little respect of civic or territorial boundaries, giving rise to other concerns, for example in such things as economic conditions and travel. [See 5.9 and 5.11] Responses to the plague were telling of such conditions and of the possibilities for significant and sustained change in many early modern societies. The outbreak, or even the threat, of plague could cut deep social fissures and inflame latent social, economic, political, and cultural tensions. The terror of the plague was both an impetus to retrenchment of customs and perspectives, but also at times a flashpoint for apocalyptic thought and action. [See 5.3] Plague could be leveraged to effect changes. It could be coopted to build community or to establish barriers and marginalize groups or individuals.[23]

Plagues could have especially significant social and political dimensions. Utilizing different forms of polemics, early modern writers could reference plague to inform and support a variety of religious and political perspectives and initiatives. [See 5.5 and 5.6] The Italian Capuchin friar Lawrence of Brindisi (1559–1619), for example, took the plague that had recently broken out in

Prague as an opportunity to preach against the Protestants when he visited that city.[24] Numerous early modern Catholic writers connected the dissemination of "heretical," that is Protestant, doctrines with the outbreak of plague, which according to their logic, was sent by God to punish Catholic sins.[25] One early modern Jesuit writer noted that when three teachers and a rector fell to the plague, the Lutherans in Graz accused the Jesuits of causing the infection by poisoning the well, though he carefully refuted that accusation by pointing out that upon a thorough cleaning nothing nefarious was revealed.[26] Returning the favor, Jesuits could blame the Lutherans. In one instance, it was claimed that a "zealous Lutheran" had introduced a pestiferous epidemic into the area.[27] Visual depictions of plagues might also have polemical uses. The Flemish painter Michael Sweerts' (1618–64) "Plague in an Ancient City" appears to have carried with it a religious polemic, supporting Catholicism as the one true faith in an age of robust Catholic and Protestant conflict.[28]

Plague could also be associated with political polemics. The critics of the Doge of Venice in 1577 linked him and his tenure with various misfortunes that struck the city. According to one contemporary writer, reporting on the illness of the Doge, upon the news of his sickness:

> all orders of the Republic showed themselves very well content, for everyone remembered how unfortunate had been the time of his Principate, even up to this present moment, for there seemed to be no kind of ill luck or catastrophe that had failed to descend upon our country under his ill-starred auspices. For it had suffered great loses of cities and of whole kingdoms, fires, floods, famines, and at last the most terrible pestilence.[29]

Already in the early modern period discussions of plague frequently hinged on particular views of geographic regions, climates, and the associated characteristics of different peoples. In 1506, Portuguese sailors fled the plague in Lisbon and arrived in the East Indies, seen by some as a haven for good health.[30] Capturing some of the early modern sensibilities that animated many political and medical discussions of early modern plague, one early nineteenth-century writer asserted that nations of the North were generally more advanced than those of the Levant, though even in the North some had made less progress than others.[31] Such geographic discrimination was hardly limited to Europe. In medieval and early modern China regionalism was seen as a determining factor in the health disposition of people and the nature and transmission of specific diseases.[32]

While not bubonic plague, the devastation wrought by other diseases on native Americans, often carried to the new world by European conquerors, was ironically seen as proof of the weakness and errors of the natives and as something like justification or approval for taking over their lands. Rev. Francis Higginson in his 1629 *A Short and True Description of New England*,[33] for example, asserted that:

> Their subjects about twelve years since were swept away by a great and grievous plague [used in a general sense] that was amongst them, so that

there are very few left to inhabit the country. The Indians are not able to make use of the one fourth part of the land, neither have they any settled places, as towns to dwell in, nor any ground as they challenge for their own possession, but change their habitation from place to place.

Or, consider a text in the name of King James, granting Plymouth Plantation's patent,[34] which noted that,

> Within these late years, there hath, by God's visitation, reigned a wonderful plague, together with many horrible slaughters and murders, committed amongst the savages and British people there heretofore inhabiting, in a manner to the utter destruction, devastation, and depopulation of that whole territory, so as there is not left, for many leagues together, in a manner, any that do claim or challenge any kind of interest therein ... whereby we, in our judgement, are persuaded and satisfied, that the appointed time is come in which Almighty God, in his great goodness and bounty towards us, and our people, hath thought fit and determined, that those large and goodly territories, deserted as it were by their natural inhabitants, should be possessed and enjoyed by such of our subjects.

Indeed, even as the outbreak of an epidemic might cause colonists fear and pause to consider their own moral improvement, it could be described more metaphorically as a weapon.[35] According to Thomas Harriot's "Briefe and True Report of the New Found Land of Virginia" (1588), the natives "were perswaded that [the plague] was the worke of our God through our meanes, and that wee by him might kil and slai whom wee would without weapons and not come neere them."[36]

Plagues were often associated with marginal and liminal groups, such as the poor, criminals, foreigners, gypsies, and especially in Europe, Jews, who were accused of spreading the disease willfully and maliciously or inadvertently through poor hygiene or criminal behavior. [**See, for example, 5.5**] To take only one illustrative example, consider the plague of the mid-1660s, which struck numerous communities along the Rhine River, with particularly virulent outbreaks in 1665 and 1666, followed by epidemics in Switzerland in 1667 and 1668. As many people fled the plague concerns arose about migrants from infected areas. Many cities took precautions to protect their citizens from people and goods arriving from infected areas or areas suspected of being infected. According to a placard posted outside Mainz on June 19, 1666:

> Afterwards it was felt that in the neighborhood and now and then on the land the contagious disease and evil plague erupted ... with great sensation, and to prevent such diseases and plagues from coming into this city admission of people coming here from already infected areas was reduced. It was made public that nobody would be tolerated to enter this electoral residence-city from such infected [places] or suspected places on pain of punishment: in the case that someone is recognized, enters here, and is found

secretly or through a pretext that he is not from an infected region, that person or his possessions shall be punished without neglect—his person or his goods. Thereby should every person concerned know how to behave and to be protected from damage.[37]

Throughout the early modern period members of these groups could be marginalized, in legislation as well as literature, though after the Black Death in the middle of the fourteenth century discrimination against these groups, physical attack, expulsion, and murder were generally rare,[38] **[See 5.1]** pointing to changing understanding of the plague and the increased emphasis on preventing and curing it.[39] At times, the discourse of plague reveals imaginative constructs that drew from many different medical, religious, and historical experiences and texts and, when it came to Jews, a long, and often complicated, history of Jewish and Christian relations. At other times, it revealed multifaceted interactions between social, ethnic, and religious groups.

Marginal and liminal segments of society: the poor, foreigners, and Jews

As noted above, in some places the poor were increasingly victims of early modern plague. The plight of the poor was graphically captured in an account from Padua in 1405 (Gatari), with people in the plague-ridden city crowded into houses, churches, monasteries, and warehouses. The author recounted the stench and putrefied air, along with great need and hunger. "And these conditions combined with other forces of darkness sparked a ferocious plague in the city of Padua," the author noted,

> with little nuts forming on some around the throat, on others, on the arms, and on some, on the thighs, along with an intolerable and burning fever with discharges of blood. With this illness the victims lived two or three days at the most and died.[40]

Treatment of the poor at times of plague was also related to changing early modern notions of and attention to poverty. In late medieval and early modern Europe a large number of poor ordinances were produced that dictated charity and prescribed behavior of and towards the poor. Increasingly, differences were noted between those who were legitimately needy and could not support themselves and those who were lazy and simply refused to work.[41] Legislation also dictated the number of beggars allowed in an area and often prescribed where and when they could beg for alms.

The poor were frequently associated with plague—due to their own filth, vagabondage, lack of food, other illnesses, etc.—as well as their possible role in carrying disease. In some cases, this led to the appointment of public doctors or doctors specifically assigned to work with the indigent. Such responses could reflect a sense of civic obligation, though at times perhaps also fear.[42] The poor could be scapegoated as a result, or even in advance, of the plague.[43] The outbreak of plague could stoke social and communal tensions and wreak havoc beyond the medical emergencies it spawned more directly. In early modern Italy, the historian Brian Pullan has demonstrated that the civic response to plague could have many dimensions and result from diverging issues and concerns.[44] "Relieving the poor," he argues, "could at once be an act of placation addressed to God and a practical measure for containing an epidemic."[45] At the same time, the plague could intensify the feeling that the poor were to be pitied for the suffering or needed for their labor;[46] and yet the poor were to be feared because of their role in spreading disease or in imagined and nefarious plots against society.[47]

The poor were often less resistant to plague and had fewer means to treat it if they did contract it. While some areas had more physicians per capita, in most cases people facing diseases utilized the services of a wide range of healers, even as medical experts were increasingly professionalized and university curricula were formalized and the number of hospitals increased in the early modern period.[48] At times, this diverse range of treatments was related to socio-economic standing, but not always. "Alternative" healers could be quite expensive as well and they frequently catered to a wealthier clientele. Reflecting different conditions and means, some early modern plague regiments in fact differentiated the medications to be used for the poor and the rich.[49] On the other hand, plague ordinances stressed equal punishments at times of plague for both rich and poor for any misbehavior,[50] suggesting the need for governmental oversight regardless of the drastically different social conditions people may have experienced.

As with the Black Death of the fourteenth century, in the seventeenth century in various locations, such as Seville (1630), concerns were raised about the possibility of conspiracies involving the production of various substances to spread the plague.[51] [See 5.7] Such conspiracy theories often focused on outsiders, notably foreigners, the poor, and Jews. These accusations had long roots, stretching well into the Middle Ages. Brian Pullan further observes that,

> Suspicion tended to spread from casual or seasonal migrants to refugee populations: in Venice it clung to Slavs and Albanians in the mid-fifteenth century, and a century later to Marranos or Portuguese New Christians from the Low Countries. The expulsion of Marranos by the senate in 1550 was prompted not only by the argument that they were bearers of heresy, mingling Christianity and Judaism or moving at will between the two faiths, but also by the fear that their squalid and overcrowded lodgings would breed disease. Hence the metaphorical plague of heresy would combine with a clinical pestilence to undermine both the physical health and the orthodoxy of Venice.[52]

Drawing from various non-Jewish sources, one late sixteenth-century Jewish historian wrote of the fourteenth-century Black Death that,

> Also in many places there occurred desolation from the inhabitants, a plague like none other. And among the Jews they did not die except a very few,

that on account of this harbored jealousy of the Jews in Spain [Sefarad], in France and in Germany, libeled them and said that they sent poison in the air and in the rivers, and they killed and they slaughtered thousands and ten thousands of Jews.[53]

[See also 5.5] Indeed, the narratives of persecution of Jews during the Black Death would come to dictate much of later plague historical writing. We possess particularly disturbing accounts of Jewish confessions under torture and resulting executions and attacks. The Jews of Savoy, to take one prominent example, were interrogated in the fall of 1348. According to documents drawn from the city of Strasbourg, ten Jews (nine men and one woman) from several cities in the county of Savoy were arrested and interrogated. Under torture they confessed to poisoning wells in order to transmit plague to Christians. Jews and other marginalized groups had been accused of poisoning at various times during the medieval and early modern periods. Such accusations and forced "confessions" under torture further incited attacks on and murders of Jews across Western Europe. According to the trial records, utilized for political purposes:

> Balavigny, a Jewish surgeon living at Thonon, was nonetheless imprisoned in Chillon because he was apprehended within the castellan's jurisdiction. He was briefly put to the question, and when he was released from torture, he confessed after a long interval of time that around ten weeks ago, Rabbi Jacob, who had come from Toledo and was staying at Chambéry since Easter [April 20], sent to him at Thonon through a certain Jewish serving boy a heap of poison about the size of an egg, which was in the form of a powder enclosed in a sack of fine, sewn leather, together with a certain letter, in which he ordered him under pain of excommunication and out of obedience to his religion to put the said poison into the greatest and most public well of the town, which was used the most often, in order to poison the people who would use the water of this well. And he was not to reveal this to anyone at all under the aforesaid penalty. It also was stated in the said letter that similar things were ordered in other mandates sent out by the Jewish rabbis of his religion to diverse and various places.[54]

As studies of inquisition records have shown, interrogators often planted in the minds and mouths of those being tortured specific details for which they were searching. The allegations in this case built upon and fed into ongoing notions that Jews—as the ultimate religious, social, and political outsiders—through extensive networks plotted against Christians. During times of plague, despite other and generally more rational minds, such accusations could serve as justifications for scapegoating, confiscation of property, and even murder. [See 5.1, 5.5, and 5.8, for example]

Attacks against the Jews during earlier periods of the second Pandemic are well known—especially during the Black Death of the mid-fourteenth century—even if some recent scholars have questioned whether the attacks were as deadly or widespread as once perceived.[55] Typical of the period is the account of events in and around Strasbourg by the late medieval chronicler Friedrich Closener:

> This epidemic also came to Strasbourg in the summer of the above mentioned year, and it is estimated that about sixteen thousand people died ... In the matter of this plague the Jews throughout the world were reviled and accused in all lands of having caused it through the poison which they are said to have put into the water and the wells—that is what they were accused of—and for this reason the Jews were burnt all the way from the Mediterranean into Germany, but not in Avignon, for the pope protected them there.[56]

Tortured Jews in parts of Switzerland confessed to poisoning wells, leading to attacks against the Jews in Basel, among other places. Bowing to popular pressure, the Bishop and city governors in Strasbourg agreed to kill the Jews, burning some 2,000. Those who accepted baptism were spared, but debts to Jews were cancelled and Jews had to surrender all pledges. Jewish possessions were confiscated and, according to the chronicler, distributed among the working class. A similar fate awaited many Jewish communities along the Rhine. Jews were banned from the city for 100 years, but were again briefly admitted by 1368.[57]

Physical violence against Jews associated with the plague appears to have dissipated and in most cases disappeared in the early modern period, however, as other explanations for plague were advanced and as political conditions changed. According to one recent historian,

> After 1350 social violence changed in most places—Quiescence, flagellant purging, and the mass murder of beggars, Catalans or Jews disappear from the records. With increasing regularity peasants, artisans and bourgeois now directed their misgivings and frustration against those in power within society.[58]

Further, while plague narratives revealed details about Jewish daily life, including the overcrowding and unsanitary conditions facing some Jews in larger ghettoized communities, they also at times belied multifaceted, and not always negative, interactions between Jews and Christians. [See 5.9, regarding this complexity]

Well into the sixteenth century, however, we can still find accusations (if not associated physical attacks) that Jews spread the plague. In December 1576 Emmanuel Philibert, based on information allegedly received from a Jew, believed that Jews had intentionally introduced the plague into Venice and that it was spreading throughout the Duchy of Savoy from Nice. The same month the papal nuncio reported that the Duke informed him that the plague was brought to Venice by the Turks through the Jews and that they were spreading it through other Jews traveling from Algiers.[59] Beyond (apparently decreasing early modern) physical violence, civic and territorial authorities often legislated against Jewish immigration and business during times of plague (as they did against other groups as well) and some plague ordinances carried with them anti-Jewish language and sensibilities.

The plague revealed at times tense relationships between Jews and their non-Jewish neighbors. The seventeenth-century Alsatian memoirist Asher Levy of Reichshofen described serious plagues on several occasions. Regarding the epidemic of 1628/29,[60] for example, he recorded that:

> The plague, it should be far from us, broke out here in Reichshofen ... in the month Cheshvan [5]389 (1628), also in Hagenau, and ... nothing decreased until Rosh Chodesh Shevat [5]389 (1629). More than a hundred people died here and almost 50 houses were polluted, but, praise God, no dog sharpened his tongue against any of the Children of Israel. And I took myself to all the officials in our surroundings in order to search a sanctuary and to flee there with my wife and my family until after the epidemic, but I found no resting place for my soul, and I remained here against my will, and God saved me along with the rest of His people Israel.[61]

Utilizing biblical metaphor, Asher recorded the general situation, noting the number of houses infected in the city. But, he was also quick to point out that no Jews perished or were harmed. Like others, Asher searched the surrounding areas for refuge from the plague, but he could not find any and he remained in the city throughout the epidemic. The situation was a bit different a few years later. Regarding the plague of 1633,[62] Asher wrote,

> I thank God for my help. On Thursday, the 19th of Elul [5]393 (1633), I returned to my house, with my wife and my children (they should live), and when I came to my house, I found it ravaged and destroyed. The windows were smashed, oven and hearth pulled down, all wooden implements thrown here and there, and that was nothing in comparison to other devastated houses of Jews. I prayed to God, my Rock, that He send me favor to dwell in my house and allow life and peace and wealth and honor and to hear good reports.[63]

At the same time, early modern plague narratives detailed many aspects of daily life, including diet, medicine, housing, and work—allowing for profitable comparisons of the experiences of different groups. Jews, like their Christian contemporaries combined traditional Jewish approaches to healing with contemporary medical and popular remedies. Jews were simultaneously particularistic, focused on the developments within their communities, and universalistic, paying careful attention to and participating in the developments of broader central European society. [See 5.9 and 5.11] Jews were clearly aware of and engaged with local and regional news and ordinances, and they negotiated with local rulers and authorities even as they were marginalized at times by volatile and inconsistent relations with their neighbors and their protectors. In any event, openly anti-Jewish violence against people and property was occasionally recorded, but often overcome, particularly when some Church leaders rejected in theory the notion that Jews malevolently spread the plague [**See 5.1**]—even if they continued to see Jews and Judaism in a generally negative light.

As it did other communities, the plague affected all segments of the Jewish community, frequently taking the lives of entire families. In times of large-scale plagues, Jews left chilling reports of the dead, who could not be buried quickly and whose corpses often rotted in the sun, as well as the death of babies and children.[64] Jewish communities had to address many different communal concerns. Moses ben Hayim Eisenstadt in the eighteenth century described the length to which some Jewish community members in Prague went to set up temporary housing and provide food for the daily increasing number of Jewish poor. "There were eight hundred sick, and sometimes this number rose to a thousand at once," he rued.[65] At times, Jewish accounts suggest inter-communal dissonance—from criticism of Jewish leaders who fled the plague[66] to the appointment of Jewish policemen or officials to guarantee that no criminal activity was taking place within the Ghetto at the time of the plague.[67] In describing the plague outbreak of 1713, Eisenstadt regretted that,

> In this state of cruelty, people rose up against each other ... no one could perform the *gemilut hesed* [kindness, good deeds], for fear of being infected himself ... I cannot be silent about what happened, how people began [to tear] each other to pieces.[68]

Recent research has stressed the extent to which responses to sickness were similar among Jews and Christians, even to the extent that Jews participated in the broader culture in which people assumed the existence of demons, consulted astrological signs, and relied on amulets, even as they consulted more formal medical theories and books.[69] In Eisenstadt's account one finds a number of common practical treatments recommended for plague. In addition to "solemn services and supplications to Heaven," beseeching God to end His wrath,[70] Eisenstadt wrote that, "When going out is unavoidable, it would be useful to wash your face and hands in vinegar, and also hold a sponge soaked in vinegar to your nose and mouth until you have returned home."[71] Like others he suggested that people apply to infected parts of the body a plaster comprised of eggs and other ingredients.[72] Jews, like Christians, also freely mixed religious and contemporary "medical" responses to the plague. [**See 5.9**]

Cultural responses to plague

Despite, or precisely because of, geographical and chronological variations and differing impacts of individual outbreaks, plague entered early modern narratives in a rich variety of ways. It was determined, and simultaneously shaped by, numerous medical, religious, social, political, and cultural concerns. Plague narratives, therefore, reveal a great deal about the spread and impact of the disease; but they can also simultaneously allow us to peer deeper into larger societal processes and issues during periods when plague was manifest, as well as periods when plague was a more distant memory or fear. [**See, for example, 5.5 and 5.8, for the narrative and polemical use of plague persecution in early modern Jewish writing**]

Some renowned writers engaged with the theme of plague in diverse ways during the period of the Second Pandemic. Indeed, the term and concept of "plague," beyond the disease itself, had long-lasting effects on early modern and modern culture. Famous and oft-cited today is Giovanni Boccaccio (1313–75), the son of a merchant from Tuscany, whose well-known work, *The Decameron* (1348–53), includes lengthy literary discussion of the Black Death. The theme of plague was also the subject of theatrical performances—ironically theaters were themselves frequently forced to close during epidemics and they were often labelled as plagues on society by their enemies. William Shakespeare's oeuvre is filled with references to plague—as curses on people, but also as real life epidemics that wrought disaster on early modern populations. Shakespeare himself lived through several severe outbreaks of plague in late sixteenth- and early seventeenth-century London. Below are included excerpts from the work of Daniel Defoe, who wrote extensively about plague. [**See 5.12**] While Defoe was writing after the plague outbreak he described, and his accounts represent a literary construction of plague—one to be sure that at times drew from a wide range of documentary sources—the ways that he thought about and presented plague to his readers can tell us a good deal about the cultural concerns and sensibilities at the end of the early modern period.

Diverse forms of literature, as well as music and art, were likewise affected by plague sensibilities in the early modern world. These works both reflected and helped to shape early modern culture and worldviews. One significant musical manuscript from the later Middle Ages, probably from the early fifteenth century, for example, reflected changes in sacred music, but the associated words could also shed light on cultural understanding of and responses to plague, including through the rather traditional call to Saint Sebastian for intercession.[73]

Plague, as we have seen, had medical and religious dimensions that were often inextricably linked. Similarly, plague was simultaneously perceived through cultural lenses and helped to shape culture itself. Early modern plague narratives built upon an extensive range of classical and medieval sources, but to this added contemporary concerns and worldviews that were shaped by a wide range of factors—some quite localized and other similar across geographical regions. But experiences with plague also shaped early modern culture in some ways that seem quite obvious and in others that appear to be more subtle. In the arts and in literature, plague could reflect cultural values and norms, even as the associated narratives could be used to criticize perspectives, policies, and priorities. Some of the later texts included in this volume reveal this tension. They present narratives of the plague that appear to be rooted in the lived experiences of past generations, yet the selectivity and refashioning that their authors engaged in made them texts of their days and not merely antiquarian accounts.

As noted in the Introduction, theories of resilience note the importance of memory and narrative, as well as communal structures and learning from experience. In that regard, although many early modern communities remained vulnerable to plague and other diseases, they also displayed a remarkable ability to use the plague in a variety of ways to address medical, religious, political, and social conditions. In a very real sense, then, plague discourse and imagination played as large a role as response to actual plague throughout the early modern period. While the death rates and impact varied tremendously from place to place, plague was a defining concept in early modern life that helped to shape worldviews and daily decision-making.

Sources

5.1 Judicial protection of Jews—theory

Author: Pope Clement VI (1291–1352, r 1342–52)

Title: "Sicut Judeis" (Mandate to Protect the Jews) (October 1, 1348)[74]

Introduction: Jews were often accused of various crimes against Christianity. Particularly noteworthy in the Middle Ages and into the early modern period were host desecration and ritual murder. Increasingly since the thirteenth century, Jews were also accused of other criminal activity—from international conspiracy to economic crimes, and even murder, especially through poisoning. While accusations against Jews for poisoning of wells and ritual murder were generally disavowed by the Church, at least in theory, they nevertheless circulated widely in secular society and in both learned and popular literature and art. The pronouncements of the Church were hardly pro-Jewish and they often did little to curtail attacks against or negative impressions of Jews in Christian society. The Church leadership believed that the Jews fell under their protection, even as they believed that the Jews were theologically mistaken and problematic. While a chronologically early document in the scope of this volume, the following decree points to the complexity of the position of Jews in Christian society as well as the notion of (and challenges to) authority during the early modern period. The decree underscores the religious as well as economic and political forces that underpinned accusations (and actions) against the Jews.

Text

... We rightly detest the treachery of the Jews, who endure in their hardness, [by which they] do not recognize the words of the prophets and their own sacred writings and moreover do not pay attention to the Christian faith and revealed salvation; nevertheless, we are attentive, because it was from these same Jews that our Savior stemmed, when he assumed mortal flesh for the salvation of the human race. We have chosen, for the sake of humanity, to support [them now that] they have called upon us for our protection and clemency of Christian piety. Favorably recalling Calixtus, Eugene, Alexander, Clement, Celestine, Innocent, Gregory, Nicholas, Honorius, and Nicholas III, Roman Pontiffs, our predecessors, [we have] inherited from the past the protection of our shield to command patience; [it being] previously established that no Christians should harm or kill these Jews personally, without the authority of the lords or officials of the land or region in which they reside; or steal their assets or extract from them forced services, except if they do so according to the habit of the time ... Recently, however, it has come to our attention through public report [fama], or truly [through] infamy, that some Christians, [with] extraordinary rashness have wickedly slayed some of these Jews, regardless of age or sex, falsely blaming them for the pestilence, [alleging them to be] seduced by the devil, even as [it is] God [Who] afflicts the Christian people, provoked by the sins of these very people. Although the Jews are prepared to submit to judgment before a competent judge concerning such a slanderous crime, this is not enough to cool the violence of these same Christians, [for whom] violence only further excites their fury. Where their error is seen and not corrected, it is endorsed. And although [for] these same Jews, when they are culpable or are perhaps guilty or knowledgeable of such outrages, any imaginable penalty, appropriate and severe, is hardly sufficient, it does not seem that the Jews are responsible for the crime that they are occasionally charged with, since it is known in different regions of the world, affecting the Jews themselves and many other nations, where there are no Jews. We order everyone by apostolic writing, and each of you who will be asked to do this, in your churches during established masses, when people are gathered, clergy and the people, to admonish them expressly upon pain of excommunication, which you may inflict on those who act otherwise, that they not presume, by any authority or their own rashness, to seize, strike, wound, or kill Jews or to exact from them forced labor. But if anyone, related to either these or any other matters, has brought the Jews before competent judges—which they may do regarding these or any other excesses committed by the Jew—they may proceed according to ordinary judicial procedures, provided it does not annul any authority.

5.2 Communal responses and social implications of the plague

Author: Ahmad ibn ʿAlī al-Maqrīzī (1364–1442)

Title: *A History of the Ayyubids and Mamluks* (fifteenth century)[75]

Introduction: Ahmad ibn ʿAlī al-Maqrīzī was born and lived in Cairo. He was a historian of Mamluk Egypt and himself a Sunni Muslim. A legal scholar and historian, he also held some lower governmental positions and served for a time as a preacher. In Damascus he was an inspector and lecturer, returning to retire in Egypt. Writing a couple generations after the events he narrated, Maqrīzī highlights the impact of plague on the religious, but also social and economic conditions of Egyptian society. He depicts abandoned and decaying cities, shortages of religious and communal functionaries, as well as the effect that depleted populations had on agricultural production and trade. Other communities suffered similar fates during particularly harsh epidemics and the rate of return to more normal functioning could vary tremendously depending on a number of factors, from internal organization and economic reserves to broader regional conditions.

Text

At the end of the month of ramadān (22 December), the sultan returned from Syria. In [the month of] šawwāl (January 1349), there appeared new symptoms that consisted of spitting of blood. The sick person felt an internal fever, followed by an uncontrollable desire to vomit, then one spat blood and died. The inhabitants of a house were affected one after the other and, in a night or two, the house became deserted. Each individual lived obsessed that he was going to die this way. He was preparing for a good death by distributing alms; acts of reconciliation were witnessed and acts of devotion multiplied.

No one had time to see doctors or take potions or drugs, so sudden was death. In the middle of [the month of] šawwāl (7 January), cadavers piled up in the streets and the steps; teams were eventually appointed to perform the burials, and pious people were standing permanently in the various places of prayer in Cairo and Old Cairo to recite the prayers of funerals. This epidemic went beyond the bounds of the understanding, and it is impossible to draw a statistic. Almost all the royal guard disappeared and the barracks of the Citadel were empty of their effects.

At the start of [the month of] dū l-qaʾda [21 January], Cairo had become an abandoned desert, and one did not see any passersby on the streets. A man could go from the Port Zuwayla to Bāb al-Nasr without coming across a living soul. The dead were very numerous, and all the world could think of nothing else. The decomposing bodies piled up in the streets. People were moving about with worried faces. Everywhere one heard lamentations, and one could not pass by any house without being disturbed by the howling. The corpses formed piles on the public highway, [funeral] processions were so numerous that they could not march without colliding, and the dead were not transported without confusion.

One Friday, after the public prayer, in the mosque of al-Hakim in Cairo, the funeral prayer was recited in front of a double row of coffins, aligned from the preacher's maqsura to the main door: the imam was standing on the threshold of the door and the people stood behind it outside the building ...

According to another estimate, there were twenty thousand deaths in a single day. The statistics of the funerals in Cairo, during the months of sa'ban and ramadān (November–December), gave the figure of nine hundred thousand, still without understanding the deaths of the non-built properties ...

One began looking for readers of the Koran for the funeral ceremonies, and a number of individuals quit their usual occupations in order to recite prayers at the head of processions; people were also devoting themselves to plastering the crypts; others presented themselves as volunteers to wash the dead or carry them; these people earned substantial salaries. For example, a reader of the Koran got ten dirhams: also, hardly had he reached the oratory before he disappeared as soon as possible in order to officiate a new [funeral]. The porters required 6 dirhams at the moment they were engaged, and then again [at the grave]. The gravedigger demanded fifty dirhams per grave. Most of the rest of these people died without benefitting from their gains. ...

Also families kept their dead on the floor, because of the impossibility of having them buried. The inhabitants of a house died by the tens and, since there was not a litter at their disposal, had to transport them gradually. On the other hand, some people appropriated for themselves without scruple the immovable and movable goods and cash of their owners after their death, but very few lived long enough to profit from this, and those who remained alive could have done without. ...

Family festivities and weddings had no more place [in life]; nobody extended an invitation to a feast during the entire duration of the epidemic, and no concert was heard. The vizier took a third of what he was owed from the woman responsible [for collecting] the tax on singers. The call to prayer was canceled in various places, and in the exact same way, those places [where prayer] was most frequent subsisted on one muezzin [the person who makes the call to prayer].

Most neighborhood mosques and chapels were closed. It has been established that during this epidemic, no child survived more than one or two days after birth, and moreover, his mother followed him in his grave.

At the end of the year, the whole Upper Egypt was invaded by the plague, and the water wheels were no longer working. ...

The men of the [military] troop and the cultivators had all the trouble in the world to finish their sowing [the fields]: The plague emerged at the end of the season or the fields were green. How many times did we see a laborer, at Gaza, at Ramleh, and along other points of the Syrian littoral, guide his plow being pulled by oxen suddenly fall dead, still holding in his hands his plow, while the oxen standing in place without an operator.

It was the same in Egypt: When the time of the harvest came, there remained only a very small number of tillers. The soldiers and their valets left for the harvest and attempted to hire workers, promising them half of the harvest; but they could not find anyone to help them gather the crops. They loaded the grain on their horses, did the sowing themselves, but, being powerless to carry out the greatest portion of the work, they gave up the undertaking.

The endowments passed rapidly from hand to hand as a consequence of the multiplicity of deaths in the army: such a concession passed from one to the other until the seventh or eighth holder, to fall finally [into the hands] of artisans, such as tailors, shoemakers, or public criers, and these mounted the horse, capped with headdress and dressed in military tunics.

Basically, no one collected the full income from his endowment, and many incumbents collected absolutely nothing. During the flooding of the Nile and the period of the sprouting of vegetation, it was difficult to procure a laborer: on only half of the lands did the crops reach maturity. Moreover, there was no one to buy the green clover [as feed] and no one sent their horses to graze in the field. This was the ruin of royal properties in the suburbs of Cairo, like Matarieh, Hums, Siryaqus, and Bahtit. In the canton of Nay and Tanan, 1,500 feddans [= 1.038 acres] of clover were abandoned where they stood: No one came to buy them, either to pasture their beasts on the spot, or to gather them and to make fodder.

The province of Upper Egypt was deserted, despite the vast area of cultivatable land: Thus, according to the surface of the lands cultivated in the territory of Asyūt, six thousand individuals were obliged to pay the property tax; now, in the year of the epidemic [1348–49], we do not count on more than 116 taxpayers. Yet, during this period, the price of wheat did not exceed fifteen *dirhams* per *ardeb* [= a little more than 5 bushels].

Most of the trades disappeared, because many artisans devoted themselves to handling the dead, while others, no less numerous, dealt with auctioning off the movable goods and clothing [of the deceased], so that the price of linen and similar objects fell by at least fifth of their real value, and still further until customers could be found.

...

Thus the trades disappeared: One could no longer find either a water carrier, or a laundress, or a domestic. The monthly salary of a [horse] groomer rose from thirty *dirhams* to eighty. A proclamation made in Cairo invited artisans to take up their old trades, and some of the recalcitrants received the stick. Because of the shortage of men and camels, a goatskin [flask] of water reached the price of eight *dirhams*, and in order to grind an *ardeb* of wheat, one paid fifteen *dirhams*.

This epidemic circulated, it is said, in various countries of the world during fifteen years. Many letters devote bits of verse to it.

5.3 Finance magistrate's book cover

Anonymous, Siena, Italy, 1437

"Allegory of the Plague"[76]

Introduction: The image of the plague was widely circulated in the later Middle Ages. This image, fashioned as an allegory of the plague shows an angel of death shooting arrows, a typical representation for plague drawn from accounts from classical and biblical literature, and the multifaceted impact of the devastating attack. Given its location and the depiction of civic officials being attacked by the plague, the image spoke very directly to both the fears and the practical impact that the plague could have on a city and its administrative functioning. As noted elsewhere, the plague could affect communities as well as individuals

Figure 5.3 Finance magistrate's book cover.
Photo Credit: bpk Bildagentur/Kunstgewerbemuseum/Saturia Linke/Art Resource, NY

and families. Core civic functions could be disrupted by an epidemic, even as these functions were particularly important mechanisms of response and control. Early modern communities would increasingly develop a range of policies and procedures for such disasters, but severe plagues, especially when combined with other conditions and disasters, might deplete community resources and leave the population quite vulnerable. In many cases, it could take years or even generations for a city or region to recover. In other cases, cities could prove to be quite resilient and rebound or develop in new ways after these setbacks.

5.4 Exegesis and plague

Author: Martin Luther (1483–1546)

Title: "First Lectures on the Psalms" (1513–15)[77]

Introduction: We met the Christian reformer Martin Luther earlier in this book [**See 2.6**]. In this brief selection from his commentary on the book of Psalms, Luther also references the plague as a flying arrow and he utilizes the image as a means to critique a range of contemporary vices that he believes attack morality and religious life in his day. Like other early modern writers Luther associates plague with punishment for sin, but here and elsewhere the concept fits into a larger program of religious reform and polemic that Luther uses to advance his own religious ideas and attack his opponents.

Text

Psalm 91:5–6

The trouble that stalks in darkness. In Hebrew: 'plague' or 'pestilence, etc.' This is the teaching that has already been poisoned. For the flying arrow is gentler, while contained in its limits, it teaches the killing letter and deals with the things that are in a human day, with glory, riches, and the power of the world, the things that appeared to be promised in the Law. [Ps. 1:1: "He does not sit in the seat of pestilence."] But there is added this blight which detracts from the truth and teaches evil about God, while it denies faith and the spirit. The flying arrow sets up its own opinion; but the pestilence also attacks another. The former boasts an earthly vanity, but the latter blasphemes also against the spiritual grace. And this is an incurable poison that quickly kills. It crawls and stalks in darkness, that is, in dark minds, for which the light of the spirit has been completely put out. [This is indeed setting up one's own righteousness; see Ps. 92:2.] For through the nighttime fear they easily catch the daytime arrow and, struck and inflamed by it toward the earthly things which the nighttime fear was afraid to lose, they begin to hate everything that is opposed to them, spit out the truth, and love vanity. Ps. 4:2 beautifully agrees when it says, 'O sons of men, how long will you be dull of heart (which the nighttime fear produces)? Why do you love vanity (which the arrow striking in the day produces) and seek lying (which the plague produces, indeed which is itself the plague in the dark)?' And notice the proper, signification of the words. Why does he not say 'nighttime love,' rather than 'fear?' Because love would not act unless it were afraid of losing. The Jewish people for a long time loved earthly things. But after Christ began to preach the Gospel and the spirit, then love began to be afraid. And thence all wretchedness arose. Then Pharaoh's heart was hardened (Ex. 7:14), because he was afraid of losing the people of Israel. ...

5.5 Jewish suffering in the exile

Author: Samuel Usque (c 1500–after 1555)

Title: *Consolation for the Tribulations of Israel* (Ferrara, 1553)[78]

Introduction: Samuel Usque was a Portuguese Marrano who settled in Ferrara, Italy. Drawing from a wide range of sources, Usque wrote in Portuguese for an audience of Marranos (Jews who had been forcibly converted to Judaism, some of whom continued to practice Judaism secretly). Written in the form of a consolation, the book reviews the tribulations faced by the Jews throughout their history. The narrator represents the Jewish People. While we cannot take the account here as a fully accurate account of actual events, it underscores the narrative value of plague for broader purposes. At the same time, the account does reflect some of the animus and violence against Jews in the medieval and early modern worlds. Significant and widespread attacks against and expulsion of Jews occurred in large swaths of Europe. Later plague epidemics may have spawned less physical attacks; however, they fed into longstanding anti-Jewish mentalities and could be used both to marginalize the Jews and to define communal and religious boundaries. Jews could serve as a metonym for more general threat to society, especially as developed in accusations of political intrigue and international conspiracy, as well as religious subversion. Along the way, Usque's account provides an overview of some key events and trajectories in early modern Jewish history.

Text

Germany. Year 5006 [5106; = 1346 CE]

... I saw envy breed such a hatred in the populace that they sought any means to plunder and destroy them [the Jews]. When a dread disease came to the land, they found the best opportunity to put their evil inclination into effect, for not many years had passed since the plague had occurred in France. They asserted that the Jews had poisoned the water in the wells and rivers, and cited the events in France for evidence. My offenses gave such force to this charge that the populace did not wait for further proof but acted on this rumor, which was circulating throughout Germany. They armed themselves and rose up against the Jews, and with sword and fire killed as many Israelite lambs as they could find.

Nor was my misfortune satisfied with these deaths in Germany. When the noxious rumor reached Catalonia and Provence, where the devastation of the contagious illness had spread similar killings and burnings were executed on my limbs. Out of fear of this punishment, some Jews changed their religion to save their lives; they escaped death by becoming Christians.

... But God's mercy saw fit to take the sword from the Enemy's hand and not to destroy me completely.

This tribulation, stemming from water, had to pass over me that these other prophecies of yours, Jeremiah, might be fulfilled: 'He will give us waters of gall to drink because we have sinned' (Jer. 8:14). 'I will deliver them into vexation and misfortune in all the kingdoms of the earth' (Jer. 24:9). ...

Italy. Year 5311 [1551]

In Italy's safest port [Ferrara], where God's mercy had ordained that I might rest from the distressing journeys I have made from Portugal and Spain, I was again harassed by my spiritual Enemy, who was aided by my iniquities.

It happened that a plague broke out somewhere in the territory of the Grisons [Swiss Canton] and in Germany. Travelers who came from those areas spread the highly contagious disease to Ferrara, and a number of people, including Portuguese Hebrews, died.

The people fancied that the Hebrews had spread the disease, since on leaving Spain and Portugal they had traveled through the Grisons and Germany on their way to this safe port. Their suspicion increased to such an extent that the lord of the region, though favorably disposed toward us and inclined to ease the desolation of the captivity we have endured throughout the world since the destruction of our Second Temple, was forced to take action against me because of the insistence of the people. Reluctantly, he tried to placate them by expelling all the Portuguese Jews in the city. They left under conditions of great hardship and wretchedness, for the populace considered them contaminated and no one could be found to help them with their departure, even for a price. ...

When they finally reached the port in such distress, they were attacked by the guards who had been stationed there by the court to protect them. ...

Still God's mercy did not permit any of these Jews to die, nor was there a single person among them who even became ill. This was evidence that they were not infected, and that the disease had not been carried by them.

But the plague continued to spread in the city, and the natives insisted that the Portuguese [Jews] abandon their beach and leave. They therefore embarked again. Some set out for Turkey; they were attacked at sea by corsairs and pirates and had to satisfy them with all the gold they desired to obtain their freedom. Others wandered across the Adriatic, not knowing where to turn, for all people at the nearby ports had readied their spears for the Jews' arrival.

Heaven's pity came to the aid of the Israelites through a son of mine, [Manuel Bichacho], one of the exiles from Portugal who lived in a town called Pesaro, in the state of Urbino. He was moved to compassion and pity for his afflicted brethren, and entreated the prince of the city to take them in. There they found rest as the storm subsided.

Others died unsheltered on Italian roads, for they were recognized as belonging to the Portuguese nation; everyone fled from them because they were rumored to be infected with the plague.

With great reason did Jeremiah say: 'I will pursue them with the sword, famine and pestilence. I will make them roam in terror unto all the kingdoms of the earth and let them be a curse, an astonishment, a mockery and a reproach among all the nations whither they shall go tired and harried' (Jer. 29.18). In this exile and the exile from Portugal, this prophecy has been effected against me.

5.6 Heresy, more pernicious than plague

Author: Jan David (c 1545–1613)

Title: *Christian Soothsayer ...* (1603)[79]

Introduction: Jan David was a late sixteenth- and early seventeenth-century Jesuit historian. In the image a book labelled "heresy" is lifted and presented from the mouth of Hell, as a crowd of people runs away. The Latin inscription at the top reads: "Heresy, the most pernicious plague." The inscription below, in Latin, Dutch, and French reads: "What is more deadly than a poisonous plague? Heresy: This darkness fosters a nest of vipers." Plague was often utilized in the early modern world in starkly polemical ways. In this case, it is through comparison with plague that heresy is described as dangerous to one's physical health, but also to spiritual wellbeing. Leveraged for a range of religious purposes, especially widespread during the theological debates and religious wars of the period of religious reform in sixteenth- and seventeenth-century Europe, the idea of plague could be a powerful tool for criticizing particular groups, practices, or ideologies. Throughout the early modern period, such use of the term was both widespread and effective, linking various opposing groups with disease, degeneration, and general waywardness.

HÆRESIS, PESTE PERNICIOSIOR. 6.

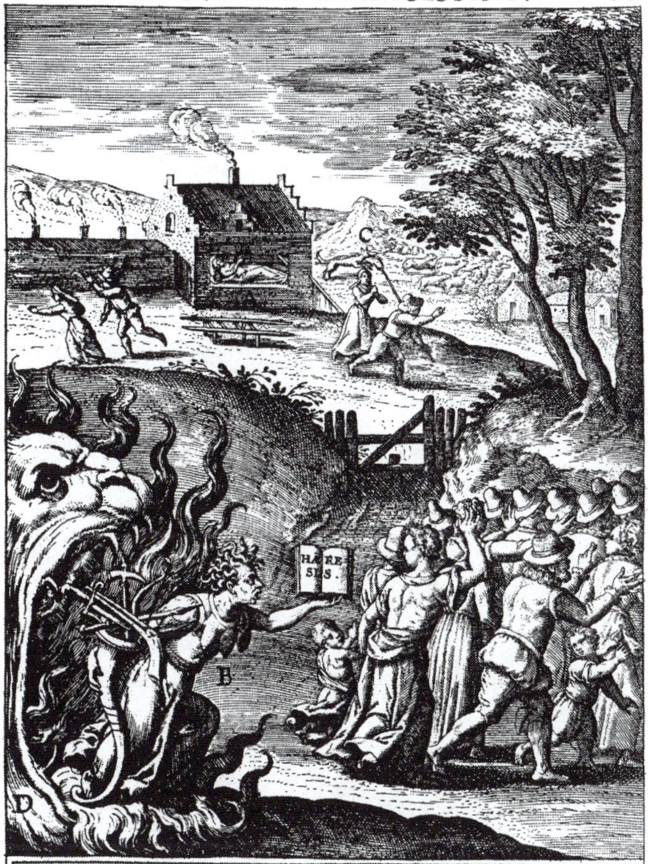

Peius letiferi vitem quid peſte veneni?
Hæreſin: hanc Stygiæ nidus confouit Echidnæ.

Wat moetmen van al die, meer ſchouwen dan de peſte?
Argheyt der Ketterie; ghebroeit in Duyvels neſte.

Y at il de reſte, Rien de plus funeſte, Que peſte, ou poiſon?
Ouy; c'eſt l'Hæreſie, Qui a prins ſa vie, Au nid du demon.

Figure 5.6 Heresy, more pernicious than plague.

Credit: Courtesy of the Pitts Theology Library, Candler School of Theology, Emory University

5.7 Engraving of the torture and execution of alleged plague carriers

Title: *Description of the Implementation of Justice Made in Milan against Some of Them Who Have Made Up and Spread the Anointed Pestiferous ...* (Milan, 1630)

Introduction: During times of plague (as well as other crises) communities often sought out scapegoats—individuals or groups who might be held responsible for initiating or facilitating evil deeds. Poor people, minorities, or foreigners were particularly common targets, to whom a variety of motivations could be ascribed. Combined with a general propensity to villainize others, these groups—which functioned on different levels, outside of society and in some cases accepted social norms—were often depicted as dangerous elements against the common good. Many plague accounts identified alleged conspirators who consciously spread the plague or used the cover of plague for a variety of criminal activities, swindling the dying and living out of their goods or taking possessions from the dead. In some cases, such crimes extended beyond individual criminal activity and were seen as acts against the commonwealth or the State.

Figure 5.7 Engraving of the torture and execution of alleged plague carriers.
Credit: Wellcome Library

5.8 Imagined power?

Author: Joseph Juspa Hahn of Nördlingen (1570–1637)

Title: *Maaseh Nissim* [*Miracle Stories*] (early seventeenth century)[80]

Introduction: Juspa Hahn of Nördlingen, the Shammash (sexton) of the community of Worms, recorded many of the customs as well as financial transactions within the Jewish community in that city. He also collected a book of miraculous stories. This tale appears to conflate events that unfolded in a different community, that of Fulda, also in Germany, during the fourteenth-century Black Death, when Jews from that community rose up to defend themselves against attack. Worms was one of the central Jewish communities in the early modern period, with a Jewish population that was approximately 10% of the total city population. The Jews were expelled in the early seventeenth century, but readmitted a short time later after a populist rebellion was put down. This tale appears to be a fictional account that could have been intended to strengthen the resolve of the Jews facing anti-Jewish activity, indicating that Jews could take actions to defend themselves. Although they might not succeed, even with divine intervention, Jews might be buoyed by the story of intellectual acumen that eventually ensured the survival of some of the remnant of the community. The tale ties the plague concretely into the experiences and memory of the early modern Jewish community.

Text

In the year 5109 [1349], the Gentiles brought a false accusation against the Jews. Many non-Jews had died that year; however, among the Jews, there was not one death. [The Gentiles], therefore, engaged false witnesses to testify that they had seen Jews leaving the [Jewish] street in the middle of the night and pour[ing] poison into the well. The [Gentiles] brought other false accusations against the Jews, and issued an evil decree to annihilate them on the tenth day of [the month of] Adar II. The Jews were very grieved, and they hurried to the bishop of Worms. The bishop puzzled over the matter while standing near an iron chain in the courtyard of the palace. Striking the chain with his staff, he said, 'Just as this little staff in my hand has no power to break that iron chain, so too are your enemies powerless to harm you!' To the distress of the bishop, however, the staff did break the chain. 'It is a Divine decree,' he proclaimed, '[that] such a sordid and strong chain should be broken by the blow of this small stick.' And he said no more to encourage or to discourage them.

When the day of the decree arrived, the Jews knew they were to die horrid deaths by sword, arrow, and spear. They decided to avenge themselves against their enemies, since death seemed inevitable in any case. The *parnasim* [lay leaders] [of Worms], twelve in number, had been ordered to appear the next day in the courthouse to hear the sentencing. Before they left, they concealed slaughter knives and small spears inside their cloaks. ...

All of the councilmen were seated together, ready to pronounce the judgment. One of the *parnasim* cried, 'Your justice is false!' Descending upon the judges with their knives, the *parnasim* killed them all.

While the *parnasim* were in the courtroom, ten or twenty mysterious figures armed with swords and spears surrounded the courthouse and attacked the burghers who passed by. They ignited the storehouses of grain, causing fires that could not be extinguished. Nothing, however, averted the threat to the Jews, and almost all of them were killed.

Several burghers took pity upon the few remaining Jews and hid them in their houses, for they knew that the accusations against the Jews were false. However, [the wicked burghers] used black magic to summon a goose that would fly to the houses in which Jews were concealed. The [merciful] burgher homeowners were forced to hand over the Jews, and because of the accursed goose, even more Jews were killed.

At that same time, a [Jewish] visitor who was an acquaintance of the local priest, arrived in Worms. This visitor was fluent in Latin, and expert in evangelical works, and well-versed in many other secular works. Since the priest held [the visitor] in high esteem, he hid in his house. When the matter of the goose became known, the priest was greatly frightened. Before he left to deliver his sermon in the church, the guest said, 'I have an idea. Dress me in priestly garments and take me with you to the church. Introduce me as a fellow priest and bestow upon me the honor of delivering the sermon. Perhaps in this way I will be able to save myself along with the few Jews that are still hiding in non-Jewish homes.'

The priest followed the Jew's advice, dressed him in priestly clothes, and honored him with the sermon in the church.

In his sermon, the visitor rebuked his audience for spilling Jewish blood without cause. He directed their attention to the scriptural injunction, 'Thou shalt not murder.' Speaking persuasively, he told them that they had sinned by invoking the sorcery of the goose, for truth is not found in witchcraft. 'I guarantee you,' he added, 'in a little while the goose will fly over the roof of this church where there is not even one Jew!' He asked [the congregation] to abandon their trust in the spirit which caused the loss of innocent Jewish lives. As he was speaking, a cry went up in the church that the preacher was right, for the goose had perched on the roof of the church. [The congregation] was amazed at the sight of the goose, and they regretted having placed confidence in its divination.

And so, the evil 'goose' decrees were annulled. [The congregants] did not realize that there had been a Jew in the church when the goose perched on the roof—namely, the visitor who was preaching to them!

A communal custom [was established] in Worms to fast on the tenth day of Adar, just as on public fast days. In the morning and afternoon prayer services, they would chant the Torah portion for fast days and recite the special supplicatory prayers [Selichot].

O merciful Father, see our suffering! Remember not only the afflictions of Worms, but also all the other evil decrees against communities and provinces in Germany, Spain, and France—afflictions that are painful even to write. May the exalted Creator have mercy upon us and send us the righteous redeemer, Amen.

5.9 Intra communal relations

Author: Anonymous

Title: "Autobiography" (seventeenth century)[81]

Introduction: Autobiographical writing became increasingly popular and wide-spread in the early modern period. This anonymous autobiography was written in Hebrew in the seventeenth century, probably in Bohemia or Moravia. It details the fine balance that Jews faced in their relations with Christian rulers and neighbors. It reveals the tensions between Jews and Christians as well as the extent of daily interaction. The account raises intriguing questions of how people practically dealt with contracting the plague—including evading quarantines and travel restrictions, and ways of interacting with others. The author raises concerns about the treatment of Jews and the suspicion under which Christians held Jews, even as he reveals close relations between Jews and Christians. The account provides insights into the role of Jews in some areas of early modern Germany—particularly through service at court and through economic efforts—as well as Jewish family dynamics. The author also provides important information about political responses to plague outbreaks, common medical treatments, and the reciprocal impact of plague and social dynamics.

Text

In the year [5]440 (1680) a plague came in the region of Bohemia, and particularly in the holy community of Prague. And then the Rabbi, R. Jacob Backofen, the author of *Minhat Yaakov*, came out from Prague with his wife Yettel and her sister Freidel, the daughters of the Rabbi, R. Wolf son of the gaon [genius] Rabbi Simon Spira, and they stayed with us in the village in our house. The humility of the above mentioned rabbi was so great that I remember that he was willing to take the trouble to teach me as a school teacher teaches little children. But his wife, who ruled over him, did not permit him to carry out the good deed [mitzvah]. In the month of Tammuz I became sick, with the symptoms of the plague. For three days and nights I had high fever, and was near death. And at the end of three days, a blister formed behind my ear on my neck, which burned like fire, and the members of the household trembled and were anxious [literally fell sick]. The rabbi mentioned above and his wife sensed it, and they fled from our house to another place, the house of his uncle in Wotitz. The plague was at the time all around our locale, and the ruler [Count?] established a lazaretto, that is, a small house of two rooms built of wood in a large forest about a *parsa* [approximately a mile and a half] away from his castle. If someone fell sick in one of the villages he was expelled from his house into that forest with all his belongings. The Count designated a plot of land some *amot* [yards] distant from his castle, which only those living in the castle were permitted to come near. He kept very few people in his castle, and he enclosed himself there, and never left it with his people. He allowed no outsider for meetings except my father, who was beloved for wisdom and knowledge of [many] matters, and he wanted him to come before him and remain with him most of the day. He admonished my father to act in the same way, and not to go out with his family or to admit strangers from other borders. He also warned him that if, God forbid, a member of his own household should fall sick, he should not conceal it, but of his own accord should lock up his house and take everything and go with everyone in his household into the forest. He warned his people that if it ever came to his attention that such a matter occurred without his knowledge, he would permit the Gentiles to set the house on fire and to burn it with everything and everyone inside.

When my father now saw that the pestilence had come and that the plague [was] in the house and that the evil mentioned above was upon him, he did not know what to do. If he carried out the order of the Count and went with his family into the forest he would subject himself to great danger, for the fact would become known to the inhabitants of the villages, who were mostly wicked men, thieves, and murderers, lying in wait for the blood and the property of Jews. Even in the cities they love to oppress and rob them in their houses, how much greater then would be the danger of their coming to annihilate us in the forest. He therefore decided to hide me in the attic, asking his father the rabbi Jacob ha-Levi to take care of me, which he did, even though he was an old man himself, such that no one else from the household had to be concerned with me nor come into the room in which I stayed, hoping perhaps that the plague would not consume any others. And so, he stood with me in this way about six days.

It happened one day that slanderers came to the Count and reported how they had seen my grandfather, of blessed memory, travel with another Jew—whose name was Saul Pollack, of blessed memory, and who stayed in our house with his wife—together to other villages in which the plague was raging to trade there. Immediately the Count decreed the expulsion of both from his territory at the risk of their lives should they be seen within the boundaries of his territory again. Then my grandfather, of blessed memory, was forced to abandon me alone on my sick-bed, for it was dangerous to hide, as they would have searched for him in all the rooms, and if I had been discovered it would have involved danger for all. Therefore, they both had to leave the territory under the eyes of the Count. But God took pity on my suffering, seeing that there was no one to attend to me, and sent me full recovery, and what was particularly fortunate, the abscess did not open again when there was no one to take care of me, but it went down daily by the grace of God. At that time the distinguished rabbi Samson Kamnitz (the brother of my wife's father, rock of Israel) came and instructed my father to take the white of an egg in a bowl with a little alum, about the size of a nut, spreading the white of the egg around in the bowl with the alum quickly until the egg was solidified. He did this and the plaster was held out for me and I applied it, although I was only a boy of twelve years. Because I was sick I was compelled to devise ways to care for myself.

And so every matter of food and drink were brought to me in the same way, by stair, and it was placed near the opening of the staircase, which was immediately closed. I had to get up out of my bed and take them. I lay there alone day and night, and once I saw visions and images. That I remained alive was against the laws of nature; and thus God through His mercy gave me strength so that I returned to my health from day to day, the fever left me, with only the place of the swelling was burning like fire and my whole face red.

And it happened one day that a voice rang out among the Gentiles, who sensing my absence, said to one another, 'see what the Jews did; one of their children certainly died from the plague and they have concealed the matter. And we faithful servants of the Count should go and tell him, and we will be able to take our revenge against the Jews.' These words reached the ears of the householders and my father cleverly ordered me to dress myself and place a linen cloth around my neck doubled, so that the redness could not be seen. He told me to be strong and courageous, and please go in the field, through the garden, and return along the river, by all the houses of the Gentiles and also by the castle. And if somebody were to ask me from where I came, I should answer that I was coming from school, that I had stayed with a teacher in the village of Měnăn two miles away, and that I had longed to come home. And so I did and thank God, who gives strength to the weary …, I ran like a young deer, and I passed the castle and the village, and was seen by many of the Gentiles, who were put to shame, and their scheme failed. Many of our neighbors came to the store to tell my father: 'Your son whom we thought dead has returned.' He responded to them, 'You are dead, but we live forever;' and a few of them almost revealed to him what had been in their thoughts. Further, in his wisdom, my father ordered my older brother, may God protect and preserve him, to place a ladder against our fruit tree in the garden and ordered me to climb the tree that extended towards the side of the road of the village so that passersby would see that I was healthy. He ordered me to laugh and to be playful with the village children, to throw fruits into their faces, and to call at them with laughter and silliness. And this I did and I laughed, while my heart was bitter. Thus it was through God's counsel that the rumors stopped. I did this several times, but I could not appear before them often, lest they should notice the change in my appearance, for I never used to go with a cloth on my neck before, and now it was already some days after I had returned from my journey. One time when I went from the road, I saw a Gentile crossing before me with his hand on his cheeks because of a toothache, and his faced looked angry; I jokingly remarked to him, 'Woe unto you, I am afraid you are ill from the plague.' I said this to show how merry and healthy I was myself, as my father had ordered. But he responded back to me, 'You are sick with the plague yourself, remove that cloth from your neck, and underneath are the spots and remnants.' I was frightened and hid myself, but God in His mercy made the Gentile blind and forgetful.

After a month I returned to the house and went with my brothers and sisters as before, eating and drinking together and no one was concerned. I grew ever more robust and healthy after this. In the year 5441 (1680) in the beginning of the month of Tishrei, the number of deaths in the city of Prague dropped, but in the region of Bohemia it spread to such an extent that people became tired of keeping away from one another. In our village many, even among the people of the castle, fell sick and died. My sister Leah, who was then six years old, got the swelling of the plague, but it was not so dangerous, even though it was discovered, since neither Leah nor my father went before the Count. And at the end of the month of Kislev, the plague was quiet but in the moth of Heshvan it raged around our area and many Jews died. In some villages all the male population died out, and only a few women were left. No one was found to take care of the dead, who could not be buried, for it was winter and the earth was as hard as marble, and there was a heavy snowfall in those parts; so they only covered them with snow and often wolves came and ate the corpses, and sometimes dogs scratched the snow off the bodies. May God have pity on their souls, and may they be bound up in the bundle of life with the other righteous. But in our house, thank God, no one died. Only Saul, of blessed memory, died during this plague, two months after the Count had expelled him, as mentioned above; and even this turned out for the good, for in this way he did not die in our house.

5.10 Plague and public space

Artist: Carlo Coppola (d c 1672)

Title: "Plague Scene in Market Square" (Naples, Italy, 1656) (detail)[82]

Introduction: Carlo Coppola was an Italian Baroque painter who was active in Naples. Reputed to have painted at night, he is said to have gone blind later in life. He also painted a series of battle scenes. The painting provides a vivid depiction of the chaos of this major plague epidemic, with scattered bodies and multiple makeshift responses. Plague rarely took a community completely by surprise, as tales of spreading plague could arrive in advance of actual outbreaks. Still, even communities that were relatively well organized and prepared for response could have difficulty predicting where plague would erupt and how quickly it would make its way through the population. Some methods of treatment and responses proved to be effective and communities that had previous experience with plague could design better plans. Yet in the throes of an epidemic even the most thoughtful plans might not take into account all variables and the sight and emotion of dying people could challenge the very fabric of society. At the same

Figure 5.10 Plague and public space. Museo Nazionale di San Martino Naples ©DeA Picture Library/Art Resource, NY.

Location: Museo Nazionale di San Martino Naples

time, visual images—just like literary narratives—were never completely objective reflections of reality and artists like authors added to the scenes they depicted from their memories and imaginations, making their works of art both records of events and tools to express messages and opinions, and, often, to critique or strengthen society, government, or even religion.

5.11 Family, community, and politics

Author: Glückel (Glikl bas Judah Leib) of Hameln (1646–1724)

Title: *Memoirs* (before 1720)[83]

Introduction: Glückel was a Jewish business woman, born in Hamburg. Her diary covers a broad range of topics, meshing personal experiences, the history of various German Jewish communities, and a broad range of popular tales (Jewish and general). The memoirs provide details about business and family life, from the perspective of an upper-class Jewish woman. Her work has been mined for many details and is particularly valuable as one of the few writings available by Jewish women in the early modern period. This selection offers a glimpse into internal Jewish family and community, including religious, life—which could be hierarchical and rigid at times and open and supportive at others. The account underscores the complexity of Jewish communities in the early modern period and the range of relations that Jews had across regions with other Jews and with Christians and Christian authorities. Glückel provides a vivid description of the emotionally charged nature associated with contracting the plague and the ways that early modern people understood and treated those with plague.

Text

In Hamburg rumors began to circulate, God forbid, that the plague was in the area. It was finally at hand, so that unfortunately three or four Jewish houses were contaminated, and almost everyone within them died, so that these houses stood almost empty. It was a time of great emergency and misery. The dead were miserably avoided, God forbid. Most families moved from Hamburg to Altona and the people had several thousand Reichsthalers of pledges, including many pledges there were between ten to thirty and one hundred Reichsthalers, for when one is engaged in the pawn-shop business one must loan against pledges of eight as well as 20 Reichsthaler. The plague was in the entire region, God shield us, and we had no rest from the people, although we knew that they were contaminated. We had to release their pledges, for even if we had already moved to Altona they would have followed us there. We therefore resolved to take our children and move to Hameln, where my father-in-law, may the memory of the righteous be for a blessing, lived at that time.

Therefore, we soon left Hamburg, the day after Yom Kippur, and the day before Sukkot we arrived in Hannover. We were guests in the house of my brother-in-law Abraham, who lived in Hannover at that time. He did not want to let us leave, since it was so close to the holiday, so we remained in Hannover for Sukkot. I had with me my daughter Zipporah—she should live—who was four years old; my two-year-old son Nathan, and my daughter Mata—may she rest in peace—approximately eight weeks old. My brother-in-law Loeb Hannover invited us to spend the first days of Sukkot in his house, in which the synagogue was located.

On the morning of the holiday, while my husband—may the memory of the righteous be for a blessing—was in the synagogue, I was below in my room and I wanted to dress my daughter Zipporah. I must now write of a small difficulty that we had during the lifetime of my husband—may the memory of the righteous be for a blessing—as well as of other difficult matters that one can not often speak of. And especially now, unfortunately, to whom should I complain or to whom should I speak? We had nobody who could support us other than our Father in Heaven. He should help us and His people Israel and gladden us in the days of our need. Indeed, I had troubles now and again during the lifetime of my husband—may the memory of the righteous be for a blessing; concerns about the upbringing of the children, part of which one can talk about and part of which one should not and cannot say. ...

To return again where I left off, when I was dressing my daughter Zipporah the child was writhing as I touched her. I said to her: 'Zipporah, darling, what is wrong?' The child responded, 'Mama dear, something hurts me very much under my arm.' So I looked to see what the child felt and there was a boil under the arm. I had my maid with me. My husband—may the memory of the righteous be for a blessing—had had a small boil, which a barber in Hannover had covered with a bit of plaster. So I said to the maid: 'Go to Haim [Glückel's husband]. He is upstairs in the synagogue. Ask him who the barber was and where he lives and go with the child there and have him apply a plaster.' I dreamed of nothing wrong.

The maid went into the synagogue and asked my husband—may the memory of the righteous be for a blessing—where the barber lived. He—may he rest in peace—said where he lived. If you want to go into the men's synagogue, you had to pass through the women's synagogue. As the maid was leaving there, my sisters-in-law Yenta, Sulka, and Esther—may she rest in peace—, who were also in the synagogue asked the maid, 'What were you doing in the men's synagogue?' The maid innocently responded, imagining nothing evil, 'Our child has a boil under the arm. Therefore, I asked my master, which barber had healed his boil. I will go with the child there as well.'

The women were mightily afraid, because they were generally very skittish in such things and because we had come from Hamburg [where the plague had broken out]. From such anxiety, they huddled up and spoke about what to do. There was also in the synagogue a beggar, an old Polish woman, who heard the story and saw that my sisters-in-law were so afraid. She said to the women, 'Do not be afraid, it is nothing. I have dealt with such matters for probably twenty years, and if you would like I will go and take a look at the little girl and soon tell you, God shield us, whether it is dangerous and I will tell you what you should do.' They said, 'yes, for God's sake, go down and ensure that we are not, God forbid, in danger.'

I knew nothing of all this. The old Polish woman came below and said, 'Where is the little girl?' I replied, 'Why?' 'I am a healer and I will give the little girl what she needs in order to get better soon.' I suspected nothing evil and brought the child to her. She examined the child and fled from her to the women and raised an alarm and said to the women: 'All of you flee from here, whoever can flee and run, for you alas have the actual plague in the house. The little girl lamentably has the plague in her, God forbid.'

You can well imagine the dismay this caused and the lamenting among the women especially among those so fearful. Women and men all ran from the synagogue and unfortunately ran from there on the holy holiday during the best prayers, and they immediately took the maid with the child and pushed them out the door. Nobody wanted to take them into the house or go. One can probably comprehend how overcome we must have been. I then bawled and cried and prayed to God and said, 'My lords, ask God what you do. My child is not sick. You can see that my child, thank God, is fresh and healthy. The child had a flowing head. Before I left Hamburg, I treated it so that the flow moved from the head to a boil. If anyone were really stricken, God forbid, there would be ten signs to show for it. See, my child plays in the grass and eats a buttered roll from the hand.'

But it did not help at all. They said that if this would unfortunately come to light and be made known to his Highness, our Duke—God raise his majesty— that such things, God forbid, occurred in his residence city, there would be such misery. And the old woman told me to my face that she would give her neck if the child did not have some kind of illness [evil]. What should we do? I prayed, 'In mercy let me stay with my child. Where my child is so will I be. Only let me go out to her.' But they would not suffer it. Shortly my brothers-in-law Abraham, Lipmann and Loeb conferred with their wives what to do, where to put the maid with the child, and how to keep everything secret from the officials, for we would be in great danger if, God forbid, the Duke became aware of anything.

It was agreed that the maid and the child should be dressed in old, torn clothing and they should go to a village that was not further than a Sabbath day's journey from Hannover. That village was named Peinholz. They should take shelter in a farmhouse and say that the Jews of Hannover did not want to house them for the holiday because they already had so many poor people so that they did not even let them in. Therefore, they wanted to stay in the village during the holiday, to stay with them and to pay them for the trouble. We also know for certain [they were to add] that the [Jewish] people from Hannover would send them food and drink for they would not allow us to suffer hunger over the holiday.

In Hannover there was an old beggar, a Polish man who they hired and also the aforementioned Polish woman; both were to spend several days with us and see how things went. Neither wanted to go from the place unless they were paid 30 Reichsthaler to place themselves in danger. Whereupon, my brothers-in-law Abraham, Lipmann, and Loeb took council among themselves and [with] the teacher of Hannover, who was a great scribe [and] who evaluated whether one could transgress the holiday in order to pay the money. They together determined that one should pay the money, for they said that there was a danger to life.

Therefore, we had to send our dear child from us on the holy festival and we were persuaded to imagine that the child, God forbid, might be infected. I will let every pious father and mother judge how difficult this was for us.

My husband—may the memory of the righteous be for a blessing—stood in a corner and wept and prayed to God, and I [stood] in another corner. It is certain that it was only by the merit of my pious husband—may he rest in peace—that God, blessed be He, answered him. As it is written, 'And he was answered.' I do not believe that the sacrifice of our father Abraham was more painful than this was for us at that time. For our forefather Abraham acted 'at the command of God and out of love for Him,' and thereby went through grief with joyfulness. But the grief came upon us from foreigners, [such] that it pierced us in the heart. Now, what should we do? One must bear everything with patience. 'Just as God blesses for the good, so must man also bless for the evil.'

I turned the maid's clothes inside out, and wrapped my child's things in a little bundle. I slung the bundle on the back of the maid like a beggar, and the child too, I dressed in old and torn rags. And so my good maid and my beloved child, and the old man and the woman marched from here to the village. One can probably imagine what blessings we repeated and with how many hundreds of tears she was sent from us. The child herself was merry and happy, as a child who knows nothing [of what is happening]. But all of us of our own who were in Hannover wept and prayed and unfortunately passed the holy festival in deep sorrow.

Now, they reached the village and were well received in a peasant house, since they had money with them—for as long as one has that it can be put to good use.

The peasant asked them, 'Since this is your holiday, why aren't you with Jews?' They answered, that there are already so many poor people in Hannover that it is forbidden to admit anyone. However, they believe that the Jews of Hannover will send them food for the holidays.

Now we went again together into the synagogue, but the prayers were already finished. At that time Judah Berlin was in Hannover. He was still unmarried and had already done business with us. Living there, too, was a young man from Poland named Michael, who taught the children and who was likewise sort of half-servant in the house, according to the German custom by which such young people had to learn with the children. Later he took a wife from Hildesheim and he lives now in Hildesheim in honor and wealth and is *parnas* in Hildesheim.

As people were now leaving [the] synagogue, [my brother-in-law] Loeb had us called to dinner, for, as already mentioned, he had invited us the day before the festival. One can probably imagine how undesirous this was. My husband—may the memory of the righteous be for a blessing—said, 'Before we eat, I must bring something to eat to my child and the others.' 'Naturally,' they said, 'you are right. We will not eat until they too have something.' It [the village] was very close, as close as Altona from Hamburg. So food was gathered together, everyone giving something. [The question now arose,] who should bring the food? And everyone shied away from fear. Then Judah [Berlin] spoke up, 'I will bring it to them.' Michael said, 'I will also go with you,' and my husband—may the memory of the righteous be for a blessing—also went along, for he—may he rest in peace— loved the child dearly. But the Hannoverians would not trust my husband—may the memory of the righteous be for a blessing—for they thought, if my husband went he could not restrain himself from approaching the child. So my brother-in-law Lipmann also had to go along. So they went together and brought the food.

Meanwhile the maid with the child and their companions, for hunger, were walking in a field. When the child saw my husband—may the memory of the righteous be for a blessing—, she was filled with joy, and wanted childlike to run to her father. My brother-in-law Lipmann cried out, they should hold the child and let the old man come fetch the food. They had to bind my husband with a rope, to keep him from coming to his dear child. He and the child bawled, for my husband—may the memory of the righteous be for a blessing—saw that the child was, thank God, fresh and healthy and yet he could not go to her.

So they placed the food and drink on the grass, and the maid and her companions fetched it away. My husband—may the memory of the righteous be for a blessing—and his friends went away. This continued until the eighth day of the Sukkot festival. The old man and the old woman were provided with plaster and ointment and everything wherewith to heal the boil. They healed it nicely, and the child was fresh and healthy and pranced about the field like a young deer.

We now said to the Hannoverians, 'How far will your foolishness lead you? You can see that my child, thank God, is fresh and healthy and that, thank God, there is no more danger. Let the child return!' So they took counsel again, and decided that the child should be allowed to come to Hannover only on the days of [the holiday of] Simhat Torah. Now, what should we do? There was nothing we could do about this. On Simhat Torah, Michael went out and brought the child and her companions back to Hannover. Who could not see at that time the joy of my husband—may the memory of the righteous be for a blessing—and myself and everyone present. We had to cry for great joy: 'The eyes weep and the heart is glad.' Everyone wanted to eat the child alive, for she was a beautiful and lovely child with no equal. And for a long while after she was called none other than the damsel of Peinholz.

5.12 Literary constructions of plague

Author: Daniel Defoe (1660–1731)

Title: *Journal of the Plague Year* (1722)[84]

Introduction: Daniel Defoe [see **4:7**] was a well-known literary figure in the eighteenth century. His extensively circulated *Journal of the Plague Year*, drew from a variety of sources, but also was crafted as a piece of literature that cannot be taken at face value as a source for the history of the plague. Still, the work does reflect the cultural construction and representation of the plague in the period, as the significance of the plague was beginning to decline at least in Western Europe. The first selection discusses the common association of the plague in the early modern world with God's judgment and the appearance of natural wonders and signs. Here Defoe presents a world of common and popular superstitions that both guided and terrified them. Inherent in the account is an opposing contemporary and more rational understanding that criticizes and undermines earlier approaches to plague. In the second selection Defoe narrates a horrifying episode related to quarantine, which like the first selection offers a nuanced critique of the quarantine house and social practices through a graphic and moving account. Such narratives reinforced modern critiques of pre-modern medical practices and plague policies, often times rather unfairly. Similarly, in the final selection, Defoe dramatizes the fissures in family relations that could be exacerbated at times of crisis. Contributing to later stereotypes of early modern family life as sad and love-less, such accounts did a disservice to the nature of family life and the love of parents and children for each other. At the same time, the account throws into relief the divisiveness that the outbreak of plague could have on families and communities. Reading the great plague epidemics of the seventeenth century, Defoe's eighteenth-century literary reflections provide a fitting way to end this volume, pointing as they do to a particular way of thinking about and representing plagues and the past.

5.12A Plague and the common man

Text

In the first place, a blazing star or comet appeared for several months before the plague, as there did, the year after, another, a little before the fire [1666]; the old women, and the phlegmatic hypochondriac part of the other sex, whom I could almost call old women too, remarked, especially afterward, though not till both those judgements were over, that those two comets passed directly over the city, and [in addition to] that so very near the houses, that it was plain they imported something peculiar to the city alone. That the comet before the pestilence was of a faint, dull, languid colour, and its motion very heavy, solemn, and slow; but that the comet before the fire was bright and sparkling, or, as others said, flaming, and its motion swift and furious, and that, accordingly, one foretold a heavy judgement, slow but severe, terrible, and frightful, as was the plague. But the other foretold a stroke, sudden, swift, and fiery, as was the conflagration; nay, so particular some people were, that as they looked upon that comet preceding the fire, they fancied that they not only saw it pass swiftly and fiercely, and could perceive the motion with their eye, but even they heard it, that it made a rushing mighty noise, fierce and terrible, though at a distance, and but just perceivable.

I saw both these stars, and, I must confess, had had so much of the common notion of such things in my head, that I was apt to look upon them as the forerunners and warnings of God's judgements, and especially when, after the plague had followed the first, I yet saw another of the like kind, I could not but say, God had not yet sufficiently scourged the city.

The apprehensions of the people were likewise strangely increased by the error of the times, in which, I think, the people, from what principle I cannot imagine, were more addicted to prophecies, and astrological conjurations, dreams, and old wives' tales, than ever they were before or since: whether this unhappy temper was originally raised by the follies of some people who got money by it, that is to say, by printing predictions and prognostications, I know not, but certain it is, books frighted them terribly; such as Lilly's 'Almanack,' Gadbury's 'Astrological Predictions,' 'Poor Robin's Almanack,' and the like; also several pretended religious books, one entitled, 'Come out of Her, my People, lest ye be Partaker of her Plagues;' another called, 'Fair Warning;' another, 'Britain's Remembrancer,' and many such; all, or most part of which, foretold, directly or covertly, the ruin of the city; nay, some were so enthusiastically bold as to run about the streets with their oral predictions, pretending they were sent to preach to the city; and one in particular, who, like Jonah to Nineveh, cried in the streets, 'Yet forty days, and London shall be destroyed.' I will not be positive whether he said 'yet forty days,' or 'yet a few days.' Another ran about naked, except a pair of drawers about his waist, crying day and night, like a man that Josephus mentions, who cried, 'Woe to Jerusalem!' a little before the destruction of that city; so this poor naked creature cried, 'O! the great and the dreadful God!' and said no more, but repeated those words continually, with a voice and countenance full of horror, a swift pace, and nobody could ever find him to stop, or rest, or take any sustenance, at least that ever I could hear of. I met this poor creature several times in the streets, and would have spoken to him, but he would not enter into speech with me, or any one else; but kept on his dismal cries continually.

These things terrified the people to the last degree; and especially when two or three times, as I have mentioned already, they found one or two in the bills dead of the plague at St Giles's.

Next to these public things were the dreams of old women; or, I should say, the interpretation of old women upon other people's dreams; and these put abundance of people even out of their wits. Some heard voices warning them to be gone, for that there would be such a plague in London so that the living would not be able to bury the dead; others saw apparitions in the air, and I must be allowed to say of both, I hope without breach of charity, that they heard voices that never spake, and saw sights that never appeared; but the imagination of the people was really turned wayward and possessed; and no wonder, if they who were poring continually at the clouds, saw shapes and figures, representations and appearances, which had nothing in them but air and vapour. Here they told us they saw a flaming sword held in a hand, coming out of a cloud, with a point hanging directly over the city. There they saw hearses and coffins in the air carrying to be buried. And there again, heaps of dead bodies lying unburied, and the like; just as the imagination of the poor terrified people furnished them with matter to work upon...

I could fill this account with the strange relations such people gave every day of what they had seen; and every one was so positive of their having seen what they pretended to see, that there was no contradicting them, without breach of friendship, or being accounted rude and unmannerly on the one hand, and pro-fane and impenetrable [insensible] on the other. One time before the plague was begun, otherwise than as I have said in St Giles's, I think it was in March, seeing a crowd of people in the street, I joined with them to satisfy my curiosity, and found them all staring up into the air to see what a woman told them appeared plain to her, which was an angel clothed in white, with a fiery sword in his hand, waving it or brandishing it over his head. She described every part of the figure to the life, showed them the motion and the form, and the poor people came into it so eagerly, and with so much readiness; 'Yes!, I see it all plainly,' says one; 'there's the sword as plain as can be;' another saw the angel; one saw his very face, and cried out, 'What a glorious creature he was!' One saw one thing, and one another. I looked as earnestly as the rest, but perhaps not with so much willing-ness to be imposed upon; and I said, indeed, that I could see nothing but a white cloud, bright on one side, by the shining of the sun upon the other part. The woman endeavoured to show it me, but could not make me confess that I saw it, which, indeed, if I had, I must have lied: but the woman, turning upon me, looked me in the face, and fancied I laughed, in which her imagination deceived her too, for I really did not laugh, but was very seriously reflecting how the poor people were terrified by the force of their own imagination. However, she turned from me, called me profane fellow, and a scoffer, told me that it was a time of

God's anger, and dreadful judgements were approaching, and that despisers such as I should wander and perish.

The people about her seemed disgusted as well as she, and I found there was no persuading them that I did not laugh at them, and that I should be rather mobbed by them than be able to undeceive them. So I left them, and this appearance passed for as real as the blazing star itself.

5.12B Escaping quarantine[85]

Text

It is most certain that, if by the shutting up of houses, the sick had not been confined, multitudes, who in the height of their fever were delirious and distracted, would have been continually running up and down the streets; and, even as it was a very great number did so, and offered all sorts of violence to those they met, even just as a mad dog runs on and bites at every one he meets; nor can I doubt but that should one of those infected diseased creatures have bitten any man or woman, while the frenzy of the distemper was upon them, they, I mean the person so wounded, would as certainly have been incurably infected, as one that was sick before, and had the tokens upon him.

I heard of one infected creature, who, running out of his bed in his shirt, in the anguish and agony of his swellings, of which he had three upon him, got his shoes on and went to put on his coat, but the nurse resisting and snatching the coat from him, he threw her down, ran over her, ran down stairs and into the street directly to the Thames, in his shirt, the nurse running after him, and calling to the watch to stop him; but the watchman, frightened at the man, and afraid to touch him, let him go on; upon which he ran down to the Still-Yard stairs, threw away his shirt, and plunged into the Thames; and, being a good swimmer, swam quite over the river; and the tide being coming in, as they call it, that is, running westward, he reached the land not till he came about the Falcon Stairs, where landing, and finding no people there, it being in the night, he ran about the streets there, naked as he was, for a good while, when, it being by that time high water, he takes the river again, and swam back to the Still-Yard, landed, ran up the streets again to his own house, knocking at the door, went up the stairs, and into his bed again; and [it seems] that this terrible experiment cured him of the plague, that is to say, that the violent motion of his arms and legs stretched the parts where the swellings he had upon him were, that is to say, under his arms and his groin, and caused them to ripen and break; and that the cold of the water abated the fever in his blood.

I have only to add, that I do not relate this any more than some of the other, as a fact within my own knowledge, so as that I can vouch the truth of them, and especially that of the man being cured by the extravagant adventure, which I confess I do not think very possible, but it may serve to confirm the many desperate things which the distressed people falling into deliriums, and what we call light-headedness, were frequently run upon at that time, and how infinitely more such there would have been if such people had not been confined by the shutting up of houses; and this I take to be the best, if not the only good thing, which was performed by that severe method.

On the other hand, the complaints and the murmurings were very bitter against the thing itself.

It would pierce the hearts of all that came by to hear the piteous cries of those infected people, who, being thus out of their understandings by the violence of their pain, or the heat of their blood, were either shut in or perhaps tied in their beds and chairs, to prevent their doing themselves hurt, and who would make a dreadful outcry at their being confined, and at their being not permitted to die at large, as they called it, and as they would have done before.

This running of distempered people about the streets was very dismal, and the magistrates did their utmost to prevent it; but as it was generally in the night and always sudden when such attempts were made, the officers could not be at hand to prevent it; and, even when any got out in the day, the officers appointed did not care to meddle with them, because, as they were all grievously infected, to be sure, when they were come to that height, so they were more than ordinarily infectious, and it was one of the most dangerous things that could be to touch them; on the other hand, they generally ran on, not knowing what they did, till they dropped down stark dead, or till they had exhausted their spirits so as that they would fall and then die in perhaps half an hour or an hour; and which was most piteous to hear, they were sure to come to themselves entirely in that half hour or hour, and then to make most grievous and piercing cries and lamentations, in the deep afflicting sense of the condition they were in. There was much of it before the order for shutting up of houses was strictly put in execution; for, at first the watchmen were not so vigorous and severe as they were afterwards in the keeping the people in; that is to say, before they were, I mean some of them, severely punished for their neglect, failing in their duty, and letting people who were under their care slip away, or conniving at their going abroad, whether sick or well. But after they saw the officers appointed to examine into their conduct were resolved to have them do their duty or be punished for the omission, they were more exact, and the people were strictly restrained; which was a thing they took so ill, and bore so impatiently, that their discontents can hardly be described; but there was an absolute necessity for it, that must be confessed, unless some other measures had been timely entered upon, and it was too late for that.

5.12C Family abandonment[86]

Text

I remember, and while I am writing this story, I think I hear the very sound of it: a certain lady had an only daughter, a young maiden about nineteen years old, and who was possessed of a very considerable fortune; they were only lodgers in the house where they were. The young woman, her mother, and the maid had been abroad on some occasion, I do not remember what, for the house was not shut up; but about two hours after they came home, the young lady complained she was not well, in a quarter of an hour more she vomited and had a violent pain in her head. 'Pray God', says her mother, in a terrible fright, 'my child has not the distemper!' The pain in her head increasing, her mother ordered the bed to be warmed, and resolved to put her to bed; and prepared to give her things to sweat, which was the ordinary remedy to be taken when the first apprehensions of the distemper began.

While the bed was airing, the mother undressed the young woman, and just as she was laid down in the bed, she, looking upon her body with a candle, immediately discovered the fatal tokens on the inside of her thighs. Her mother, not being able to contain herself, threw down her candle, and screeched out in such a frightful manner that it was enough to place horror upon the stoutest heart in the world; nor was it one scream, or one cry, but the fright having seized her spirits, she fainted first, then recovered, then ran all over the house, up the stairs and down the stairs, like one distracted, and, indeed really was distracted, and continued screeching and crying out for several hours, void of all sense, or, at least, government of her senses, and, as I was told, never came thoroughly to herself again. As to the young maiden, she was a dead corpse from that moment; for the gangrene, which occasions the spots, had spread over her whole body, and she died in less than two hours. But still the mother continued crying out, not knowing anything more of her child, several hours after she was dead. It is so long ago that I am not certain, but I think the mother never recovered, but died in two or three weeks after.

Notes

1 Clusters, according to Edward Eckert, *The Structures of Plagues and Pestilence in Early Modern Europe: Central Europe, 1560–1640* (Basel, 1996).
2 Samuel K. Cohn, Jr, "Changing Pathology of Plague," in *Le interazioni fra economia e ambiente biologico nell'Euopa preindustriale, secc. XII–XVIII*, 33–56, here at 46ff, 50; Lilith K. Whittles and Xavier Didelot, "Epidemiological Analysis of the Eyam Plague Outbreak of 1665–1666," *Proceedings of the Royal Society* B 283 (May 2016): electronic download, 5–6.
3 Cohn, Jr, "Changing Pathology of Plague," 53.
4 Pierre Galanaud, Anne Galanaud, and Patrick Giraudoux, "Historical Epidemics Cartography Generated by Spatial Analysis: Mapping the Heterogeneity of Three Medieval 'Plagues' in Dijon," *PLoS ONE* 10:12 (2015): 1–24 (electronic version), here at 1, 10.

5 Neil Cummins, Morgan Kelly, and Cormac ÓGráda, "Living Standards and Plague in London, 1560–1665," *The Economic History Review* 69:1 (February 2016): 3–34, here at 20; Whittles and Didelot, "Epidemiological Analysis of the Eyam Plague Outbreak of 1665–1666," 5.

6 Samuel K. Cohn, Jr and Guido Alfani, "Households and Plague in Early Modern Italy," *Journal of Interdisciplinary History* 38:2 (Autumn 2007): 177–205, here at 194.

7 See Galanaud et al., "Historical Epidemics Cartography Generated by Spatial Analysis," 12–13.

8 Ernst L. Sabine, "Butchering in Medieval London," *Speculum* 8:3 (July 1933): 335–53, here at 339, 343.

9 Klaus Schwarz, *Die Pest in Bremen: Epidemien und freier Handel in einer deutschen Hafenstadt 1350–1713* (Bremen, 1996), 94.

10 Frank Hatje, *Leben und Sterben im Zeitalter der Pest: Basel im 15. bis 17. Jahrhundert* (Basel, 1992), 91, 162.

11 Ibid., 232.

12 See Fabian Crespo and Matthew B. Lawrenz, "Heterogeneous Immunological Landscapes and Medieval Plague: An Invitation to a New Dialogue between Historians and Immunologists," in *Pandemic Disease*, 229–57, here at 232–33, 237, 249, 251; see also Andrew Cunningham, "Transforming Plague: The Laboratory and the Identity of Infectious Disease," in *The Laboratory Revolution in Medicine*, ed. Andrew Cunningham and Perry Williams (Cambridge, 2002 (orig., 1992)), 209–44, here at 221, regarding causes and predispositions.

13 Crespo and Lawrenz, "Heterogeneous Immunological Landscapes and Medieval Plague," 231–2.

14 Lynn A. Martin, *Plague? Jesuit Accounts of Epidemic Disease in the 16th Century* (Kirksville, 1996), 148.

15 Ibid.

16 Ibid., 149.

17 Florence 1400; in Gene Brucker, *The Society of Renaissance Florence* (New York, 1971), 141–2, quoted in Joseph P. Bryne, *Daily Life during the Black Death* (Westport, 2006), 178.

18 Christian Jörg, *Teure, Hunger, Großes Sterben: Hungersnöte und Versorgungskrisen in den Städten des Reiches während des 15. Jahrhunderts* (Stuttgart, 2008), 357ff.

19 In Jacob R. Marcus, *Communal Sick-Care in the German Ghetto* (Cincinnati, 1947), 214–15.

20 Paul Slack, *Plague: A Very Short Introduction* (Oxford, 2012), 96.

21 John Henderson, "Coping with Epidemics in Renaissance Italy: Plague and the Great Pox," in *The Fifteenth Century XII: Society in an Age of Plague*, ed. Linda Clarke and Carole Rawcliffe (Woodbridge, 2013), 175–94, here 181.

22 Hanna Wegrzynek, "Shvartze Khasene: Black Weddings among Polish Jews," in *Holy Dissent: Jewish and Christian Mystics in Eastern Europe*, ed. Glenn Dynner (Detroit, 2011), 55–68, here 55–8.

23 David Herlihy, *The Black Death and the Transformation of the West*, ed. Samuel K. Cohn, Jr (Cambridge, MA, 1997), 59.

24 Joseph M. Davis, *Yom-Tov Lipmann Heller: Portrait of a Seventeenth-Century Rabbi* (Oxford, 2004), 47; see also Hatje, *Leben und Sterben im Zeitalter der Pest*, 55.

25 Franco Mormando, "Introduction: Response to the Plague in Early Modern Italy: What the Primary Sources, Printed and Painted, Reveal," in *Hope and Healing: Painting in Italy in a Time of Plague 1500–1800*, ed. Gauvin Alexander Bailey, Pamela M. Jones, Franco Mormando, and Thomas W. Worcester (Chicago, 2005), 1–44, here at 19.

26 Martin, *Plague?*, 44–5.

27 Ibid., 57: January 10, 1600 in a letter of Henricus Vivarius to Aquaviva.

28 See Mormando, "Introduction," 15.

29 David Chambers and Brian Pullan, eds, *Venice: A Documentary History, 1450–1630* (Toronto, 2001), 76.

30 Mark Harrison, *Disease and the Modern World: 1500 to the Present Day* (Cambridge, 2004), 27, 29.

31 Cited in Daniel J. Schroeter, *The Sultan's Jew: Morocco and the Sephardi World* (Stanford, 2002), 50.

32 See Marta E. Hanson, "Northern Purgatives, Southern Restoratives: Ming Medical Regionalism," *ASME* 2:2 (2006): 115–70.

33 Introduced and redacted by John Beardsley. http://winthropsociety.com/doc_higgin.php.

34 In Cristobal Silva, *Miraculous Plagues: An Epidemiology of Early New England Narrative* (Oxford, 2011), 37.

35 Ibid., 135.

36 Ibid., 58.

37 Walter G. Rödel, "Pestepidemien in Mainz im 17. Jahrhundert," *Scripta Mercaturae* 15:1 (1981): 85–103, here at 97.

38 See Samuel K. Cohn, Jr, "The Black Death and the Burning of Jews," *Past and Present* 196 (August 2007): 3–36, and Paolo Preto, *Epidemia, paura e politica nell'Italia moderna* (Bari, 1987).

39 Cohn, Jr, "The Black Death and the Burning of Jews."

40 Samuel K. Cohn, Jr, *The Black Death Transformed: Disease and Culture in Early Renaissance Europe* (London and New York, 2002), 230.

41 See Kristy Wilson Bowers, *Plague and Public Health in Early Modern Seville* (Rochester, 2013), 36–7.

42 Ibid., 38.

43 See Alfred Haverkamp, "Die Judenverfolgungen zur Zeit des Schwarzen Todes in Gesellschaftsgefüge deutscher Städte," in *Zur Geschichte der Juden im Deutschland des Späten Mittelalters und der Frühen Neuzeit*, ed. ibidem (Stuttgart, 1981), 27–93.

44 Brian Pullan, "Plagues and Perceptions of the Poor in Early Modern Italy," in *Epidemics and Ideas: Essays on Historical Perceptions of Pestilence*, ed. Terence Ranger and Paul Slack (Cambridge, 1992), 101–23.

45 Ibid., 105.

46 Ibid., 117.

47 Ibid., 106, 118.

48 See, for example, Lawrence I. Conrad, Michael Neve, Vivian Nutton, Roy Porter, and Andrew Wear, *The Western Medical Tradition, 800 BC to AD 1800* (Cambridge, 1995), 238.

49 Katharina Kellner, *Pesthauch über Regensburg: Seuchenbekämpfung und Hygiene im 18. Jahrhundert* (Regensburg, 2005), 129.

50 Ibid., 132.

51 Bowers, *Plague and Public Health in Early Modern Seville*.

52 Eckert, *The Structures of Plagues and Pestilence in Early Modern Europe*, 113–14; Pullan, "Plagues and Perceptions of the Poor in Early Modern Italy," 113–14.

53 David Gans, *Zemah David*, ed. Mordechai Breuer (Jerusalem, 1983), 355–6, for the year 1348. He notes that these attacks were at the hands of the mobs and not the authorities and they were decreed from heaven.

54 John Aberth, *The Black Death: The Great Mortality of 1348–1350: A Brief History with Documents* (Boston, 2005), 145–50. Trans. from German in *Urkunden und Akten*

der Stadt Strassburg, ed. Wilhelm Wiegand et al., 15 vols (Strasbourg, 1879–1933), 5:167–71.

55 See Haverkamp, "Die Judenverfolgungen zur Zeit des Schwarzen Todes in Gesellschaftsgefüge deutscher Städte." See also Cohn, Jr, "The Black Death and the Burning of Jews."

56 From Jacob R. Marcus, ed., *The Jew in the Medieval World: A Sourcebook: 315–1791* (Philadelphia, 1938), 45–47.

57 Ibid.

58 Cohn, Jr, "The Black Death and the Burning of Jews," 11. See also 27. See also Samuel K. Cohn, Jr, "Jews and Violence in the Early Modern Period," http://fordham.bepress.com/emw/emw2013/emw2013/3/ [last visited August 13, 2017].

59 Renata Segre, ed., *The Jews in Piedmont* (Jerusalem, 1986–90), 3 vols, docs 1239–40, 583.

60 Compare the autobiography of Leon Modena in Venice for the years 1630/31, *The Autobiography of a Seventeenth-Century Venetian Rabbi: Leon Modena's Life of Judah*, trans. Mark R. Cohen (Princeton, 1988), 134–7.

61 *Die Memoiren des Ascher Levy aus Reischshofen im Elsass (1598–1635)*, trans. M. Ginsburger (Berlin, 1913), 38 (German).

62 For a discussion of the demographic implications of the plague in the seventeenth century, see Christian Pfister, *Bevölkerungsgeschichte und historische Demographie, 1500–1800* (Munich, 1994), especially 11ff.

63 *Die Memoiren des Ascher Levy*, 62 (German).

64 Sylvie Anne Goldberg, *Crossing the Jabbok: Illness and Death in Ashkenazi Judaism in Sixteenth- through Nineteenth-Century Prague*, trans. Carol Cosman (Berkeley, 1996), 164.

65 Ibid., 165.

66 Ibid., 197.

67 Ibid., 195.

68 Ibid., 164–5; Chava Turniansky, "Yiddish Song as Historical Source Material: Plague in the Judenstadt of Prague in 1713," in *Jewish History; Essays in Honour of Chimen Abramsky*, ed. Ada Rapoport-Albert and Steven J. Zipperstein (London, 1988), 189–98, here at 194.

69 Nimrod Zinger, " 'Our Hearts and Spirits Were Broken:' The Medical World from the Perspective of German-Jewish Patients in the Seventeenth and Eighteenth Centuries," *Leo Baeck Institute Yearbook* 54:1 (2009): 59–91, here at 62, 69, 90, 66; for a discussion of Jewish uses of Christian saints in the Middle Ages, see Ephraim Shoham-Steiner, "Jews and Healing at Medieval Saints' Shrines: Participation, Polemics, and Shared Cultures," *Harvard Theological Review* 103:1 (2010): 111–29.

70 Goldberg, *Crossing the Jabbok*, 169.

71 Ibid., 170.

72 Ibid.

73 Margaret Bent, *Bologna Q15: The Making and Remaking of a Musical Manuscript. Introductory Study and Facsimile Edition* (Lucca, 2008).

74 Aberth, *The Black Death: The Great Mortality of 1348–1350*, 158–9. My own translation from the original in Shlomo Simonsohn, ed., *The Apostolic See and the Jews*, 8 vols (Toronto, 1988–91): 1:396–99.

75 Aberth, *The Black Death: The Great Mortality of 1348–1350*, 84–7. My own translation from the French translation in Gaston Wiet, "La Grande Pest Noire en Syrie et en Egypte," *Etudes d'orientalisme dediees a la memoire de Levi-Provencal*, 2 vols (Paris, 1962), 1:375–80.

76 www.artres.com/C.aspx?VP3=ViewBox_VPage&VBID=2UN365CFKDZSU&IT
    =ZoomImageTemplate01_VForm&IID=2UNTWA9G8J1M&PN=3&CT=Search
    &SF=0. Details: Kunstgewerbemuseum, Staatliche Museen, Berlin, Germany.
77 Martin Luther, *Luther's Works*, vol. 11: First Lectures on the Psalms II, Psalms, 76–
    126, ed. Hilton C. Oswald (Saint Louis, 1968), 217–18.
78 Samuel Usque, *Samuel Usque's Consolation for the Tribulations of Israel*, trans. Martin
    A. Cohen (Philadelphia, 1965), 192, 213–14.
79 *Christeliicken waerseggher: de principale stucken van t'christen geloof en Leuen int cort
    begrijpende. Met een rolle der deugtsaemheyt daer op dienende. Ende een schildt-wacht
    teghen de valsche waersegghers, tooueraers, etc./Deur den e. Heer P. Ioannes David,
    priester der Societeijt Iesu.* http://pitts.emory.edu/dia/detail.cfm?ID=10550.
80 Shlomo Eidelberg, *R. Juspa, Shammash of Warmaisa (Worms): Jewish Life in Seventeenth
    Century Worms* (Jerusalem, 1991), 76–78; trans. from the Hebrew text, 74–6.
81 Alexander Marx, "A Seventeenth-Century Autobiography: A Picture of Jewish Life in
    Bohemia and Moravia. From a Manuscript in the Jewish Theological Seminary," The
    Jewish Quarterly Review 8:3 (1918): 269–304. Translated from the Hebrew edition,
    187–91.
82 www.artres.com/C.aspx?VP3=ViewBox_VPage&VBID=2UN365CFKDZSU&IT=Z
    oomImageTemplate01_VForm&IID=2F3C2S0IM7L&PN=49&CT=Search&SF=0.
83 The Memoirs of Glückel of Hameln. https://de.wikisource.org/wiki/Die_
    Memoiren_der_Gl%C3%BCckel_von_Hameln/Drittes_Buch; from the German 76–
    85. See 161–69 in the Yiddish version.
84 *Daniel Defoe's Journal of the Plague Year*, ed. George Rice Carpenter (New York:
    Longmans, Green, and Co., 1896), 23–7.
85 Ibid., 159–62.
86 Ibid., 55–6.

Bibliography

Works cited

Aberth, John. *Plagues in World History*. Lanham, 2011.

Aberth, John. *The Black Death: The Great Mortality of 1348–1350: A Brief History with Documents*. Boston, 2005.

Adventures of Baron Wenceslas Wratislaw of Mitrowitz. What he saw in the Turkish Metropolis, Constantinople, experienced in his captivity; and after his happy return to his country, committed to writing in the year of our Lord 1599. London, 1862.

Alchon, Suzanne Austin. *A Pest in the Land: New World Epidemics in a Global Context*. Albuquerque, 2003.

Alexander, John T. *Bubonic Plague in Early Modern Russia: Public Health and Urban Disaster*. Oxford, 2002.

Alfani, Guido. "Plague in Seventeenth-Century Europe and the Decline of Italy: An Epidemiological Hypothesis." *European Review of Economic History* 17 (2013): 408–30. Online at ftp://ftp.igier.unibocconi.it/wp/2011/377.pdf.

Alkofer, Erasmus Siegmund. "Regenspurgisches Pest- und Buß-Denckmahl Wegen Der im Jahr Christi 1713. allhier grassirten Seuche der Pestilentz/ In sich haltend Einige Pest- und Buß-Predigten" (Regensburg: Seidel, 1714). www.hab.de/ausstellungen/seuchen/expo-19.htm. 19 (Kat. Nr. 39).

Archambeau, Nicole. "Healing Options during the Plague: Survivor Stories from a Fourteenth-Century Canonization Inquest." *Bulletin of the History of Medicine* 85 (2011): 531–59.

Attewell, Guy. "Islamic Medicines: Perspectives on the Greek Legacy in the History of Islamic Medical Traditions in West Asia." In *Medicine across Cultures: History and Practice of Medicine in Non-Western Cultures*, ed. Helaine Selin (London, 2003), 325–50.

The Autobiography of a Seventeenth-Century Venetian Rabbi: Leon Modena's Life of Judah. Trans. Mark R. Cohen. Princeton, 1988.

Ayalon, Yaron. *Natural Disasters in the Ottoman Empire: Plague, Famine, and Other Misfortunes*. Cambridge, 2015.

Ayalon, Yaron. "Religion and Ottoman Society's Responses to Epidemics in the Seventeenth and Eighteenth Centuries." In *Plague and Contagion in the Islamic Mediterranean*, ed. Nükhet Varlik (Kalamazoo, 2017), 179–97.

Baker, Don. "Oriental Medicine in Korea." In *Medicine across Cultures: History and Practice of Medicine in Non-Western Cultures*, ed. Helaine Selin (Dordrecht, 2003), 133–53.

Baldeus, Philippus. "Nauwkeurige en Waarachtige," 28–33 in Ishrat Alam, *Smallpox and Its Treatment in Pre-Modern India* (Kumar, 2001), 85–93.

Bent, Margaret. *Bologna Q15: The Making and Remaking of a Musical Manuscript. Introductory Study and Facsimile Edition.* Lucca, 2008.

Blazina Tomic, Zlata and Vesna Blazina. *Expelling the Plague: The Health Office and the Implementation of Quarantine in Dubrovnik, 1377–1533.* Montreal, 2015.

Bondy, G., ed. *Zur Geschichte der Juden in Böhmen, Mähren und Schlesien: von 906 bis 1620.* 2 vols. Prague, 1906.

Bos, Kirsten I. et al. "Eighteenth Century *Yersinia pestis* Genomes Reveal the Long-Term Persistence of an Historical Plague Focus." eLife 2016;5:e12994 (online).

Bowers, Kristy Wilson. *Plague and Public Health in Early Modern Seville.* Rochester, 2013.

Brucker, Gene. *The Society of Renaissance Florence.* New York, 1971.

Bulmuş, Birsen. *Plague, Quarantines, and Geopolitics in the Ottoman Empire.* Abingdon, 2012.

Byrne, Joseph P. *Daily Life during the Black Death.* Westport, 2006.

Campbell, Bruce M. S. *The Great Transition: Climate, Disease and Society in the Late-Medieval World.* Cambridge, 2016.

Carmichael, Ann G. "Plague Persistence in Western Europe: A Hypothesis." In *The Medieval Globe* 1 (2014), *Pandemic Disease in the Medieval World: Rethinking the Black Death,* ed. Monica H. Green (Kalamazoo, 2014), 157–91.

Carmichael, Ann G. "Universal and Particular: The Language of Plague, 1348–1500." *Medical History Supplement* 27 (2008): 17–52 (electronic version).

Carus, Titus Lucretius. *De Rerum Natura.* Trans. W. H. D. Rouse. Cambridge, MA, 1937.

Catalano, Abraham. "A World Turned Upside-Down." Ed. Cecil Roth, *Kobetz al Yad* (Kalamazoo, 1946), 67–101.

Cavallo, Sandra and Tessa Storey. *Healthy Living in Late Renaissance Italy.* Oxford, 2013.

Celebi, Evliya. *An Ottoman Traveller: Selections from the Book of Travels of Evliya Celebi.* Ed. and trans. Robert Dankoff and Sooyong Kim. London, 2010.

Chambers, David and Brian Pullan, eds. *Venice: A Documentary History, 1450–1630.* Toronto, 2001.

Chopra, Ananda S. "Ayurveda." In *Medicine across Cultures: History and Practice of Medicine in Non-Western Cultures,* ed. Helaine Selin (Dordrecht, 2003), 75–83.

Cipolla, Carlo M. *Cristofano and the Plague: A Study in the History of Public Health in the Age of Galileo.* Berkeley, 1973.

Cohn, Norman. *The Pursuit of the Millennium: Revolutionary Millenarians and Mystical Anarchists of the Middle Ages,* revised ed. (New York, 1970).

Cohn, Samuel K., Jr. "The Black Death and the Burning of Jews." *Past and Present* 196 (August 2007): 3–36.

Cohn, Samuel K., Jr. *The Black Death Transformed: Disease and Culture in Early Renaissance Europe.* London and New York, 2002.

Cohn, Samuel K., Jr. "Changing Pathology of Plague." In *Le interazioni fra economia e ambiente biologico nell'Euopa preindustriale, secc. XII–XVIII* (Florence, 2010), 33–56.

Cohn, Samuel K., Jr. *Cultures of Plague: Medical Thought at the End of the Renaissance.* Oxford, 2009.

Cohn, Samuel K., Jr. "Jews and Violence in the Early Modern Period." http://fordham. bepress.com/emw/emw2013/emw2013/3/ [last visited August 13, 2017].

Cohn, Samuel K., Jr. and Guido Alfani. "Households and Plague in Early Modern Italy." *Journal of Interdisciplinary History* 38:2 (Autumn 2007): 177–205.

Conrad, Lawrence I. and Dominik Wuastyk. *Contagion: Perspectives from Pre-Modern Societies.* Aldershot, 2000.

Conrad, Lawrence I., Michael Neve, Vivian Nutton, Roy Porter, and Andrew Wear. *The Western Medical Tradition, 800 BC to AD 1800.* Cambridge, 1995.

Cook, Harold J. *Matters of Exchange: Commerce, Medicine, and Science in the Dutch Golden Age.* New Haven, 2007.

Coste, Joël. *Représentations et comportements en temps d'épidémie dans la littérature imprimée de peste (1490–1725)*. Paris, 2007.

Crenshaw, Jane L. Stevens. *Plague Hospitals: Public Health for the City in Early Modern Venice*. Farnham, 2012.

Crespo, Fabian and Matthew B. Lawrenz. "Heterogeneous Immunological Landscapes and Medieval Plague: An Invitation to a New Dialogue between Historians and Immunologists." In *The Medieval Globe* 1 (2014), *Pandemic Disease in the Medieval World: Rethinking the Black Death*, ed. Monica H. Green (Kalamazoo, 2014), 229–57.

Crown, Alan D. "The World Overturned: The Plague Diary of Abraham Catalano." *Midstream* XIX:2 (February 1973): 65–76.

Cummins, Neil, Morgan Kelly, and Cormac ÓGráda. "Living Standards and Plague in London, 1560–1665." *The Economic History Review* 69:1 (February 2016): 3–34.

Cunningham, Andrew. "Transforming Plague: The Laboratory and the Identity of Infectious Disease." In *The Laboratory Revolution in Medicine*, ed. Andrew Cunningham and Perry Williams (Cambridge, 2002 (orig., 1992)), 209–44.

Curry, John J. "Scholars, Sufis, and Disease: Can Muslim Religious Works Offer Us Novel Insights on Plagues and Epidemics among the Medieval and Early Modern Ottomans?" In *Plague and Contagion in the Islamic Mediterranean*, ed. Nükhet Varlik (Kalamazoo, 2017), 27–55.

Curtis, Daniel R. *Coping with Crisis: The Resilience and Vulnerability of Pre-Industrial Settlements*. Aldershot, 2014.

Davis, Joseph M. *Yom-Tov Lipmann Heller: Portrait of a Seventeenth-Century Rabbi*. Oxford, 2004.

Daniel Defoe's Journal of the Plague Year. Ed. George Rice Carpenter. New York: Longmans, Green, and Co., 1896.

Dewitte, Sharon N. "The Anthropology of Plague: Insights from Bioarcheological Analyses of Epidemic Cemeteries." In *The Medieval Globe* 1 (2014), *Pandemic Disease in the Medieval World: Rethinking the Black Death*, ed. Monica H. Green (Kalamazoo, 2014), 97–123.

Dinanah, Tah. "Die Schrift von Abi G'far Ahmed ibn 'Ali ibn Mohammed ibn 'Ali ibn Hatimah aus Almeriah über die Pest." *Archiv für Geschichte der Medizin* 19 (1927): 49–87.

Dols, Michael. *The Black Death in the Middle East*. Princeton, 1977.

Dongwon, Shin. "Measures against Epidemics during Late 18th Century Korea: Reformation or Restoration?" *Extrême-Orient, Extrême-Occident* 37 (2014): 91–110.

Duffy, John. *Epidemics in Colonial America*. Baton Rouge, 1953.

Eckert, Edward. *The Structures of Plagues and Pestilence in Early Modern Europe: Central Europe, 1560–1640*. Basel, 1996.

Eidelberg, Shlomo. *R. Juspa, Shammash of Warmaisa (Worms): Jewish Life in Seventeenth Century Worms*. Jerusalem, 1991.

Fineman, Martha Albertson and Anna Grear. *Vulnerability: Reflections on a New Ethical Foundation for Law and Politics*. Farnham, 2013.

Flamm, Heinz. *Die ersten Infektions- oder Pest-Ordungen in den österreichischen Erblanden, im Fürstlichen Erzstift Salzburg und im Innviertel im 16. Jahrhundert*. Vienna, 2008.

Fracastorii, Hieronymi. *De contagione et contagiosis morbis et eorum curatione, Libri III*. Trans. Wilmer Cave Wright (New York, 1930).

Friedrichs, Christopher R. *The Early Modern City 1450–1750*. London, 1995.

Galanaud, Pierre, Anne Galanaud, and Patrick Giraudoux. "Historical Epidemics Cartography Generated by Spatial Analysis: Mapping the Heterogeneity of Three Medieval 'Plagues' in Dijon." *PLoS ONE* 10:12 (2015): 1–24 (electronic).

Gans, David. *Zemah David*. Ed. Mordechai Breuer. Jerusalem, 1983.

Gerrard, C. M. and D. Petley. "A Risk Society? Environmental Hazards, Risk and Resilience in the Later Middle Ages in Europe." *Natural Hazards* 69:1 (2013): 1051–79.

Goldberg, Sylvie Anne. *Crossing the Jabbok: Illness and Death in Ashkenazi Judaism in Sixteenth- through Nineteenth-Century Prague.* Trans. Carol Cosman. Berkeley, 1996.

Grasmüller, Heinrich. *Krancken-Buch Oder Gebether Und Trost-Sprüche Für Krancken und Sterbenden. Zum andermahl vermehret heraußgegeben.* Hamburg, 1681. Wolfenbuttel: www.hab.de/ausstellungen/seuchen/expo-18.htm. 18 (Kat. Nr. 37).

Graus, František. *Pest, Geissler, Judenmorde: Das 14 Jahrhundert als Krisenzeit.* Göttingen, 1987.

Green, Monica H. "Editor's Introduction." In *The Medieval Globe* 1 (2014), *Pandemic Disease in the Medieval World: Rethinking the Black Death,* ed. ibidem (Kalamazoo, 2014), 9–26.

Green, Monica H. "Taking 'Pandemic' Seriously: Making the Black Death Global." In *The Medieval Globe* 1 (2014), *Pandemic Disease in the Medieval World: Rethinking the Black Death,* ed. ibidem (Kalamazoo, 2014), 27–61.

Hanson, Marta E. "Northern Purgatives, Southern Restoratives: Ming Medical Regionalism." *ASME* 2:2 (2006): 115–70.

Harrison, Mark. *Climates and Constitutions: Health, Race, Environment and British Imperialism in India 1600–1850.* Oxford, 1999.

Harrison, Mark. *Disease and the Modern World: 1500 to the Present Day.* Cambridge, 2004.

Hatje, Frank. *Leben und Sterben im Zeitalter der Pest: Basel im 15. bis 17. Jahrhundert.* Basel, 1992.

Haverkamp, Alfred. "Die Judenverfolgungen zur Zeit des Schwarzen Todes in Gesellschaftsgefüge deutscher Städte." In *Zur Geschichte der Juden im Deutschland des Späten Mittelalters und der Frühen Neuzeit,* ed. ibidem (Stuttgart, 1981), 27–93.

Hays, Jo N. "Historians and Epidemics: Simple Questions, Complex Answers." In *Plague and the End of Antiquity: The Pandemic of 541–750,* ed. Lester K. Little (New York, 2007), 33–56.

Henderson, John. "The Black Death in Florence: Medical and Communal Responses." In *Death and Towns: Urban Responses to the Dying and the Dead, 100–1600,* ed. Stephen Bassett (Leicester, 1992), 136–47.

Henderson, John. "Coping with Epidemics in Renaissance Italy: Plague and the Great Pox." In *The Fifteenth Century XII: Society in an Age of Plague,* ed. Linda Clarke and Carole Rawcliffe (Woodbridge, 2013), 175–94.

Herlihy, David. *The Black Death and the Transformation of the West.* Ed. Samuel K. Cohn, Jr. Cambridge, MA, 1997.

The History and Description of Africa of Leo Africanus. Vol. 1. London, 1896?

Homer. *The Iliad.* Book I, Internet Classics Library. http://classics.mit.edu/Homer/iliad.1.i.html.

Hopley, Russell. "Contagion in Islamic Lands: Responses from Medieval Andalusia and North Africa." *Journal for Early Modern Cultural Studies* 10:2 (Fall/Winter 2010): 45–64.

Hornstein, Jakob. *Sterbens Flucht; Das ist Christlicher vnd Catholischer Bericht/von Sterbenslauff der Pest.* Ingolstadt, 1593.

Horrox, Rosemary. Trans. and ed. *The Black Death.* Manchester, 1994.

Hsia, R. Po-chia. *A Jesuit in the Forbidden City: Matteo Ricci 1552–1610.* Oxford, 2010.

Hymes, Robert. "Epilogue: A Hypothesis on the East Asian Beginnings of the Yersina Pestis Polytomy." In *The Medieval Globe* 1 (2014), *Pandemic Disease in the Medieval World: Rethinking the Black Death,* ed. Monica H. Green (Kalamazoo, 2014), 285–308.

Jacobs, Louis. *Jewish Mystical Testimonies.* New York, 1977.

Jannetta, Ann Bowman. *Epidemics and Mortality in Early Modern Japan.* Princeton, 1987.

Janzen, John M. and Edward C. Green. "Continuity, Change, and Challenge in African Medicine." In *Medicine across Cultures: History and Practice of Medicine in Non-Western Cultures*, ed. Helaine Selin (London, 2003), 1–26.

Jingfeng, Cai and Zhen Yan. "Medicine in Ancient China." In *Medicine across Cultures: History and Practice of Medicine in Non-Western Cultures*, ed. Helaine Selin (London, 2003), 49–73.

Jörg, Christian. *Teure, Hunger, Großes Sterben: Hungersnöte und Versorgungskrisen in den Städten des Reiches während des 15. Jahrhunderts*. Stuttgart, 2008.

Kasper-Holtkotte, Cilli. *Die Jüdische Gemeinde von Frankfurt/Main in der Frühen Neuzeit: Familien, Netzwerke und Konflikte eines jüdischen Zentrums*. Berlin, 2010.

Kellner, Katharina. *Pesthauch über Regensburg: Seuchenbekämpfung und Hygiene im 18. Jahrhundert*. Regensburg, 2005.

Kinzelbach, Annemarie. *Gesundbleiben, Krankwerden, Armsein in der frühneuzeitlichen Gesellschaft: Gesunde und Kranke in den Reichsstädten Überlingen und Ulm, 1500–1700*. Stuttgart, 1995.

Kinzelbach, Annemarie. "Infection, Contagion, and Public Health in Late Medieval and Early Modern German Imperial Towns." *Journal of the History of Medicine and Allied Science* 61:3 (2006): 369–89.

Kohn, George C., ed. *Encyclopedia of Plague and Pestilence: From Ancient Times to the Present*. New York, 2001.

Kumar, Deepak, ed. *Disease and Medicine in India: An Historical Overview*. New Delhi, 2001.

Kuriyama, Shigehisa. "Epidemics, Weather, and Contagion on Traditional Chinese Medicine." In *Contagion: Perspectives from Pre-Modern Societies*, ed. Lawrence I. Conrad and Dominik Wujastyk (Aldershot, 2000), 1–22.

La Rue, George Michael. "Treating Black Deaths in Egypt: Clot-Bey, African Slaves, and the Plague Epidemic of 1834–1835." In *Histories of Medicine and Healing in the Indian Ocean World, The Modern World*, Vol. 2, ed. Anna Winterbottom and Facil Tesfaye (Basingstoke, 2016), 27–59.

Leibowitz, Joshua. "The Plague in the Roman Ghetto (1656) according to Zahalon and Cardinal Gastaldi." *Korot* 4:3–4 (1967): 155–69.

The Life and Letters of Ogier Ghiselin de Busbecq. 2 vols. London, 1881.

Lindemann, Mary. *Medicine and Society in Early Modern Europe*. 2nd ed. Cambridge, 2010.

Little, Lester K., ed. *Plague and the End of Antiquity: The Pandemic of 541–750*. New York, 2007.

Little, Lester K. "Plague Historians in Lab Coats." *Past and Present* 213 (November 2011): 267–90.

Liu, Michael Shiyung. "Disease, People, and Environment: The Plague in China." Unpublished paper.

Lowry, Heath W. "Pushing the Stone Uphill: The Impact of Bubonic Plague on Ottoman Urban Society in the Fifteenth and Sixteenth Centuries." *Osmanli Araştirmalari* 23 (2003): 93–132.

Luther, Martin. *Luther's Works*, vol. 11: First Lectures on the Psalms II, Psalms, 76–126. Ed. Hilton C. Oswald. Saint Louis, 1968.

Luther, Martin. *Luther's Works*, vol. 43: Devotional Writings II. Ed. Gustav K. Wiencke. Philadelphia, 1968.

Mackenzie, Catriona, Wendy Rogers, and Susan Dodds. "Introduction: What Is Vulnerability, and Why Does It Matter for Moral Theory?" In *Vulnerability: New Essays in Ethics and Feminist Philosophy*, ed. ibidem (Oxford, 2014), 1–29.

Marcus, Jacob R. *Communal Sick-Care in the German Ghetto*. Cincinnati, 1947.

Marcus, Jacob R. ed. *The Jew in the Medieval World: A Sourcebook: 315–1791.* Philadelphia, 1938.

Marien, Giselle. "The Black Death in Early Ottoman Territories: 1347–1550." MA thesis, Bikent University, 2009.

Marre, Katharina. "Components of Risk: A Comparative Glossary." In *Measuring Vulnerability to Natural Hazards: Towards Disaster Resilient Societies*, 2nd ed., ed. Jörn Birkmann (Tokyo, 2006), 569–618.

Martin, A. Lynn. *Plague? Jesuit Accounts of Epidemic Disease in the 16th Century.* Kirksville, 1996.

McNeill, William H. *Plagues and Peoples.* New York, 1976.

Mead, Richard. *A Discourse on the Plague.* 9th ed. corrected and enlarged. London, 1744.

Die Memoiren des Ascher Levy aus Reischshofen im Elsass (1598–1635). Trans. M. Ginsburger. Berlin, 1913.

Mengel, David C. "A Plague in Bohemia? Mapping the Black Death." *Past and Present* 211 (May 2011): 3–34.

Mikhail, Alan. *Nature and Empire in Ottoman Egypt: An Environmental History.* Cambridge, 2011.

Moote, A. Lloyd and Dorothy C. Moote. *The Great Plague: The Story of London's Most Deadly Year.* Baltimore, 2004.

Mormando, Franco. "Introduction: Response to the Plague in Early Modern Italy: What the Primary Sources, Printed and Painted, Reveal." In *Hope and Healing: Painting in Italy in a Time of Plague 1500–1800*, ed. Gauvin Alexander Bailey, Pamela M. Jones, Franco Mormando, and Thomas W. Worcester (Chicago, 2005), 1–44.

Naphy, William G. *Plagues, Poisons, and Potions: Plague-Spreading Conspiracies in the Western Alps, c 1530–1640.* Manchester, 2002.

Noordegraaf, Leo and Gerrit Valk. *De Gave Gods: De pest in Holland vanaf de late middeleeuwen.* Bergen, 1988.

Nutton, Vivian. "The Reception of Frascatoro's Theory of Contagion: The Seed That Fell among Thorns?" *Osiris* 6 (1990), 2nd series: 196–234.

Obringer, Frédéric. "Wu Youxing and Pestilential Epidemics: A Medical Expert in Late Ming China." *Revue de synthèse/Centre international de synthèse* 131:3 (2010): 343–72.

Panzac, Daniel. *La peste dans l'empire Ottoman: 1700–1850.* Leuven, 1985.

Pearson, Michael. "Medical Connections and Exchanges in the Early Modern World." *PORTAL Journal of Multidisciplinary International Studies* 8:2 (July 2011): 1–15.

Pfister, Christian. *Bevölkerungsgeschichte und historische Demographie, 1500–1800.* Munich, 1994.

Pomata, Gianna. "Observation Rising: Birth of an Epistemic Genre, 1500–1650." In *Histories of Scientific Observation*, ed. Lorraine Daston and Elizabeth Lunebeck (Chicago, 2011), 45–80.

Preto, Paolo. *Epidemia, paura e politica nell'Italia moderna.* Bari, 1987.

Procopius. *History of the Wars, Books I and II.* Trans. H. B. Dweing. London, 1971; first printed 1914, XXII–XXIII. www.gutenberg.org/files/16764/16764-h/16764-h.htm#BOOK_II.

Pullan, Brian. "Plagues and Perceptions of the Poor in Early Modern Italy." In *Epidemics and Ideas: Essays on Historical Perceptions of Pestilence*, ed. Terence Ranger and Paul Slack (Cambridge, 1992), 101–23.

Rawcliffe, Carole. *Urban Bodies: Communal Health in Late Medieval English Towns and Cities.* Woodbridge: The Boydell Press, 2013.

Rödel, Walter G. "Pestepidemien in Mainz im 17. Jahrhundert." *Scripta Mercaturae* 15:1 (1981): 85–103.

Rogers, Wendy. "Vulnerability and Bioethics." In *Vulnerability: New Essays in Ethics and Feminist Philosophy*, ed. Catriona Mackenzie, Wendy Rogers, and Susan Dodds (Oxford, 2014), 60–87.

Rosenberg, Charles. "What Is an Epidemic? AIDS in Historical Perspective." *Daedalus* 118:2 (Spring 1989): 1–17.

Royer, Katherine. "The Blind Men and the Elephant: Imperial Medicine, Medieval Historians and the Role of Rats in the Historiography of Plague." In *Medicine and Colonialism: Historical Perspectives in India and South Africa*, ed. Poonam Bala (London, 2014), 99–110.

Russell, Alexander. *Natural History of Aleppo*. London, 1756.

Ryrie, Alec. *Being Protestant in Reformation Britain*. Oxford, 2013.

Sabine, Ernst L. "Butchering in Medieval London." *Speculum* 8:3 (July 1933): 335–53.

Sallares, Robert. "Ecology, Evolution, and Epidemiology of Plague." In *Plague and the End of Antiquity: The Pandemic of 541–750*, ed. Lester K. Little (New York, 2007), 231–89.

Schretter, Bernhard. *Die Pest in Tirol 1611–1612: Ein Beitrag zur Medizin-, Kultur- und Wirtschaftsgeschichte der Stadr Innsbruck und der übrigen Gerichte Tirols*. Innsbruck, 1982.

Schroeter, Daniel J. *The Sultan's Jew: Morocco and the Sephardi World*. Stanford, 2002.

Schwarz, Klaus. *Die Pest in Bremen: Epidemien und freier Handel in einer deutschen Hafenstadt 1350–1713*. Bremen, 1996.

Segre, Renata, ed. *The Jews in Piedmont*. 3 vols. Jerusalem, 1986–90.

Seifert, Lisa, et al. "Genotyping *Yersinia pestis* in Historical Plague: Evidence for Long-Term Persistence of *Y. pestis* in Europe from the 14th to the 17th Century." *PLOS One* 11:1 (January 13, 2016): online.

Shoham-Steiner, Ephraim. "Jews and Healing at Medieval Saints' Shrines: Participation, Polemics, and Shared Cultures." *Harvard Theological Review* 103:1 (2010): 111–29.

Silva, Cristobal. *Miraculous Plagues: An Epidemiology of Early New England Narrative*. Oxford, 2011.

Slack, Paul. *Plague: A Very Short Introduction*. Oxford, 2012.

Slavin, Philip. "The Fifth Ride of the Apocalypse: The Great Cattle Plague in England and Wales and Its Economic Consequences, 1319–1350." In *Economic and Biological Interactions in Pre-Industrial Europe from the 13th to the 18th Centuries*, ed. Simonetta Cavaciocchi (Firenze, 2010), 165–79.

Spyrou, Maria A., et al. "Historical *Y. pestis* Genomes Reveal the European Black Death as the Source of Ancient and Modern Plague Pandemics." *Cell Host & Microbe* 19 (supplemental information): 874–81.

Stathakopoulos, Dinonysios. "Crime and Punishment: The Plague in the Byzantine Empire, 541–749." In *Plague and the End of Antiquity: The Pandemic of 541–750*, ed. Lester K. Little (New York, 2007), 99–118.

Sudhoff, Karl. "Pestschriften aus deb ersten 150 Jahren nach der Epidemie des 'schwarzen Todes' 1348." *Archiv für Geschichte der Medizin* 5 (1911): 36–87.

Tlusty, B. Ann. *Augsburg during the Reformation Era: An Anthology of Sources*. Indianapolis, 2012. Trans. from German, *Paul Hector Mairs 1. Chronik von 1547–1565*, Beilage VIII, 485–94.

Toubert, Pierre. "La Peste Noire (1348), entre Histoire et biologie moleculaire." *Journal des Savants* (2016): 17–31.

Turniansky, Chava. "Yiddish Song as Historical Source Material: Plague in the Judenstadt of Prague in 1713." In *Jewish History; Essays in Honour of Chimen Abramsky*, ed. Ada Rapoport-Albert and Steven J. Zipperstein (London, 1988), 189–98.

The Tuzuk-i-Jahangiri; or, Memoirs of Jahangir. Trans. Alexander Rogers. Ed. Henry Beveridge. London, 1909.

Ulbricht, Otto. "Angst und Angstbewältigung in den Zeiten der Pest, 1500–1720." In *Gotts verhengnis und seine strafe—Zur Geschichte der Seuchen in der Frühen Neuzeit* (Wiesbaden, 2005), 101–12.

Usque, Samuel. *Samuel Usque's Consolation for the Tribulations of Israel.* Trans. Martin A. Cohen. Philadelphia, 1965.

Varlik, Nükhet. *Disease and Empire: A History of Plague Epidemics in the Early Modern Ottoman Empire (1453–1600).* Doctoral Dissertation, University of Chicago, 2008.

Varlik, Nükhet. "From 'Bete Noire' to 'le Mal de Constantinople:' Plagues, Medicine, and the Early Modern Ottoman State." *Journal of World History* 24:4 (December 2013), 741–70.

Varlik, Nükhet. "New Science and Old Sources: Why the Ottoman Experience of Plague Matters." In *The Medieval Globe* 1 (2014), *Pandemic Disease in the Medieval World: Rethinking the Black Death*, ed. Monica H. Green (Kalamazoo, 2014), 193–227.

Varlik, Nükhet, "'Oriental Plague' or Epidemiological Orientalism? Revisiting the Plague Episteme of the Early Modern Mediterranean," in *Plague and Contagion in the Islamic Mediterranean*, ed. ibidem (Kalamazoo, 2017), 57–87.

Viesca, Carlos. "Medicine in Ancient Mesoamerica." In *Medicine across Cultures: History and Practice of Medicine in Non-Western Cultures*, ed. Helaine Selin (London, 2003), 259–83.

Voigtländer, Nico and Hans-Joachim Voth. "The Three Horsemen of Riches: Plague, War, and Urbanization in Early Modern Europe." Unpublished essay; www.anderson. ucla.edu/faculty/nico.v/Research/Horsemen.pdf [last viewed March 29, 2016]. Subsequent publication in the *Review of Economic Studies* 80:2 (2013): 774–811.

Webster, Noah. *A Brief History of Epidemic and Pestilential Diseases.* 2 vols. Hartford, 1799.

Wegrzynek, Hanna. "Shvartze Khasene: Black Weddings among Polish Jews." In *Holy Dissent: Jewish and Christian Mystics in Eastern Europe*, ed. Glenn Dynner (Detroit, 2011), 55–68.

White, Sam. "A Model Disaster: From the Great Ottoman Panzootic to the Cattle Plagues of Early Modern Europe." In *Plague and Contagion in the Islamic Mediterranean*, ed. Nükhet Varlik (Kalamazoo, 2017), 91–116.

Whittles, Lilith K. and Xavier Didelot. "Epidemiological Analysis of the Eyam Plague Outbreak of 1665–1666." *Proceedings of the Royal Society* B 283 (May 2016): electronic download.

Zahalon, Jacob. "The Treasure of Life." Trans. in Harry A. Savitz, "Jacob Zahalon, and His Book 'The Treasure of Life,'" *NEJ of M* (July 25, 1935) 213:4: 167–76.

*Zakour, Michael J. and David F. Gillespie. *Community Disaster Vulnerability: Theory, Research, and Practice.* New York, 2013.

Ziegler, Michelle. "The Black Death and the Future of the Plague." In *The Medieval Globe* 1 (2014), *Pandemic Disease in the Medieval World: Rethinking the Black Death*, ed. Monica H. Green (Kalamazoo, 2014), 259–83.

Zinger, Nimrod. "'Our Hearts and Spirits Were Broken': The Medical World from the Perspective of German-Jewish Patients in the Seventeenth and Eighteenth Centuries." *Leo Baeck Institute Yearbook* 54:1 (2009): 59–91.

Zysk, Kenneth G. *Medicine in the Veda: Religious Healing in the Veda.* Philadelphia, 1996.

Further reading

Aberth, John. *From the Brink of the Apocalypse: Confronting Famine, War, Plague and Death in the Later Middle Ages.* New York, 2000.

Amelang, James, trans. and ed. *A Journal of the Plague Year: The Diary of the Barcelona Tanner Miquel Parents, 1651.* Oxford, 1991.

Amundsen, Darrel W. "Medical Deontology and Pestilential Disease in the Late Middle Ages." *Journal of the History of Medicine* 32 (1977): 403–21.

Ansari, B. M. "An Account of Bubonic Plague in Seventeenth Century India in an Autobiography of a Mughal Emperor." *Journal of Infection* 29:3 (November 1994): 351–2.

Appleby, Andrew B. "Epidemics and Famine in the Little Ice Age." In *Climate and History: Studies in Interdisciplinary History*, ed. Robert I. Rotberg and Theodore K. Rabb (Princeton, 1981), 63–83.

Arnold, David, ed. *Imperial Medicine and Indigenous Societies.* Oxford, 1988.

Bailey, Gauvin Alexander, Pamela M. Jones, Franco Mormando, and Thomas W. Worcester, eds. *Hope and Healing: Painting in Italy in a Time of Plague, 1500–1800.* Worcester, MA, 2005.

Baldinucci, Giovanni. "Memoirs of the Plague in Florence (1613–48)." In *Italy in the Baroque: Selected Readings*, ed. and trans. Brendan Dooley (New York, 1995), 183–207.

Baldwin, Martha R. "Toads and Plague: Amulet Therapy in Seventeenth-Century Medicine." *Bulletin of the History of Medicine* 67 (1993): 227–47.

Baldwin, Peter. *Contagion and the State in Nineteenth-Century Europe.* New York, 1999.

Barnes, Linda. *Needles, Herbs, Gods, and Ghosts: China, Healing and the West to 1848.* Cambridge, 2005.

Beier, Lucinda McCray. *Sufferers and Healers: The Experience of Illness in Seventeenth-Century England.* London, 1987.

Ben Zaken, Avner. *Cross-Cultural Scientific Exchanges in the Eastern Mediterranean 1560–1660.* Baltimore, 2011.

Benedict, Carol. *Bubonic Plague in Nineteenth-Century China.* Stanford, 1996.

Benedictow, Ole J. *The Black Death, 1346–1353: The Complete History.* Woodbridge, 2004.

Benedictow, Ole J. *What Disease Was Plague? On the Controversy over the Microbiolgical Identity of Plague Epidemics of the Past.* Leiden, 2010.

Bergdolt, Klaus. *Die Pest: Geschichte des Schwarzen Todes.* Munich, 2006.

Bergdolt, Klaus. *Der Schwarze Tod in Europa: Die grosse Pest und das Ende des Mittelalters.* Munich, 1994.

Bertran, Jose Luis. *La peste en la Barcelona de los Austrias.* Lleida, 1996.

Biraben, Jean-Noel. *Les hommes et la peste en France et dans les pays europeens et mediterraneens.* 2 vols. New York, 1989.

The Black Death: A Chronicle of the Plague. Compiled by Johannes Nohl from contemporary sources. Trans. C. H. Clarke. London, 1924.

Boeckl, Christine M. *Images of Plague and Pestilence: Iconography and Iconology.* Kirksville, 2000.

Boeckl, Christine M. "Plague Imagery as Metaphor for Heresy in Rubens' *The Miracle of Saint Francis Xavier*." *Sixteenth Century Journal* 27 (1996): 979–95.

Borsch, Stuart. "Plague Depopulation and Irrigation Decay in Medieval Egypt." *The Medieval Globe* 1, 125–56.

Bowsky, W. M., ed. *The Black Death: A Turning Point in History?* New York, 1971.

Bowsky, W. M. "The Impact of the Black Death upon Sienese Government and Society." *Speculum* 39:1 (1964): 1–34.

Brighetti, Antonio. *Bologna e la peste del 1630.* Bologna, 1968.

Buxton, Jean. *Religion and Healing in Mandari.* Oxford, 1973.

Calvi, Giulia. *Histories of a Plague Year: The Social and the Imaginary in Baroque Florence.* Trans. Dario Biocca and Bryant T. Ragan, Jr. Berkeley, 1989.

Campbell, Anna Montgomery. *The Black Death and the Men of Learning.* New York, 1931.

Cantor, Norman F. *In the Wake of the Plague: The Black Death and the World It Made.* New York, 2001.

Capasso, Luigi and Arnaldo Capelli. *La Epidemie di Peste in Abrizzo dal 1348 al 1702.* Cerchio Aquila, 1993.

Carlin, Claire, L., ed. *Imagining Contagion in Early Modern Europe.* New York, 2005.

Carmichael, Ann G. "Contagion Theory and Contagion Practice in Fifteenth-Century Milan." *Renaissance Quarterly* 44:2 (1991): 213–56.

Carmichael, Ann G. *Plague and the Poor in Renaissance Florence.* Cambridge, 1986.

Carmichael, Ann G. "Plague Legislation in the Italian Renaissance." *Bulletin of the History of Medicine* 57:4 (1983): 508–25.

Chimin Wong, K. and Wu Lien. *The History of Chinese Medicine.* 2nd ed. Shanghai, 1936.

Christakos, George, et al. *Interdisciplinary Public Health Reasoning and Epidemic Modelling: The Case of the Black Death.* Stuttgart, 2006.

Ciecieznski, N. J. "The Stench of Disease: Public Health and the Environment in Late-Medieval English Towns and Cities." *Health, Culture and Society* 4:1 (2013): 92–104.

Cipolla, Carlo M. *Fighting the Plague in Seventeenth-Century Italy.* Madison, 1981.

Cipolla, Carlo M. *Miasmas and Disease.* New Haven, 1992.

Cohn, Samuel K., Jr. *The Cult of Remembrance and the Black Death: Six Renaissance Cities in Central Italy.* Baltimore, 1992.

Cohn, Samuel K., Jr. *Plague and Its Consequences.* Oxford, 2010.

Conrad, Lawrence I. "Arabic Plague Chronologies and Treatises: Social and Historical Factors in the Formation of a Literary Genre." *Studia Islamica* 54 (1981): 51–93.

Conrad, Lawrence I. "Epidemic Disease in Formal and Popular Thought in Early Islamic Society." In *Epidemics and Ideas,* ed. Terrence Ranger and Paul Slack (Cambridge 1992), 77–99.

Conrad, Lawrence I. "Ta'un and Waba: Conceptions of Plague and Pestilence in Early Islam." *Journal of the Economic and Social History of the Orient* 25 (1982): 291–301.

Conrad, Lawrence I. "'Umar at Sargh: The Evolution of an Umayyad Tradition of Flight from the Plague." In *Story-Telling in the Framework of Non-Fictional Arabic Literature,* ed. Stefan Leder (Wiesbaden, 1998), 488–528.

Cook, Alexandra Parma and Noble David Cook. *The Plague Files: Crisis Management in Sixteenth-Century Seville.* Baton Rouge, 2009.

Cook, David Noble. *Born to Die: Disease and New World Conquest, 1492–1650.* Cambridge, 1998.

Cooke, Jennifer. *Legacies of Plague in Literature, Theory and Film.* New York, 2009.

Coulton, G. G. *The Black Death.* London, 1929.

Crosby, Alfred. *The Columbian Exchange: Biological and Cultural Consequences of 1492.* Westport, 1972

da Costa Roque, Mario. "A 'Peste Grande' de 1569 em Lisboa." *Anais de Academia Portuguesa da Historia,* II serie, 28 (1982): 71–90.

de Cunha, Xavier. *Revoadas de Peste Bubonica em Lisboa nos Seculos XVI e XVII: Velharias Recopiladas.* Lisbon, 1893.

Deaux, George. *The Black Death. 1347.* New York, 1969.

Del Panta, Lorenzo. *Le epidemie nela storia demografia italiana (secoli XIV–XIX).* Turin, 1980.

Dols, Michael W. "The Comparative Communal Responses to the Black Death in Muslim and Christian Societies." *Viator* 5 (1974): 269–87.

Dols, Michael. "Ibn al-Wardi's Risalah al-Naba an al-Waba, a Translation of a Major Source of the History of the Black Death in the Middle East." In *Near Eastern Numismatics, Iconography, Epigraphy and History: Studies in Honor of George C. Miles,* ed. D. K. Kouyijan (Beirut, 1974), 443–55.

Dunstan, Helen. "The Late Ming Epidemics: A Preliminary Survey." *Ch'ing-shih wen-t'I* III:3 (1975): 1–59.

Dyer, Alan D. "The Influence of Bubonic Plague in England, 1500–1667." *Medical History* 22 (1978): 308–26.

Einbinder, Susan L. *After the Black Death: Plague and Commemoration among Iberian Jews.* Philadelphia, 2018.

Ell, Stephen R. "The Venetian Plague of 1630–1631: A Preliminary Epidemiologic Analysis." *Janus* 73 (1986–1989): 85–104.

Elmer, Peter and Ole Peter Grell. *Health, Disease, and Society in Europe, 1500–1800: A Source Book.* Manchester, 2004.

Emery, R. W. "The Black Death of 1348 in Perpignan." *Speculum* 42 (1967): 611–23.

Fabbri, Christine Nockels. "Continuity and Change in Late Medieval Plague Medicine: A Survey of 152 Plague Tracts from 1348–1599." Dissertation, Yale University, 2006.

Filliozat, Jean. *The Classical Doctrine of Indian Medicine: Its Origins and Its Greek Parallels.* Delhi, 1964.

Flinn, Michael. "Plague in Europe and the Mediterranean Countries." *Journal of European Economic History* 8 (1979): 131–48.

Gamal, Adil, ed. *Medieval Islamic Medicine: Ibn Ridwan's Treatise "On the Prevention of Bodily Ills in Egypt."* Berkeley, 1984.

Garza, Randall P. *Understanding Plague: The Medical and Imaginative Texts of Medieval Spain.* New York, 2008.

Gentilcore, David. *Healers and Healing in Early Modern Italy.* Manchester, 1998.

Gentilcore, David. *Medical Charlatanism in Early Modern Italy.* Oxford, 2006.

Gilman, Ernest B. *Plague Writing in Early Modern England.* Chicago, 2005.

Greenberg, Stephen. "Plague, the Printing Press, and Public Health in Seventeenth-Century London." *Huntington Library Quarterly* 6:4 (2004): 509–27.

Grell, Ole Peter. "Conflicting Duties: Plague and the Obligations of Early Modern Physicians towards Patients and Commonwealth in England and the Netherlands." In *Doctors and Ethics: The Earlier Historical Setting of Professional Ethics,* ed. Andrew Wear, Johanna Geyer-Kordesch, and Robert French (New York, 1993), 131–52.

Hanson, Marta. *Speaking of Epidemics in Chinese Medicine: Disease and the Geographic Imagination in Late Imperial China.* New York, 2011.

Hatcher, John. *Plague, Population, and the English Economy, 1348–1530.* London, 1977.

Hatty, Suzanne E. and James Hatty. *The Disordered Body: Epidemic Disease and Cultural Transformation.* Albany, 1999.

Hays, Jo N. *Epidemics and Pandemics: Their Impacts on Human History.* Santa Barbara, 2005.

Hecker, J. F. C. *Epidemics of the Middle Ages.* London, 1944.

Henderson, John. "Epidemics in Renaissance Florence: Medical Theory and Government Response." In *Maladies et societe (XII–XVIII siecles): Actes du colloque de Bielfeld, Novembre 1986,* ed. Neithard Bulst and Robert Delort (Paris, 1989), 165–84.

Herlihy, David. "Population, Plague and Social Change in Rural Pistoia, 1201–1430." *Economic History Review* 18 (1965): 225–44.

Herring D. Ann and Alan C. Swedlund, eds. *Plagues and Epidemics: Infected Spaces Past and Present.* Oxford, 2010.

Hirshleifer, Jack. *Disaster and Recovery: The Black Death in Western Europe.* Santa Monica, 1966.

Jarcho, Saul, ed. *Italian Broadsides Concerning Public Health Documents from Bologna and Brescia in the Mortimer and Anna Neinken Collection.* New York, 1986.

Jennings, Ronald. "Plague in Trabzon and Reactions to It According to Local Judicial Registers." In *Humanist and Scholar: Essays in Honor of Andreas Tietze,* ed. Heath W. Lowry and Donald Quataert (Istanbul, 1993), 27–36.

Jolly, Julius. *Indian Medicine.* New Delhi, 1994.

Jones, Colin. "Plague and Its Metaphors in Early Modern France." *Representations* 53 (Winter 1996): 97–127.

Klairmont, Alison. "The Problem of the Plague: New Challenges to Healing in Sixteenth-Century France." *Proceedings of the Fifth Annual Meeting of the Western Society for French History* 5 (1977): 119–27.

Kleinman, Arthur. *The Illness Narratives: Suffering and Healing and the Human Condition.* New York, 1988.

Kulikowski, Michael. "Plague in Spanish Late Antiquity." In *Plague and the End of Antiquity: The Pandemic of 541–750,* ed. Lester K. Little (New York, 2007), 150–70.

Leibowitz, Joshua O. "Bubonic Plague in the Ghetto of Rome (1656)." *Korot* 14 (2000): 65–68.

Leslie, Charles, ed. *Asian Medical Systems: A Comparative Study.* Berkeley, 1976.

Lieberman, Victor. *Strange Parallels: South-East Asia in Global Context 800–1830.* 2 vols. Cambridge, MA, 2003, 2009.

Little, Lester K. "Life and Afterlife of the First Plague Pandemic." In *Plague and the End of Antiquity,* ed. ibidem (New York, 2007), 3–32.

Lloyd, Geoffrey. *Adversaries and Authorities: Investigations into Ancient Greek and Chinese Science.* Cambridge, 1996.

Lloyd, Geoffrey and Nathan Sivan. *The Way and the Word: Science and Medicine in Early China and Greece.* New Haven, 2002.

Lockhart, James, ed. *We People Here: Nahuatl Accounts of the Conquest of Mexico.* Berkeley, 1993.

Lopez, Austin "Sahagun's Work on Medicine of the Ancient Nahuas: Possibilities for Study." In *Sixteenth Century Mexico: The Work of Sahagun,* ed. Munro S. Edmonson (Albuquerque, 1974), 205–24.

Lucenet, Monique. *Les grandes pestes en France.* Paris, 1985.

MacKay, Ellen. *Persecution, Plague, and Fire: Fugitive Histories of the Stage in Early Modern England.* Chicago, 2011.

MacLeod, R. and L. Milton, eds. *Disease, Medicine and Empire: Perspectives of Western Medicine and the Experiences of European Expansion.* London, 1988.

Marshall, Louise. "Manipulating the Sacred: Image and Plague in Renaissance Italy." *Renaissance Quarterly* 47:3 (1994): 485–532.

Mate, Mavis E. *Daughters, Wives, and Widows after the Black Death: Women in Sussex, 1350–1535.* Woodbridge, 1998.

Matlock, Derbyshire, ed. *The Plague Reconsidered: A New Look at Its Origins and Effects in Sixteenth- and Seventeenth-Century England.* Cambridge, 1977.

Meier, Mischa, ed. *Pest: Die Geschichte eines Menschheitstraumas.* Stuttgart, 2005.

Meiss, Millard. *Painting in Florence and Siena after the Black Death.* Princeton, 1951.

Melhaoui, Mohammed. *Peste, Contagion et Martyre: Histoire du fleau en Occident musulman medieval.* Paris, 2005.

Melville, Elinor G. K. *A Plague of Sheep: Environmental Consequences of the Conquest of Mexico.* Cambridge, 1994.

Mormando, Franco and Thomas Worcester. *Piety and Plague: From Byzantium to the Baroque.* Kirksville, 2007.

Nappi, Carla, "Bolatu's Pharmacy: Theriac in Early Modern China." *Early Science and Medicine* 14:6 (2009): 737–64.

Nappi, Carla. *The Monkey and the Inkpot: Natural History and Its Transformations in Early Modern China.* Cambridge, MA, 2009.

Neustadt, David. "The Plague and Its Effects upon the Mamluk Army." *Journal of the Royal Asiatic Society of Great Britain and Ireland* 1 (April 1946): 67–73.

Norris, John. "East or West? The Geographic Origin of the Black Death." *Bulletin of the History of Medicine* 51 (1977): 1–24.

Nutton, Vivian, ed. *Pestilential Complexities: Understanding Medieval Plague*. London, 2008.

Nutton, Vivian. "The Seeds of Disease: An Explanation of Contagion and Infection from the Greeks to the Renaissance." *Medical History* 27 (1983): 1–34.

Ormrod, W. M. and Phillip G. Lindley, eds. *The Black Death in England*. Lincolnshire, 1996.

Osheim, Duane J. "Plague and Foreign Threats to Public Health in Early Modern Venice." *Mediterranean Historical Review* 26:1 (June 2011): 67–80.

Palmer, Richard. "Girolamo Mercuriale and the Plague in Venice." In *Girolamo Mercuriale: Medicina e cultura nell'Europa del cinquecento*, Alessandro Arcangeli and Vivian Nutton (Florence, 2008), 51–65.

Panzac, Daniel. "La Peste Smyrna au xviiie siècle." *Annales: Economies, Societies, Civilizations* 28 (1973): 1071–93.

Parker, Geoffrey. *Global Crisis: War, Climate Change, and Catastrophe in the Seventeenth Century*. New Haven, 2013.

Parker, Geoffrey. *Global Interactions in the Early Modern Age, 1400–1800*. Cambridge, 2010.

Pas, J. de, and M. Lanselle. "Documents sur la peste de 1596 a Sant-Omer." *Bulletin de la Societe Francaise d'Histoire de la Medecine* 23 (1928): 206–16.

Patterson, T. J. S. "The Relationship of Indian and European Practitioners of Medicine from the Sixteenth Century." In *Studies on Indian Medical History, Groningen*, ed. G. Jan Meulenbeld and Dominik Wujastyk (England, 1987 (Reprinted: New Delhi, 2001)), 119–29.

Payne Crawford, Raymond Henry. *Plague and Pestilence in Literature and Art*. Oxford, 1914.

Pearson, M. N. *Towards Superiority: European and Indian Medicine 1500–1700*. Minneapolis, 1989.

Phillips, William. "Peste Negra: The Fourteenth-Century Plague Epidemics in Iberia." In *On the Social Origins of Medieval Institutions: Essays in Honor of Joseph F. O'Callaghan*, ed. Donald J. Kagay and Theresa M. Vann (Boston, 1998), 47–62.

Platt, Colin. *King Death: The Black Death and Its Aftermath in Late Medieval England*. Toronto, 1996

Porter, Roy. *Disease, Medicine and Society in England 1550–1860*. London, 1987.

Post, John D. "Famine, Mortality and Epidemic Disease in the Process of Modernization." *Economic History Review*, 2nd series, 39 (1976): 14–37.

Puglisi, Catherine R. "Guido Reni's *Pallione del Voto* and the Plague of 1630." *Art Bulletin* 127:3 (September 1995), 403–12.

Ranger, Terrence and Paul Slack, eds. *Epidemics and Ideas: Essays on the Historical Perception of Pestilence*. Cambridge, 1992.

Reff, Daniel T. *Disease, Depopulation, and Culture Change in Northwestern New Spain, 1518–1764*. Salt Lake City, 1991.

Reff, Daniel T. *Plagues, Priests, Demons: Sacred Narratives and the Rise of Christianity in the Old World and the New*. Cambridge, 2005.

Richards, John. *Unending Frontier: An Environmental History of the Early Modern World*. Berkeley, 2003.

Rodenwaldt, Ernst. *Pest in Venedig, 1575–1577: Ein Beitrag zur Frage der Infektkette be idem Pestepidemien West-Europas*. Heidelberg, 1953.

Rodrigues, Teresa. *Crises de Mortalidade em Lisboa: Seculos XVI e XVII*. Lisbon, 1990.

Rosenberg, Charles E. *Explaining Epidemics and Other Studies in the History of Medicine*. Cambridge, 1992.

Salomon, Xavier. *Van Dyck in Sicily: 1624–1625 Painting and the Plague*. London, 2012.

Sarris, Peter. "Bubonic Plague in Byzantium: The Evidence of Non-Literary Sources." In *Plague and the End of Antiquity: The Pandemic of 541–750*, ed. Lester K. Little (New York, 2007), 119–49.

Schamiloglu, Uli. "The Rise of the Ottoman Empire: The Black Death in Medieval Anatolia and Its Impact on Turkish Civilization." In *Views from the Edge: Essays in Honor of Richard W. Bulliet*, ed. Neguin Yavari et al. (New York, 2004), 255–79.

Scot, Susan and Christopher Duncan. *Return of the Black Death: The World's Greatest Serial Killer*. Hoboken, 2004.

Selin, Helaine, ed. *Medicine across Cultures: History and Practice of Medicine in Non-Western Cultures*. Dordrecht, 2003.

Shatzmiller, Joseph. "Les Juifs de Provence pendant la Peste Noire." *Revue des Etudes Juives* 133 (1974): 457–80.

Shefer-Mossensohn, Miri. *Ottoman Medicine: Healing and Medical Institutions. 1500–1700*. Albany, 2009.

Shrewsbury, J. F. D. *A History of Bubonic Plague in the British Isles*. Cambridge, 1970.

Shrewsbury, J. F. D. "The Plague of Athens." *Bulletin of the History of Medicine* 24 (1950): 1–25.

Sigerist, Henry. *Early Greek, Hindu, and Persian Medicine*. New York, 1961.

Signoli, Michel, D. Chevé, and A. Pascal, eds. *Peste: Entre Epidémies et Sociétés*. Florence, 2007.

Singer, Dorothea Waley. "Some Plague Tractates (Fourteenth and Fifteenth Centuries)." *Proceedings of the Royal Society of Medicine* 9 (1916): 159–212.

Slack, Paul. *Impact of Plague in Tudor and Stuart England*. London, 1985.

Stathakopoulos, Dionysios. *Famine and Pestilence in the Late Roman and Early Byzantine Empire: A Systematic Survey of Subsistence Crises and Epidemics*. Aldershot, 2004.

Stearns, Justin. "Enduring the Plague: Ethical Behavior in the Fatwas of a Fourteenth-Century Mufti and Theologian." *Muslim Medical Ethics: From Theory to Practice*, ed. Jonathan Brockopp and Thomas Eich (Columbia, SC, 2008), 38–54.

Stearns, Justin K. *Infectious Ideas: Contagion in Premodern Islamic and Christian Thought in the Western Mediterranean*. Baltimore, 2011.

Sterans, Justin. "New Directions in the Study of Religious Responses to the Black Death." *History Compass* 7:5 (2009): 1363–75.

Sticker, Georg. *Abhandlungern aus der Seuchengeschichte und Seuchenlehre*. Giessen, 1908–12.

Sublet, J. "La peste aux rets de la jurisprudence: Le Traite d'ibn Hagar Al 'Asqalani sur la peste." *Studie Islamica* 33 (1971): 141–9.

Syros, Vasileios. "Galenic Medicine and Social Stability in Early Modern Florence and the Islamic Empires." *Journal of Early Modern History* 17:2 (2013): 161–213.

Totaro, Rebecca. *The Plague in Print: Essential Elizabethan Sources, 1558–1603*. Pittsburgh, 2010.

Twigg, Graham I. *The Black Death: A Biological Reappraisal*. London, 1984.

Varlik, Nükhet. *Plague and Empire in the Early Modern Mediterranean World: The Ottoman Experience, 1347–1600*. Cambridge, 2015.

Vaught, Jennifer C., ed. *Rhetorics of Bodily Disease and Health in Medieval and Early Modern England*. London, 2010.

Velimirovic, Boris and Helga Velimirovic. "Plague in Vienna." *Reviews of Infectious Diseases* 11 (1989): 808–26.

Venezia e la peste 1348–1797. Venice, 1980.

Von Kremer, Alfred. *Über die Grossen Seuchen des Orients nach Arabischen Quellen*. Veinna, 1880.

Wahrmann, Carl Christian. *Kommunikation der Pest: Seestädte des Ostseeraums und die Bedrouhung durch die Seuche 1708–1713*. Berlin, 2012.

Wallae, Lars. *Plague and Population: Norway 1350–1750*. Oslo, 1995.

Warde, Paul. *Ecology, Economy and State Formation in Early Modern Germany*. Cambridge, 2006.

Watts, Sheldon. *Epidemics and History: Disease, Power and Imperialism*. New Haven, 1981.

Webster, Charles, ed. *Health, Medicine and Mortality in the Sixteenth Century*. Cambridge, 1979.

White, Sam. *The Climate of Rebellion in the Early Modern Ottoman Empire*. New York, 2011.

Williman, Daniel, ed. *The Black Death: The Impact of the Fourteenth-Century Plague*. Binghamton, 1982.

Wilson, F. P. *The Plague in Shakespeare's London*. Oxford, 1927.

Xianqing, Zhang. "The Metaphor of Illness: Medical Culture in the Dissemination of Catholicism in Early Qing China." *Frontiers of History in China* 4:4 (2009): 579–603.

Zanette, Laura. "Tre pedicatori per la peste: 1575–1577." *Lettere italiane* 42 (1990): 430–59.

Zentner, Howard M. *Human Plague in the United States*. New Orleans, 1942.

Ziegler, Philip. *The Black Death*. New York, 1969.

Index

Taylor & Francis Group
an **informa** business

Taylor & Francis eBooks

www.taylorfrancis.com

A single destination for eBooks from Taylor & Francis
with increased functionality and an improved user
experience to meet the needs of our customers.

90,000+ eBooks of award-winning academic content in
Humanities, Social Science, Science, Technology, Engineering,
and Medical written by a global network of editors and authors.

TAYLOR & FRANCIS EBOOKS OFFERS:

A streamlined
experience for
our library
customers

A single point
of discovery
for all of our
eBook content

Improved
search and
discovery of
content at both
book and
chapter level

REQUEST A FREE TRIAL
support@taylorfrancis.com

Routledge
Taylor & Francis Group

CRC CRC Press
Taylor & Francis Group

Made in the USA
Monee, IL
29 August 2023

41827253R00166